Scoring Human Motives: A Manual

SCORING HUMAN MOTIVES: A Manual

by JOHN DOLLARD
Professor of Psychology
Yale University

and FRANK AULD, JR.
Associate Professor of Psychology
Wayne State University

New Haven
YALE UNIVERSITY PRESS
1959

Published on the Louis Stern Memorial Fund

"With clumsy fingers man has fumbled over the keyboard of a vast organ. He has called forth only a few shy notes, but of a sweetness so piercing that we tremble at the thought of the harmonies to come."

Max Mason, physicist, in a dedication speech at the Mt. Palomar Observatory

ACKNOWLEDGMENTS

WE WISH to express acknowledgments as follows: to the idea of a university (peerless Yale, if you wish) which made our work possible by providing the temper of life, the setting, and much of the funds for it; to the National Institutes of Health, Public Health Service, which supported our research in part by research grant M-648 from 1953 to 1960 (in this connection we cannot suppress a note of citizen's pride in the care with which these funds are expended as well as the scientist's satisfaction at the way in which public procedures are tailored to the special requirements of scientific research); to the John and Mary R. Markle Foundation and the Social Research Foundation for providing the funds to build and equip the rooms in which the therapy sessions were conducted and recorded; to our psychiatric colleagues at Yale for their help in many different ways; to a well-ordered Department of Psychology which demands research activity from its members and, in addition, permits it; to our friend and colleague, Dr. James E. Dittes for his work of research and writing in preparing Appendix A; to Alice M. White, our research assistant, for scholarly activity, editorial assistance, and administrative work on the book; to Mrs. Nina Wolfson for assistance in statistical computations, in typing manuscript, and in preparing the recorded interviews included in the book; to Armin Hemberger for drawing the graphs; to Mrs. Alice Boone for assistance in transcribing, typing, and proofreading materials; to Mrs. Barbara Young, Mrs. Ann Byler, and Mrs. Margaret Vranesh for help in recording and transcribing interviews. The permission of International Universities Press, Hogarth Press, the Journal Press, Charles Griffin and Company, M. G. Kendall, Professor R. F. Bales, and the American Psychological Association to quote from their publications is likewise gratefully acknowledged.

JOHN DOLLARD
FRANK AULD, JR.

New Haven, Connecticut
May 1959

TABLE OF CONTENTS

CHAPTER 1

Can Talk Be Fragmented?

THIS BOOK is a manual. It defines a way of marking off the sentences of a dialogue and, once they are marked off, of sorting these sentences into categories such as "fear" or "sex." One can count the number of items falling into each of these categories and say, for instance, that a specific hour of a case contains n fear sentences but no sex sentences. It may then turn out that a patient having n fear sentences and no sex sentences is a good prospect for therapy (or a poor prospect)—and thus the time of good psychotherapists, always in short supply, can be more intelligently rationed. This, in a nutshell, is our project.

In a larger sense the subject matter is that of human interinfluencing, or communicating, of signaling on the one side and responding on the other—of which psychotherapy is a special and critical example. Ours is an attempt to come nearer to the heart and meaning of human affairs, to the play of intellect and emotion which occurs when two humans are brought together. Our attempt may seem poor when judged by the majesty of the goal toward which we are moving, but progress in this unshaped area must be judged by inches rather than yards. No leaps on the tiptoe of cognition seem to occur here; rather, the investigator drags his body along the rugged ground, leaving behind portions of his clothes and even of his person as testimony to the pain of learning. Many will find our attempt dishearteningly prosaic and will feel that the beauty of unconscious emotional interaction has been lost or destroyed by the gritty work of scientific analysis. The therapist, in particular, who knows the splendor of unconscious interaction, who can feel the answer generating the question, may be appalled at our too simple-seeming categories. Perhaps his will prove to be the intelligent response to our effort: "too soon, too simple."

But another voice arises within us to ask: If not this, what are you going to use for data? Surely not what a man thinks he said, or thinks another man said, some hours or days before. Data, in the case at hand, must be more than memories. It must be the living stuff of the conversation with all relevant emotional signs attached. This conversation, when electronically recorded, is available to the cultivated senses of a second or third observer. Transcribed, it can be provisionally divided into units and the units assigned to categories. These categories can be tested, and accepted or rejected. Such a transaction is "public" in the sense that science uses the word. It is our belief that no other method will suffice. No units, no science; no categories, no science; no numbers, no science.

What is known now in psychotherapy—and we include psycho-analysis—we regard as, in the best and highest sense of the word, exploratory. Good exploration is an absolute precondition of good scientific work. Generally considered, it is a part of science but not the terminal act of science. Good exploration discerns new variables such as the role of unconscious fear in personal life, the structure of the Oedipus situation, or the influence of a negative self-image; but these variables are seen at first darkly, and they require extended treatment by the methods of science to give them exact limits and make them quantities as well as qualities.

Measurement can best begin in any area when the exploratory work has been properly done. Has it been done in this area of psychotherapy? We believe that it has, magnificently so. Freud almost managed to forge a science with his bare hands; but the verdict has to remain *almost*. There is nothing in the nature of knowledge itself which determines that Freud's work cannot be examined, verified, and extended by the usual methods of science. In the case at hand these "usual methods" are those of behavior science; their steady application will turn intuition into positive knowledge, hunch into reliable practice.

Behavior, especially talk, is indeed hard to fragment. One need only try it to understand the mortifying difficulties. In a new field all initial perceptions and discriminations are hard to come by. How to signify in the face of confusion is one of the most cruel tasks. Technique by itself is always sterile; nothing can be called science which omits from the description of a situation the variables which are truly significant in it. In the case of psychotherapy, scientific no-tation will capture the play of feeling and emotion as well as the sentences which accompany and describe a response. If the human whole is to be hacked to pieces, the pieces should be at least natural and unitary parts of the whole. Sentences divested of their proper emotional accompaniments would be unnatural units. For us, the sentence and the emotion always belong together. The lawfulness which is obscurely but powerfully evident in human interaction can never be discerned unless this fact is understood: Sentences always have defining emotional and other reactions attached to them.

Our purpose then is to describe such sentence units, summarize them, render them comparable, and eventually predict what may co-occur when they appear. By counting crudely as we must now do we hope that some of the crucial relationships between variables will show through despite our rough measures.

The system is built to show growth, progression, and change within the patient—if there is any—and the evolution of the relationship between patient and therapist.

In this connection we may ask: What is the scorer's act? What does he actually do? The following is a provisional answer. The scorer takes the interview data which has been recorded and transcribed and marks it up into sentence units. Then he faces the problem of sorting these units into categories such as "aggression," "resistance," or "dependence." In order to sort by motivational category the scorer must feel the emotion "attached" to the sentence as best the transcript permits him to feel it. In crucial cases of doubt the scorer can recur to the sound recording from which the transcript was made. Moot points can often be decided by doing so. In most cases the transcript alone will suffice. It might seem that the ability to discern emotion attached to a written sentence would be rare. We think, however, that this is not the case. Although emotions are originally learned to spoken sentences they are apparently transferred to the written version of the live sentence. Emotional response to the written word is thus, we believe, a common and not a rare skill. If it were not so, the empathic reading of novels or dramas would be impossible. Just as sentence and emotion are tightly linked in daily life so they are still linked when the sentence appears in written form. It is this widely shared ability to respond emotionally to the written sentence which makes content scoring possible.

Though our eventual hopes for this kind of work as we and others may carry it on are high, our present task is a humble one. We have been doing an engineering job. We are trying to create units and thus to invent measures. In order to create a unit one must prove that two people, at least, can recognize it and handle it in the same way. The unit must be shown to be reliable—steady, serviceable. In a field in flux this is no mean task and is well worth the effort we have given it and much more. With the further and seemingly more rewarding task of showing how our new units are related to other reliable units (the task of validation) we have been able to do much less; but we are sustained by the faith that a good measure will somehow be needed and used—and improved. At this stage of things in research on psychotherapy the invention of measures cannot be underestimated as a task. The physical scientists did not find the microscope lying about in an attic; they had first to invent it and then, continuously, to perfect it. As it was improved, knowledge of the subvisible world increased enormously. We believe that matters will follow a similar course in the case of psychotherapy. No measure, no science; new measures, new science.

In developing our coding system we deliberately adopted a naïve viewpoint. We came, as it were, fresh to the material and tried to see what kind of system of analysis it called for. If the data seemed to be crying aloud to have a certain sign we grudgingly adopted it, but only on probation; if further experience did not justify the sign, we dropped it. Many variables were suggested by theory and by the work of other investigators. We resisted inventing a sign to meet any theoretical system or adopting one merely because someone else had used it. We believe therefore that our signs are close to the material from which they arose. This is of course a merit, but there is an attached demerit: Our repertory of signs is limited by the nature of material available to us. During the development of our system we scored sixty-eight interviews by six different therapists with eight patients and one normal person. This material has many limitations. The cases were mainly carried on by student apprentices who, of course, use psychotherapeutic methods least well. The interviews are mainly beginnings of cases, the early hours of what, if carried to conclusion, would have been a long therapeutic process. Thus we do not have the terminal hours of protracted—successful— therapy cases. It may well be that some of the "best" material was thus denied us, material which, if analyzed, would have made our system look different and better than it does (though we do not apologize for what we have been able to do). An urgent need of the field, as our experience shows, is the recording of extensive materials by the best therapists.

Every scientist has his ancestors, near and remote, and every book similarly has a frame of reference larger than its content. Our frame of reference might be called "Conditions-Principles." Human behavior, all that is psychological, occurs under specific conditions— social conditions. It is unthinkable without such conditions. Our patients share a common American culture and they are members of a specific social class. The wise therapist pricks up his ears at all references to the early cultural formations which guided and coerced the first contacts of the patient with the world. Religion may be important; the mother's concept of her maternal role can be decisive; the presence of the companion-father may set up an enduring source of inward strength. The class and culture of the patient define the world in which his first adaptive efforts must be made, those efforts whose outcome gives permanent form to the nuclear personality. The role of class and culture in the issues of psychotherapy is still, we believe, too little understood and valued.

But if the "conditions" element of our frame is important, so also is the "principles" aspect. Neither culture nor class works with precision effects. The human being can be seen as a kind of "marker" stamped out by culture only if viewed from a great distance; seen close up, we observe that culture stamps quite unevenly. Some part of this unevenness is due to the fact that cultural conditions are not a mechanical form, are not uniform throughout a society; and some great part is also due to the fact that the bodies presented to culture for indoctrination are different one from the other. The organism has its lawfulness as the culture has its. The infant, clinging to the dress and breast of culture, discerning her smiling face, has the capacity for fierce passion as well as for blissful repose; as his brain and body mature his individualistic features become more prominent, his capacity for rebellion and dissent more obvious. Acutely vulnerable to gestures of weal and woe from its environment, the infant takes off on his course of life—at once a thing of the centuries and a new separate thing seething with individual needs and motives.

Freud's towering work, still so little understood, still so uncertain in some respects, is part of our broad frame. To say that Freud has dethroned reason seems to us a misleading comment; rather he has enormously increased its importance by showing that the scope of reason in human life can be increased to a point somewhere near that of mastery. To be sure, before Freud's time the nature of the intellectual aspect of man was not well understood. Intellectual functions were thought to occur somewhat without regard to man's passions. Freud better described the unruly forces over which reason is the uneasy master, and sometimes the unwitting servant. Freud saw man as each of us inwardly feels himself to be—as smoking hot, urgent, impelled. Nor did Freud fail to describe realistically and tolerantly the infantile motives which are often the antecedents of the sterilized traits and aspirations of adult life. Nothing, neither the lowest reaches of the animal in man nor his highest achievements, was strange to Freud. Freud noted also the coarse coercion of adult life by the conscience implanted in childhood. This unconscious childhood conscience sometimes coalesces with the civilized demands the adult makes on himself and sometimes stands aside, crying havoc, mewing and gibbering, creating panic in the domain of the civilized personality.

Freud noted that much of our emotional life is unconscious, that it consists of ambiguous sets and stances, that we are governed by obscure images of other and self, that we are perversely swayed by planted emotional tropisms, that daily life (and national life) is influenced by the ground swell of mood, both negative and positive. The niceties of a purely rational view of man had to yield before the invigorating, and in some ways frightening, picture drawn by Freud. Yet Freud recognized that the proudest claim of the conscious self is that it is able to gentle the terrified child within us and guide us to action which will safely reduce our unruly drives.

No theory of human personality which does not take these factors into account, exactly the factors Freud specified, can be realistic. Every personal act and, no less, the chained actions of man's history become more intelligible if one supposes man to be the kind of creature that Freud depicted. The time is almost at hand when every scientific student of behavior will be also, to some degree, a Freudian.

The reader must not be misled by the fact that we call Freud's tremendous sketch "exploratory." There is nothing disparaging in that word. We mean only that in order to be more than exploratory Freud's work must be better attested and clarified, must meet the ordinary canons of science; must be made more teachable and learnable; must grow by orderly and explicit means and not by unobtrusively giving a new sense to old formulae. (We picture Freud, who was not, as he himself once said, a Freudian, smiling indulgently at these thoughts.)

Learning theory, like Freudian theory, is part of the frame of reference in which we work. All professional students of culture believe that social behavior is somehow learned. The question is, how? Does culture fall on the human seedling like rain on the planted seed? Or is it somehow passed on from generation to generation by means we know not of? Neither notion seems correct. The best belief seems to be that cultural traits and habits are learned, lawfully learned, and, if changed, lawfully changed.

The work of a generation of behavior scientists has created a body of principles which we may view as laws of learning. These men include Thorndike, Hull, and a host of modern experimenters. These principles indicate that the crucial element in selecting and preserving culture traits and individual habits is drive reduction. Those responses which get tried out are preserved when followed by a reduction of a drive. Thus the image of the mother's face is preserved as a comforting sign by reinforcement—the reduction of the hunger drive. The feeling of the infant that help will always come is similarly reinforced. Suspicion of others can be learned if such an attitude occurs by inadvertence, just before a reinforcing event occurs. Presumably one's deepest images of self, benign or malignant, can be acquired in the confusing learning dilemmas of early childhood.

As in the case of Freudian theory, it seems to us that learning theory can act as a great organizing force in the understanding of human events. Much clarification follows immediately when one tries to pick out in any human situation the crucial variables recognized by learning theory: when one tries to identify motive, to recognize what response must be tried if learning is to occur, to sense the relevant cues to which the learned response must be attached, and to inquire whether or not drive reduction follows rather immediately after the response-cue connection which is to be strengthened. Learning theory also has a clear-cut answer to the question: How are already learned responses unlearned? and it can tell us much about how responses are generalized and discriminated to different sets of cues. In the present confusion of social science theory, learning theory is a rock.

Our concern with content analysis did not begin with the present work. One of us (Dollard and Mowrer, 1947) had worked with an earlier form called the D.R.Q. This was an interesting measure but too rough in its nature for refined work. It seemed to have no chance of capturing the detailed events of the psychotherapeutic transaction. We had therefore somewhat lost interest in the problem of content analysis. Our interest in the problem was reawakened by the vigorous work of E. J. Murray, who took content analysis of psychotherapy as a thesis problem. He devised a more elaborate content system and showed that it could be reliable, i.e. that a more complex system than that of the D.R.Q. could be made to work. Murray, though technically a thesis advisee, worked with a minimum of aid from those of us (e.g. N. E. Miller, Irving Janis, Auld, Dollard) who at various times acted as his thesis advisers. Excited by Murray's original work and stimulated by the advances he had made, we took up again the problem of content analysis. At first we began fiddling with Murray's categories to check on their reliability. Then we became interested in the categories themselves and, as we warmed to our task, in various new problems, i.e. the desirability of signs to represent unconscious processes, the elaboration of the sign system to give more adequate coverage, the problem of teaching scorers, and the reliability with which scorers could sort individual sentences. The path that Murray had opened turned out to be a high road of new problems and challenges. The result is this book. It is attractive to think of the work of science as one of interactive stimulation and one where a graduate student of talent * can show his professors a thing or two.

* Dr. Murray is now assistant professor of psychology at Syracuse University.

CHAPTER 2

Dividing the Interview into Sentences

ANY STUDY of the therapeutic process requires some sort of division of the material into units. Freud, for example, in describing his treatment of Frau Emmy von N. divided the treatment into days, making then such statements as "Today she was in a good mood" or "I found her in a state of great anxiety" or "Her chief complaint today was of sensations of cold and pain in her left leg." Again in his account of the case of Fräulein Elisabeth von R., Freud spoke of "the first period" of the treatment, of a "second, fruitful period" of the treatment, and of a third and final period (Breuer and Freud, 1895). Scientific communication necessitates some division of the material; quantitative study requires a *precise* division of the material.

When we come to ask: Are these two scientists talking about the same thing when they use such words as "resistance," "transference," or "anxiety"? we discover another reason for dividing the material into units. In order to determine whether different scientists agree on their definitions, we have to know what part of the material they are talking about when they employ technical terms. To know what part of the material they are talking about, we must identify the various parts; i.e. we must unitize.

Finally, we need units when we are teaching the system. If we want to test whether the learner is correctly identifying resistance, dependence, interpretations, and so on, we must be able to point to individual instances of these and to determine, for each one, whether the learner's judgment was correct.

LARGE AND SMALL UNITS

What kind of division one should make depends, of course, on the researcher's aims. If one wishes to get an over-all view of a whole case without paying attention to details, one may use a whole series of interviews as the unit ("the first period," "the second, fruitful period," "the third period"). One may want a medium close-up view of the therapy, for which a whole hour of the case will serve as the unit. One may wish to study the psychotherapy in even greater detail, choosing a topic or theme within an hour, an utterance (what the patient or therapist says until the other one speaks), or a sentence as the unit.

For our research we wished a unit that is very small, so that we would be able to study the detail of the interaction between therapist and patient. By definition, the sentence is the smallest portion of speech that can be fully understood by itself; it is, linguists say, a "minimum free utterance." Thus the sentence seemed appropriate to our aims, and we chose it as our unit.

SCORED, CONTEXTUAL, AND SUMMARIZING UNITS

Before we tell how an interview is divided into sentences, we must briefly turn aside to consider the various ways in which a researcher divides the material he is studying. Not only does he divide it into portions that he measures—for example, sentences each of which he rates or classifies—he also divides it into *contextual* and *summarizing units*. The contextual unit consists of that portion of the interview that is considered when one assigns a score to the *scored unit*. The summarizing unit consists of a number of scored units about which the researcher makes some statement. Considerable confusion arises if these three types of units are not recognized.

Whenever the scored unit is scored in isolation, without the scorer's having knowledge of any other material, the scored unit is the same as the contextual unit. To produce such isolation the researcher may find it necessary to type each sentence on a card, shuffle up all the cards, and present them in random order to the scorer. So far as we know, only Bordin and his co-workers have tried to score units in isolation, and this was not their usual way of working. Researchers do not have scorers consider units in isolation because lack of context makes it difficult to understand the units.

Consider the following three sentences:

> And it comes to me. And I'm—I don't know, I guess I don't want the responsibility. But I'll have to take it, that's about the size of it.

Now let the reader imagine that each of these sentences is presented to him by itself, typed on a card, and that the card has been mixed in with thousands of other cards having sentences that are quite unrelated. Could the reader understand any of these sentences by itself? Could the reader, indeed, understand these sentences if he had only the several sentences of context given above? Consider "And it comes to me." Taking this sentence by itself, or with the sparse context above, the scorer does not know what "it" refers to. For other reasons, too, this sentence is virtually unscorable in isolation. To understand what is being communicated emotionally by the quoted sentence one has to know that the patient is talking about the possibility that her mother may come to live with her after the patient's father dies. One has to know, further, that the patient has just said that her brother is accepting no responsibility for her mother's welfare, so the burden falls on the patient. Thus the three sentences quoted mean: The patient doesn't want to accept responsibility for her mother's well-being, but she feels that she has to. With this much context—the description of the setting just given—the scorer can understand what the patient is trying to say.

A contextual unit could consist of only slightly more than the scored unit or of considerably more than that. How large the contextual unit is depends on the arrangement of the scoring task, for instance on whether the scorer takes the material consecutively. If the scorer has scored consecutively all of the case up to the scored unit, he is influenced to some degree by everything that comes earlier. The researcher cannot eradicate such influence by sternly advising the scorer to consider only the preceding page. It seems to us, therefore, that the wisest course for the researcher is to describe the whole set of arrangements and instructions for scoring, so that any scientist examining the study can estimate for himself what kind of context the scorer had. The arrangements used in our work are described in Chapter 3.

The summarizing unit, including usually a number of scored units, consists of that part of the material about which the researcher makes a summary statement. For example, the summarizing unit can be an hour of a case, which the researcher characterizes as having only a few, or a moderate number, or a great number of sentences that are resistant. Again, the summarizing unit may be the successive ten-minute periods during an interview; the researcher reports the characteristics of such periods occurring early and late in the interview. For real examples of summarizing units the reader may turn to Chapter 8.

METHOD OF IDENTIFYING SENTENCES

Having decided to use the sentence as our unit to be scored, we faced the task of identifying sentences. In developing instructions for dividing interviews into sentences, we built on the work of grammarians and linguists, especially the work of Leonard Bloomfield (1933) and of Charles Carpenter Fries (1952). Fries defined a sentence as a single free utterance—free in the sense that it is not included in any larger structure by means of any grammatical device. Starting from this definition, he sought to identify the cues in a person's speech that signal to the listener, "This is a sentence." In framing our rules for unitizing we invented instructions for finding and responding to the cues that Fries has shown perform this signaling.

Fries and his colleague Kenneth L. Pike (see Pike, 1945) have shown that the structural features of a person's speech usually provide the cues for discriminating what is a sentence from what is not. Before the studies of Pike and of Fries, many linguists believed that sentences are regularly marked off by patterns of pitch. Bloomfield, for instance, said that "secondary phonemes of pitch mark the end of sentences" (p. 170). Fries made phonographic recordings of fifty hours of conversation, then studied these conversations to find out what features signaled a sentence. His findings leave no doubt that while intonation sometimes provides the distinctive contrasts between sentence and nonsentence, it does so much less frequently than grammatical structure does. Let the reader notice that we are talking here not about whether intonation affects the meaning of what is said; we are only considering whether intonation tells the hearer what is a sentence.

THE RULES FOR UNITIZING

Orienting remarks. A sentence is a single free utterance—free in the sense that it is not included in any larger structure by means of any grammatical device. The single free utterance may be a minimum free utterance, having only the barely necessary structures for a communication that could stand alone, or it may be an expanded free utterance (Fries, p. 25). A sentence may be a greeting or fare-well, a call, a question, a request, or a statement (Fries, pp. 41–53).

Speeches of the patient and of the therapist are to be separately unitized. However, what the patient says may influence the unitizing of the therapist's speech, and what the therapist says may influence the unitizing of the patient's speech, as noted in rules 5, 7, and 8.

The unitizer should first go through the typescript of the interview, dividing the material into units as he reads. He should put a separating vertical line between the sentence units which may be discriminated grammatically. Whenever he comes upon a passage where intonational cues provide the distinctive contrast between sentence and nonsentence, he should make a check mark on the typescript. Then he should listen to the tape recording of the interview, making such changes in his placement of the unit markings as are shown by the intonational pattern to be appropriate.

In order to understand the references to intonation in the rules, the unitizer must familiarize himself with the system of marking and notation developed by Pike (see also Fries, pp. 26–8). According to this system there are four levels of relative pitch that include all the intervals essential for American English:

No. 1. Extra high
No. 2. High
No. 3. The usual voice level
No. 4. Low

In illustrating intonational sequences we will represent these levels graphically, using a line that rises for rising pitch and falls for falling pitch,

$$
\begin{array}{c}
1 \overline{} \\
2 \underline{} \\
{}_3 \underline{\text{You were studying sci}|\text{ence}}
\end{array}
$$

$$
\begin{array}{c}
2 \overline{} \\
{}_3 \underline{\text{No}}\,{}_3 \underline{|\text{not exactly}} \\
4 \underline{}
\end{array}
$$

This must not be taken to mean that the voice maintains exactly the same pitch throughout all the syllables on a given line, since the lines are schematic and call attention to the significant points on the intonational contour.

The division into units should be determined by structure whenever possible. Intonational contour should, in our opinion, have second place in this determination. We therefore advise the unitizer as follows:

a. Allow grammatical structure to determine the division into units whenever the structure is unambiguous.

b. When the structure is ambiguous, for example when a group of words could be joined to either the preceding or the following independent clause, allow the intonational pattern to decide the matter of division whenever possible.

c. Only when both the intonational pattern and the structure are ambiguous, let the pattern of pauses be decisive. A final pause is indicated by the symbol //, a tentative pause by the symbol /. By "pause" we mean a signaling of the end of a clause (in the case of tentative pause) or of the end of sentence (in the case of final pause) by a slowing and/or stopping of speech. The final pause is usually longer than the tentative pause: The slowing up is more marked, or the gap between words is longer, or both. Usually accompanying this slowing up and pausing there is a drop in pitch or a level of pitch below what it would have been if the speaker had not intended a final pause. (Of course in interrogation there is sometimes a rise in pitch accompanying the slowing of speech and the pause.)

Punctuation is used in written materials to signal certain structural features of utterances which in speaking are signaled by intonation, pause, and stress. Since the interview is originally a spoken communication, it is not appropriate to consider the typist's punctuation as authoritative when dividing the interview into sentences; rather one should be guided by the signals actually given by the communicator—features of form and arrangement, intonation, pauses, and stress. Ideally, therefore, the unitizer would work from unpunctuated transcripts. If doing so is awkward, he should at any rate try to ignore the punctuation, relying instead on hearing the original tape when the verbal signals alone are insufficient.

The rules are given immediately below. Extensive examples that clarify the application of the rules are presented in Appendix B.

1. A noun or noun substitute tied to a verb comprises an *actor-action* construction (Bloomfield, pp. 172, 184–5; Fries, p. 176). Such an actor-action construction is sufficient for a complete sentence except in any of the following cases:

a. The verb is transitive and there is no noun or noun substitute in the construction of direct object (Fries, pp. 189–201).

b. The verb belongs to a list headed by the forms of *be* (*be, seem, sound, feel, become;* Fries, p. 80) and there is no noun or noun substitute in the construction of predicate nominative and no adjective in the construction of predicate adjective (Fries, pp. 187–201; Okerlund and Vinson, 1942, p. 49).

c. The verb is incompletely modified—i.e. a phrase or dependent clause was intended as a modifier, but only the function word introducing the phrase or clause was spoken, not the function word with noun (for a phrase) or the function word with actor-action construction (for a dependent clause); or some other kind of modification was intended but not carried out, for instance modification by an infinitive verb (Fries, p. 230).

d. The verb is an auxiliary and is not joined to a main verb.*

e. One of the following words or phrases, or some other subordinating conjunction, stands before the actor-action construction, signaling a dependent clause: *after, although, as, because, before, in order that, if, since, when, where, while, that, what, who, why, how, which, whenever, wherever, whatever, whoever, whichever, whether, so that* (Fries, p. 253).

The word *that* as signal of a subordinate clause is often omitted in conversational English. Because of this, the unitizer may have to know what the intonational pattern is in order to distinguish between a subordinate clause from which the introductory *that* has been elided and an independent clause which should be counted as a separate unit.

2. Do not join two actor-action constructions into a single so-called compound sentence; instead, treat each actor-action construction as a separate sentence unless one of the signals of inclusion listed above in 1e stands before it (Fries, pp. 251–2). The following coordinating conjunctions are not to be considered signals of inclusion: *and, but, however, yet, nevertheless, also, moreover, besides, likewise, otherwise, therefore, thus, consequently, accordingly, furthermore, similarly, so.*

3. In order to determine whether a group of words (phrase or dependent clause) belongs with the preceding or with the following sentence, it is sometimes necessary to listen to the sound recording to get the cues of patterns and pauses. A dependent clause more frequently belongs with what follows than with what precedes. When it belongs with the preceding independent clause, that clause

* Auxiliaries are treated by Fries as function words rather than as Class 2 words ("verbs"). See Fries, pp. 90–1, 96–7.

has a 3–2–3 intonational pattern * at the end, signaling continuation (Fries, p. 254).

4. Certain conventional expressions may lack an actor-action construction, yet be sentences. These include the following:

> Seems that it concerned you a great deal (*Seems that* is a conventional substitute for *it seems that.*)

> See you next week (*See* is a conventional substitute for *I'll see,* when used in this farewell.)

5. A complete sentence may consist of a question that lacks an actor-action construction. Such a question is signaled by repetition, with rising intonation at the end, of a part of a statement sentence uttered by another speaker, usually immediately after the statement has been made (Fries, p. 157).

6. Another kind of complete sentence, sometimes not having the actor-action construction, is the supplement question, which is signaled by special words such as *what* and *which* (Fries, pp. 98–9; Bloomfield, p. 171).

7. Answers to questions may be complete sentences, though lacking an actor-action construction, if they are complete when considered within the frame of the question to which they are answers.

a. *Yes* or *no* or an equivalent word is to be considered a complete sentence, as is *yes* or *no* supplemented by a statement utterance. *Yes* or *no* supplemented by a statement utterance is to be considered only one sentence. What follows *yes* or *no* is to be counted supplemental if no final pitch or final pause (//) comes at the end of the *yes* or *no* (Fries, pp. 165, 102–3).

b. A completive sentence may be of any form called for by the question that it completes (Fries, pp. 167–72).

8. Occasionally one speaker may complete a sentence begun by another speaker. Such completions are to be considered sentences even when they lack an actor-action construction, if they are complete when considered within the frame of the speech that they finish (Bloomfield, pp. 176-7). Example:

> PATIENT And I think that's going to be a great asset in his work if he's able to make then speedy decisions when the time comes and
>
> THERAPIST Yeah and make a study

* See the discussion of intonation above and refer to Fries, p. 27.

9. Continued attention, signaled by "mm-hmm" or an equivalent form, constitutes a sentence (Fries, pp. 49–50).

10. False starts do not count as sentences and are not to be scored by the content-scorer. Put the division mark before the false start. Falterings like *uh* or *ah* may be bracketed as not belonging to a sentence (Fries, p. 23 n.; Bloomfield, p. 186, "anacoluthon").

a. Very occasionally it is necessary to listen to the sound recording to determine whether one is dealing with a false start. Intonational patterns in these instances give the cues as to whether the function words were signals of inclusion of the dependent clause with the preceding or the following independent clause.

11. No words are to be "understood" or "supplied" by the unitizer. In particular, an actor-action construction *must* have an explicitly stated noun or noun substitute and an explicitly stated verb.

12. Some words and phrases are to be included, by the construction of parataxis, in the adjoining sentence: *goodness, I guess, you know, I think, isn't it* (Bloomfield, p. 185). Phrases and clauses following *I mean* are to be included with the preceding independent clause if there is 3-2-3 intonational pattern signaling continuation at the end of that clause. Example:

I divided sex up into ⌐ two classes in my mind I mean sexual feeling

13. Some actor-action constructions which, if they stood alone, would be considered complete sentences are to be included with the sentence that surrounds them. These *parenthetic* clauses can be identified by the fact that they interrupt the surrounding sentence (Bloomfield, p. 186). Example:

> While my husband and I get along well together uh-as I told you before he's very easygoing very easy to get along with still there's within me sometimes a turmoil of dissatisfaction (Parenthetic or included sentence consists of: *as I told you before he's very easygoing very easy to get along with.*)

14. Greetings, farewells, and calls are treated as sentences (Fries, pp. 42–5).

15. Requests and commands, signaled by the infinitive verb alone or by the infinitive verb followed by a noun or noun substitute not tied to the verb, are considered sentences (Fries, p. 145).

16. A quotation is to be included in the quoting sentence, even if

the quotation consists of several sentences each of which, except for the quotation device, could stand alone. Certain grammatical devices (words like *said,* for example) are the usual signals of quotation; sometimes, however, intonational patterns, not the arrangement of words or the words used, supply the cues needed for deciding that the speaker is quoting (Bloomfield, p. 148).

17. Weeping, laughter, and sighing of the patient are to be unitized. Each instance of weeping, laughter, or sighing is to be designated as at least one unit; if it lasts for more than seven seconds it is to be counted as more than one unit, the number of units being the number of five-second intervals occupied by the behavior, to the nearest five seconds. Weeping, laughter, and sighing are to be designated as separate units even when occurring in the midst of speech. In this case both the speech and the emotional behavior are to be unitized and scored. Included in weeping are all sorts of responses such as sobbing, sniffling, and talking through tears.

18. Each period of silence lasting five seconds or longer is to be designated by unit markings. Each five seconds of silence is to be counted as one unit, the counting to be done to the nearest five seconds. However, when weeping or laughter occurs while the patient is not talking, the time occupied by the weeping or laughter is not to be counted as silence when determining the number of units of silence. When the therapist is having the patient use the couch, silences at the beginning of the hour should be counted from the moment the patient lies down.

RELIABILITY OF UNITIZING

To test the reliability of unitizing, we taught two intelligent persons to unitize, using as instructional material the rules just presented and the examples given in Appendix B. No oral instruction of any kind was given. Therefore the results of this test represent what can be accomplished by using these rules when the unitizer has no chance to receive supplemental oral instruction or to reach a consensus with a partner on how to solve certain problems.

The material used in this test consisted of excerpts from five psychotherapy cases. An excerpt contained ten pages of completely unpunctuated, uncapitalized transcription taken from a randomly selected place in each of the cases. Altogether the material included about 900 sentences. The results are presented in Table 1. In summary, the two workers agreed on the placement of 86% of the unit marks. Agreement ranges from 83% on the poorest case to 91% on the best.

TABLE 1. RESULTS OF TESTING RELIABILITY OF UNITIZING

	Unit marks agreed on by both scorers	Mark by A, none by B	Mark by B, none by A
Case 1	155	20	41
Case 2	138	17	34
Case 3	221	11	33
Case 4	135	23	31
Case 5	123	10	31

It is apparent that Scorer B had a tendency to divide the material into more units than Scorer A. In actual application of the unitizing, of course, the unitizers would have the benefit of close supervision as they were learning this task; and so such tendencies to make too many divisions or too few would be corrected, and misunderstandings of the instructions could be quickly spotted and corrected.

We consider this amount of agreement in unitizing to be satisfactory, especially in view of the rigorous conditions of the test.

PRACTICE MATERIAL ON UNITIZING

Chapter 6 and Appendix D, which are presented in order to illustrate the scoring of interviews, can also serve to illustrate the application of the unitizing rules. Anyone who wishes to develop his skills in unitizing should carefully study these two interviews.

The reader who has carefully studied the rules and has thoughtfully read the two illustrative interviews may then wish to test his understanding of the unitizing procedure. To enable the reader to do this we present in Appendix C several extracts from interviews. The correct unitizing is given on the facing page for the first excerpt, and at the end of the appendix for the other two excerpts.

CHAPTER 3

The Approach to the Scoring Task

THE RESEARCHER who wishes to use our content-analysis method must understand a number of assumptions, attitudes, and procedures. These bases of the method constitute the subject matter of the present chapter.

PREPARATION FOR SCORING

If one hopes to score psychotherapy interviews intelligently, one cannot plunge right into the task without preparation. For sensible results it is necessary to prepare oneself by going through the following steps:

1. Listen to the tape recording of the first hour of the case that is to be scored. The purpose of this is to get an impression, from the auditory stimuli, of the patient's way of talking and of relating to the therapist.

2. Arrange for the preparation of an accurate typescript of each hour of the case (see the suggestions at the end of this chapter).

3. Arrange for the division of the material into sentence units, according to procedures outlined in Chapter 2 of this book.

4. Have at hand sheets of paper with numbers running from 1 to 100, on which you can write the scores.

5. Make sure that you know what has happened in the case up to the point where you begin scoring, whether or not you score each hour of the case. For example, if you score only the odd-numbered hours, be sure to read all the even-numbered hours also.

6. Score the case, so far as possible, as it would be seen by the therapist at the time of the sentence that is being scored—i.e. as it would be seen by a perfect therapist who understood fully what was going on, or, rather, as fully as anyone could at that point. Therefore

you should know whatever the therapist knew up to the time of the hour being scored, but you should know nothing more than this. The idea is that the scorer should see the case unfolding just as the therapist saw it. His judgment about the meaning of the unfolding events may differ from the therapist's, but he should at any rate have before him the same data that were available to the therapist at the time. Only thus can the scoring capture the therapeutic process as an unfolding interaction between patient and therapist.

7. Read through the whole page that you are scoring before you write down any scores. Then start through it again, writing down the scores as you go. The purpose of this procedure is to control the amount of context that different scorers of the same hour will have. We have found that it is sometimes necessary to read ahead a bit to understand the point of a certain utterance. But how far should one be permitted to read ahead? "How far" proved difficult to define. We finally settled on letting the scorer go to the end of the page as a usual thing, and a little further than that if necessary to complete the topic the patient is discussing. We want to allow the scorer at least as much freedom as the therapist has, *not* to have to respond immediately, to be able to delay making a formulation. In allowing the scorer to read ahead for a few pages, if necessary, we were guided, too, by the belief that establishing this procedure would help the scorer to respond more to the case as a unified, on-going interaction between patient and therapist rather than as a collection of separate items. In other words, we wanted to help the scorer to see the forest as well as the trees.

ATTITUDES TOWARD SCORING

We have found it helpful to put in writing, for our own guidance, certain general principles that should be followed in scoring.

Scorer tries to understand the interaction. Since the aim of the content-analysis system is to identify the interaction between patient and therapist and highlight the most significant therapeutic variables, the scorer should approach the task with the aim of allotting scores that bring out just these aspects as well as can be done. Thus the scorer has to understand what is going on in the case. In doing this, he will in our opinion be greatly helped by a knowledge of psychoanalysis. He will do well to be familiar with Freud's distinction between manifest and latent content (first applied to dreams

[Freud, 1900]), since some of the more important currents of the therapy run below the surface.

In general the scorer should ask himself, when scoring a sentence of the patient: What is it, mainly, that the patient is trying to communicate? What does the patient mean? In scoring a sentence of the therapist he should ask: What is the main effect of this in the interaction? It often helps to bring out what the patient's communication means if the scorer asks himself: What would the therapist (if acting most adaptively) do about this behavior? When the scorer sees, for instance, that the therapist would have to make a certain kind of interpretation of resistance, then he sees clearly that the patient's sentence is, indeed, resistant.

Scorer focuses on the most important aspect of the sentence. The scorer attempts to deal with the most important—usually the most obvious—aspect of the material. The primary meaning is scored, the secondary meanings are neglected.

In deciding what is more important, when a sentence of the patient has several equally clear aspects, the scorer should be guided by the following table of priorities:

1. Anything concerning the therapist is of greatest importance.

2. Resistance is next in importance.

3. Evidence of reasoning, generalization, or discrimination comes next.

4. Motivational conflicts or simple motives are next in importance (e.g. an aggression-fear conflict or an uncomplicated expression of aggression).

5. Finally, *Unsc* (for "unscorable") should be used as a last resort.

For the therapist's sentences the rule of priorities is as follows: Interpretive activity of the therapist should be noted first, if present; only if the therapist's sentence is not interpretive should some other sign than *Interp* (for "interpretation") be used.

Scorer stays close to the material. So far as he can, the scorer stays close to what the patient has said. The scorer resists guessing about motives that are unknown to him. He does not "reach" for scores. The inferences that he does make, he makes according to the rules set forth in Chapters 4 and 5.

However, the scorer does make reasonable inferences. Sometimes the patient is inexplicit in expression, not saying everything that is required for full understanding. For example, a patient who was apparently worried over money problems (particularly over the financial problems she would face if she got a divorce and then herself had to support her infant son) spoke of being concerned about "the terrible problem." She didn't specifically say what the "terrible problem" was; but one could reasonably infer that it was the problem of taking care of the baby without the father's help. When it does happen that a patient isn't explicit enough, the scorer is justified in making reasonable inferences. Even so, he should strive to keep such guessing to a minimum. Furthermore, the fact that the patient is vague may in itself be a most important feature of the communication, a feature not to be neglected or glossed over in the scoring.

The scorer doesn't assume motives that according to theory *should* be present; he scores what is, not what ought to be. For example, the scorer should not automatically assume the frustration-aggression sequence (see Dollard *et al.,* 1939). If the patient is frustrated the scorer does *not* assume that the patient is angered, consciously or unconsciously, by the frustration unless there are specific cues of resentment.

Scoring is from patient's point of view. The scorer tries to identify the meaning of each utterance for the patient, since it is the patient who is in therapy and it is in his life that therapeutic effects, if any, will occur. For example, if the patient's sister is described as wanting a baby, don't score what the sister wants; score how the patient views this, its relevance to her.

Score as of the time spoken of. The scorer takes each sentence of the patient as an expression of the patient's feeling and behavior at the time to which the sentence refers (unless it is clear that the sentence, though ostensibly referring to the past, has a transference or resistance meaning).

If a speaker says of his childhood, "I was a trusting child," that sentence is scored as a loving reaction (*L parents*). If, then, he adds a second sentence, "But now I think I was a fool to be so trusting," this reaction should be scored as a self-critical reaction of the present day, probably *H/self.* The rule to score as of the time spoken of presents difficulties when the patient's reaction to a past event is unclear. For example, if a patient says, "My sister used to tattle on me to Mother," giving no further information as to his reaction, the scorer must somehow infer what the patient's reaction was at the time in order to score correctly. If he feels that he can safely infer hostility toward the patient's sister, he would assign the score *H sister.* If it were clear, however, that in speaking of tattling the patient was indirectly complaining that the therapist wasn't keeping confidences, the scorer would consider the sentence as an indication of transference attitudes and might score it *h-a therapist.*

Take each sentence for itself. The scorer considers each sentence in and of itself—though allowing himself to be somewhat influenced by the context—and in particular he does not anticipate future developments in the case by scoring a denouement before it happens. The reader will appreciate the importance of this rule if he considers that the patient's understanding of some aspect of his behavior may change in the course of an hour, perhaps as a result of an interpretation by the therapist; and that in such a case the scorer would not want to attribute to the patient at an earlier time what he learned only later. Furthermore, different feelings of the patient may come to the fore at different times: satisfaction, guilt, and self-justification about something he has done may successively appear in the speech of a patient. Each of these feelings, when it dominates, should receive notation.

Though each sentence is scored separately, and is scored for itself, context must be considered. Many sentences could not be scored at all in isolation; their meaning depends on the surrounding sentences. We believe, furthermore, that the scorer should not so fix his attention on the single sentences that he loses his sense of what is going on in the case. His sense of the whole flow of the case is of utmost importance to proper scoring.

Special features of the method. Some special features of the scoring must be mentioned:

1. There is no differential weighting of the sentence units. A strong expression of hostility counts for no more than a mild expression; each is one unit of *H.* We expect that strength of motive will be shown by an increase in the number of sentences of a particular kind—the stronger the motive, the more sentences expressing it. At any rate, no attempt is made in this system to scale individual sentences for strength of motive.

2. Conscious thoughts and feelings are represented by scoring abbreviations beginning with capital letters; unconscious thoughts and feelings by abbreviations starting with small letters.

3. If the patient makes clear who the object of his feeling is, we note this. For example: *L wife,* for "patient expresses love of his wife."

Empathic reactions of the scorer. The scorer tends to be influenced in his scoring by his sense of what he himself would feel in the situation described by the patient. Such empathic response is, of course, necessary to sensible scoring of the emotional transaction that is presented in psychotherapy protocols. Empathy is the instrument of understanding.

However, the scorer has to be on guard against carrying such identification too far, against assuming that what he feels is what the patient felt. The patient, for example, may report receiving an affront which would have made the scorer angry. But the patient might not have had such a reaction of anger; indeed, it may be part of the patient's neurotic problem that he *doesn't* react with anger to such a frustration. In such an instance, empathy is the scorer's—and the therapist's—means of seeing in what way the patient is neurotically different. (An example of this point: One of our patients described how her family had always forgotten her birthday when she was a child. She made excuses for their forgetting; after all, since her birthday came on July 5, they were naturally preoccupied with the holiday and couldn't be expected to remember, and so forth. One of the scorers credited the patient with hostility toward her family; but there is no evidence in what the patient said that she felt any anger toward them. Evidently the scorer, imagining himself in the situation, felt angry.)

At times, the unconscious needs of the scorer influence his scoring, producing confusion. The conflict represented in the patient's utterances may be one that the scorer has not adequately resolved in his own life. Even the psychologically most composed person is likely to find scoring stressful, because reacting empathically to the patient's suffering produces pain in the scorer, and coming upon a problem of the patient's that is similar to an unresolved conflict of one's own is especially unsettling. The scorer who is hampered by unconscious forces in himself may either overemphasize or underemphasize certain scores that are connected with his own conflicts. Personal factors in the scorer will cause the most trouble when the cues from the therapeutic material are most ambiguous; unconscious conflicts of the scorer will have much less effect when the material is quite clear.

One is tempted, in order to avoid these problems of the scorer as he identifies with the patient and tries to understand what is going on, to try to make the scoring a quite routine matter in which empathy would play no part. One could attempt to convert the scoring into the following of a set of easy rules. For example, one might give this instruction in connection with the dependence category: *Score as "dependence" any mention of birthdays, of getting letters, of feeling cheated, or of wanting more affection.* (Undoubtedly the list would have to be longer than this.) It wouldn't matter, then, what the patient said about these events or what his feelings were; the scorer would just routinely apply the rule. The rules would have to be long and complex, full of lists of items to be scored this way or that. Such an approach to achieving reliable scoring is possible, but we did not choose to adopt it. We chose rather to suffer with the difficulties of allowing the scorer to react freely to the material, in order to let him make use of the incomparable empathic instrument of understanding.

The questions arise then: Who can do this scoring? Must the scorer be relatively free of neurotic conflicts? Should he have been psychoanalyzed? Does he need to have had graduate training in psychology? Does he need to have had postdoctoral training in psychoanalysis? Do the answers to these questions depend on the individual—can some talented people who haven't the formal training mentioned do the scoring adequately whereas less talented persons cannot? We must admit that we don't know the answers to these questions. Our best judgment—out of our experience in scoring therapy interviews—is that the scorer must have freedom from severe neurotic conflicts in himself, and that it is likely that especially talented persons do not need a personal analysis or special training in psychoanalysis, though these would certainly be advantageous. We believe that these questions can be answered adequately only by having different kinds of persons try their hands at the scoring. We have not done this as yet—all of the scoring on which this book is based was done by the two authors—and so it remains to be determined who can score.

RÉSUMÉ OF RECOMMENDED ATTITUDES

1. Ask: What is it, mainly, that the patient (or the therapist) is trying to say?

2. Score the most important aspect. In deciding what is important be guided by the following order of priorities: anything concerning therapist, resistance, reasoning, motivation, unscorable. For the

therapist's sentences give interpretation (if present) priority over other categories.

3. Resist dubious inferences. Score what is, not what (according to theory) ought to be.

4. Score from the patient's point of view.

5. Score as of the time spoken of.

6. Take each sentence for itself, but do consider context when necessary.

7. Allow empathic reactions to have some role in the scoring, but be on guard against imputing to the patient feelings that you have but he does not.

WHAT IS MEANT BY CONTENT ANALYSIS?

We sometimes speak of our method of classifying sentences in the psychotherapy interview as a content-analysis method.* What is meant by this phrase? Content analysis, in its general social-science definition, means the classification of what is said according to some set of categories. As we understand the term, content analysis does not imply any particular kind of categories. Rather, the set of categories can be chosen so as to be appropriate for the problem being studied.

Perhaps it is unnecessary to make this point. Yet we fear that readers who are accustomed to thinking of the word "content" as one that defines a certain kind of category-set may misunderstand what we are doing. We fear that they will look not at our categories but only at the name, "content analysis," and reject our system because it has a name that has been applied to things they don't like.

Therefore we warn the reader: By calling our system a content-analysis method we *don't* mean to compare it with the content analysis of Rorschach practitioners (who contrast "content" with "determinants"). We *don't* intend any contrast between "form" and "content"; some of the formal aspects of meaning—such as the tempo of speech—do enter into our scoring. We *don't* mean to say that our system deals with the "historical content" that is reported in psychotherapy rather than with "current interaction with therapist"; far from it. It is unlikely that anyone who has read what we have said up to now would fail to see that our system is intended to

* A review of "Previous Studies Bearing on Content Analysis of Psychotherapy" is provided in Appendix A.

deal with the emotional and interpersonal events of psychotherapy
and that we consider these to be the really important variables.
Finally, by "content analysis" we *don't* mean a study only of the
surface or manifest elements in the therapy. Again, it is unlikely
that anyone who has read the prior pages of this book would misunderstand; but we want to make the point crystal clear.

RECOMMENDATIONS FOR STUDYING THIS BOOK

The reader who wishes to learn to score by our system should, we
believe, read the book in the following manner:

1. Read Chapters 4 and 5. Be sure to read both before trying to
score, so that you will be familiar with both patient's and therapist's
categories. If one doesn't score the therapist's sentences at the same
time as one is scoring the patient's, one tends to neglect and pass over
the therapist's role in the interaction. Therefore one needs to know
how to score the therapist's sentences in order to score the patient's
sentences adequately.

2. Read and study Chapter 6. Refer to Chapters 4 and 5 as you
feel the need to do so, while studying 6.

3. Score the hour printed in Appendix D, referring to the rules
as needed. Then check your scoring at the end of the appendix.
Where you don't understand the scoring, and the authors' comments
don't help, go back to the definitions in Chapters 4 and 5.

4. Score other materials. Prepare the typescripts as suggested at
the end of this chapter; unitize according to the rules given in
Chapter 2. The person who unitizes must study Chapter 2 and do
the practice exercises in Appendix C.

PREPARING TRANSCRIPTS OF THERAPY INTERVIEWS

1. The recording equipment must be of sufficiently high fidelity
to record an ordinary conversation, at normal voice levels, intelli-
gibly. The room in which the recording is made must be adequate
acoustically; the finest recording machine is useless in a room that
has the acoustics of a tile bathroom.

2. It is recommended that a technician be made responsible for
operating the recording equipment. The technician should pretest
the equipment before each session, preferably by making a test recording. If possible, the technician should monitor the recorder

throughout the session in order to make sure that the recording level is appropriate and to be on hand in case of any mechanical mishap.

3. The person employed to type the interviews should be of high intelligence, with a wide vocabulary. Otherwise she will not be able to understand a mumbled word. The typist must be persistent in playing back, over and over, sections of the recording that at first seem unintelligible. And she shouldn't guess at what is said if she doesn't understand. Nor should she clean up the patient's and therapist's grammar; she should write down exactly what they said.

4. Even though we have warned the unitizer not to rely on the typist's perceptions of intonations and pauses, we concede that in practice he will be influenced by them. If the typist punctuates the typescript accurately, this influence will be useful rather than harmful. The typist naturally indicates a final pause (see Chapter 2 for definition) by a period. When she notes changes in pitch indicating that the speaker is quoting, she inserts quotation marks. She should also try to indicate by parentheses when an independent clause is interrupted by a parenthetic statement. However, we do not expect that the typist can identify all of the parenthetic clauses; some of these will be discovered only later, by the unitizer.

5. The typist should time all pauses with a stop watch and write down how long each is; and she should note all weeping, laughing, and sighing.

CHAPTER 4

The Signs of the Content-Analysis System: Categories for Patient

THE SIGNS we use arose from the struggle to categorize actual case material. A sign was invented only when it seemed to deal with a problem which posed itself repeatedly in the clinical data. We use no imaginary examples; every example given occurred in an actual case. Even when we paraphrase or summarize we are always referring to a real experience of a real person. With analytic or behavior theory as a guide, many other signs could have been invented; unless our material forced us to add a new sign, we did not do so. Others faced with new problems in material might elaborate or abridge our system for special purposes; thus it could easily be adapted to code expressions of anxiety in newspaper editorials. Certainly our system will have to be elaborated before it can catch the full scope of the transaction in psychoanalysis between patient and analyst. So be it; we have forced the matter as far as we were able at this time and have made what we consider a suitable first try.

CRITERIA FOR SCORING UNCONSCIOUS MOTIVES

Before discussing the rules for scoring individual signs we will present a schematic account of our views on the conscious-unconscious problem. In connection with the individual signs, many examples of scoring unconscious motives will be found. We wish to introduce these examples by a more general discussion.

BEHAVIOR IS MOTIVATED

No matter how complex or bizarre an item of behavior may seem, it is our firm assumption that each such item of response is motivated. The neurotic, like the member of a foreign culture, may seem to be acting without motivation; closer inspection of his behavior will show that he has "learned motives" which are strange to us. The layman may dismiss strange behavior as of no importance to him; the behavior scientist is obliged to search for the motives which may lie behind seemingly inscrutable action.

BEHAVIOR IS LAWFUL

Another of our basic assumptions is that behavior is never nonsensical but is always lawful. If a behavior sequence does not make ordinary sense, it makes some kind of extraordinary sense. We assume that behavior proceeds from motive to response to reward (or lack of it); each behavior sequence must be studied from this standpoint. We sense something "wrong," the play of hidden motive, if an individual cannot adequately describe what he is doing. In an overwhelming preponderance of cases, as we have found, enigmatic behavior loses its strange character when a sequence is carefully examined to discover what are the motives and what the rewards. The observer needs this conviction of lawfulness if he is to penetrate to the heart of an incident. If he does not have it, he will be easily thrown off by minor difficulties and apparent contradictions. As mysteries yield and riddles of behavior are solved, the assumption that behavior is lawful becomes ever stronger in the mind of the observer.

DO WE NEED THE CONCEPT OF THE UNCONSCIOUS?

We certainly do not need the notion of the unconscious in any formal or philosophical sense, but as a practical matter it is indispensable. Without it, the facts of daily life as they are evident to anyone cannot be understood. It is to these facts, not to the concepts which govern them, that we are loyal.

Behavior problems which require us to impute unconscious motive are known to every normal adult person. Perhaps uneasily, the normal adult will notice aspects of his own feeling and action for which he cannot account. When this adult acts as observer and has available to him the span of behavior about a single person which is presented to an analyst, the use of the category "unconscious motive" becomes mandatory. The evidence for unconscious motive can be discovered in every printed record of a psychotherapeutic transaction.

LABELING

Labeling or naming of human motive, act, cue, and reward is the distinctively human attribute; apparently it was achieved in some ten million years of human development. Labeling is learned by the in-coming child from the supply of labels provided by his culture. Apparently labeling is learned by typical reinforcement processes brought to bear on the innate vocalizing tendencies of the child. Labeling is first acquired in the great learning episodes of childhood, those episodes having to do with feeding, cleanliness training, aggression control, and sexual orientation.

The learning of labels to match the significant events of life turns out to be quite imperfect. Even in the best of cases, the labels learned do not enable the individual to explicate completely his emotions and feelings; much less do they provide him with an accurate history of what has happened in the course of his socialization. For all the centuries before Freud, this singular and stunning fact failed to impress observers of human psychology.

Neurotics are those who have been able to do only an unusually poor job in conscious description of their mental and emotional life; the result in behavior is that neurotics are afflicted with un-resolvable conflict—unresolvable because, literally, inexpressible. If one misses one's first chance to label the emotional world accurately, there is usually no second chance available. Until modern times the neurotic person was doomed to a lifetime of misery. Even today there is no second chance for most people. But for a few there is the resource of psychotherapy, which in its best form is psychoanalysis. By carefully re-arousing the neurotic conflicts which went unlabeled and often unnoticed in the first push of childhood, psychotherapy can attach labels to these active emotions. Once these emotions have been labeled, all the resources of higher mental life can be brought to bear to resolve conflict.

CONSCIOUS VERSUS UNCONSCIOUS

For us, "conscious" means the named or nameable; "unconscious" means the unnameable or unlabelable. Any or all units in a behavior chain can be unconscious: motive, response, cues to which subject reacts, or rewards which occur. Neglecting to name a motive (because of distraction or because one can't say everything at once) does not make it unconscious. A motive or a pattern of cues is unconscious only when it cannot be named at all.

CHARACTERISTICS OF CONSCIOUS BEHAVIOR

Conscious behavior is variously said to be intelligent, adaptive, ingenious, creative, problem-solving, stress-reducing, goal-achieving. Conscious behavior is intelligent exactly because it depends on clear and complete labeling. Clear naming permits the subject to make sharp and adaptive discriminations (e.g. of what is dangerous from what is not); it allows appropriate generalizations of problem solutions (such that one repeats successful solutions and avoids failures). Foresight is, so to say, the juggling of labels (and linked emotions) so that one can correctly anticipate future problems and compose designs for their solution. Planning ties foresightful responses together and binds the mental units to the gross-behavioral actions in a tight (and ready-to-use) pattern. What we are stressing here is that intelligence is intelligible. Intelligence itself is lawful. It has to do with a correct description of the great inner as well as the great outer world.

CHARACTERISTICS OF BEHAVIOR IMPELLED BY UNCONSCIOUS CONFLICT

Behavior motivated by unconscious conflict is denounced, in various ways, as stupid, inflexible, repetitive, or incautious. Higher mental processes do not seem to operate in the case of such behavior; important discriminations and generalizations fail to occur; anticipation of the future is inaccurate; ingenious planning does not appear. Since the elements of the conflict cannot be named, they cannot appear in a foresightful calculation of consequence. Neurotic behavior appears more like that of children than of adults, and, indeed, it is more under the influence of the chaotic "primary process" (Fenichel 1945, p. 16) than is adult behavior.

Neurotic behavior is no mere innocent or intellectual deviation. A heavy price is exacted of the neurotic: suffering, constant dreadful suffering. Occasional life circumstances, not easily found or maintained, will "turn off" this suffering for a brief time. Sleep may reduce it. Obsessed activity may milden it. Symptoms ameliorate it. Drugs too damp it down; but it is always present waiting for its next moment of resurrection. The motive to relieve neurotic suffering is one of the most humane of all scientists' motives. The challenge to end neurotic suffering is surely one of the highest goals of a culture influenced by science.

The penalties and embarrassments of failure to label are illustrated by the experience of a male patient. The following is a paraphrase of his report: *

Patient met a young man on a bus and fell into conversation. The stranger proved agreeable and patient had the feeling of having known him better than the passage of time would warrant. The stranger invited patient to visit him the next time he came to New York. Patient did go to New York on his vacation and did visit his acquaintance of the bus trip. The man on the bus turned out to be a young actor, and he took patient to various actors' parties, took him behind the scenes of a Broadway show, and generally made a fuss about him. On one particular evening, patient was elaborately wined and dined. He went to the apartment of the actor for a further talk. The actor played some (supposedly) incendiary music and invited patient to lie down on a couch to listen to it. Patient complied. When the actor began kissing him furiously, patient rose and explained that he was not interested in the kissing and would like to go home. The actor could hardly believe his ears but, not wishing a scene, he allowed patient to break up the situation.

Patient did indeed have unconscious motives and they impelled him toward the actor—but they were not, as the actor had hoped, explicit homosexual motives. Patient had a deep unconscious need for care and love; at the same time, he felt himself a "bad" and worthless person. These were the motives that were suddenly re-

* In the case histories and interviews cited throughout this volume all identifying references have been disguised so as to protect the patients. Some of the illustrative passages quoted have been silently condensed and edited from the original transcriptions of interviews to eliminate irrelevancies and repetition, but otherwise they are accurate reproductions of what was actually said.

duced by the various attentions of the homosexual prospector. Patient did not ask himself why his new friend was so devoted; he was pleased to have what he thought was a simple-hearted devotion from anyone, woman or man. Not knowing his own needs, he was unable to foresee the embarrassing course of behavior in which he became involved. Failure to be able to label his dependent needs made it impossible for him to behave foresightfully. In many such cases "innocence" is not a protection but a threat to well-being.

BEHAVIOR MYSTERIOUS TO SUBJECT

Unconsciously motivated behavior is often mysterious to the subject himself. He refuses to comply with some routine of life, he flares out at some friend or is phobically prejudiced against some situation—and he turns and asks himself, "Why did I do that?" His response is bafflement. He does not know and has no means of finding out why he did what he did. After a moment of attention, the patient hopelessly drops the problem and turns to other matters. Our point is that the victimized person often records the operation of unconscious motives by his sense of being baffled about one of his "slips."

The disturbing experience of bafflement can be escaped if a rationalization for mysterious behavior can be found. Every act may be "overdetermined," i.e. more than one motive is almost invariably operating to produce a specific action. If the conscious member of a bundle of motives can be accented while the unconscious one is slighted, we have a rationalization for behavior. Thus:

> *A young businessman reported in psychotherapy that his work had been interrupted by getting erections while he was sitting at his desk. He was at a loss to explain this behavior and was much vexed at it. He concluded that it must be because "his pants had been rubbing against his penis" at the time that he got the erection.*

This was indeed true; trousers have a way of rubbing against the genitals, not just once in a while but all the time. What the patient was leaving out of account was the new secretary who had come to the office two weeks before. The patient was plainly attracted to

her but was not at all aware of how direct and deeply genital his attraction was. It was against his code to admit that he was sexually
attracted to an unauthorized woman. His response, unconsciously
determined, was to have the erection, in isolation from all thoughts
and intentions regarding the girl. His remark that the erection was
caused by "pants-rubbing" was a rationalization which concealed
the guilty fact of his sexual attraction to the girl and dismissed the
"mystery."

BEHAVIOR MYSTERIOUS TO OBSERVER

The behavior of others is often mysterious to the casual observer.
This "mystery" can arise because the others withhold facts, known
to them, which would make their behavior intelligible. An account-
ant who has been stealing money by long-standing falsification of
his books can hardly behave in a way which is entirely sensible to
other persons. He is bound to be covering up in ways that create
mysteries.

If, however, the observer has accessible the most complete information that the subject can provide, mysteries created by conscious withholding of facts do not arise; but in this closer look one
will still find mysterious actions. An apparently unmotivated response will seem mysterious and will cause inquiry, especially if the
observer is a therapist, as to what motive is exciting it. Stupid behavior in an intelligent person will lead to puzzlement; why, in this
situation, is Baker unable to act at his intellectual level? Causeless
misery will attract attention; what dammed up motives does the
suffering represent? Behavior seems sensible to us when we understand, or think we do, the motive, the response, the concurrent cues,
and the apparent goal or reward. Motive without response or response without motive arouses our curiosity; similarly we pay attention when we hear of a behavior sequence but do not know the cues
to which the subject is reacting. Goalless behavior is implicitly mysterious; what, after all, is there in it for Baker that he acts so?

Often one cannot sense a mystery when one knows only a single
detail of behavior; we don't expect ourselves to understand behavior
in fragments, and we dismiss such fragments as not challenging. It
can then happen that, as details are added to our original meaningless fragment, the true proportions of a mystery emerge. The following case report will illustrate this fact:

*One of our patients was a former soldier. He had been a suc-
cessful enlisted man and was cited for a field promotion to
officer's status. He refused this promotion and remained in the
ranks. Several years later, at the time of his ostensibly much
looked-forward-to discharge from the army, he was unable to
answer his name at the discharge proceedings.*

Either refusal of promotion or inability to respond in the mus-
tering-out situation might have been dismissed by a casual observer;
however, when taken together they constitute a mysterious circumstance. Why refuse a promotion? Was it that the officer's task was
more dangerous? Why be struck mute at the joyful moment of release from long routine and servitude? Why should a man who
doesn't care enough about the army to accept higher status nevertheless be unable to make the response which would separate him
from the military organization?

As in every human incident, a bundle of motives was operating.
Patient was indeed somewhat more afraid to be an officer than a
private. There were also some repellent circumstances of civilian
life which made release from the army unwelcome. But there was
a dominant unconscious reaction which linked the two situations together. The patient valued his *dependent* status in the army; thus
he rejected the officer's role because it would have forced autonomy
on him at a time when he felt especially in need of "dependent supplies." Release from the army had, for this patient, approximately
the same meaning as promotion from the ranks. The patient felt
that civilian life would demand a more independent and aggressive
role than he had been playing in the military. He recoiled from
this role though he believed, at the conscious level, that he wanted
nothing more than separation from the service. Unconscious fear
of playing an adult male role also contributed to his avoidance of
civilian life. This fear and unconscious craving to remain in the
military embrace made him unable to pronounce the words which
would lead to his release. The accumulation of details of this kind
enables the skilled therapist to detect unconscious conflicts when
they are invisible to the very naked eye of the lay observer.

The therapy situation can be established by interest and warmth,
but it cannot move except as unconscious dilemmas are perceived
and labeled. The mystery must be identified before the new naming
procedures can be put into effect.

ALWAYS a WITH S

In illustrating the criteria for unconscious scoring, we have decided to draw our examples from the sexual sphere. The general sign for sex is *S. s* indicates an unconscious sexual motive. *s-a* could be translated as "an unconscious sexual motive rendered inexpressible by unconscious anxieties." The sign *s-A* is also serviceable; it might be translated as "an anxiety in the sexual sphere which is apparently causeless but conscious." We never use the *s* sign alone. We argue that *s* would be *S* if some force were not keeping it unconscious. Even if the inhibiting force is not named, we argue that it must be present. We know that it exists by its effect, i.e. that a sex motive which is operative nevertheless cannot be named.

HOW TO DISCERN UNCONSCIOUS MOTIVES

There is no problem in evaluating a conscious motive. The subject names his emotion. He is "sexy"; he is angry; he is guilty; he is afraid. We do not score a motive as unconscious if a subject merely *neglects* to name it; a motive is deemed unconscious only when the reporter is *unable* to name it. A person may fail to name a motive when he could do so, because his description is synoptic or hasty, because he assumes we understand that he was motivated, or because other facts reported imply conscious motive.

1. *Inference of unconscious motive from situation.* We will not be wrong many times out of a hundred if we impute to a participant that motive which the environing situations should evoke. For instance, strife evokes angry emotions, situations of fear evoke fear, and so forth. If, having been in such a situation, a person denies having experienced the appropriate emotion, we will often conclude that the suspected motive was active but unconscious. Indeed, it would support our inference if it is just a timid person who denies anger where anger would be called for or just an inhibited person who cannot claim sexual motives in a situation of saturnalia. Even though there are limits to this principle, there are also great advantages to it; it will enable us to detect unconscious motives in many cases where we would otherwise miss them.

Here is an example: An extremely inhibited man had come to us after his discharge from the army. He had had a singular experience

with the army of occupation in a foreign country. We will paraphrase it as follows:

> *Patient had come to a great city with two soldier friends to*
> *spend a weekend of leave. The three soldiers found it extremely*
> *difficult to get a place to sleep. Finally they hit upon a single*
> *small hotel bedroom with three cots. Patient's two friends went*
> *out on the town and he was composing himself for a night's*
> *sleep when the friends returned with two women. The two*
> *prostitutes and the two friends made no to-do about having*
> *intercourse before patient. Patient viewed the details atten-*
> *tively. When reporting on his experience, he claimed that the*
> *scene had had no particular effect on him; he had had only a*
> *rather casual interest in it, was not sexually excited, and had*
> *no tendency to imitate his friends. He felt that he was cooperat-*
> *ing with his two pals by allowing them to use the room for their*
> *own purposes, it being hard to find a bed, etc.*

It was certainly true that the patient was somewhat immature and
that the genital components in his nature were poorly developed.
They were not, however, nonexistent. Rather than conceive of a
person incredibly immune to such a scene, we prefer to attribute an
unconscious sex excitation to patient and to assume that it was inhibited by fear. Thus we would infer from the situation that the
patient was sexually aroused as any person would likely be. We do
not at all assume, however, that any person, though he felt conscious sex excitation, would wish to imitate the abandoned couples.
Many a person would walk away from such a scene in its earliest
stages; others might protest at invasion of their own privacy; still
others might be revolted. If one has to make a choice, however, as to
whether a scene like this would or would not produce sex excitation in the witness, it seems to us far safer to assume that it would.

2. *Score unconscious if bodily mobilization occurs.* A person exposed to a provocative situation may react with signs of mobilization
for action which he himself does not recognize—that is, does not
label correctly. A slamming heart or quickened breathing or fearful
perspiration may testify to an active but unconscious motive. A vir-
tuous housewife may experience the quickened pulse which accom-
panies the weekly chat with the cheerful trashman but have no
knowledge that she is experiencing, and responding to, a sexual
temptation. We, however, as observers, may be willing to put her

down for an unconscious sex reaction whose naming is inhibited
by the aid of a good conscience.

Soldiers were taught during the last war (with the aid of a book
written by one of us; Dollard, 1943) to identify the physiological
symptoms characteristic of fear and call them by their proper name.
Through the specific permission of Army authorities, soldiers were
permitted not to repress their fear but to identify it and confront it.
If a soldier should show all the signs of fear motivation yet maintain
that he was not afraid we would allot him, nevertheless, a score for
unconscious fear.

3. *Score unconscious if avoidant response reported.* If a person
in a provocative situation reports an avoidant response while denying
the motive appropriate to the situation, we tend to credit him with
an unconscious motive. Why avoid the situation, we ask, if no approach motive has been bestirred? Very often the avoidant reaction
will be one of actual physical escape from a situation; at another
time it will be one of anxious alarm. Ordinarily what would be
noticed would be the fear or avoidance reaction, whereas the person
would deny any positive motive to remain in the situation. These
matters can be best clarified by an example from one of our woman
patients.

> *This attractive young woman was much inhibited in sexual*
> *matters and had come for treatment because of her husband's*
> *complaints on this score. His considerable enthusiasm for her was*
> *spoiled by fearful and evasive responses on her part. She claimed*
> *to be anesthetic in her sexual relations with her husband. She*
> *claimed not to be interested in or attracted to the sexual side*
> *of life. She was house-bound with a phobia, fearing to go alone*
> *to movie theaters, to ride on busses, or to shop in the large*
> *markets. Nevertheless, isolated in her apartment as she was,*
> *she fell into conversation with the man downstairs who hap-*
> *pened to be home alone. In the course of this conversation, she*
> *volunteered the information that she was in psychotherapy. The*
> *willing neighbor gladly led her on in this discussion, and the*
> *question was raised whether a person in psychotherapy always*
> *had sexual problems. The patient suddenly found herself on*
> *the verge of a discussion, the like of which she denied even to*
> *her husband. Startled, she arose and fled back to her own apart-*

ment. She subsequently added the man downstairs to the list of her phobic objects.

The therapist, and perhaps the humanist, will gladly note that although the patient is inhibited she is not sexually "dead." We reject the notion that housewives casually fall into sexual discussions with neighbors unless they are motivated to do so. The patient's sharp reaction of recoil has to be a reaction to some stimulus; we score her as having an active but unconscious sexual motive which led to the discussion in the first place, which was accelerated by the circumstance of the lonely apartment—and which finally became strong enough to set off a striking response of escape. The escape response itself testifies to the activity of the unconscious striving. It goes without saying that the patient reported no sexual emotion in discussing her experience; her emphasis was entirely on the fear and the escape. The crucial elements here are: an excitatory situation, strong inward inhibitions, no label, but a course of behavior which is meaningless if not explained by an unconscious motive. The aversion, so to speak, is the best witness for the existence of the attraction. The incident would be scored *s-A*.

4. *Naming but no report of arousal.* We do not like very well to follow the practice we are now recommending but have been constrained to do so. If, in a situation which arouses fear, a patient is able to name the motive which would normally evoke fear, we are inclined to credit him with said motive even though he denies feeling anything. We argue that if a person can name a motive some inward representation of that motive will exist even though it is not strong enough to deserve labeling.

The characteristic situation would be the following:

Modern fathers are supposed to have some kind of confrontation with their sons whereby they protect the son against ignorance of sexual matters. One of our patients reported the efforts made in this direction by his earnest but ungifted father. The father had taken him on a little trip to a neighboring town. The pair was walking along the street when the father pointed out a cloistered dwelling which was approached by a sidewalk covered by a concealing trellis. Pointing out the house, the father said, "Do you see that place? That's a place men go to sleep with women. The women live there and sleep with a lot

of different men. The men pay five dollars. Do you know what
I mean?" The son, confused and embarrassed, said that he did
know what the father meant and the subject was dropped. The
work of enlightenment had come too late.

When the son described this incident, he emphasized his shock
and embarrassment. He had not wanted to talk with his father about
these matters. At fourteen he already knew far more than his father
supposed. He did not report sex excitement during this conversation, and denied it when asked. We put him down, nevertheless, for
an *s-A* score. The words "sleep with" women (and the boy knew a far
stronger verb) did, we assume, arouse some fragmentary sex mobilization. Unlabeled, it deserves to be called unconscious. The general
principle is this: We take it for likely that a person will have in some
minimal form, at least, the reaction appropriate to a word which he
can utter. We agree that this principle is not entirely satisfactory,
but we affirm that, on balance, the assumption is better made than
not.

SKILL IN NOTING MYSTERIES

Any skill possessed by a psychological specialist is likely to be
possessed by the general population though in lesser degree; the
aptitude is heightened and sharpened in the specialist. A psychoanalysis is like its social counterpart, conversation, in some ways and
very different in others. Unconscious interstimulation and response
occur both in analysis and in free-wheeling social life. Our point is
that the basic equipment needed for a specialized psychological skill
will also be possessed by individuals generally. Thus we believe it
to be the case that people tend to be alerted when the behavior of
others doesn't make sense. They tend, perhaps, to be slightly uncomfortable. They comment mildly. They wonder a little why such-
and-such a beautiful woman never married. It's her own business,
they feel, and yet it's odd. People are more comfortable when they
feel that they can understand the motives of others and can see the
goals they strive for. They tend to be a little uncomfortable when
the behavior of others is obscure or mysterious.

This alerting reaction, when behavior is enigmatic, is probably
learned in childhood. If we can predict the motives of others correctly, we are better able to secure the rewards we want; if others'

motives are inscrutable, we are more likely to be helpless and disappointed. Not to have a suitable account of the motives and goals of other people thus itself arouses a kind of response which we have called "alerting." We recognize at once that it is a widespread talent, though perhaps much more sharply developed in some people than in others.

The therapist is, of course, a specialist in being on the alert for signs of unconscious motives. Several circumstances are of help to him. The first is that he usually gets much more information from his patients than is available to the casual witness. With or without the free-association instruction, a warm interview situation will encourage any patient to show himself as he truly feels himself to be. In the course of thus showing himself he will present the therapist with much data, not evaluated by the patient as such, which is mysterious; when first exposed to view in the therapy situation human behavior becomes much more, rather than much less, curious than it had seemed to be before. The powder and paint of convention wiped off, the quaking soul is seen near at hand.

Not only does he have more information, but the therapist also has a specially developed skill (best developed, incidentally, by psychoanalysis): He has freedom from many of the repressions which prevent the clear identification of dilemmas; his labeling of his own feelings, and therefore of the feelings of others, is much more adequate than that of the patient or the casual observer; finally, his theory enables him to identify and decode the first enigma, after which is revealed a series of others.

The idea is that therapists begin with psychological mysteries. The mere identification of such mysteries implies the existence of unconscious motives. The identification of unconscious motives and their activation in the therapeutic situation permits the loan of new labels to the patient who needs them so urgently. From this standpoint, the therapist is a kind of semantic expert. His shingle could say, "Labels for Loan—Permanent Possession Guaranteed if They Fit."

WHAT HAPPENS IN THE BODY WHEN UNCONSCIOUS MOTIVES ARE ACTIVE?

We have already hypothecated that quite strong reactions may occur (fear or anger, for instance) even though these reactions are not labeled. Without saying so, we have been assuming that only verbal cues are attached to emotional reactions. This need not be true. Emotional reactions may, for example, be attached to imageal cues or to proprioceptive (muscle tension) cues. Thus a person having an unconscious reaction may, to be sure, have no word attached to said reaction—but he may have an image or a proprioceptive signal. Of course, unless such a signal is labeled the presence of such cues cannot be indicated to others, i.e. these cues may excite only internal reactions.

It is also possible that the inward mobilization of, say, a fear motive may be so faint that no labeling response can be attached to it. The inward mobilization can vary from, for example, the sharp pang of fear to a "faint hum" or "central buzz" of fear—too slight to be labeled at all, yet nevertheless a stimulus to which reactions (like flight or alerting) can be attached. It seems to us necessary to assume some kind of hum or buzz of a distinctive type even when strong mobilization cannot be demonstrated or even labeled by the subject. It seems to us possible that such a faint reaction as described may occur whenever certain words are pronounced, even though the subject has no conscious feeling of being activated. In the case of the boy getting sex instruction from his father, it seems possible that a not-to-be-sensed hum occurred when he heard the words "sleep with." So far as he could tell, he was not sexually mobilized at all; but something within him occurred of sufficient stimulus strength so that he could attach a heightened avoidance reaction to it as a result of his conversation with his father.

The Sign A

I. DEFINITION OF A

A refers to an internal stimulus which might be called apprehension, distress, tension, or fear. Anxiety is the sequel or residue of painful experience. If the outward stimulus is known and believed adequate to cause a reaction (e.g. mad dog), we speak of fear; if it is vague or unknown we speak of anxiety. In either case the appropriate score is *A*. Anxiety is a disturbing and upsetting condition. He who causes another anxiety does that other a real damage.

A should be scored when: (1) a patient reports manifest anxiety,

(2) the patient reports being under tension, (3) the patient describes a situation where anyone would be bound to be afraid, (4) the patient reports making an avoidant response which could be motivated only by anxiety, (5) the patient reports guilt, or (6) the patient reports embarrassment.

II. THEORY OF A

Anxiety is learned (long before the patient comes to therapy) in situations that produce pain, intense motivation, or loss of love; when the cues reminiscent of such situations recur, the person feels anxious (Freud, 1926). The anxiety reaction can be completely automatic, that is, evoked by unnoticed cues. It can be evoked by processes within the subject, such as thoughts, as well as by external stimuli. In either case the anxiety can be conscious, that is, labeled as anxiety, or it can be unlabeled or unconscious. "Anxiety" is commonly used to designate fear reactions when they are unconscious or attached to vague or poorly labeled stimuli; "fear," on the other hand, is often used to designate those cases in which the stimuli to which the person reacts, and the reaction itself, are sharply and clearly labeled. Our scoring system, however, includes both *anxiety* and *fear* in the category *A*.

Anxiety is often revealed by the avoidant responses of a person. Thus we conclude that a person is afraid, because he is seen to be running away. Indeed, without such evidence anxiety would often go unnoticed. When the patient has anxiety attached to one of his strong motives or wishes we speak of *conflict*. When the positive motive impels approach to some goal, whereas anxiety motivates avoidance of the goal, we call it an approach-avoidance conflict; such conflicts are particularly important in neurotic behavior (Dollard and Miller, 1950). Thus in scoring the protocols of neurotic persons one has frequent occasion to identify utterances as simultaneously representing opposing tendencies, positive tendencies such as sexual or aggressive feelings and negative feelings like anxiety.

III. EXAMPLES OF A

Though conflict is the rule in cases of anxiety, the scorer frequently does not have enough information to identify the elements of the conflict. All he can do in such a case is to identify the anxiety component or state. The two examples which follow will illustrate this kind of situation.

1. *The patient describes a manifest anxious disturbance*

a. A teacher who was a patient said:

> [1]I don't know why. [2]But every time Jones talks in my class I get upset. [3]Somehow, he has me off balance. [4]I get confused. [5]After class I can think of a perfectly good answer to his question. [6]But I'm not able to do so on the spot. [7]I wish I could get this reaction under control because it bothers me so much in practical situations.

b. A woman patient said of her husband:

> [1]But it was just that I was trying to please him. [2]Or I thought I had to please him. [3]But no matter how I tried I never succeeded. [4]I never wanted to do the wrong things. [5]I wanted everything to be perfect, to be the best mother, the best housewife. [6]But I never managed to do it no matter how I tried.

2. *Hectic activity.* Hectic or driven activity comes under suspicion as being motivated by anxiety. Such activity does not seem to be arranged to accomplish rational ends or to yield understandable pleasures. A patient described such activity as follows:

> [1]My wife's sister and her husband joined us for the weekend. [2]That made four adults and five kids in our small house. [3]The kids weren't in our hair too much. [4]We had some activities, picnics and whatnot. [5]But I-uh . . .* seem to have trouble . . . entering into the spontaneity of situations like that. [6]And after they were gone my wife asked me whether I had enjoyed myself. [7]It's a peculiar situation to be in. [8]I don't really know whether I enjoyed myself or not. [9]The whole thing seems sort of fuzzy and indefinite. [10]Of course I interrupted my other work to be available for the visitors.

Such a passage should be scored *A*.

3. *Situation of overt danger.* A situation where anyone would be bound to feel fear is scored *A*. Here is an example from the report of a soldier-patient:

---

* An ellipsis (. . .) is used throughout to indicate a pause less than five seconds long. Pauses of five seconds or more were timed, and the exact length is given in parentheses.

> ¹I have a couple of medals for Zeros which I was s'posed to have shot down, yes. ²But on our missions we had maybe a dozen planes flying together with-ah-two, three, four . . . about ten machine guns on each one. ³And . . . we were attacked by about eighty Zeros and everything else in the world. ⁴I mean it was just flak. ⁵And they had a Japanese bomber over us dropping sulphur bombs at our planes and Zeros coming in from every angle and with a hundred B-24's shooting.

Even though the patient does not emphasize that he was afraid, one may safely impute it here and score *A*.

4. *Avoidant response.* Avoidance of a neutral stimulus situation indicates anxiety. Thus a woman patient said, in commenting on our recording room:

> ¹Uh . . . I think it's perhaps because there are no windows in here . . . sort of stymied me a little bit, uh-never having been in a room like this before with no windows. ²And-uh-the first impression wasn't a very good one. ³And-uh-I have been thinking of it. ⁴In fact, ⁵(*She laughs anxiously*) I almost dreaded to come tonight for that reason. ⁶All I could think of was the several doors and not being able to get out of here if I wanted to.

Patient is phobic for the interviewing room, which is surely not in itself a dangerous place.

Another example of avoidant behavior follows:

> *A high-school boy who did not dance well nevertheless made an engagement to go to a dance. As the fated day approached he became more and more upset. He felt he could not carry out his commitment to go to the dance, and yet he empathized with the girl whom he would have to disappoint at the last minute. Finally, he took what he considered the cowardly way out—he wrote the girl a letter, withdrawing his invitation.*

Whatever else may be involved here from a motivational standpoint, anxiety is certainly present. The student avoided the mysteriously frightening situation of the dance. The example should be scored *A*.

5. *Guilt.* Self-reproaches, remorse, and other evidences of guilt should be scored as *A*.

*In the course of her free-associations a woman patient recalled
the fact that her aunt had died a couple of years before. Patient
was still concerned about her own behavior during the period
of the aunt's illness and death. Patient had been in the very
city where her aunt was dying and had not gone to see her; she
had wanted to visit the aunt but was somewhat afraid of the
aunt's husband. The husband was spoken of as "queer," and
he did not encourage visits from anyone. Nevertheless, the
patient blamed herself because she had not performed this
parting duty to her aunt. She said:*

PATIENT   [1]I just felt terrib-terribly guilty that I hadn't made
it my business to get there. [2]I don't even know if he would have
let me in if he got there—if I had gotten there because from
what I understood he didn't want anybody to know that she
wasn't well. I—

THERAPIST   [3]So this wasn't exclusive to you then?

PATIENT   [4]Oh no, oh no.

THERAPIST   [5]But still you blame yourself?

PATIENT   [6]But I feel like I should have tried. [7](7-sec. pause)
[8]And I feel like maybe if I haven't been so—if I hadn't been
so darn wrapped up in myself I would've made it my business
to have been there.

Patient felt remorse at not having seen her aunt and criticized
herself as being "so darn wrapped up in myself." The sources of her
guilt are undoubtedly unconscious, though the guilt itself is conscious; she was really hindered from seeing her aunt, so she had no
real reason for blaming herself. Patient's sentences should be scored
A.

6. *A for embarrassment.* Another aspect of behavior included
under the *A* sign is that of embarrassment, the wish "to fall through
the floor." The following is an example:

*The high-school boy referred to in a previous example told a
lie when he wrote to his date. He said he was sick. By bad luck,
as he felt it, he met the girl on the street on the day after the
dance. She cut him dead. The boy was seized by intense embarrassment and shame.*

In the absence of other defining information this reaction should
be scored *A*.

IV. COMBINED SIGNS

The use of *A* as a single sign is the exception rather than the rule. It is far more frequently seen in combination with other signs. *A* is likely to be used alone when the scorer's information about the speaker is limited or inadequate. In such a situation one uses *A* alone rather than make an adventurous assumption about motives which might be connected with it. *A* can be combined with signs such as *H* (for hostility), *S* (for sex), *Mob* (for mobility strivings), and others. Both *A* and any combined sign may be either conscious or unconscious. Some of the paradigmatic possibilities will be exemplified here using the signs *S* and *A*.

1. *S-A*. This sign indicates, of course, a conscious sexual motive to which a conscious anxiety reaction is attached. The anxiety reaction may or may not be strong enough to prevent the occurrence of a sexual act. In the case of a young businessman it was strong enough, as the following report will reveal:

> [1]This . . . uh . . . new secretary has been around the office for about a week. [2]And I have felt vaguely that there was something between us. [3]She has been given the keys to the vault downstairs. [4]And when anyone wants to get something from the vault she goes down to open the vault. [5]Yesterday I had to get some canceled checks. [6]And I asked Miss Jones to come down and open the vault for me. [7]Uh . . . when we got downstairs I had the strongest feeling that I could and should do something with her. [8]I . . . uh . . . I wanted to kiss her the worst way. [9]I felt she wouldn't mind. [10]But my heart was slamming as if it would . . . uh . . . jump out of my chest. [11]I got my checks. [12]But I didn't kiss her. [13]Afterwards, I felt sort of regretful and silly.

Patient was certainly conscious both of his sexual wish and of the alarm reaction which it created in him.

2. *S-a*. This is the symbol for an inhibition, that is, for a conscious sexual wish which is mysteriously inhibited by unconscious anxiety. A married male patient reported:

> [1]Recently something funny has been happening between my wife and me. [2]When we are fooling around before we go to bed, I am sexually interested in her and excited. [3]But-but when we

get into bed with our clothes off I lose my erection. [4]That makes it hard for her and embarrassing for me.

Patient had some fears concerning his wife of which he was not conscious at the time this was spoken.

3. *s-A*. This is the case where an unconscious wish stirs conscious anxiety. Sometimes one can, and sometimes one cannot, safely infer the nature of the unconscious motive; if one cannot infer it one simply scores *A*. Such was the case, and such the score, in the incident of the high-school boy who broke his date for the dance. At a later time in therapy the youth brought up the matter of this broken date a second time and reported:

> [1]I had many thoughts about her in which I would tear off her clothes and play with her breasts and body. [2]I thought she would probably let me if I wanted to. [3]I felt very guilty about these thoughts and never indulged in them when she was near by.

When patient was with the girl or planning to be with her, he was aware only of his anxiety; nevertheless it seemed that there were some unconscious wishes present. With the new information available one could score the earlier report as an unconscious sex wish opposed by anxiety, *s-A,* or possibly an unconscious aggressive wish opposed by conscious anxiety, i.e. *h-A*. It is not possible in our system to score *s-h* so the scorer would have to pick whichever one of the unconscious motives seemed most closely connected to the anxiety.

4. *s-a*. This is the case where a mysterious event must either be allowed to stand as nonsensical or unconscious motives must be posited to explain it. Since our assumption is that human behavior is invariably lawful, we consider in such a case whether plausible unconscious motives can be assumed. The following case report will exemplify this dilemma and its solution:

> *A student therapist was repeatedly advised by his supervisor to announce to the patient the forthcoming end of treatment. The student steadily failed to tell his patient that treatment must end. When the student was later taken into treatment himself it turned out that he was strongly romantically interested in his patient. However, such an interest was entirely incompatible*

with his role as therapist. Even to be aware of his sexual motive would have cost him strong anxiety and precipitated a crisis for the student. His solution was to fail to inform the patient of the end of treatment and tell his supervisor each week that he had forgotten.

Rather than suppose that an intelligent apprentice could regularly fail to take an action which was thoroughly explained and explicitly advised, we assumed unconscious motivation must be working. Further investigation showed that the student did have both a sexual wish and a strong shock reaction to the existence of such a wish, both of these being unconscious. In this case the plea of "forgetting" was a rationalization.

5. *A:r.* The *r* sign is an interesting one and is likely to be valuable in any system which works with a theory of drive reduction. Here the *r* is attached to an *A* to indicate reduction in anxiety.

A woman patient who had severe anxiety attacks when left alone at home reported:

> [1]And I told you, too, that first night I was talking to you that-uh-I feel very safe like in my house-uh-if there are doctors around, someone that if I—the feeling goes through me all the time-uh-that if-uh-if I got bad, i-if this thing gets bad that-that comes over me, there will be a doctor around. [2]And he will talk to me. [3]Even talking to the doctor on the phone helps.

The patient has told us in a bumbling way that when she is sure she can get to a doctor, or when she actually talks to one, her anxiety drops. The score *A:r* is appropriate (and of course the occurrence of this reward did strongly strengthen the habit of keeping telephone contact with a physician). A second example from the same patient is reported as follows:

> [1]And-I-of course, this panic as I've told you had subsided. [2]But still there was this-uh-feeling inside me that I kept. [3]I couldn't sit.

The patient reported that her panicky condition subsided but that she was still so anxious she couldn't sit still. The first unit should be scored *A:r* if the scorer estimated that the drop in anxiety is sufficient to reinforce some response; the latter two units are scored *A*.

V. DISCRIMINATION AND BORDERLINE CASES

Every system of ordering or dividing the wild diversity of nature will break down at some point. Contradictions, difficult discriminations, and borderline issues will arise. In this section we discuss a few such issues which center around the score *A*.

1. *The case where one is sure conscious anxiety is present and suspects, but is not certain, that unconscious anxiety is also involved.* In such a case the preferred scoring is, as has been said, *A*. One does not reach wildly for unconscious scorings; one uses them only when it is more stupid to omit than to employ them. This point of view will be shortly exemplified again.

2. *The case where unconscious anxiety can be firmly discerned but conscious anxiety is also present.* In such a case the unconscious factor, as the more important one, is scored. It is precisely the purpose of therapeutic investigation to identify unconscious fears.

At this point we will present one complex example which will illustrate both of the above cases. A woman patient presented, more or less in series, the following incidents, all of which had an anxious or self-critical tone.

a. *The patient felt that she had advised her son badly in discouraging him from playing football (though he has been generally successful in college).*

b. *Patient felt that she had been too irascible with her adolescent daughter (though the girl was developing nicely and no particular effects of maternal criticism were evident).*

c. *Patient felt she had failed to do all possible for her dead father (though she had cared for him in her own home with her own hands for three years before he died).*

d. *Patient felt she should not have gotten into a quarrel with a neighbor and given vent to an angry outburst (though the right was on patient's side and the provocation extreme).*

e. *Patient reported that she had cheated on a comprehensive examination when she was graduating from college (though the event was twenty years in the past and could have had but little effect on a generally outstanding record).*

f. *Etc.*

g. *Etc.*

The unwarned scorer would certainly score items *a* and *b* (above) as conscious anxiety (*A*). He might have a slight feeling that patient was "reaching" for it, but he could nevertheless admit that anxious self-blame might be justified.

At *c*, however, he might begin to wonder and be in doubt. He might think something of this sort: She is certainly blaming herself a lot in this series. The facts that none of the incidents reported is really so very "bad" and that all have compensating features might begin to strike him. In short, something new about the behavior would begin to register vaguely, such as the feeling: This material is somehow patterned in a way not obvious.

When the scorer comes to items *d* and *e* he becomes openly suspicious. He begins to ask himself: Why so many self-damaging references occurring one after the other? Why doesn't she think of something cheerful in between? Are these incidents somehow connected? Finally, he would put to himself the big question: Does the self-blame asserted arise from the events as reported individually or, on the contrary, is a chronic attitude of self-blame excited which then, so to say, selects and emphasizes a series of incidents in which some degree of realistic self-blame was involved? Is the realistic blame involved sufficient to account for the recital of the items in the series? The therapist might well conclude that taken individually there seems to be some reason for self-blame in each case, but taken as a pattern the incidents point rather to a continuous force of self-blame, a sense of guilt, not to a series of individual examples, each of which involves anxious self-depreciation.

When the scorer comes to *f* and *g*, the "et ceteras," his doubts would almost certainly disappear. Such a series of self-damaging thoughts could hardly come to mind each by independent inspiration. They must be connected. The more important thing about them must be that they represent a well-lodged unconscious sense of guilt which seizes upon and magnifies, in ostensibly reasonable fashion, any incident where the patient can blame himself at all. When the scorer comes to this conclusion he should use the score indicating unconscious self-blame, i.e. *h-a/self,* and not *A*. He can if he wishes return to the first items in the series which he has already scored *A,* and change his scoring to *h-a/self;* or he may leave his scoring as was, changing from *A* to *h-a/self* only when he became certain that it was *h-a/self* that was involved. We recommend the latter practice. We score them as the baseball umpire calls strikes, i.e. as they come, and we do not change our calls. This is a case where the pattern is the distinctive stimulus which evokes a particular score.

3. *Can* s *or* h *be scored alone?* It is our practice that s and h shall not be scored alone. If s is judged to exist and a scoring of s-A is not appropriate, we would assume that some unconscious anxiety must be inhibiting the s factor. The same reasoning obtains in the case of h. We thus recognize the dynamic fact that some force must exist which keeps the unconscious motive from becoming conscious. In this connection we discuss an example already cited, the student therapist who could not follow the instruction to forewarn his patient about the termination of therapy. From his own fantasies we were able to discern that he had sexual motives toward his patient. In his case we have concrete evidence that the student was unconsciously anxious about these motives; had we not had such evidence, however, we would have risked inferring that it was present. An unconscious motive cannot remain unconscious unless some force keeps it so.

4. *Sense of pressure,* A *or* H? Many patients report feelings of pressure or compulsion, a sense of being forced, of inward stress and tension. We score these sentences A unless there is some definite evidence that resistance or opposition is involved. In general we stand by the frustration-aggression hypothesis, but in this particular instance we ask evidence that the distressing experience has actually aroused aggression. For example, a busy young husband reported his feelings of stress and uneasiness when playing with his children at his wife's insistence. Often he felt he would prefer to be doing something else:

> PATIENT   [1]What is the feeling? [2]Oh, it's like this. [3]I don't and haven't felt at all times as though it were completely spontaneous, as though I-I-uh wanted—as though it-it-uh was a natural outburst on my part that I want to mix with them. [4]And there's uh-just that premeditation that-that seems to bother me a little.
> THERAPIST   [5]As if you were forcing yourself?
> PATIENT   [6]Yeah, yeah, against-uh-forcing myself against-uh-well, not playing with them, whatever I might—might have been taking myself from, either reading or-uh . . . listening to music, or watching TV, relaxing.

The patient may indeed be angry that his children take him away from his reading or from the TV set, but all one can be reasonably certain of is that he is miserable. The sense of being ill at ease when playing with his children, the pressure, and stress should be scored *A*. By way of another discrimination, it is worthy of note that he does not blame himself for not doing something, or having done something wrong, thus the score could not be *H/self*.

Another patient, a woman, reported the same sense of pressure or of being driven, this time in the sexual sphere. She said of her husband:

> [1]Uhm, after the-uh . . . terrific for me anyway, pace of last weekend in the way of sex relations with my husband where he had four orgasms in three days, uh-in which he said the more he gets the more he wants, I don't know exactly why it should be. [2]But it's a little bit of a relief to find that that edge of his has worn off considerably. [3]The demands made on me aren't nearly what they were during the past weekend.

The patient shows in these sentences her awareness of her husband's coercion and seems to be "afraid" of him in some way. We recognize the pressure here as *A;* we would wait for some more definite evidence of resentment before scoring *h-a* or *H*. Thus we recognize that *A* may cover a complex set of drives in the patient which result in a stressful condition, Freud's *Unlust*.

5. *Discrimination of* A *from* Res. Utterances laden with anxiety, or coming out of a context where conscious anxiety is obvious, may nevertheless serve resistant purposes. Thus a patient who was all but crawling up the walls of the interviewing room with phobic anxiety nevertheless found time to say:

> [1]But has there ever—I've never had a physical examination, a complete physical, never, except my—when I had my two children. [2]And that wasn't what you'd call a physical, a good physical examination. [3]Uh-is there anything in one's make-up that could cause anything like I have?

The patient had been thoroughly examined physically before being admitted to therapy. Her statements here are just not true. Though obviously exhibiting anxiety, and prompted by anxiety, the statements are also resistant. The preferred scoring would be *Res* rather than *A*.

Such a *Res* scoring may interrupt a series of sentences which are scored *A* or with some modification of *A*. Thus the same patient spoke as follows:

> [1]And I was able to stay up there by myself, but then became so bad that-uh each and every time my mother-in-law went out I had to go out. [2]I bundled the baby up. [3]Or the baby wasn't a baby. [4]She was, as I say, she was past two years old then. [5]I bundled her up whether it was winter or summer and got out of there as fast as I could. [6]And that I did for the rest of the time we lived up there until I moved into town. [7]And in the meantime why my doctor suggested I have another baby. [8]He said that that would cure everything, that that would make my nerves [9](*She sighs*) steady again. [10]Well, as you can see, I'm here. [11]And it hasn't made me any steadier. [12]Or I haven't gotten over my fears or phobias. [13]In fact, they're worse than they ever were. [14]In fact, I'm not able to, well, control them as-as good as I used to be able to. [15]And that's why I told you in the beginning tonight that I do have to take something. [16]And I don't want to be like that and dependent on something like that for the rest of my days.

In the example above, units 1–6 should be scored *A*. Units 7–14 should be scored *Res*. Units 15 and 16 should be scored *A* again. We are not debating the point here as to whether or not it was wise for her doctor to suggest a baby as a cure for a neurosis; it probably was not wise. But the patient is failing to make the discrimination between a physician acting outside his area of competence and the trained therapist she faces. She is saying in substance, "Doctors are no good, and thus you are no good, and thus you can't help me, and thus there is no use in my being here." Spelled out in this way, it is plain to see that the attitude is resistant. The failure to discriminate between the obstetrician and the therapist is unconsciously willful. The sentences recording this attitude are hence scored *Res*.

THE SIGN Conf

I. DEFINITION

Conf is the score used for a particular response by the patient to an interpretation by the therapist. To be called *Conf* the response must have two characteristics:

1. The patient must show that he understands the interpretation, even if only in a minimal way.

2. The patient must react in such a way as to "confirm" the interpretation.

Confirmation could consist either of bringing forward new information (new in the sense that it had not been previously available to the therapist) * or of displaying a pertinent emotional reaction.

II. THEORY OF Conf

An interpretation, successful in content and timing, should change the balance of forces in the mind so that formerly repressed materials and emotional reactions can emerge. In order to be confirmatory, such reactions do not need to stem from earliest years of childhood. Current as well as long past material can qualify. Nor does the reaction need to be one which has been deeply repressed; recall of preconscious material can constitute a *Conf*. In order to exclude empty agreement on the patient's part, however, the confirmatory material must be new. Usually it has a surprising quality.

The interpretative transaction ending in a *Conf* is a complicated one. For instance, the patient must *rehearse* the interpretation, that is, play it over on his own "psychological piano." In order for him to rehearse, repressive effects must have been lessened. In the total interpretation-*Conf* transaction *labeling* undoubtedly occurs. Formerly disavowed ideas or feelings are named. The learned abilities of *generalizing* and *discriminating* are often important in the total transaction. Intelligent patients, those who are skillful at generalizing and discriminating, can speed the work of therapy by correctly adapting the interpretation to novel circumstances.

III. EXAMPLES OF Conf

1. The following interpretation-*Conf* transaction took place between a Freudian analyst and his woman patient: The therapist pointed out a humorous way of talking which the patient used, by

* Freud writes as follows in connection with the confirmation of an interpretation (1937, p. 364): "The 'Yes' has no value unless it is followed by indirect confirmations, unless the patient, immediately after his 'Yes,' produces new memories which complete and extend the construction." In this paper, "Constructions in Analysis," Freud considers the various circumstances by which an interpretation or "construction" can have therapeutic effect.

which she made light of her own problems and feelings; was this
humorous tone, he asked, a way of pretending that her own feelings
were not real or serious?

> PATIENT   ¹That's funny . . . ²I just . . . I remember I was
> reading some paperback volumes of Freud's. ³There were six
> of them in the series. ⁴I entirely skipped the one on wit and
> humor. ⁵(*Embarrassed laugh*)
>
> THERAPIST (*Laughs*)
>
> PATIENT   ⁶I read all the rest of the volumes. ⁷And I didn't
> think about that until just this minute, ⁸(*Embarrassed laugh*)
> 'cause it just seemed . . . what connection? ⁹Now I . . . I see
> a little in that.

Evidently patient rehearsed and swiftly understood the interpretation and brought forth new information. Her remark, if decoded,
would seem to be to this effect: "Maybe you are right; perhaps I
don't want to understand the technique of humorous disguise since
I didn't read the one of Freud's books which might have robbed
me of this defense."

2. A married male patient was telling his therapist about his
sexual relations with his wife. The patient said he enjoyed these relations but that his wife frequently rejected his sexual approaches
on the ground that she was "too tired." The transaction went on:

> THERAPIST   ¹Quite apart from sexual things, did you feel
> "rejected" when your wife said she was too tired?
>
> PATIENT   (*After a less than 5-sec. pause*) ²I guess I did. ³I
> tend to-uh unconsciously pull—go back and not-uh I just
> rather—uh-to go into a fantasy about—uh-something that's
> greener on the other side of the—of the fence.
>
> THERAPIST   ⁴As if your reaction meant, "If she won't have
> me, maybe some other woman will."

It would seem that the rejection interpretation was correct; at
least the patient makes a response consistent with it. When his wife
was "too tired," he thought of "something greener."

3. The following transaction took place between a student therapist and his married woman patient:

> *This patient showed a remarkable shyness with men. Her ex-*
> *periences with men had generally turned out badly. She was*

*trying to plan her life to do without the male element. Thera-
pist also noticed, though no connoisseur in such matters, that
she was poorly dressed, less well than her income would have
permitted her to be and than her personal taste might have dic-
tated. One day he raised this question: Was she showing avoidant tendencies toward men in the way she dressed?*

PATIENT   [1]This business . . . about the clothes, ah . . . I'm
trying to do . . . do something about myself. [2]Most of my
clothes are too large for me. [3]I buy . . . I have a tendency to
buy things too large. [4]Uh . . . well anyhow, this . . . this has
borne some fruit, I hope. [5]I . . . I . . . I bought a spring coat
this week. [6]And I . . . I had a nice . . . very dark blue tint
picked out. [7]It was just about black. [8]And . . . and I said, "No,
Sadie, you're doing the same thing again." [9]So I got one that's-
that's real flashy. [10]And my first thought after I got it was, "Ah
. . . what's Mother going to say when she sees it?"

The patient showed in her response that she had been half-aware
of selecting clothes for their ugliness rather than their beauty and
suitability. The affirmatory effect of her statement is especially great
because she not only accepted but also used the interpretation. What
therapist said was not only illuminating but also permissive. The
nature of the fear which kept her away from men is suggested by
her last response, "What's Mother going to say when she sees it?"
   4. The following example is taken from the same case but four
hours later.

*The "fear" of mother, so casually discovered in an earlier hour,
turned out to have ever increasing importance in the patient's
mental life. At first, patient accounted for the fear in terms of
the fact that her mother was a formidable person even in patient's adult life. Therapist doubted that current criticism from
the mother could account for the depth and strength of patient's
fear; he guessed it must stem from earlier occasions. No
thoughts came immediately to patient's mind, but at the beginning of the following hour she said:*

[1]About being afraid of my mother. [2]Uh-uh . . . something—I
never even thought about it. [3]But . . . uh—on my—on my
way down here, uh-I-I thought of something I've never told
you. [4]And-and-uh-I guess, I didn't think it was important. [5]I-I

mean I never thought about it. [6]You remember-uh I told you last week—I never could sleep-uh with my door closed. [7]And-and I was thinking about that. [8]And I know definitely that started when I was—I was—uh very small. [9]I wanted to hear if mother was coming. [10]And I always—always left my door open a crack. [11]Uh . . . and now I've gotten so I don't like to sleep in a room with a door closed.

Patient's response is clearly confirmatory and should be scored *Conf*. It does not yet tell us just how a fear of her mother was implanted, but it takes us a step along the road of discovery. She kept her door open to forewarn her of the frightening, stealthy maternal approach.

5. This is an example again from same patient and therapist, but two hours later. In some connection patient reported that she had envied the ability of her brother to stand up and urinate:

> THERAPIST   [1]Was it that you wanted to have a penis like he had, also?
>
> PATIENT   [2]Uh . . . I-I've been told many times by my mother, and less frequently by other people, that I should have been a boy. [3]That's-uh-it's sort of a-uh cliché. [4]The reason that that is said is because-uh I apparently uh-uh-well, I have-uh . . . high aptitudes along mechanical lines. [5]When I was younger . . . my father would take me down the cellar and-and show me how to-how to make things—how to do carpentry and-and-and explain things to me. [6]And-uh-he taught me a lot of things that-that would normally be taught to a boy. [7]I mean I could fix doorbells or a lock that got stuck or take care of the furnace. [8]I wanted to do all the things that boys could do. [9]For instance, I wished I could go to sea. [10]I thought if I was a boy—I would leave home and sign up on a ship.

The patient went on with yet more specific associations concerning her wish to be a boy. The therapist's interpretation was felt as permissive and produced a flood of unique confirmatory material, events so tightly knit into her life and character that they could not have been faked or dreamed up for the purpose of obliging therapist. The score *Conf* is indicated for all these sentences.

IV. COMBINED SIGNS

Conf is not combined with any other sign.

V. DISCRIMINATIONS AND BORDERLINE CASES

We interpret *Conf* very narrowly rather than broadly. The relation between an interpretation and a confirmatory response is a murky matter at best; only the plainest and strongest signs of confirmation should be accepted. Thus one is most sure of *Conf* when it occurs swiftly after an interpretation. In scoring practice the *Conf* utterance should appear within a page or two (of a transcript) after the interpretation. If intervening events are allowed to occur it is hard to identify the stimuli to which patient is reacting. If, however, at a later time, patient recalls and repeats an earlier interpretation ("something that you said lingered in my mind . . ."), scoring *Conf* for the confirmatory reaction is justified. If patient agrees in order to be agreeable, or to dismiss the topic, or merely passively reflects the interpretation, *Conf* is not scored.

Interpretation must be understood. It is not enough that an interpretation produces confirmatory data; patient must also understand the interpretation, must register it, rehearse it, get its meaning at least in minimal form. In the regular course of analytic work, interpretations constantly produce new information (from the therapist's standpoint) even when they do not register with the patient. An interpretation could be adjudged as correct (from the standpoint of the therapist or outside observer) without being confirmed (from the standpoint of the patient). Thus the production of new symbolic information could not be scored *Conf*.

> *In response to adequate cues therapist had surmised that patient had some fear of genital damage.*

> PATIENT [1]Well, I played a lot of soccer in college and high school, and-uh-took some pretty good beatings, uh-came very close to having my eye kicked out. [2]I know I've gotten direct kicks all over my face.

Using all the knowledge he had available as context for this incident, therapist might be justified in supposing that patient's factual report was a kind of symbolic confirmation of his interpretation, the valued eye replacing the valued genital. However, the utterance could not be scored *Conf* because patient does not realize the connection between the interpretation and the symbolic recollection. This example enables us to emphasize again that the scorer should be tight-fisted in allotting *Conf*.

THE SIGN Dep

I. DEFINITION OF Dep

Dep is, of course, short for "dependence." Although *Dep* is a powerful notion there is no brief, handy definition of it. It has to do with one person's relying on another for support, maintenance, or help when helping is one-sided rather than reciprocal. Behavior is dependent when one person makes claims on another or waits for another person to act instead of acting himself; when one tries to coerce another by expecting things of him; when one of a pair fails to initiate necessary planning (at the mental level) but instead relies on the other to do it; when a patient expresses helplessness, self-pity, yearning, or nostalgia. Failing to make decisions and to act while awaiting signals from others as to what to do is dependent. Passivity, helplessness, and loneliness are all related to *Dep*.

Dependent needs can be conscious or unconscious and are then scored respectively *Dep* or *dep*. Exaggerated attitudes of independence may, strangely enough, compensate for unconscious dependent needs.

Dep is related to anxiety and the discrimination of the two presents a vexing problem.

Dep is a constant phenomenon in the psychotherapy situation; such a reaction as expecting miraculous help from the therapist while showing but little tendency to tackle one's own problems is obviously dependent.

II. THEORY OF Dep

Dep originates in the helpless situation of the new-born infant. It is understood by Freud to be related to frustrations in the "oral phase" (Freud, 1905). Feeding frustrations are undoubtedly one of the most potent sources of *Dep* motivation. The situation may be pictured as follows: The infant is frustrated when hungry or by the failure of the environment to reduce some other important drive. The infant thereupon produces its limited repertory of behavior. It cries, struggles, becomes intensely mobilized (rage), and exhausts itself in the most vehement activity of which it is capable. Eventually "ache in the throat" inhibits crying and fatigue slows down muscular activity. If nothing the child can do brings relief, it may have re-course to a passive waiting attitude, meanwhile bearing hunger or whatever drive is operative. This attitude should be conceived of not as merely passive but as one of suffering and waiting. Since it cannot help itself, the child must await help from others. *Dep* is thus seen to be a complex condition of painful stimulation.

Anxiety about the recurrence of a similar painful *Dep* condition is likely to be learned by the child. If punished for actions designed to relieve the *Dep* condition, the child may also experience fear in relation to *Dep*. During the later socialization, and because of later punishments for *Dep*-motivated activities, the child may come to blame itself for having *Dep* motives. It can even get cause and effect reversed and learn to assume that the reason it was frustrated was because it was "bad." Whether by the means just outlined or by some kind of innate connection, it occurs in adult cases that people who are seriously frustrated will immediately react with self-blame. Thoughts such as the following are illustrative: "If I had been a good girl, Mother would have loved me," "If I had done my home-work, Daddy wouldn't have gone away."

Though *Dep,* with all its ramifications, is an exceedingly impor-tant state of affairs, scoring *Dep* has proved, for the moment, trouble-some. It is often hard to say what is anxiety, what is passivity, and what is dependence. It is hard to form a rule on which portion of a sequence of actions one should note and score. Should it be the frustration itself, the ensuing struggles, the rage, the motivated yet passive-seeming waiting, or the guilt? Should one merely label a ter-rific unconscious complex of forces without trying to discriminate details? Should one identify motive or response? Such perplexing circumstances as these make the proper coding of *Dep* a man-size task.

III. EXAMPLES AND DISCUSSION

1. *The sign* Dep *for conscious dependence.* Whenever conscious dependence (*Dep*) is present, unconscious dependence (*dep*) is al-most invariably present also; however, one scores the known, con-scious *Dep* and not the assumed unconscious *dep* unless the "mys-tery" which indicates the operation of an unconscious force can be detected. In the latter case, one scores it *dep*. We will begin with ex-amples of conscious dependence.

a. A married male patient who was constantly being neglected and rejected by his wife spoke as follows:

> Ah . . . and at the other extreme, ah . . . I feel-ah as though I'd be the most desolate man on earth if I didn't have my family and my children and the . . . the constant . . . ah . . . turmoil that accompanies family life and that what a . . . a . . . what a lost soul I'd be if I didn't have . . . have that situation.

This quote expresses, we believe, more than affection for his family; it expresses the desolation and helplessness he would feel at separation from them; the patient was exploitable because of the strength of his dependent motivation on his wife.

b. The following quote is from the same patient. Because of his failure to jump speedily at command, his wife was giving him the "remote" treatment, speaking to him only about necessary matters.

> [1]Now yesterday I admitted something to my wife that I had never told her before. [2]And that is that . . . I would appreciate being brought back into her . . . ah . . . well, confidence isn-isn't the word I mean—but being brought back to a point where . . . ah . . . she could feel that . . . ah . . . [3](*He sighs*) . . . she could talk to me and . . . ah . . . ask my opinion on things and discuss ideas and thoughts.

The patient has appealed to his wife for reinstatement. Her withdrawal of loving participation has aroused intense dependent motives in patient; his response is to plead to be taken back. Since the patient is aware of his motive (though not of its unconscious causes) the passage (excepting the *sigh*) should be scored *Dep*.

c. The following example shows how a husband manipulated his wife's dependent fears.

> PATIENT   [1]I don't know, I guess I was afraid. [2]I-I don't know. [3]. . . I-I wanted to—I wanted to be with him. [4]. . . And-and I know that he would . . . go off if—I mean, I knew that, because-because . . . he-he had a habit of going off anyhow when he'd just . . .
> THERAPIST   [5]Mm-hmm.
> PATIENT   . . . [6](*Tearfully*) at the slightest provocation would disappear. [7](*Tearfully*) [8]We used to go to parties and things together. [9](*She sobs*) [10]And he'd walk off and leave me. [11](*She sobs*)
> THERAPIST   [12]Mm-hmm.

PATIENT   [13](*Weeping*) [14]And I had to go home alone. [15](*She sobs*) [16]And everyone knew about it . . .

The submission of the wife, and the feelings of desolation and abandonment (units 1, 3, 4, 8, 10, 14, and 16) are properly scored as *Dep.*

d. The same woman patient showed marked dependent feelings in other connections. For example, her family never made enough fuss about her birthdays, she felt. An example follows:

[1]I-my birthday is the fifth of July. [2]It's the day after the Fourth. [3](*She sighs*) [4]On the Fourth people are always going off somewhere. [5]It-the Fourth is a holiday. [6]Everybody gets sunburned and exhausted. [7]And then the fifth is the day after, when they all go back to work. [8]It's a terrible day. [9]Ah . . . always ever since I can remember, my birthday has been the least important birthday in the family . . . ah . . . for that reason, I know it. [10]I mean it's-it's just common sense. [11](*She sighs*) [12]Ah . . . for one reason, it comes at a time when people-people don't think-ah about your birthday when they're planning for a holiday. [13]They have other things to think about. [14]And then all of a sudden it's the fifth of July. [15]And they haven't gotten you anything. [16]Ah . . . the other birthdays which are scattered through the year are-are-are events of a sort-ah with cakes and-and . . . [17]Ah . . . this sounds too childish for words. [18]But I must say I-I never, I-I-I've never gotten as many presents as anyone else in the family has. [19]And-and I always felt sort of bad about that. [20]This year, well, I felt bad about it this year too.

This passage seems to emphasize how the patient missed getting the presents (love) that she needed when she was a child. For this passage, one would consider a scoring of *H* for aggression, but this scoring should be rejected. A good guide for scoring is to try to answer the question: What should the therapist react to in the utterance? In the case at hand we think that he should react to the feeling of being rejected, to being slighted, to the demanding, dependent motivation which the patient is evidently enduring. Passage should be scored *Dep.*

e. We have said that nostalgia and yearning should be treated as dependent reactions. The following is an example from a woman patient. She has been speaking of her father, who died when she was an adolescent girl.

> PATIENT   [1]Oh, I-I came to the point of even crying, oh, not sobbing or anything but just sort of like filling up for a moment. [2]And then I caught hold of myself.
>
> THERAPIST   [3]About what? [4]I mean what were you thinking about?
>
> PATIENT   [5]Well, everything seems so hopeless, even the treatment. [6]And-and oh, I think perhaps feeling a little bit sorry for myself. [7]*(She sighs)* [8]Perhaps I don't know.

The patient is feeling consciously blue and sorry for herself. She is evidently hoping that the therapist will do something kind for her. This mood has been evoked by thinking about her father and has presumably called up some of the feelings which were appropriate at the time of his death. The passage should be scored *Dep.*

2. *The score* dep. The sign *dep* has the same criteria as that for conscious dependence except that there must be a mystery present— the mystery which identifies an unconscious motive.

a. We will take as an example a woman patient whose husband managed her ruthlessly by exploiting her dependent feelings, forcing her to get an abortion. The patient had at last succeeded in freeing herself from her husband and was living separately; occasionally, however, the husband begged her to see him again. Despite all her bad experience with him, she finds it impossible to refuse his request. Why is she still vulnerable? The following example will clarify this situation.

> [1]I-I saw him last week. [2]I-I . . . I never had any idea that we'd get together again. [3]I couldn't stand living with him. [4]He-he's-he-he's done too many things to me. [5]I know it's not his fault. [6]But-uh-I don't love him. [7]I really don't. [8]I haven't wanted to hurt him. [9]I mean I-I felt that. [10]But-uh . . . it-it's sort of letting go of the last straw, you know? [11]But-but I see that it's a foolish situation. [12]I saw him this week. [13]Now, when we were first separated I told him I didn't want to see him. [14]And then he begged me. [15]And it went on. [16]And then I-I don't know, to avoid trouble, I gave in to him. [17]That's-that's about the size of it.

The solution of the mystery seems to lie in the patient's dependent feelings. Though her former husband has bitterly abused her she also identifies with him and feels the frustration *he* would have to bear if she should refuse to see him. These feelings are so painful that they impel her, against good reason, to see her husband again. Obviously, these feelings are unconscious. They should be scored *dep-a,* since we assume a counterforce keeping these motives out of awareness. The therapist could not free patient of being thus exploited unless he made clear to her her unconscious identification with her former husband.

b. Another patient had been mysteriously moved by a passage in the book *The Wind in the Willows* by Kenneth Grahame. She remembered this passage all her life. She has never understood why it haunted her, though it keeps coming back to memory. In the book two animals, Mole and Rat, are treated as human beings. The patient spoke of the matter as follows:

> PATIENT   ¹I haven't told you the story yet. ²I couldn't get to it. ³Uh—Mole-uh-they're running through the woods to get home. ⁴And it's a dark winter night. ⁵And-and-uh-they go by Mole's old home. ⁶And he smells it. ⁷And it's described how it comes to him. ⁸And-and-uh-he-he gets a shock. ⁹And he doesn't know what it is. ¹⁰And then he realizes it's his old home . . . and-and-uh stops. ¹¹Uh-he-he sort of lost it. ¹²But-uh-he stops. ¹³And-and while he-he's trying to-to get his bearings uh Rat goes racing on ahead. ¹⁴And he-he waited. ¹⁵And he calls to Mole to hurry up and come along. ¹⁶And Mole uh well, he just gives up the idea of looking for his old home and runs after Rat. ¹⁷And-and while he's going along he starts to cry. ¹⁸And-and Rat asks him what he's crying about. ¹⁹And he-he tells him. ²⁰And then Rat slaps him on the back and says, "Why didn't you say so, old man?" and-and, "Of course we've got to find it." ²¹They go back. ²²And they find his-his home in the ground.
>
> THERAPIST   ²³Well, why would this—why should this upset you? ²⁴What-what are your thoughts about that?
>
> PATIENT   ²⁵I don't know. ²⁶I-I don't know. ²⁷When I was—when I was little and I read it I-uh-I liked to read it. ²⁸But-uh-but the reason I think I liked to read it was because I was always so happy when-when Rat said, "Come on, let's go and look for

it." [29]Uh-and . . . that uh was worth all the agony. [30]Uh I don't know. [31]I suppose it's some sort of a wish fulfillment. [32]Uh I couldn't tell you.

THERAPIST   [33]What do you mean by that?

PATIENT   [34]I-I-uh-I felt like Mole did. [35]I wanted something. [36]And Mole got it. [37]I mean I knew just how he felt. [38]I could—I could feel for him. [39]I never thought of it that way when I was little. [40]But it must have represented something I experienced.

It would seem that the patient is here reporting in symbolic form on an important event in her own childhood. She remembers a little tale from *The Wind in the Willows* because it is the vehicle which carries the emotions of an important event. One infers that sometime in her childhood, probably very early, the patient suffered an acute experience of rejection and abandonment by her mother. The longing to be lovingly reunited with her mother persists, as it is wont to do, throughout life. She felt this when she read the story as a child and was consoled by the story of Mole. She remembered it in therapy, and thus repeated in miniature the noxious traumatic experience and the consoling fantasy. Like Mole, she found her way home again if only in imagination. Naturally, this recollection also constituted an invitation to the therapist to understand her problem and administer aid and comfort. Since the scoring must be as of the time of childhood, the sentences telling the story should be scored *dep-a*.

c. Children often show unconscious dependence reactions, waiting speechlessly for adults to divine the thing they want. The following reaction is from an adult woman patient, recalling her childhood:

The patient said that as an adolescent girl she would never ask for things as other girls did. She did not besiege her mother with a clamor for clothes; indeed, as the usual thing her mother bought dresses for her without patient having to ask for them:

[1]I never would say I wanted a dress. [2]Someone had to offer it to me.

The intense, passive waiting constituted a kind of silent demand on her mother. But why shouldn't she ask for clothes or have a clothes allowance as other girls did? This is the mystery. The apparent answer is that she didn't want it, she preferred to have gifts, to have others understand her need by intuition and meet it. The patient herself had no explanation for this mystery, but we conceive that an unconscious dependent motive is operating. When the clothes were given unasked, they were much more than a practical gift; they were also a needed testimony of love.

d. A married male patient found himself in the situation where his wife had left for a two-week vacation with her parents. His response to her departure was to develop dizziness and feelings of apprehension. There seemed no sensible reason for such feelings. Consciously, patient looked at the matter as follows:

> [1]My wife does need a vacation. [2]The children enjoy their grandparents. [3]And so they will be well off with her. [4]I am perfectly capable of taking care of myself. [5]There is no reason to think that my wife will not come back. [6]I know she loves me.

Unconsciously, however, the patient felt quite differently. Constantly susceptible to the slightest signs of rebuff, he had felt her leaving as an abandonment. It was in response to this unconscious evaluation of the situation that he developed symptoms (which in his childhood would have called the solicitous attention of adults to him). The scores should be *dep-a*.

IV. SIGNS COMBINED WITH Dep

1. A small *r* can be attached to the sign *Dep* to indicate reduction of dependent motivation. The following is an example:

> *A twenty-year-old girl, suffering from obesity, had particularly stormy relations with her father. During the course of therapy they had a dramatic quarrel, and the patient moved out of her parents' home. Apparently alarmed, her father responded by buying an automobile for patient. The patient's reaction to the car was singular; it brought her more joy, she said, than she had ever experienced before. It was more than a means of transportation, more than a valued present. She reacted to it by complete remission of her eating symptom (and by a similarly complete lack of motivation to continue therapy). The car was constantly in her thoughts and seemed to pre-empt every other consideration in her life.*

The car was, indeed, more than a car. It was a symbol of her father's love and willingness to nurture and supply her. The patient's intense dependent need, in every way unconscious, had been the motive behind her symptom and her wish for therapy; when the need was suddenly stilled, the responses to it dropped out. Thus a strong unconscious need was reduced. The scoring should be *dep-a:r*.

2. *The sign* Dep-A. A person may be aware of but yet fear his dependent motives; for example, the married man whose wife went on the vacation was apprised of the reason for his symptoms of dizziness and apprehension. As time passed he became aware of the strength of his dependent needs. He also became somewhat afraid of them, thus:

> [1]I know I shouldn't let my wife do for me all of the things that she does. [2]She treats me just like one of the children, picks up after me, babies me. [3]I don't do many of the things that other husbands do around the house. [4]And she lets me get away with it.

As the patient became aware of his dependence he developed some anxiety lest letting himself be indulged would unman him completely. This reaction should be scored *Dep-A*.

3. *Other cases.* Undoubtedly other signs than those we have indicated could be combined with *Dep*. Other users of the scoring system may find circumstances, which did not appear in our material, to use *Dep* in combination.

V. DISCRIMINATIONS AND BORDERLINE CASES

1. Dep *versus* A. As the reader may suspect from the theoretical section, the scoring *Dep* shades into scores for other reactions by degrees which are often insensible. Thus *Dep* and *A* are sometimes hard to distinguish. A woman patient described how her mother would disappear in order to exact "good behavior" from her:

> PATIENT   [1]Every once in a while she'd get in a huff and just disappear . . . which was extremely alarming.
>
> THERAPIST   [2]This alarmed you then, worried you?
>
> PATIENT   [3]Yes. [4]Every time she did it I thought maybe she wouldn't come back. [5](*Anxious laugh*) [6]She always did. [7]But-but

. . . and I wasn't sure that she would. [8]I mean every time it was, "Well, this is it." [9]I mean [10](*Anxious laugh*), "Last time didn't count, this is—it."

Is the patient describing here the suffering due to dependent motivation or that due to fear? We decided the scoring should be *Dep* because the form of the mother's behavior is a threat by absence, which would presumably mobilize strong dependent motivation. No specific reason for fear is indicated. Yet, as the reader will probably agree, the decision is a close one. It could go the other way and no one could count himself foolish.

2. Dep *versus* L. Dependence could be thought of, and some have thought of it, as a need for love. This understanding of the matter puts the accent on the goal rather than on the motive. It is true that *Dep* motivation is reduced by loving response from others; nevertheless it seems worth while to have a sign which indicates the motive itself, the mixture of stimuli which compose the *Dep* motive. Where we score *L*, as between people, the motive and response are more likely to be reciprocal and more or less equal; one doesn't get the unbalance which exists, say, in the relationship between mother and child. It is likely also that *L* is shaded more toward sexual meanings, although by no means defined by them. Unfortunately, *dep* frequently underlies relations which, on the surface, resemble reciprocal loving relations. Crisis may strip away the appearance of equality and reveal stark dependent demands exerted on the one person by the other. Surely, in an adequate love relationship all kinds of needs will be met, both conscious and unconscious, both one-sided and reciprocal, sexual needs, sheer needs for care and babying, support of self-esteem, and the like. In this fluent river of response to stimuli—simultaneous, complex, and interchained—we are trying to isolate, by appropriate definition, a few rocks to which the witness can cling. For the moment, *Dep* is a slippery rock because of its relatively low reliability of scoring.

THE SIGN DREAM

I. DEFINITION OF Dream

The sign *Dream* is used for the text of a dream when it is first told. If details which are a part of the dream are added later, they are also scored *Dream*. When dream elements are taken as starting points for association, said associations are scored not as *Dream* but according to content. Resistant material, such as deprecating the importance of a dream, whether appearing before or after the dream, is scored *Res*. The Sign *Dream* is never combined with any other.

II. THEORY OF Dream

Freud's brilliant dream theory (Freud, 1900) is our standard. The dream represents a compromise between a disavowed wish or motive and a hindering force. The basic motive of the dream is camouflaged according to the laws of the primary process (Fenichel, 1945, p. 47). Dreams have both a manifest and a latent content. What we score *Dream* is the manifest content; that is, it is what the dreamer remembers and reports as his dream.

III. EXAMPLES OF Dream

A married male patient dreamed the following:

> [1]The dream I had this morning-uh—last night, whenever it was—is-uh that one of them was, somebody was tapping my lungs, very [2](*Anxious laugh*) uh-ingenious device that they jabbed through my ribs into my lungs. [3]And they were going to drip some medicine in there because I had a cough in my chest. [4]My wife was there. [5]And she-uh was watching the procedure. [6]Then-uh my wife was to go to the doctor to see when she would have-uh- [7](*Anxious laugh*) be allowed to have sexual relations with-with me again. [8]And-uh somehow I was floating around. [9]And I could pick up conversations that my wife couldn't. [10]And I-I heard the doctor say to someone else or to me, "Oh, she couldn't because this—there's uh-uh-a chance of-of-uh starting a cancer-uh with uh-uh-the irritation there." [11]Uh-now uh and this became more confused. [12]And uh-uh-I-I began to feel kind of desperate-uh.

The foregoing units (excepting the laughs) should, of course, be scored *Dream;* there seems no point to illustrating this category further.

IV. BORDERLINE CASES AND DISCRIMINATIONS

There are a number of useful discriminations which one can make in respect to the sign *Dream*.

1. *Emotions in the dream*. Emotional reactions occurring in a dream are not scored by content but are simply scored *Dream*. Thus the fear and sex elements in the dream just presented are not scored as *A* or *S* but are scored *Dream*.

2. *Resistant material*. Resistant material appearing before, during, or after the telling of a dream *is* scored as resistant. The following statement was made by a particularly intimidated married male patient:

> [1]And then I-uh-I dozed off just for a few minutes, maybe five at the most, fell asleep, and promptly had a dream, then woke up again . . . yeah, almost . . . short order, almost. [2]That was the-the exact impression that I had, that well, you haven't had a dream up till now; if you fall asleep again for a few minutes, have one. [3]And . . . so the dream was uh-uh-it wasn't uh-features-like. [4]It was more of a short subject, I guess.

In this example the patient stalls, tells the circumstances of the dream, but does not report the dream itself. The material is viewed as resistant and should be scored *Res*.

3. *Associations to a dream*. Associations to a dream are scored by content. The following example of a dream by a timid male patient will exemplify the matter:

> [1]I think my dreams are still uh difficult to understand. [2]But I don't have any I remember very often except last night I can remember there being a dream. [3]Uh-you know I was [4](*Anxious laugh*) uh sort of half betwixt and between . . . sleep and being awake. [5]And I thought there was somebody buzzing the back doorbell. [6]We don't have a back doorbell. [7]But there was somebody buzzing the back doorbell. [8]And then they were trying the lock. [9]And they came in. [10]And then I suspected that I was lying in-in bed. [11]And I-this figure-uh was there. [12]And I was very scared, and-uh until I completely woke up and realized that I was looking in the—in the wrong direction, that there was-was nothing there.

The therapist then asked the patient to give his associations to the elements of the dream, and the patient said:

> [13]Well, I can recall uh about the fear-uh. [14]This approximated the-the this kind of panic feeling that I have had in the past and which I recall having for some reason last night uh-to a—to a small degree sometime either when I'd just gone to bed or on —just before the dream or sometime. [15]Uh-I think I do recall . . . a mild wave of it.

In the passage shown above units 1 and 2 should be scored *Res* because they tend to belittle the dream and delay the telling of it. Units 3–12 should be scored *Dream;* they are the manifest dream. Units 13–15 are associations which should be scored according to content; in this case the content is fearful so these latter units should be scored *A*. The understanding of dreams will become continuously a more important matter as research on psychotherapy advances.

THE SIGN H

I. DEFINITION OF H

H is the sign used for a hostile *act* or *motive*. *H* is social, defined by the culture in which it occurs. A *hostile* action is one which would tend to injure another person. A physical assault would, of course, be hostile but so also would behavior which tends to put another person in his place, lower his self-esteem, or cut him down to size. Criticism and gossip are hostile.

Hostile *motives* are those which give rise to actions which would injure others. Anger, enmity, envy, jealousy, spite are hostile motives. If allowed free rein they would excite actions which would be dangerous to other people.

Hostile motives or actions are not necessarily pathological. Capability for hostile actions is a necessity of normal living. Defense of self, of family, or of country is required of the average person; hostile motives and means are necessarily involved.

Smug contemplation of the misfortunes of others can reveal hostile motives. The idea is: "I smile, or falsely lament, while fate does the dirty work." Newspapers offer many opportunities for such secret hostile satisfaction; they show the culpable foibles of the great, and occasionally they depict the mighty brought low.

H can be conscious or unconscious. If scored as unconscious (*h*) the cues of a mystery must be present. *H* can be combined with other signs, and it appears especially frequently in combination with anxiety (*A*). The appropriate control and expression of *H* is a leading problem in both individual and collective life.

II. THEORY OF H

The raw material of *H* is the strong, innate, vague "gesture against" or "movement against" of the infant. Such gestures or movements include crying, struggling, flailing with the limbs, batting. There is also some kind of inward mobilization which occurs at the same time as the gesture. If the "gesture against" attracts attention and brings relief, it is rewarded and strengthened. Such gestures seem to be evoked when tension builds within the organism. It is a matter of choice whether or not one calls such rising tension "frustration." It seems to be a fact that non-cooperation by the environment in reducing strong drives provokes "gestures against." Such non-cooperation might be called frustrating.

Overt gestures and inward arousal occur at the same time. The aggressive complex (gesture and emotion) is strengthened by reward (feeding the infant when it is hungry and cries). Presumably, also, this complex can be weakened by extinction. The idea is that aggressive gestures and emotions are fatiguing. If reward does not occur, fatigue will stop them after a period of time. The end condition, after protracted non-cooperation, is the disappearance of crying and protesting. The resulting state is one of infant despair, helplessness, passivity, or lack of initiative. If the circumstances of learning such despair are not noticed, the learned reactions may easily be misunderstood as constitutional.

Even when infant aggression has been properly rewarded, as it ought to be, the learning of aggression control must proceed at a later time. Thus punishments occurring when the aggressive complex is active may strengthen responses which successfully compete with aggressive responses, i.e. passivity. The cues for permitted and not-permitted aggressive mobilization must be learned. Effects of punishment can transfer from aggressive actions to aggressive emotions and can inhibit both. Punishment effects may further transfer to the words which label action or emotion. Since the words are compounded into thoughts, it follows that aggressive thoughts can be inhibited. According to the customs of the society, the child learns *what* aggressive actions are permitted and what are not (striking but not biting), *when* aggressive actions may occur (in case of self-defense), *how* they may occur (between siblings of equal age but not between older and younger)—and all the multitude of circumstances which define aggression (for example, verbal but not physical hostility may be tolerated).

There are many flaws and errors in the training relating to aggression. Sometimes the caretakers of the child do not realize that their actions have the effect of aggression training on the child. The inward conscience-barrier against aggression may be imposed with too great rigor. Uninstructed, and this being its first time around in life, the child may come to believe, even from gestures which seem innocent to the parents, that horrible aggressive acts will be initiated against it—acts which parents would not perform and which the culture would not tolerate. The child may get an entirely mistaken notion of the potency of its own aggressive acts when the tendency to carry them out arises.

The life needs and the aggressive intentions and actions of the child are closely, and often curiously, connected. The child may learn that only aggressive acts will help it gain its goals, or that no aggressive acts are efficient. Since aggression is often the occasion of bringing the child attention, relief, and love, aggression may be inappropriately used to compel love. Occasionally a murderer acts as if the following were a true statement of his predicament: "I killed her in order to get her to love me."

Although frustration seems very frequently connected with aggression and can, on many occasions, be shown to excite aggressive acts (Dollard *et al.*, 1939), the occurrence of frustrating circumstances is not sufficient to justify a scoring of aggression, conscious or unconscious. If aggression is to be scored there must be some kind of direct evidence for it, either the motive or the act itself or the enigma which calls attention to an unconscious angry emotion. The inhibition of aggression will be illustrated in our section on combined signs.

III. EXAMPLES OF H

1. *Actions likely to injure others.* By injury, in this context, we mean to damage others, to hurt them physically, to cause them psychological pain, etc.

a. One of our male patients recorded his adolescent defiance of his parents as follows:

> [1]And around that time, also, was-uh . . . when I started sneaking away to the movies. [2]And it's quite possible that uh if my parents went to church I, I would head for the movies if I had the price.

The patient's very religious parents would have been pained indeed had they known of these secret visits.

b. The same patient was quite capable of expressing a roundabout aggression toward his therapist. He acknowledged the fact by saying, "Gee, I've yawned three times already today." Since yawning is recognized as a social affront which calls for an apology, and since none was made, the correct scoring of this utterance would be *H*.

c. A man patient had been much put-upon by his wife and had been exceedingly passive in his relations with her. As therapy progressed he reported a change in his behavior, as follows:

> [1]When I'm irritated she knows it to a greater extent than she ever did before. [2]We exchange a few sharp words every now and— [3]That never used to happen. [4]In the past I-I wouldn't allow myself to get into that position.

This passive patient was apparently acquiring a more nearly normal capacity for opposition to his wife. Units 1 and 2 should be scored *H*. (The note of gratitude to therapist for helping patient change is faintly but sensibly present; but it is judged that the aggressive content is dominant. While one may recognize a minor or secondary implication of such a passage, the dominant implication is always scored.)

d. A communication intended to cause chagrin or embarrassment to another should be scored as aggressive; thus from a patient:

> [1]Well, I have sort of a difficult time getting in touch with you. [2]Uh-the switchboard operator-uh couldn't locate you or-or didn't know. [3]And I had to explain to her about this building. [4]Well, anyway, we were able. [5]And when I thought I had gotten a-hold of you someone else spoke, on the phone. [6]Is that your extension, 2121?

The patient needed the therapist but had trouble reaching him by phone. Her remarks are at once a request for information and a reproach. The element of reproach seemed to us dominant and we scored the passage *H*.

e. There can be no doubt about the aggressive nature of the behavior which was reported to us by a woman patient as follows:

> [1]Once I was at a party. [2]And I was tight. [3]And a man said, "You don't know what you are talking about." [4]And I threw the glass in his face. [5]I threw the Scotch right in his face.

This woman's version of a blow should certainly be scored *H*. The act was typical of a psychopathic streak in this patient.

f. As already stated, aggression can and should be a possibility of normal behavior. A passive male patient suffered much from the aggressions of his wife. She was accustomed to put pressure on him to have intercourse with her at times when he was not at all in the mood. If he tried to evade she would return to the attack, in the case at hand by asking, "Are you ducking me by staying in the bathroom?" The patient resisted her pressure as follows:

> [1]I told her I didn't want my actions doubted or misinterpreted or anything else. [2]I just wasn't interested. [3]And-uh-I thought we were both agreed that if I wasn't interested we weren't going to go through any motions that usually resulted in-uh-in a dismal failure, you know, in the way of lack of—losing the erection.

Every such forced attempt at intercourse and resulting failure of potency had a wounding effect on patient. His well-justified opposition should be scored *H*.

2. Motives as well as verbal or physical actions can be scored as hostile. They should be so scored if putting them into effect would result in damage to the other person.

a. One of our women patients gave the following hostile evaluation of her marriage:

> [1]Our marriage is just a flop. [2]I could never get together with him again. [3]I just have a negative feeling I can't control.

Much abuse by her husband and unforgettable incidents passing between them had left this patient with a residue of hostile feeling which she could not and did not wish to control. The sentences should be scored *H*.

b. Another woman patient had a very negative reaction to her grandfather:

> ¹My grandfather was a very domineering man. ²He was a very selfish old man. ³I think that my grandfather did something to all his children. ⁴He spoiled their whole lives.

The patient's conscious hostility toward her grandfather needs no further comment. It should be scored *H*.

c. Describing socially disapproved behavior of another person with the implication that one joins in condemning it is ground for scoring *H*. For example a woman patient described her brother's unfeeling behavior toward her mother saying:

> ¹My brother is a lost cause. ²My brother is a real psycho. ³And he hates my mother quite openly. ⁴He makes no secret of it. ⁵Between my brother and his wife, between them . . . they have an income of about three hundred dollars a week. ⁶He's never given my parents a cent since all this trouble come up. ⁷And Father hasn't worked since last year. ⁸He doesn't give a damn. ⁹That's about the size of it.

The patient feels that she is speaking for all reasonable people in describing and condemning her brother's behavior. The culture has it that when one's parents are ill and more or less destitute, children should help. The passage should be scored *H*.

d. The same patient criticized her brother in a similar vein on a later occasion. His wife was deathly ill and had to spend Christmas in a TB sanitarium. The patient spoke as follows:

> ¹The whole thing was absolutely nauseating. ²How could any-one act like that . . . with someone who is dying, not even to send any note. ³I mean it wasn't that he didn't know. ⁴He knew then that she was . . . and-and-and . . . ⁵Then it was just—it-it—seemed absolutely heartless to me.

The patient's hostile motives toward her brother, which seem so well justified, are entirely evident from this passage. The fact that she judges the brother "heartless" apparently keeps her from having guilt in expressing such motives. The passage should be scored *H*.

e. It seems that there are plenty of complaints against husbands in our cases, and it is certainly true that one finds such complaints among neurotic married women. A dependent wife said:

> [1]I get very annoyed with him. [2]He was away all weekend. [3]And
> I was alone. [4]Men are awfully selfish, I think. [5]They only think
> of themselves. [6]A woman is so different. [7]I hate men.

The fact that the patient says "A woman is so different" gives a
hint of other content in connection with this hostile utterance; but
the main meaning is an aggressive one and the passage should be
scored *H*.

IV. COMBINED WITH OTHER SIGNS

H can be combined with other signs and is, especially frequently,
combined with variants of *A*.

1. *H-A*. This sign identifies the situation where a person is angry
and is afraid to carry out his angry intention, or does carry it out
and is afraid of consequences; both anger and fear are conscious.

a. Here is a report of another telephone incident; a woman patient said:

> [1]When I first came to your office, you remember, I had to change
> the date. [2]I tried to reach you for about an hour by telephone.
> [3]And no one around here had even heard of you. [4](*Embarrassed
> laugh*) [5]I'm very sorry! [6]That isn't quite flattering to you.
> [7](*Laughing anxiously*) [8]Is it?

Here the patient speaks out her disparaging estimate of therapist
but, with a mixture of guilt and warmth, apologizes. The belittling
impulse is swiftly modified by anxiety. The scores of 5, 6, and 8
should be *H-A*.

b. A man patient, reflecting back on his boyhood, said the following:

> [1]I know I would steal some from my—from the change at the
> grocery store. [2]And-uh-and I remember being caught at it once
> and being . . . quite soundly spanked.

This little saga of crime and punishment deserves to be scored
H-A.

2. *H-a*. This sign describes the situation in which a person is
aware of angry feelings but cannot, for some mysterious reason, express them. A man patient gave us an illustration suitable for this
sign when he described what happened to him in a schoolroom:

¹That was a funny deal. ²I never could recite in Miss Smith's class. ³She used to make jokes about my Polish name and jeer at me because of my accent. ⁴I was fuming inside. ⁵But I never could answer her. ⁶Nor could I volunteer to recite in class. ⁷Funny, wasn't it?

No, it wasn't funny, nor even amusing, but it was interesting from a psychodynamic standpoint. The patient's angry feelings were opposed by a mysterious force which could be called "unconscious anxiety." This anxiety inhibited not only the angry retort but all other attempts to speak out in class. Evidently anxiety generalized from the nascent angry utterance to the originally neutral recitation responses. This situation deserves to be scored *H-a*. This sign is frequently used for an inhibition or symptom.

3. *h-A*. This sign describes the situation where a person feels strong overt anxiety with no apparent reason for it; there is no reason, that is, so far as the patient can see, but if one inspects the wider context of the situation a reason, and a hostile one, can be divined.

a. A woman patient reported suffering a severe anxiety attack which came on without any reason. The dialogue between her and the therapist went as follows:

PATIENT ¹I had this terrible feeling last night late in the evening. ²My heart was slamming so I thought it would jump out of my chest. ³And I could hardly breathe. ⁴I was so nervous I couldn't stand up or sit down. ⁵Uh-there didn't seem to be any particular reason for it. ⁶It just sort of came on.

THERAPIST ⁷It's hard to believe that such a thing could happen to you for no reason at all. ⁸Something must have happened. ⁹Or something came up in your thoughts.

PATIENT ¹⁰I don't think so. ¹¹⁻¹⁴(*20-sec. pause*) ¹⁵ What comes to mind now is that earlier in the evening Jim and I were talking about my budget. ¹⁶I ran seventy dollars over last month. ¹⁷I told him the reasons for it. ¹⁸He had insisted on giving a party that we couldn't afford. ¹⁹⁻²⁰(*10-sec. pause*) ²¹But-but he was very unreasonable. ²²He told me ²³(*Weeping*) that if I weren't feeb-feeble-minded I could make it come out right.

After this incident the patient had gone away to her room to prepare for bed, and while she was doing so her heart began to slam as

earlier described. In further discussion between patient and therapist the true state of affairs emerged. The patient had felt the husband's words as a sharp rejection. She had felt the impulse to answer angrily at the time but had smothered it as was her custom.
The motive, although disavowed and repressed, continued active
and the patient went to her room mobilized and tense. Her anxiety
expressed itself, nevertheless, in physical form as an "attack." Units
1 through 6 of this passage, in which the patient described a causeless
fear, should be scored *h-A*.

4. *h-a*. In the case of this sign both motive and inhibitory force
are unconscious. The result is frequently a symbolic utterance.

a. An Othello-like reaction of one of our male patients will illustrate the use of this sign. About two years after their wedding, the
patient's wife had been unfaithful to him. Apparently in order to
inflict maximum torture she had confessed the fact but had refused
to name her lover. The patient's reaction at the time was one of pro-
found grief. The world seemed to collapse and become empty. After
some time he recovered in part; at least he recovered enough to
enter psychotherapy. In the course of his therapy he managed to
explain to his wife how he really felt without himself knowing what
he was doing. His report of this incident is as follows:

> ¹There's been one-ah outcome of that test that-ah-ah neither
> you or Dr. Smith would ever guess, ah-which is I think apropos.
> ²Wednesday night after that Thematic Apperception Test, ah-
> my wife asked me-ah the type of thing that I had-ah just taken,
> what type of tests were they. ³She didn't want to ask any details.
> ⁴And-ah I gave her a "for instance," which was a picture of a
> fully clothed man-ah going away from a low bed on which a-ah
> woman that was naked from the waist up was lying. ⁵And-ah
> the man going away from the bed had his-ah forearm over his
> eyes. ⁶And-ah I mentioned that to my wife. ⁷Are you—are you
> familiar with that picture? ⁸Do you recall it? ⁹The-ah that's fu-
> ture, or past, present, and future story that I was to weave out
> of my imagination on that picture was that-ah the man had been
> in jail for a year and had been told that his wife was unfaithful
> or that she was unfaithful many times. ¹⁰He brooded over that.
> ¹¹Several times, that was it. ¹²And he brooded over that incident,
> and-ah decided that he would kill his wife upon return, as a
> result of this infidelity-ah which she had just done. ¹³And he

realized that she'd died, and he was getting—going away from the bed that-ah he still loved her. [14]And that was the, well, the future was that he went to a phone and told the police what he'd just done.

In the course of describing his test, the patient managed to communicate to his wife the hatred and revengeful feelings which he had had, but had repressed, at the time of her infidelity. The communication was symbolic; under the disguise of a fantasy it went directly from his unconscious mind to hers, and there was reason to think that it registered with her. The patient's unconscious aggression was inhibited by unconscious anxiety, and both elements operated to produce a conscious fantasy. The patient did not realize, of course, that the motives involved were his own. This passage should be scored *h-a*.

b. One of our male patients had been reared in a religious school for boys. He had turned out to be a very "good" person, which translates as "obsessive and restricted." One of his college friends used to goad him about religious matters, asking him for instance whether or not he believed in a certain Biblical miracle. The patient responded:

> PATIENT   [1]I never allow the question to remain in my brain long enough to formulate it.
>
> THERAPIST   [2]You mean you had no opinion that it was true or not true?
>
> PATIENT   [3]I never allow the question or the thought to remain in my brain long enough to formulate in my own mind the way I thought about a particular question that he might have of that nature.

The patient responded to his friend's goading with an inhibition; he had a kind of mental blackout. His prim and frozen speech correctly indicates the inner emotional freezing which he had experienced. Evidently he was hostile to religious figures and ideas and institutions but reacted with "blackout" to the least stimulus which might invite expression of this hostility. The mystery in this case is: Why, in our free-speech society, should anybody be afraid to state that he did not believe in miracles? We infer that an unconscious hostile motive was operating and that it was opposed by unconscious fear. The surface result was an inhibition. The correct scoring is *h-a*.

c. A woman patient was openly hostile to her mother. The mother had recently given the patient a string of beads for her birthday. On the first day the patient wore the necklace she broke the string and scattered the beads. She described the incident as follows:

> [1]And I wasn't conscious of it when I did it. [2]I mean I'm not a bead fiddler. [3]Wasn't—I know I fiddle with matches. [4]But I don't fiddle with beads. [5]Ah-I just-uh out of the clear blue sky, I just bent over and gave it a hard yank. [6]And the beads scattered.

The mystery is, why the unaccountable yank? Although patient was consciously hostile to her mother she was evidently also unconsciously hostile, and she was so to a degree which she did not at all appreciate. The symptomatic yank was, seemingly, motivated by a strong unconscious hostility; her unawareness of this motive presumably represents the effect of strong fear. The scoring *h-a* is appropriate for this symptomatic state of affairs.

d. The overcautious mother who is unconsciously hostile to her child is a classic figure of psychopathology. Such a mother testified:

> [1]I get terribly panicky when Jody gets sick. [2]What makes me so panicky when my daughter gets sick? [3]Is it because I have a guilty feeling? [4]Is it because I am afraid my mother will be furious if I don't do the right thing about my daughter? [5]I am terribly nervous when she gets sick. [6]I get panicky. [7]I am not concerned about myself. [8]I think Jody is going to get very sick and die.

The overconcern of such a mother is mysterious; why doesn't she take the doctor's word for degree of illness as other mothers do? Therapeutic experience has taught us that a hostile motive may underlie such undue concern, a motive which is opposed by unconscious anxiety and cannot be expressed. Nevertheless, in the case at hand some of this anxiety about her aggressive wish flows over and becomes conscious. The basic transaction should be scored *h-a*. Though both the death wish and the fear are expressed openly they are not taken "for real"; though both conscious and unconscious anxiety are present the more crucial unconscious factor is scored. If unconscious anxiety can be only surmised, when conscious anxiety is known to be present, we score the known conscious factor; but if both are present and the unconscious factor can be reliably inferred, we score the unconscious factor.

e. A woman patient reported on a dreadful conflict which she experienced as a small girl. She learned that her father had a mistress but supposed that her mother was not aware of this fact. The patient was mysteriously impelled to blurt out the facts to her mother. She described the situation as follows:

> ¹But at the time I found out about it, I think—I don't know-ah what I said about my age—but I think it was about thirteen. ²I've been trying to place it. ³But I-I think it was at the end of my grammar school. ⁴And-and I was in a state of panic for two or three years-ah-ah for fear that my mother would find out about it through me. ⁵At that time I didn't know that she knew. ⁶Ah-ah-and-and I used to worry that I might talk in my sleep or . . . ⁷Well-well, it's like this obsession I have about saying dirty words. ⁸It's-uh I just was afraid that I would suddenly say something I shouldn't.

Evidently the patient was impelled to blurt out her knowledge and yet feared to do so. Why did she not quietly forget about the matter? Because other and unconscious motives were operating. It seems possible that her mysterious wish to tell could have been based on an aggressive wish to humiliate her mother, or to revenge herself on the father's mistress, or to strike back at the father who had twice "rejected" her. It seems likely that such unconscious motives gave a peculiar force to her conflict and that such discreditable motives were anxiously rejected by her. What remained was the fear of talking in her sleep or blurting out the truth. Though conscious anxiety is present, its presence cannot explain the peculiar symptom; thus we score the more important transaction, the conflict between unconscious hostile and anxious motives. The correct scoring is *h-a*.

V. DISCRIMINATIONS AND BORDERLINE CASES

1. *Sense of pressure.* A sense of pressure not further defined should not be scored as *H* or any of its variants. It should be scored as *A*.

2. *Invidious comparison as aggression.* Favorable statements about one person may turn out to have hostile meaning toward another.

When the comparison is invidious the scoring should be *H* not *L*. A woman patient spoke thus:

> [1]I-I just know that—I mean, I—it seems as though I can talk to my mother-in-law easier, ah-than I can to my own mother. [2]Oh, I can talk to her. [3]But it-it isn't the same. [4]My mother-in-law is such wonderful fun to talk to.

This passage continues a hostile train of thought which the patient has had toward her own mother. The hostility is slightly but not effectively disguised because it appears in the guise of praising someone else. Lurking in the background are other meanings; perhaps the patient is unconsciously frightened of her mother; perhaps she is implying in a very roundabout way that her mother rejects her. These minor or more distant meanings are neglected and the dominant one is scored, i.e. *H mother*.

3. *Various forms of H in one passage.* One of our married women patients was severely phobic for her own house. She endured a tortured apprehension when she had to stay at home alone. The presence of her young children was no help. During past years she had escaped from the house whenever possible or tried to make sure that some adult was present with her; in the passage that follows she is contemplating the pros and cons of a more decisive escape, to wit, going back to work and taking up a semi-independent career. She speaks as follows:

> [1]The baby is three months old. [2]Ah-I don't know perhaps-ah I sound sort of cynical to you. [3]Ah-I really don't care. [4]I mean I'm trying to express myself the way I feel. [5]Ah-you know, for instance, now, ah-like my mother-in-law, she-ah you see, that's why I think I have the wrong slant on life. [6]She is all for the home, marriage, home, children. [7]She thinks it's just wonderful. [8]And she disapproves of anyone that goes to work or has a-a life of their own. [9]Ah-for instance, I have thought, given it thought that-ah if I was ever-ever able to again, I'd like to. [10]And my child has another year to be home with me. [11]And then she will be in school. [12]And then my two youngsters will be going to school. [13]And I thought that perhaps I'd like to go back to work. [14]But my gosh, ah-I would be-ah—it would be terrific. [15]That's not the place. [16]The place for mother is home!

One senses from what the patient says that there is something more than the push of the phobia which is driving her away from home; there might be also the pull of "a life of one's own." The anxious debate of the patient should be scored as follows: Sentences 1–4 show a kind of defiant response. The patient is stating an egocentric wish but feels that she has to justify herself, as though some unconscious anxiety were working against her wish. If her intention is innocent, why justify herself? The correct scoring for these sentences is *H-a.*

In sentences 5–8 both elements of the conflict are expressed, i.e. the wish to leave home and the anxious expectation of criticism from her mother-in-law. The correct scoring for these units is *H-A.*

In sentences 9–13 the patient states, without modification by anxious expectation, what she would like to do. Although she views her intention to "leave home" as hostile toward her family, she states it without modification. The correct score is *H.*

In sentences 14–16 the patient is still contemplating leaving home but now the anxiety is more fully represented; she pictures her mother-in-law making a scene which would cause embarrassment and apprehension. Thus both elements in a conscious conflict are represented, both the egoistic intent and the fear. The correct scoring is *H-A.*

The Sign H/self

I. definition of H/self

H/self is scored when the patient makes critical remarks about himself, expresses negative thoughts concerning himself, or describes punishing himself.

II. theory of H/self

H/self is given a separate sign because it is an important category of behavior. *H/self* is a reaction learned in social life. Self-criticism is not a primordial human reaction. It is acquired by identification with some other person who criticizes oneself. In earliest life self-criticism is accepted by the parents as a kind of apology, and it is rewarded by escape from punishment and reduction of the fear of punishment.

The ability to review a course of action, to assess praise and blame, and thus learn by experience is an important skill of responsible living. In the course of such a review one often has occasion both to praise and to blame oneself. One would expect, therefore, to find self-critical remarks in the utterances of every normal person. Self-blame has rational uses as in the case where a person warns himself against a known mistake which he is about to repeat. Self-blame is, however, not always adaptive or conscious. It can be concealed and compensated for in various ways. Thus a ruminative undercurrent of self-blame can be hidden by a bright façade of comic antics. Self-blame can be defensive as when it conceals and counterbalances anger. Obsessional self-reproaches could be scored either *H/self* or *Obs*. In the particular cases we have examined no classic obsessional case has appeared; the discrimination between *Obs* and *H/self* is one on which we do not take a position until we are forced by actual data to do so.

III. EXAMPLES OF H/self

The following examples will illustrate various aspects of the problem of scoring *H/self*.

1. In the following example the dominant note is the negative judgment of himself by the patient. The patient had talked about being anxious on the preceding day.

> THERAPIST   [1]Were you anxious throughout the whole day?
>
> PATIENT   [2]It was as though I was procrastinating and-uh ducking an issue, and that while I was enjoying myself, uh-my duty was in that room. [3]And there was my-uh rationalizing temperament coming up again. [4]And I wasn't grabbing the bull by the horns and wasn't doing things that were staring me in the face. [5]And I was using excuses like family activity and not feeling well. [6]All those things kept preying on my mind.

Among other things patient is obviously reporting anxiety in such statements as "things kept preying on my mind." However, the dominant impression is one of self-castigation. The patient criticizes his own "rationalizing temperament" and asserts that "he wasn't doing things" that he should have done. The dominant voice is that of guilty self-reproach. The preferred scoring is *H/self*.

2. The patient of the following excerpt has been charged by his

wife with various failings as a husband. The patient responds in a manner highly characteristic of him—not by defense or counter-aggression but by self-blame.

> And . . . in other words, I felt . . . two things, I think: in-adequate for one thing, because I realized more and more that I haven't been doing enough independent thinking and decid-ing . . . plus the fact that I know what a-ah . . . barrier or wall that I've built up between us—my wife and I—by that constant rebuffing of her in one form or another, so that, as she said yesterday, she feels she wants to talk to somebody and . . . get their slant.

In scoring *H/self* for this utterance we disregard a number of other aspects of the problem. For example, we don't score the wife's supposed frustration, nor do we score her aggression against him in blaming him. We do not put the patient down for feelings of re-jection by his wife because of her criticism, nor do we assume counteraggression on his part, conscious or unconscious. Instead we score the end result, what actually happened. He took up his wife's criticism and admitted blame. He asserts that it is he who has "built the wall" and he who must change his attitude and behavior.

3. The woman patient involved in this example had a father who was fatally ill of cancer. Between sobs, she has been telling of her concern for him and her attempts to care for him. Checking her weeping for a moment, she said:

> PATIENT   ¹I just think that possibly it's selfish, my crying.
> THERAPIST   ²How "selfish"? ³I don't understand why that should be selfish?
> PATIENT   ⁴Well, I mean, am I crying for my father? ⁵Or am I crying for myself?

It would seem that the patient has been blamed for weeping as a child, that adults criticized her and told her "big girls don't cry." True to her training, she calls her weeping selfish, evidently expect-ing the therapist to join in with her self-reproach. In the last sen-tence this patient of high ability asks herself a significant question. The patient's utterances should be scored *H/self*.

4. This woman patient has a husband who has been mentally ill; so strong is her impulse toward self-blame that his illness is not for

her a sufficient excuse for her failure to help him. She must rectify whatever is wrong in the world without regard to feasibility:

> [1]I guess I've done a lot that's wrong. [2]I've made plenty of mistakes. [3]I tried to encourage him and help him along. [4]But I did a miserable job. [5]I didn't do any good.

Failure to perform the impossible after making a good try is not seen by the patient as a good reason for reprieving herself. All she seems to know is that she was "responsible" and that she failed. Her remarks should be scored *H/self*.

IV. COMBINED SIGNS

A self-critical reaction can be conscious, in which case it is represented by the sign *H/self*, or it can be unconscious. If it is unconscious the sign *h-a/self* is used. One would never write *h/self*, but would always combine the *h* with *a* in the sign *h-a/self*.

1. This problem has already been discussed in connection with marginal cases of the sign *A*. We gave an example of a set of incidents each of which seemed to reveal conscious anxiety. At about the third or fourth one the scorer discerned that some pattern appeared to connect the separate events. Taken together they seemed to reveal a sense of guilt which could only be described as unconscious. This guilty tendency to blame self should be given the combined sign *h-a/self*. It is regrettable, but it is a fact of life, that it takes an expert in matters of the unconscious to notice such a patterning. Failure to notice a guilty self-destructive trend would obscure relationships in a case, but the scoring of these incidents as *A* would not be entirely inappropriate.

2. A man patient, describing his boyhood, remarked that he had passed through a phase where he injured himself repeatedly. He said:

> PATIENT   [1]There was a-uh three or four months phase in my life . . . when that was going on.
> THERAPIST   [2]Yeah.
> PATIENT   [3]I seemed to be falling every—every couple of days. [4]And it was always on the same knee and always reopening . . . the same wound. [5]And I'd be getting it bandaged up again. [6]It would seem that as soon as I'd get the bandage off I'd trip. [7]Or maybe I wouldn't even have a bandage on it.

The quotation seems to refer to a period when the patient was unconsciously punishing himself. He himself notices that his behavior was somehow "peculiar." It did not seem to be connected with the particular games he was playing or with his particular companions or with any new circumstances that were known to him. The patient did not seem to be anxious, at least not consciously anxious, about falling; certainly conscious anxiety about hurting himself did not prevent his continuing to hurt himself. Since the falling was not intentional, it could not be scored *H/self*. A person who hurts himself repeatedly without intending to do so can be described as unconsciously intending to hurt himself. The score we propose for this state of affairs is *h-a/self*.

V. DISCRIMINATIONS AND BORDERLINE CASES

1. H/self *versus* A. The danger of confusing the foregoing signs is particularly great. Ambiguous instructions and poor learning of clear instructions are two important sources of error variance. The following example will highlight the situation:

> [1]I've-ah been in a rotten mental attitude . . . and just sort of a . . . inadequate feeling about almost everything that I'm in contact with now, a pessimism. [2]And inadequacy and pessimism are strange feelings for me. [3]I've never . . . experienced them to the degree that I am feeling them now.

There is a minor note of self-criticism in these sentences, but it is minor. The major effects seem to be those caused by anxiety. For the patient to say that he is "inadequate" shows his helplessness but does not reveal self-blame. A state of anxious, pessimistic, or inadequate feeling, without negative judgment on self, should be scored *A*. If one has to use the score *H/self*, self-criticism should be plain and explicit.

2. *Score conspicuous element.* The same patient made a statement in which the slanting is plainly toward self-blame rather than fear:

> At home, ah-I'm inclined to . . . relax from that feeling of responsibility and-uh . . . do at home just what would amount to the line of least resistance, I would imagine, ah . . . don't pitch right in and do what should be done around the house . . . uh don't make any of the decisions of what should be done . . . more or less look to my wife for-uh chores to do, probably things that should be evident to myself.

Although there's an anxious undercurrent to this passage the main emphasis is on self-blame. If two kinds of feeling are represented in the passage, one minor and one major, the dominant one should always be selected for scoring. In the case at hand it is *H/self.* In following this practice, some minor meanings will be missed but the important ones will be conserved.

THE SIGN L

I. DEFINITION OF L

L is, of course, shorthand for "love." *L* is an indescribable but delightful emotion. When shown toward *persons,* it takes the form of actions and sentiments such as liking, approaching, taking care of, highly evaluating, sparing, pitying, cherishing, valuing, affiliating, appreciating them. *L* can also be felt and shown toward things, places, or *activities,* such as sports and hobbies.

II. THEORY OF L

In our system *L* is not used to describe sexual motives or action, though it can be a derivative of sex rewards. It may be ventured that originally the infant does not love although it is innately capable of learning to do so (Balint, 1952). Love is, so to say, what is left behind after strong drives have been reduced. The gusty consumption of food by an infant is not *L;* rather it is described as a primary *reward,* reducing a primary *drive;* but a succession of such events can result in love for the food, the bottle, the breast, the attending mother, or any other concurrent circumstance. The sunny looking-forward to the next feeding situation would be a primitive form of *L.* Nor is the impassioned consummation of coitus by an adult properly viewed as love (as we define it); it is a terrific primary reward, but it is not love. However, love can arise as a result of sexual consummation. If the first experiences with primary drives and rewards proceed favorably, love is learned as an inevitable and lawful consequence. The detailed mechanisms by which loving is learned are well understood by behavior scientists. (Dollard and Miller, 1950, pp. 133–6.)

Love is akin to pity and to the cherishing and protecting of a person or object. It is also connected to identification with a person.

Love and loss are somehow related, too. It is believed that interference with strong primary rewards in earliest life can damage the capacity to love. Just as drive reduction favors learning to love, the endless bearing of strong internal stimuli makes it difficult to learn to love.

Love is a potent emotion. Infants desperately need the help which loving parents provide but, perhaps just as much, they need to learn to love. To be able to love, to be one of a circle of loving people, is one of the highest rewards and comforts of life; to be unable to love is the clearest conception of hell which man has ever been able to form.

Love can arise, we have posited, on the basis of the reduction of any strong primary drive. Thus one may run through the repertory of the infant's strong motives and assume that the reduction of any one of these can condition the infant to loving. Feeding, sexual satisfaction, urinating, relief from pain, warming when cold—these and other primary rewards can each have their effect on the capacity to love. Indeed, such rewards may have a common pleasure element. Freud (1905, 1916–17) made such an assumption, or one similar to ours, when he formed the hypothesis of the libido theory. Freud thought of libido as a transmuted sexual drive, one robbed of its direct sexual object and direct sexual actions; the loving residue he called libido. Our hypothesis has it that libido can be generated by any primary reward, not just sexual ones. As time passes we will try to test which hypothesis is more serviceable in describing the complex inner life of man.

III. EXAMPLES OF L

The study of the neurotic is surely not the best avenue to understanding the full range of loving feelings and activities since, by definition, the neurotic suffers an incapacity to love. Inward pain rather than outward-flowing loving feeling is the hallmark of neurosis. Nevertheless the neurotic inhibition of love is never complete, and neurotic cases do provide some examples of love. We should expect, however, to make much more use of the sign when we study the cases of normal people or patients in the terminal phases of the cure of neurosis. One, but only one, of the quantitative signs that cure is on its way should be an increase in the use of the symbol L.

The following examples of the use of L have arisen in our data:

1. A male patient spoke as follows of an automobile drive that he took with his wife:

> [1]We had a lot of congeniality and a lot of fun. [2]And uh it was about a twenty-mile drive. [3]And we discussed our problems . . . coming back. [4]And . . . we're both . . . fairly optimistic along the lines of . . . uh . . . [5](*He sighs*) when we get this business straightened out and when I get straightened out that it's very probable and quite possible that we have a terrific marriage as we do enjoy each other so much for the most part. [6]And uh . . . it was real cozy, I guess you'd call it, on that twenty-mile ride.

In this case *L* is an inference from a description of pleasure, warmth, and hope. For this one time at least the patient was happy with his wife. The patient felt himself both beloved and loving.

2. The woman patient of this example had a father who was deathly ill of cancer. Although the patient was not living at home, and the father was not dependent on her economically, she felt an intense empathy for him. She said:

> [1]With my father, I mean, it's something you just can't do anything about. [2]I mean, it's absolutely hopeless. [3]And to me, that's uh-uh the kind of situation that-that-that upsets me. [4]I like to feel that there's something I can do. [5]I feel that I must do something. [6]I just can't sit back and let this situation go on without taking part in it. [7]I can't.

The patient's pity for her father was a loving emotion. In this case love was an active force. The frustrated need to "do something" was felt as a positive pain. The patient wanted to love, protect, and hearten her unhappy father. No inheritance from him was at stake. The unit should be scored *L*.

3. This male patient was speaking of his years in the army. The patient had had a mischievous friend, a "big guy" to whom he played opposite as the "little guy." He said:

> [1]Well, I was the little fellow in this particular case. [2]And we were really fast friends. [3]I got him out of lots of scrapes. [4]And we had some . . . a lot of fun and some hilarious incidents.

Plainly, the patient "loved" his bigger and older friend. They had fun together and became fast friends. The patient made his loving thought serviceable to his friend by "getting him out of scrapes." This item should be scored *L*.

4. One of the rewards which may produce liking is suggested in the following example:

> [1]I always like to see Joe. [2]He has a calming effect on me. [3]If you tell him your troubles he always thinks of something cheerful. [4]Some guys give you the "heebie-jeebies" just to be with them. [5]But not Joe. [6]I think the world of Joe.

The patient has a load of chronic anxiety which Joe manages to reduce whenever they meet; as a result the patient is drawn to Joe. The sudden reduction of anxiety is one of the strongest rewards. The patient's reaction to Joe deserves the scoring *L*.

5. The foregoing examples have shown *L* being used to ticket loving reactions toward persons; it is also possible to feel *L* in regard to *activities,* such as hobbies or games. Human beings can variously like to watch football, play chess, read detective stories, converse, paint—all the varied activities of life. These activities are, necessarily, always sublimated activities. One of our patients, an expert tennis player, comments on his sport as follows:

> [1]I always look forward to the tennis season. [2]Of course I enjoy the competition. [3]In fact I get really involved in tennis. [4]I love the glow which comes when one is resting after a hard game. [5]Tennis gives me a kind of rest, too. [6]I get all my cares and concerns off my mind for the time being. [7]You can't follow the ball and think about anything else. [8]Summer, or life either, wouldn't be the same without tennis.

Sublimated activities play a great part in many lives and well deserve inclusion under the heading of love actions. The above passage should be scored *L*.

6. Another patient describes a recreational activity as follows:

> [1]During the winter months I often dream about being out sailing. [2]You know, we have a boat at our summer camp. [3]When we are on vacation I spend a part of every day sailing. [4]I'm teaching my son to sail.

The reader will agree that the patient likes to sail. His utterance would be scored *L*.

7. Aesthetic activities can provide great rewards and thus be beloved. The following appears in the protocol of one of our patients:

> [1]The best part of the trip to San Francisco was visiting the art gallery to see an exhibit of Renoir's paintings. [2]I can't remember anything for a long time that has given me so much pleasure.

L is the appropriate scoring for such a passage.

IV. COMBINED SIGNS

We are tempted to say that *L* should not be combined with any other sign. Being a sublimated activity, *L* should not have inner opposition. In general it seems best to let *L* stand alone. However, to bring out the problem clearly we will quote an example where an emotion that might be called *L* does seem to be opposed by unconscious anxiety:

> [1]Well uh . . . for some reason I was thinking of a labyrinth . . . where instead of heading directly for an objective which, for instance, may be a welling inside of me, or emotion which wants to come out and to tell my wife that that emotion exists, and that uh . . . uh she's got a husband that loves her dearly, and uh appreciates her completely . . . and to say it as—as though I meant it. [2]Instead of heading for that objective, I start ducking or darting to one side, or thinking about something else, or doing something else. [3]Or when I say something it isn't what I originally felt, because I . . . diffused it, or sublimated it, or squelched it.

On the face of it, it would seem as though this patient had some anxiety about expressing tenderness to his wife; but why should he be afraid to do so? Is it that his wife seems in some way dangerous to him and that a movement toward her would put him in a threatened position? Is the tender motive infiltrated by sexual desire which *does* have anxiety attached to it? The best solution would seem to be to leave this issue on probation. For the moment we will tentatively give a combined score *L-a* to the above paragraph; but we are still leaving in serious doubt the whole issue as to whether other signs should be combined with *L*.

V. DISCRIMINATIONS AND BORDERLINE CASES

The sign *L* is most frequently confused with the sign *Dep*. It is often difficult for a patient to decide whether he *cares* for someone else or wishes to be *cared for* by someone else. The scorer, however, should keep this distinction firmly in mind and notice the cues for the one or the other reaction.

A discrimination is particularly difficult when the need for care is evidenced by a passive waiting and expecting and when the loving tropism is also shown by mute behavior. The matter has been discussed in connection with the sign *Dep* as one of its borderline cases. Other borderline issues proper to *L* will be considered here.

1. *The use of* r. *r* is a separate sign and the reader can refer to the discussion of it. It is used to record a kind of unanalyzed "feeling good" or "being happy." Patients sometimes have these *r* reactions without relating them to any particular person or activity.

2. *Inferring* L *from context*. The *L* reaction may not be verbally explicit and may have to be inferred from behavior. Thus one of our male patients said:

> [1]And incidently, a couple of times I got that-uh direct thought that-that you had-uh mentioned, that this is your penis. [2]And uh . . . uh maybe it's too early to tell, but I think it helped.

This patient had been pressed by his wife to have intercourse to a degree beyond his need or even his capacities. When he failed to oblige he suffered severe chagrin. The therapist had reminded him that his genital was, after all, still within his own control. This view of the matter had greatly reduced his guilt about not complying with excessive sexual demands, and his response was one of (earned) gratitude to the therapist. The reaction may be scored *L* although the scoring of *Conf* would also be acceptable.

3. H *versus* L. It may seem strange that these two reactions should be confused. Perhaps they never are, but certainly the reports of patients are often confusing to the scorer. In the following quotation a woman patient gives much negative information about her father but only to emphasize that she really cares for him:

> PATIENT [1]My father, I—oh, he-hh—it's-it's not right to say if it sounds as if I were saying that my mother's all bad and my father's all good. [2]And that isn't so. [3]My father has a great

many faults. [4]He-he . . . he has had weaknesses. [5]I mean, he was weak with his parents . . . [6]But-but he-he's-he's so absolutely good to me.

THERAPIST [7]Mm-hmm.

PATIENT [8]He-he never—I can't ever remember him ever doing anything deliberately to hurt me. [9]I—sometimes he's done things that I haven't liked . . . in recent years . . . maybe drank too much. [10]He-he used to drink on weekends. [11]And I think he drank just to get out of his-his situation. [12]But I-I got terribly upset about that. [13]I-I hate to see anyone drinking.

THERAPIST [14]Mm-hmm.

PATIENT [15]And . . . well, but things like that-that he's done that have upset me have not been-been directed against *me*.

Beginning with unit 3, the patient's remarks should be scored *L father*, despite their negative elements. The dominant point is the stress on her father's goodness to her and her loving reaction to him. Indeed, she tells of his faults as if to say "despite all, I love him."

4. *Transference love.* Love is no less love because it is generalized or transferred from one person to another; it is also no less love because the similarity between the one from whom it is transferred and the one to whom it is transferred is unknown. Transference love should therefore be called love, and the appropriate scoring is *L therapist.* For example:

> [1]I remember when I first came here I liked you right away. [2]I don't know what it was about you. [3]But I immediately felt at home. [4]I had the kind of secret feeling that even though I didn't know you you were a friend of mine, or you could be.

The patient's feelings are plainly tranferred. Her liking for the therapist must have been based on some unnoticed similarities between him and someone she had loved at an earlier time. She could, of course, have been severely disappointed, as people who accord transferred love to others sometimes are.

5. *Earned, rather than transferred, love.* Though the therapeutic situation can profit by transferred affection it can also produce earned affection. By his work and skill the therapist brings about benign changes in the patient's mental life, and the patient responds with gratitude. In the final hour of her treatment one of our patients said:

[1]Since I've been coming here I've developed a sort of *joie de vivre* that I never had in my life. [2]Uh-people . . . I feel like laughing a great deal. [3]I mean . . . I feel happy. [4]When I'm by myself I feel happy. [5]Sometimes the unpleasant things happen. [6]And I get upset. [7]But . . . I seem to be able to throw it off. [8]It seems to me as if they . . . well, almost as if I had a fresh start in life, and-uh . . . and all these vexatious things can be overcome somehow or other.

One can never be dead sure; there may be some transferred elements in this feeling of gratitude; it may even be that part of her happiness is in escaping from therapy. But it is unmistakable, also, that she has profited from therapy. When she is happy "by herself" she is not trying to flatter the therapist. This item also should be scored *L therapist*.

THE SIGN Lf

I. DEFINITION OF Lf

Lf is an abbreviation for "laughter." One could use a dictionary definition of laughter or even construct a schematic behavioral definition, but our position is that laughter is detectable by intelligent people with their ordinary social training. Thus we rely on those who transcribe our records to be able to tell a laugh when they hear one. Apparently they can. In studying the laughter behavior in our records, we discovered that two kinds of laughter can be distinguished:

1. A kind of laughter which we call "relaxed," expressing mirth and gaiety; to this we give the sign *Lf+*.

2. Anxious or embarrassed laughter, which expresses tension rather than tension-release; to this second type we allot the sign *Lf—*.

II. THEORY OF Lf+ AND Lf—

About all we can say as to theory is that *Lf+* seems to indicate reduction of tension and relaxation whereas *Lf—* indicates increase of tension, anxiety, or embarrassment. The occurrence of *Lf+* in a therapy situation is an important indication that a warm atmosphere surrounds therapist and patient. Therapy can go forward in the presence of such an atmosphere. We would like to see some *Lf+*

signs in the case record of any friend or child of ours who was in therapy or analysis.

The *Lf—* kind of laugh is obviously some kind of "cover-up." Behind it may be concealed anxiety or hostility, self-depreciation or sabotage. It is not an agreeable kind of behavior to experience. The laugh is often short and often heard and described as a "half laugh." It indicates some kind of inward disturbance in the one who laughs, and also a disturbance in the process of communication with the therapist.

Each instance of laughing is designated as at least one unit; if the laugh lasts for more than seven seconds it is counted as more than one unit, the number of units being the number of five-second intervals occupied by the behavior, to the nearest five seconds. Laughing is designated as a separate unit when it occurs in the midst of speech, and both the speech and the emotional behavior are to be unitized and scored.

III. EXAMPLES OF Lf+

1. The following example is drawn from the case of a woman patient who showed a morbid sense of self-depreciation. Every fact she reported about herself turned out to have some damaging implication for her. It was obvious that unconscious guilt was working within this patient as a massive force. Against this force, the therapist presented an ironic spoofing front, refusing, by his attitude, to admit that there was any reality to the guilty self-accusations of the patient. Here is a typical transaction:

> PATIENT   [1](*She sighs*) [2]Strange and peculiar how we want to be what you're not.
>
> THERAPIST   [3]Well, that's pretty bad. [4]The outlook is very dismal for you, eh?
>
> PATIENT   [5]It ain't good, McGee, I'll tell you. [6](*Relaxed laugh*) [7,8](*11-sec. pause*)
>
> THERAPIST   [9]Why don't you ever tell me some jokes? [10]I'm sure you know lots of cute ones.
>
> PATIENT   [11]I don't remember them any more; [12]I guess I don't want to be happy. [13](*Relaxed laugh*)

The therapist's sentences 3 and 4 are ironic. His sentences 9 and 10 might be called spoofing. The net effect conveyed is that the therapist absolutely refuses to concur in the patient's dismal estimate of herself. The patient's relaxed laugh represents genuine decrease in dreadful tension. The spoofing is intended to show her that she cannot convince the therapist that she is really so "bad."

2. A second example from the same patient will illustrate the point in a slightly different way:

> PATIENT ¹But I'm on my knees constantly. ²I live like that.
>
> THERAPIST ³Well, how about getting up and doing a little cha-cha?
>
> PATIENT ⁴This I like too. ⁵(*Relaxed laugh*) ⁶Two Scotches and sodas and a cha-cha, yes.

Sentence 3 is obviously a frivolous statement by the therapist, but it has the effect intended. The therapist resolutely refuses to comply with the patient's dismal self-estimate. In this example and the one above the units marked "relaxed laugh" should be scored $Lf+$.

IV. EXAMPLE OF $Lf-$

The laughing behavior called $Lf-$ often occurs as protective coloration for some critical remarks, and it seems then to represent the increased anxiety accompanying such veiled criticism. In the following example we find a woman patient criticizing the physical setting of the therapeutic hour and also the time of the interview:

> PATIENT ¹I think I'll have to buy some Air-Wick and ss . . . put it in the corridor outside your office. ²Have you noticed that odor?
>
> THERAPIST ³Smells bad, does it?
>
> PATIENT ⁴Ooohh—⁵(*Embarrassed laugh*)—understatement. ⁶Each week I keep trying to see how long I can hold my breath going along there. ⁷(*Laughing anxiously*) ⁸And I can never quite get through it.
>
> THERAPIST ⁹Mmm.
>
> PATIENT ¹⁰But . . . very . . . nasty atmosphere. ¹¹I . . . um . . . have wished this week, as I did last, that . . . the interviews were at a different time . . . in the week because it seems like ¹²(*Embarrassed laugh*) such strain and stress comes in between and then by the time I get here I'm kinda calm and collected again and . . . and it's . . . ¹³It doesn't seem useless.

[14]But it's . . . in these more trying periods I've . . . wished that I could . . . get things . . . [15](*Laughing anxiously*) out of my system then.

Units 5, 7, 12, and 15 should be scored *Lf*—. The therapist accepts the patient's criticism in a good-natured way. It should be obvious to the reader that there is no "comfort" in this kind of laughter; it is a warning that tension may be increased rather than reduced—or a record that tension has already been increased. Possibly there is something apologetic in the embarrassed laugh.

THE SIGN Mob

I. DEFINITION OF Mob

The sign *Mob* is a contraction of the words "social mobility." Social mobility is used in the sense defined by Warner and Lunt (1941, p. 82) and refers to a change of social position in the system of social classes, and to all activities and habits related to such a change. Indeed, we have extended the term beyond Warner's use of it to include any reference to stable status as well as to change in status.

II. THEORY OF Mob

Americans exist in a social-class system. They are born into a social class which imparts to them a characteristic personal shape and way of life. Except perhaps for those belonging to the topmost stratum in our system, all individuals are under some pressure to change their social position. When they are successful in doing so we say that they are socially mobile. Social mobility can occur both upward and downward in the class structure.

Thus wishes or motives to improve social position or activities designed to change position would be scored *Mob*. Such activities need not be consciously chosen for mobility purposes; strivings for social mobility may be at least partly unconscious. If the aim of the striving is change of social position, the activity is scored *Mob*. Any data describing the original status of a man's family or his neighborhood is also scored *Mob*.

Tendencies toward social mobility and neurotic tendencies may interact. Excessive strivings for mobility can have an invisible under-pinning in a neurotic anxiety; in such cases change of status is mis-takenly seen as a way of reducing anxiety. So far as we know, class placement and neurotic tendencies can vary independently as well as together, neurotics and healthy people being found in all social classes (Hollingshead and Redlich, 1958).

III. EXAMPLES OF Mob

As we have said, the sign *Mob* may indicate change of status or define a stable status.

1. *Change of status.* The records of neurotic patients are full of intimations concerning status problems and motives. These are often overlooked by the therapist in favor of the attempt to under-stand underlying unconscious motives.

a. In the following example a foreign-born boy told how he was first integrated into a "real American" group. In fifth grade he had been rather shy and subdued. He continued:

> [1]And then in sixth grade, I was more the outgoing type, as much probably as I've ever been. [2]I remember playing tackle on the cement sidewalk of a school. [3]I was going to and-uh, well, going through the line and making a big gain. [4]I was being tackled and got tackled right at the foot of a . . . a very stern teacher that I had had in the fifth grade. [5]And I remember her looking down at me. [6]I was on the ground. [7]And she said, "My how you've changed."

The patient had been changing indeed in the year in which he had been in an American school. The reaction of the teacher was a recognition of this change—football-playing being the mark of the normal American boy. This item should, of course, be scored *Mob.* except for unit 7 which should be scored *Mob:r.*

b. Emerging professional and educational skills are, of course, a promise of successful mobility. One patient gave the following description of his success as a practice teacher:

> [1]While I was at normal school I developed an integrated cur-riculum for the children around the theme of waterways. [2]I taught the kids the history of water routes and tied everything in with that—history, music, drama, trade, art, poetry. [3]This

integration made up one solid five-months course. [4]And it was a great success.

Such an achievement in the life of a young teacher is not merely a local success but is prophetic of future achievement. As such, it is a step in a mobility campaign. A *Mob* scoring is indicated for units 1–3; unit 4 is scored *Mob:r*.

c. One has to keep his ear attuned for all types of "advancement," and for struggles to gain it, in order to score *Mob* correctly; thus joining a fraternity in high school or college can be a mobility gesture, or even attending night school or taking a correspondence course. One of our male patients luxuriated in the following event:

> [1]Well . . . last night I was elected vice-president of the Cashiers' Club . . . which is a new challenge and responsibility. [2]If you recall I've been editing a book on the duties of the cashier. [3]And-uh-Friday I was approached by a-uh—it's in an established New York school. [4]This school or institution has heard about the book. [5]And-uh-uh they are feeling me out now for using the book as a course. [6]They propose a royalty basis and ask that I submit what I've written so far for their approval. [7]It's kind of appealing to me also.

Living the hard-pressed life that he did, always short of money and even more short of social recognition, the patient viewed the book as a sign of better things to come. He was keeping himself overworked and constantly short of personal time for enjoyment in order to be able to write it. He knew the lesson that successful mobility is a long-range matter and was able, thus, to work for remote goals. The item should be scored *Mob* except for unit 1 which should be scored *Mob:r*.

d. Joining the church, or changing from one church to another, can be a mobility maneuver; the finding of new friends which is often the goal of such a change can turn out to be a search for better-placed friends. A patient described such a change of church as follows:

> [1]I was born a Baptist. [2]Or rather it is truer to say that I was born into a Baptist family and joined the church as an adolescent. [3]I have always gone to the Baptist church, not regularly, but enough to feel that I was a member. [4]Recently I talked it over with my wife. [5]And we decided to change. [6]We

are now members of the Episcopal church. [7]I have nothing against the Baptists, you understand. [8]But I thought I would enjoy more associating with the people at the Episcopal church. [9]And my wife felt it would be good for the children. [10]She thought that the children in the Episcopal Sunday School were nicer than those in the Baptist Sunday School. [11]I didn't care much either way. [12]So I went along with her.

The mobility aspirations of this family are plainly showing. "Nicer," whether applied to adults or children, is the equivalent of "higher status." Of course we do not mean to say that no change of religious affiliation occurs for any other reason than that of seeking status, but such transactions should be watched from the status standpoint. The above units should be scored *Mob*.

e. Skills and hobbies can be put to use in the search for status. The following is an example:

A woman patient described becoming a member of a music-study club and through this club making the acquaintance of a well-known composer. It turned out that the composer belonged to one of the city's "old families." Through this association our patient was introduced to yet other persons and activities which had an important effect in raising her status. As she later said, "It all went back to the music-study group."

We could not determine how "conscious" the original move toward the music-study group had been. People are constantly acting in terms of vaguely perceived status symbols but without feeling that they are "cuddling up to" a better-placed person. It is likely that this kind of activity always has some conscious purposive element even though the striver may not be willing or able to admit it. Such an item should be scored *Mob*.

2. *Stable status.* Many people do not change their social rank in the course of a lifetime; they have a single, stable status. All indications of such a position should also be scored *Mob*. The description of a person's original status—his childhood family status—should be similarly scored.

a. Commenting on her childhood status, a woman patient said:

[1]The neighborhood we lived in as a child wasn't too good. [2]We weren't happy there. [3]But we couldn't afford anything better. [4]The kids were always quarreling and fighting. [5]There was a

Polish woman next door. [6]Podolski was her name. [7]She must have been a neurotic woman because she was inclined to do a lot of yelling at all of us. [8]And . . . well, we used to get out of her way when we were playing around the house.

Evidently the patient lived in a lower-class area, though she would like now to claim that her family was not lower class. The woman next door may indeed have been neurotic, but her behavior sounds very much like that of a woman in a lower-class area. The patient's testimony shows that though she didn't like the Podolski family, she nevertheless played freely with the children and frequented their house. These facts give evidence of social participation with the Podolski neighbors, which would tend to indicate that the patient's family was also a lower-class family.

b. Severe financial limitations go with lower-class and lower-middle-class membership. In the case to be reported the patient came from a lower-middle-class family. Their penuriousness is represented in the following quotation:

[1]I had to wear short pants much longer than the other boys. [2]I imagine it was for financial reasons. [3]My father was never too well off. [4]Of course I was never ragged or in shreds or anything like that. [5]But I guess I had to outgrow what I had, before I got anything new.

The skimping respectability of the patient's childhood home is well conveyed by his report. *Mob* is the correct scoring.

c. Status—in this case a stable lower-class status—can be indicated by referring to a specific area in a town. Thus one of our patients, still a lower-class man, said:

[1]Uh . . . when I was a kid, we lived in a . . . in a more or less, the poorer section of Detroit. [2]It was down near the warehouse district. [3]There were a lot of rooming houses around where we lived.

The patient still lives in a housing development that has been created in a slum area. Indications of his present as of his past status are scored *Mob*.

IV. COMBINED SIGNS

Activities leading to social mobility often evoke anxiety. Such anxiety can arise because the environment itself is threatening and tends to resist the effort of the mobile person to better himself. At other times one suspects that anxiety is present because the mobility activity is conceived of as aggressive by the person himself, and because fear is already attached to the aggressive motive. At still other times it seems as though mobile and aggressive motives are fused and that both the realistic and the "already learned" fears are similarly condensed. It is not always possible, nor always necessary, to unravel motives and distinguish realistic from unrealistic anxiety. Here follows a set of examples where anxiety was found to be attached to a mobility activity:

1. *Mob-A.* This sign is used in cases where mobility tendencies touch off fear.

a. In the following excerpt a patient who was a teacher reports on his first experience as a practice teacher:

> [1]And-uh-as a teacher I never got-uh never got straightened out, and never felt physically well. [2]And-uh I never really got squared off on feeling at ease and-uh behaving naturally and exerting any personality I might have had on the children. [3]I was always-uh—it was a miserable three or four months anyway. [4]And-uh, I must have been placed on probation.

The practice-teaching situation was important since it could be predictive of the patient's later success as a teacher. Having to teach under the eye of a supervisor evoked strong anxieties in the patient, so strong as to cause feelings of illness. The fear is of course conscious and thus is called *A*. It would seem that his fear was excessive, not a reaction to dangers inherent in the activity but transferred to the situation from private or former experiences. *Mob-A* is indicated.

b. One of our patients was a young businessman who had just been made temporary head of his department. This success produced not, as would be expected, elation and self-steeling for the task, but anxiety and recoil. He reported:

> [1]And-uh already I realize that it's the first time that I've been placed in a situation like that. [2]I've always had-uh-uh supervision over me uh to an extent. [3]I've had someone I could shove the blame to, let's say, if anything came up, because at all times I've been either a clerk or an assistant. [4]I was never the big cheese. [5]And that-uh-uh I had always stepped into and worked in an organization that I had not set up.

The new position was, of course, a vital step in the patient's career, a crucial link in the chain of acts leading to social mobility. His fear is conscious, but again it seems excessive. It would seem that, in addition to a legitimate degree of conscious anxiety lest he fail, there was a large component of unconscious fear transferred to the new job situation; but the score should be *Mob-A*.

c. Another businessman patient had been asked to assume new responsibilities on his job without having management mention increased compensation. The additional rank was "fine," he felt, but where was the money that should have accompanied it? In brooding about the matter, he said:

> [1]But I do have uh a little doubt as to whether I'm getting paid enough with the increased responsibility. [2]I've been hemming and hawing in my own mind about how much actual or figurative . . . pounding on the desk I should do. [3]I ought to be getting a higher salary. [4]But if I do that how much will it be construed by management as "going-to-my-head" sort of thinking?

In the last sentence above the patient can be seen picturing management as being in a critical mood toward him. He puts the words of self-damnation, as it were, into their mouths. He has demonstrated his zeal for mobility by seeking and taking more work, but he fears to ask for appropriate compensation. This should be scored *Mob-A*.

d. A young woman patient was acting as a free-lance copy writer, selling her services to various advertising agencies. When she began this activity she hoped for gain in income and independence but nevertheless had some fear of the situation. She said:

> [1]I don't believe that I'm cut out for it 'cause I don't have the proper competitive spirit. [2]I don't . . . I don't enjoy gambling-uh . . . and it is a gamble. [3]And-uh it has a lot of tricky things you have to do to get ahead. [4]I'm not up to dirty tricks like trying to steal accounts and things like that. [5]Uh . . . it's a cutthroat racket. [6]Sometimes I think I'd be much happier if I had a job and I didn't have all this . . . worry and running around.

The patient has some anxiety about the unknown and the uncertainty of income, but she also feels she will not be capable of the ruthless competition required by her work. There may or may not be an unconscious element in the latter fear. It was a status advantage to be independently employed, but she asked, "Am I up to it?" The scoring is *Mob-A*.

e. Marriage is often a fateful event so far as status is concerned. It may fix a person permanently in present status, or it may load the dice for upward or downward mobility. An upper-middle-class patient was thinking of marrying a foreign-born girl whom his parents had never seen. With some apprehension the patient had planned to bring her to meet his parents. He reported:

> [1]I feared they'd have some difficulty in accepting my wife.
> [2]Before we were married . . . um . . . I wanted to be—I wanted to be, before I—before I committed myself, I wanted my parents to meet this girl. [3]And she couldn't understand this. [4]I think I understand it now. [5]I was—uh in a way—uh wanted approval. [6]And they didn't give it immediately. [7]I as—as a matter of fact it was a very unsatisfying relationship. [8]I took her home. [9]Uh-and I'd written ahead that a-uh-this was the girl that I intended to marry. [10]And then I got there. [11]And I got a kind of cold wall.

The patient had a number of reasons for wanting his parents' approval. For one thing, they had mobility aspirations for him and he didn't wish to disappoint them. For another, they were people of some means—not wealthy, but certainly able to help the patient substantially. Doubtless other anxieties were present at the prospect of presenting his fiancée to his father and mother. It will be noted that the girl opposed him, undoubtedly sensing her status inferiority and fearing the influence of his parents on the patient. The patient bore his anxiety and married the girl. The episode should be scored *Mob-A*.

2. *Mob-a*. At times a mysterious resistance opposes the carrying out of activities designed to bring about a change in status. This was the case with a writer who was one of our patients:

> [1]So far I have written seven or eight chapters of our book and outlined the rest. [2]But-uh I find myself or I find it impossible and find myself very reluctant to put my own thoughts and conclusions on paper. [3]As a result, I do a lot of extra uh research to find out how other people say it, and then paraphrase what-

what they say. ⁴Or even I use it verbatim, plagiarizing I guess
might be the word, to a certain extent.

The patient's reluctance to write out her own thoughts and
judgments is an inhibition. It reveals some secret anxiety which is
plaguing her and hindering her writing. Remarkably enough, it
seemed less "evil" to her to steal the work of others than to commit
the affront of asserting her own judgment. Correct scoring is *Mob-a.*

3. *Mob:r.* Successful (though usually temporary) reduction of a
mobility motive can be indicated by attaching *r* to the Mob sign. In
the educational field the high school diploma, the Phi Beta Kappa
key, and the graduate scholarship are all symbols of mobility
achievement; even certification as a practice teacher can do the job.

a. At another point in his treatment, the teacher mentioned
earlier overcame a bad start and did satisfactory work. He stated:

¹As a prospective teacher I had during the next term another
eighteen weeks of teaching. ²This time I had a very sympathetic
supervisor. ³I felt better about the whole thing. ⁴And I worked
up a teaching program that was a smash success.

We infer that the "smash success" brought him great satisfaction
and strengthened his determination to go on as a teacher. A defeat
would have meant the end of the line as far as advancement through
teaching was concerned. Undefeated, the patient was able to lay
down his burden for a moment and reward himself with the thought,
"So far, so good." Correct scoring is *Mob:r.*

b. Our worried free-lance writer also had a victory to report. After
some months of work she said:

¹But the past-past uh month I've been extremely busy. ²It's
the first time it's happened since I've been free-lancing. ³I
worked about seventy hours last week. ⁴And this week will be
about the same, I think.

The patient breathes a sigh of relief when her gamble pays off.
She has launched a promising independent career. Score should be
Mob:r.

c. Skipping grades, even in elementary school, may be looked
upon by teachers and parents alike as a sign that a child is suited for
social mobility. Praise makes the step in mobility a memorable event

in the mind of a child. One of our patients spoke of a room which appeared in one of his dreams:

> [1]The room in the dream was like the one in which I spent my second-grade year. [2]And that was the room that I must have done pretty well in. [3]I was skipped two grades from there, from second to fourth I think it was.

Indications like grade-skipping help parents who might be in doubt to realize that they have children of ability and often make them willing to plan higher education for their talented children. Since educational advancement is the American method of mobility, early signs of talent are eagerly greeted; they are often the first step of a prolonged adventure in social mobility. *Mob:r* is the correct score.

V. DISCRIMINATIONS AND BORDERLINE CASES

1. Legitimate *Mob* activities are sometimes hard to differentiate from circumstances where *H* is the appropriate score. There is probably always some *H* infiltrated into every *Mob* activity; in plain English, it takes some gumption to be socially mobile.

In the following case there was a question as to whether *Mob* or *H* was the appropriate score. The dilemma is that of a young business-man:

> [1]Uh . . . one of the . . . well, to go back a little, in my-my present job I'm an assistant to a man who didn't hire me. [2]I was hired over him by top management, brought in as his assistant. [3]And-uh I have uh no respect for him as far as ability is concerned—at least in my line. [4]And-uh he hasn't taught me anything. [5]And there is a build-up of resentment at having to take-uh orders from him with that lack of respect that I have for him.

This kind of case will stop the scorer. He will sense the mobility implications of the patient's wish to be the boss himself. On the other hand, the patient plainly says that he resents his pseudo boss and does not respect him. Our decision was that resentment was the more prominent feature of the passage, and we scored it *H*. However, the scorer will run into many a touchy problem like this one, and some error will always arise because different scorers will make different decisions.

2. Mob *frustration*. If mobility wishes are frustrated should one in some way indicate this fact? We faced this problem and decided against doing so. If *Mob* exists and is frustrated, it is presumably still *Mob*. Thus a patient reported the following about his school career:

> [1]I got high grades and was an important member of the class in grade school. [2]But when I went to high school everything changed. [3]I didn't make the football team. [4]I was never up for class office. [5]I never led any particular group. [6]It was a very run-of-the mill existence through high school and later through college. [7]It was only afterward that I was able to get underway again.

The patient had had a taste of mobility reward in grade school which strengthened his aspirations. But in high school and college he was frustrated. Frustration did not change the situation; it simply meant that the mobility drive remained in action but perhaps at a somewhat lower strength than would have been the case had he found reward in high school and college. The preferred scoring of this report is simply *Mob*.

3. *Downward mobility*. *Mob* can be used to indicate status lost as well as status gained. One of our women patients thus reported a loss in status by her parental family:

> [1]You see, when I was very little my family had—were quite comfortably fixed. [2]My father had a good income.[3]My grandfather had money, too. [4]And then my father lost his job. [5]And my grandfather lost his money in the stock market. [6]And so, when I was in school we were very short of money. [7]I—for years, I-I wore someone else's shoes. [8]And it just—it always—it always bothered me.

In the patient's childhood her family enjoyed a comfortable upper-middle-class status. Through loss of money (and accompanying loss of residential status and social associations) the family was downwardly mobile. If downward mobility were extremely common we might have invented a separate sign for it, but since it is rather uncommon we have not done so. The example given would be scored simply *Mob*.

THE SIGN N

I. DEFINITION OF N

N is the sign for negation. Any negation not expanded and not considered resistant is scored *N*. This score is never combined with any other.

II. THEORY OF N

Negation occurs, and one must find some way to score it. It may indicate a disagreement with the therapist, a refusal to act as requested, or a different understanding of fact. A large *N* count would certainly indicate that the patient has the firmness to oppose the therapist; taken together with a large count for *Res (denial)* it could indicate a tendency to obsessional negation—the automatic "no" to any assertion by another.

III. EXAMPLES OF N

The following are examples of plain or simple *N*, that is, a negation which is not considered resistant and which is not further elaborated. In most cases such negative answers are preceded by a question from the therapist.

1. In an initial interview the following exchange occurred:

> THERAPIST   Have you always lived in New Haven?
> PATIENT   No.

The negation is not elaborated by further information nor is it, so far as we know, resistant.

2. Other examples:

> THERAPIST   Have you been trained as a secretary?
> PATIENT   No.

> THERAPIST   Did you take a major in psychology?
> PATIENT   No.

> THERAPIST   Do you have a job for next year?
> PATIENT   No.

THERAPIST   Is German a required course?
PATIENT   No.

In all the preceding cases we see a simple negation. The "no" is not qualified by further information, and there is no reason for suspecting that the statement is resistant.

IV. DISCRIMINATIONS AND BORDERLINE CASES

If the "no" is accompanied by additional information or is resistant it is not scored as *N*. In deciding that the "no" is supplemented, we rely on the intonational pattern, which shows that the following clause belongs with the "no." Further discussion of this point is given in Chapter 2.

1. *Cases where "no" is accompanied by supplementary information*

a. The following exchange took place between a therapist and a man patient:

THERAPIST   [1]Did you get your degree from a teacher's college?
PATIENT   [2]No, it was a regular four-year school.

In this case the negation is supplemented by additional information, which follows without intervening final pause or drop to intonational level 4. The patient wants it understood that he graduated from a regular liberal arts college. Graduating from such a college is a matter of importance to him as a status point. The negation is not scored *N* but rather according to content, i.e. *Mob*.

b. The patient has been telling the therapist about a dark closet which was a problem during his childhood:

THERAPIST   [1]Did you enter the dark closet?
PATIENT   [2]No, I was too frightened to go in.

Here again the patient—without pausing or dropping in pitch—gives additional information which indicates fear; therefore the scoring is *A*.

2. *Cases where there is reason to believe that "no" is resistant*

a. The following example is taken from a therapy situation in which the patient showed many signs of resistance. The therapist had just returned from his vacation. During his absence the patient had "forgotten" to pay the bill for his treatment. This matter was under discussion as follows:

> THERAPIST Did you feel that I had rejected you when I went away on my vacation?
> PATIENT No.

There was excellent reason for thinking that the patient had interpreted the therapist's leaving as a rebuff or an abandonment. Thus the patient's "no" was not a simple factual disagreement; it functioned rather to deny a sense of loss and resentment at his "rejection." The "no" is implicitly resistant and should be scored *Res* (as a denial).

b. A businessman patient had been passed over for promotion; his response was a fit of depression in which he blamed himself excessively. The following conversation between therapist and patient occurred:

> THERAPIST ¹It seems strange that when you were passed over you ended up by blaming yourself instead of expressing resentment toward the boss. ²Is it possible that you were a little bit angry when you got the news?
> PATIENT ³No.

If in a case like this other items of a patient's behavior show plainly that he was angry, his negation should be interpreted as a denial—hence resistant—and the score should be *Res*. The behavior of denial is important because it has to be further examined and explained. In the case at hand the patient denied that he was angry at the boss and failed to express this anger in real life because he feared that if he did so further punishment would follow upon the rejection he had already experienced. The denial thus points to his fear of admitting and expressing his anger.

THE SIGN Obs

I. DEFINITION OF Obs

Obs is obviously the first letters of the word "obsessional." Any sentence describing an obsessional thought or act is scored *Obs*. The obsessional event is mysterious; it is not related to the on-going current of mental events. It is intrusive. It is strongly motivated, but the source of motivation is unknown. Ambivalent behavior, that which shows rapidly alternating feelings of love and hate, is scored as obsessional. This sign is never combined with any other.

II. THEORY OF Obs

Obsessional thoughts and actions are believed to have their origin in the cleanliness-training situation of early childhood (Freud, 1913). During cleanliness training the child faces, for the first time, a culture which is absolute in its demand for performance. There are no "grays" in cleanliness training; there are only blacks or whites, absolute goodness or badness, utter freedom or dread guilt. When cleanliness training is undertaken too early or pushed too severely, the basis for lifelong obsessional attitudes may be laid. Overdone cleanliness training has a kind of either-or logic: either one loves or one hates, one is good or one sins, one complies absolutely or one revolts; there is no middle ground. Overdone cleanliness training can produce profoundly negative attitudes toward self. It can leave behind a basis for scatological interests and blasphemous antagonisms. When the obsessional dichotomies are transferred to the money sphere they can produce peculiar attitudes (and opposites) such as hoarding, compulsive spending, and peculiar notions about honesty.

Obsessional behavior is often mysterious, because the emotional accent is shifted from one act to another. Once the obsessional orientation is established in early childhood it colors succeeding phases of development and becomes interlaced with later values and habits. It may merely color a personality, giving an orderly basis to a life adjustment, or obsessional traits may be so severe as to constitute a neurosis. Obsessional conflict can be extreme and the suffering it causes, most intense.

III. EXAMPLES OF Obs

Our cases have not produced the great variety of symptoms and rituals which a wider survey might reveal, but they have presented enough obsessional material to demand its categorization and its recognition by a sign. We will present a selection of examples drawn from our cases.

1. A male patient who suffered severely from inability to make necessary decisions about his work reported as follows:

> ¹It's just . . . if I am . . . doing nothing and I see wood, well, I, I'll knock on it. ²And I think to do it, if—even if it isn't wood, I mean. ³That's how silly it is. ⁴I was sitting on one of these new trains. ⁵They have a plastic cover on the seat. ⁶And I'll just tap on that when there isn't any wood available. ⁷Now it's just so . . . apparently ridiculous.

Now it will be noticed that though the action is compelled it is recognized by the patient as nonsensical. Very occasional knocking on wood could be considered as culturally accepted, but when knocking on wood is extreme, as in this example, it is safely called obsessional. The proper scoring is *Obs*.

2. An intruding image, which appears like a foreign body in the midst of sensible thoughts, can reasonably be designated as obsessional. A male patient who was by turns stubborn and submissive said the following:

> THERAPIST ¹Why did you stop just then?
>
> PATIENT ²Um . . . just . . . there was an image that came in my mind then. ³There was a-ah . . . ah . . . just a thumb and forefinger with a-uh-a-uh . . . a watch uh wheel or gear, you know, that makes the watches go, that seemed to be there. ⁴There was somebody or something holding it. ⁵And it was spinning. ⁶It was completely unrelated to anything.

At the time of first reporting, the intruding image could only be noticed. It could not be dealt with therapeutically. The patient had no amplifying thoughts in connection with it, nor could he relate it to anything else in his experience. The unit should be scored *Obs*.

3. A male patient who suffered severely from obsessional guilt and remorse reported the following ritual:

> ¹There is something I haven't told you although I have been doing it every day for the last year and for many years before that. ²When I go to the bathroom to urinate a funny thought comes into my mind. ³I say to myself the words "Dongo, dongare, dongavi, dongarus." ⁴What I seem to be doing is to take the word "dong," a slang word for penis, and decline it as if it

were a Latin verb. [5]I have often wondered why I do this. [6]That doesn't bother me when I do it. [7]But it seems to come to mind again and again. [8]I don't feel compelled to do it. [9]But I like to do it.

This action is a typical obsessional ritual. There is evidently some irreverent pleasure in combining the obscene word with the august Latin conjugation. The gesture also seems to have some sexual meaning. This intellectual patient was blandly indifferent to the presence in his thoughts of such an infantile and irrational element. The correct scoring is *Obs.*

4. An obsessional patient who had been reared as a Roman Catholic reported the following curious behavior:

When this patient was shaving in the morning he would sing in a curious way. Imitating the intonations of a priest saying Mass, he would chant a kind of nonsense Latin with obscene words mixed in; these obscene words would be given Latin endings. This eccentric behavior was casually reported by the patient. He got a certain amount of idle pleasure out of the singing. He did not recognize his behavior as symptomatic and had no curiosity about it.

The singing proved to be a new version of blasphemous thoughts with which the patient was afflicted when he attended Mass as a child. Such thoughts, in childhood, aroused the most acute horror, and he struggled desperately to suppress them. Indeed, attending Mass became an occasion of pain for him because of the unwanted intrusion of these thoughts. The conflict of the child survived in the nonsensical behavior of the adult. The correct scoring is *Obs.*

5. Obsessional thoughts and doubts often cling to religious practices. A devout Baptist patient had such moments of doubt, and these doubtings were strengthened by conversing with her husband. She reported as follows:

[1]Well, I agree with him to a point because of course he never goes to church. [2]Uh he feels very doubtful uh about religion. [3]Oh, now, he isn't an atheist. [4]I don't mean that. [5]Uh-but-uh he feels as though he'd like to be shown . . . much more proof that there is a-a supreme being. [6]Uh . . . and sometimes, too, I feel after talking to him that . . . uh [7] (*She sighs*) there is

a problem there. [8]I-I-I can't say that I have doubts. [9]But I think about it, many times, as I think perhaps people do.

The patient's own ambivalence is strengthened by repeating her husband's thoughts and doubts. Doubting the existence of God is for her not a philosophical act but a kind of blasphemy for which she still pays with punishing guilt. The correct scoring is *Obs*.

6. A compulsive man patient referred in more general terms to obsessional thoughts as follows:

[1]Then I had the little thoughts that pop into your mind uh . . . unpleasant or nasty or against something. [2]And . . . they seemed to bother me very much. [3]I mean I . . . the thought will come and I'll . . . I'll hate myself for thinking it and think why the . . . why do I think it?

Frequently indeed the content of obsessional thoughts is nasty or hostile. The threat of having obsessional notions can lead to the attempt to think only "pure" thoughts, and energy can be withdrawn from the outside world to conduct this inward battle. Who cares that the soup boils over so long as one's thoughts are pure! Such a report as that just cited should be scored *Obs*.

7. A male patient talked about how it feels to be afflicted with obsessional thinking. He said:

[1]Well, after I—pointing out with the—that business about the taxi and about the students and . . . just every moment of the day and every occurrence that my subconscious or something is . . . I'm always two-sided. [2]And whatever happens I take it in and have this opinion and that opinion, and should it be this way, or would it be better that way? [3]But I mull over the past and present and—and the future all at once. [4]If it's only a matter of spilling a glass of milk on the kitchen table or something like that, I give it importance.

No wonder this writer couldn't write; he was in constant internal conflict. His mental life was a kind of battleground where one force said "yea" and the other "nay." This struggle should be regarded as *Obs*.

8. Ambivalence of feeling, as of thought, is characteristic of the obsessional person. A woman spoke of her mother-in-law as follows:

¹I mean, I like her. ²She just makes me feel upset. ³I don't know why. ⁴And yet I couldn't tell you any more because I like her. ⁵And I've told you that-uh the fact uh religion and things like that. ⁶And-uh I lived with her. ⁷And I got to know her as well as I did my own mother. ⁸And yet she makes me feel that way. ⁹And yet I feel at ease with her. ¹⁰Now, how can you be sort of two different personalities in one? ¹¹Feel at ease with her and still yet you feel nervous with her and perspire.

The patient herself correctly identifies the ambivalence of feeling and is surprised at it; since she cannot trace it to its source she cannot change her feelings. Score *Obs*.

IV. DISCRIMINATIONS AND BORDERLINE CASES

Since *Obs* appears frequently in conjunction with aggressive utterances it is sometimes a problem to distinguish between *Obs* and *H*. The following utterance from a woman patient illustrates the problem. The patient has been wondering whether she should resume living with her schizophrenic husband. She said:

¹But . . . uh-uh when I see him, I feel that-that uh I'm-I'm —I have a responsibility towards him that I'm not fulfilling. ²And uh—the only way I can ³(*She sighs*) see to do it would be uh-uh a-at a cost to myself that I'm not willing to-to-to face. ⁴He wants to-to uh come back. ⁵He has for a long time. ⁶And uh . . . that's all he wants. ⁷I don't think I could ever get together with him again.

Although the patient oscillates, canvassing arguments back and forth, she does seem to have come to a decision; at the end she is not ambivalent. She has decided to reject her husband, a gesture which from her standpoint is aggressive. The sentence expressing that decision—sentence 7—should be scored *H* and not *Obs*. The other sentences could be scored *L,* as indicating concern for her husband.

THE SIGN PSS

I. DEFINITION OF PSS

PSS is a sign chosen to stand for "psychosomatic symptom." The idea is that some emotional factor produces a physical symptom.

One is most likely to score a physical symptom *PSS* when medical examination has failed to reveal a physical cause, when the symptom seems to appear and disappear in response to mental or social cues, and when a psychosomatic mechanism for the particular symptom is known and has been demonstrated in other cases.

II. THEORY OF PSS

Some physical symptoms are plainly somatic in that they are produced by invading organisms or by demonstrable tissue damage. In other cases physical mechanisms are plainly involved, but they are brought into play by emotional causes. Thus repressed anger can produce a tension headache. The angry emotion presumably causes a tightening of the muscles of the head and neck and a stretching of the temporal arteries. The net effect is "headache." Of course, to the patient the symptom is "real" no matter what its cause. Psychosomatic symptoms are important because they can often be influenced by psychotherapy, whereas symptoms of physical origin cannot. Important as psychosomatic symptoms are, our knowledge of psychosomatic causation is still poor and uncertain. Therefore we advise the attitude of a cautious physician, who calls a symptom psychogenic only when solid evidence is present.

One very convincing kind of evidence that a symptom is psychogenic is that it appears and disappears in response to emotional events. What makes the matter difficult is that such emotional events are often unconscious; one sees the symptom, but one does not understand the emotional cues or circumstances which trip it off. In most cases only protracted psychoanalysis (which we have not been able to attempt in carrying on our research) will identify the pertinent cues.

III. EXAMPLES OF PSS

It is likely that examples of psychosomatic symptoms surround us at all times. It is one thing to identify such a symptom as emotionally caused and another matter to say exactly what the emotional cause is. To give a detailed account of origin and mechanism usually requires a protracted study.

1. A young businessman gave the following account of a blushing symptom:

[1]The blushing would come when an argument was going on in the office. [2]Several people were involved including my boss. [3]And I was contributing to whatever was under discussion. [4]I'd find myself sitting there with . . . ah . . . could feel the blood uh throbbing, coursing through my veins whenever there seemed to be a higher pressure in the discussion. [5]And uh I had a definite feeling that my face was getting redder.

Perhaps we should remind the reader that the blushing in question was an agonizing symptom. It was also felt to be a severe business disadvantage by the patient. The symptom seems to appear in response to a pattern of social cues, i.e. those connected with an argument about business matters. Even though we do not understand the dynamics of the symptom, it should be scored *PSS*.

2. A woman patient was referred to us after exhaustive examination had shown that she did not have heart disease, as she had suspected. She described a typical attack in the following way:

[1]I never know uh-when these uh-attacks will come on. [2]But uh my heart will begin slamming as if it would jump out of my chest. [3]Then I get short of breath uh as if I had been running. [4]. . . And at the same time I will feel terribly afraid. [5]I try every way to deal with it. [6]But nothing seems to work. [7]I am so anxious . . . I can't sit down or stand up. [8]Nobody can seem to talk to me or do anything with me.

At first this symptom was entirely mysterious. It seemed to come and go without any relation to accompanying events in her life. The first illumination came when she reported having had an attack the night previous to the therapy hour. The therapist asked what had happened, and the patient explained that her husband had called her long-distance from another town and told her that he could not get home that night. When she put down the telephone she noticed the beginnings of an attack. A second attack occurred sometime later just after the hour when the therapist had told her of his vacation plans. While she was driving home in the car after the hour, the attack began, and it was in full course by the time she reached home. It began to seem as though sudden loss of support—emotional support, that is—was one of the cues for the symptom. With this information we would not hesitate to score the episode as *PSS*.

3. A male student patient reported the following symptom:

[1]Uh-uh at least once in the past ten days and-uh quite—well, once every two weeks or so, I get-get a case where I look down at my hand. [2]And it's actually shaking . . . from some sort of . . . tension. [3]And that uh tension-feeling results in a sort of general weakness, where if I don't look pale, I feel-feel pale, if there is such a thing.

The tremor which the patient reported was a more or less chronic thing. It seemed to have no somatic base but to be connected with a chronic timidity. Even the slightest, and sometimes not observable, anticipation of stress would set him to shaking. The *PSS* interpretation seemed to have high probability of being correct.

IV. COMBINED SIGNS

PSS is combined with one other sign only, namely *r*. Thus *PSS:r* would indicate the sudden termination of a psychosomatic symptom, which is accompanied by marked reduction in stress. The following circumstances will illustrate such a scoring:

A woman patient suffered from strong anxiety and a sharp pain in her side when she was left alone at home. If she could get someone to visit her the fear and the pain disappeared. If her mother could stay in the house with her the symptoms did not appear at all. If she had an attack and could even reach her doctor by phone, the pain would disappear at the reassuring sound of his voice. Needless to say, her doctor found her a tormenting patient.

The sentences describing the sudden disappearances of pain would be scored *PSS:r;* those describing the symptom itself would be scored *PSS*.

V. BORDERLINE CASES

The borderline problem for *PSS* is obviously the one of discriminating it from a physical symptom with a somatic base. Thus a reference to influenza or epilepsy is not scored *PSS*. Indeed, we think that *PSS* should be used cautiously and not freely or extravagantly. We do not have a special scoring for physical symptoms with a somatic base; we use the general scoring *Unsc* (for "unscorable") as the sign for such symptoms. We use *Unsc* because we see no point to scoring somatic symptoms in this kind of protocol, but others might disagree and wish to use a sign for physical symptoms with somatic causation.

THE SIGN r

I. DEFINITION OF r

r is the sign for reward or reduction in drive. The reward sign is added as a kind of postscript to the sign for the drive that has been reduced; for example, $A{:}r$ is used for reduction of anxiety, $S{:}r$ for reduction of sex drive. Relaxation of tension, pleasure, and comfort are evidences of reward. Any sentence of the patient describing his own experience of drive reduction, relaxation, pleasure, or comfort should be scored with the subscript r attached to the symbol for motive. r can be used alone in one case only: for the state of affairs described by the sentence "I feel happy," provided that the speaker gives no further evidence as to why he feels happy. Thus an un-analyzed feeling of well-being would be scored r.

II. THEORY OF r

Reward is important theoretically because it strengthens the responses which have just preceded it. These strengthened responses are said to be "learned" to the concurrent cues. Primary drives, like hunger, are reduced by primary rewards, like food. Secondary or learned drives are similarly reduced by secondary rewards; thus the cues of safety will reduce the learned drive of fear. A train of thought itself can produce the cues for a reward reaction, and in this sense a person can administer rewards, or comforting thoughts, to himself. Another person, such as a therapist, can "lend" comforting thoughts to a patient; a parent similarly can comfort a frightened child.

The outward signs of primary reward are clearly visible, as in the case of food as a reward to a hungry person. Reward can, however, be an inward thing. Looked at from the human standpoint a secondary reward means the end of a state of painful tension. Tension in the psychic apparatus, as Freud said (1916–17, pp. 343–9), can destroy peace of mind to a terrifying degree; the reduction of such tension (as by psychoanalytic interpretation) can be one of life's most crucial rewards. It is most unfortunate that an event of such transcendent human importance often occurs without any obvious outward indications.

III. EXAMPLE OF SIMPLE r

Although usually used in combination with another sign, r can be used alone to indicate "feeling happy" as a result of some unmentioned or unanalyzed circumstance. Thus one of our patients reported a happy moment of childhood:

> [1]Uh-I remember once uh right before I got this way, of-of feeling, I think it was a feeling of happiness. [2]Oh, one time we had a quite bad, very bad snow. [3]I'm just showing you for an example now. [4]Uh we had a very bad snow storm. [5]And we just couldn't get out of the house. [6]And uh I felt very happy and . . . [7]Well, I felt contented with myself. [8]And I felt good because we had warmth. [9]And we had enough to eat. [10]And I thought, well, gee, even if it was a few days . . . I mean, it gave me sort of a warm feeling that I felt good.

Even though the patient is miserable now, she can interrupt her misery long enough to remember a happy time. The score is r.

IV. COMBINED SIGNS

Ordinarily r is combined with a motivational sign, the particular one which r reduces. We present a series of examples of the varied uses of the sign.

1. Any mention of the sexual orgasm is scored using r. The orgasm is, of course, an example of a primary reward. A married male patient said:

> [1]After the interruption by the baby we began having intercourse again. [2]And that night we both came swiftly to orgasm. [3]It was very satisfying and relaxing.

The obvious scoring is S:r. The score would be the same even if the patient had not mentioned relaxation or satisfaction. If the orgasm occurs, reward is assumed. No matter how spoiled or minimized a man's orgastic satisfaction may be, we assume there is always some satisfaction for the male if ejaculation occurs.

2. If a painful symptom disappears, we are justified in inferring that reward has occurred. A young businessman who had been having neurotic pains in his stomach said:

> [1]I've been exceptionally busy recently, chasing around the state and lining things up for the fall. [2]It's funny. [3]But I've lost these uh-stomach pains that I had. [4]And . . . after that hectic hustle and bustle of traveling, then . . . the spasms or whatever it was seemed to go away.

There was independent evidence for believing that the patient's stomach pain was a psychosomatic symptom. It seemed to appear and disappear as tension mounted or fell in the office. Cessation of the traveling evidently brought relief from the symptom. The correct scoring is *PSS:r*.

3. A married patient of weak potency found it onerous that his wife expected more sexual activity from him than he felt able to provide. When her expectation suddenly declined he spoke as follows:

> [1]And I felt . . . uhm . . . less compelled to start the process because uh I for the first time, I believe, felt pretty secure in the fact that she wasn't interested either . . . if you follow me. [2]And I felt comfortable because for the first time, or well, for one of the very few times, I realized she didn't care one way or the other. [3]And it was just a-a plain fact. [4]There was no-no mulling around, or wondering, or doubts, or worry what she was thinking, and how that would effect, you know, all of this silly cycle that I get involved in in regard to sex.

The patient felt his wife's expectation of intercourse as a coercion which threw him into serious conflict; he had strong anxiety lest he should fail, and feelings of resentment at her coercive behavior. When she withdrew her pressure he experienced a sudden reduction in tension. This kind of tension reduction is correctly scored *A:r*.

4. The loan of comforting thoughts is illustrated in the passage to be quoted. A woman patient spoke apprehensively of her hostile feelings for her husband:

PATIENT   [1]You know, I just hate him. [2]I find myself wishing that he would have an auto accident. [3]So many people have to die who would really be missed. [4]Why can't he be one of them? . . . [5]And yet, saying this makes me feel dreadful. [6]I shouldn't even be thinking it. [7]How can I ever be well when I have such thoughts as these?

THERAPIST   [8]Feeling angry at your husband and doing anything to bring about his death are two entirely different matters. [9]Thinking is not doing. [10]You haven't *done* anything against your husband. [11]It's one thing to think and talk, but quite another thing to act in real life.

PATIENT   [12]That's true. (*Silence as she thinks about the interpretation.*)

The therapist noticed that the patient felt the guilt associated with *doing* an evil act. In the patient's mind there was on this issue no distinction between thinking and doing. By making the discrimination the therapist succeeded in reducing the guilt attached to merely thinking. Sentence 12 should be scored *A:r*. Naturally, such a reduction of anxiety will be only temporary, but this fact permits us to remind the reader that a partial or temporary reduction of anxiety is acceptable as evidence for scoring *r*. Reduction of anxiety does not need to be total or permanent to justify this score.

5. Neurotic anxiety can reach terrifying proportions, and the effort to reduce it can lead to desperate acts. In order to illustrate the matter swiftly, we paraphrase the facts from the life of one of our patients:

> *The patient had been having intercourse with another man's wife. The other man was a friend of the patient. The affair had been going on for several years, and the patient had had occasional moments of anxiety lest he be discovered. One day the patient got a letter from the husband. The letter was ambiguous. It seemed to have to do with how far a tiger would have to move to attack a lion under such-and-such conditions. The letter seemed on the face of it to present a mathematical puzzle. To the patient it seemed certain, however, that the puzzle had a deeper meaning—that it contained a hint that the older man suspected the patient as paramour of his wife. The patient fell*

swiftly into a horror of anxiety. Days of dreadful misery passed. He had just about concluded that he would have to confront his friend and "have it out" to the death, if necessary, when he ran into a second friend. This second friend was a young man like the patient. This man also mentioned having received the letter with the puzzle in it. The patient was swept by a tidal wave of relief. He realized that he had not been singled out to receive the mysterious letter, that there was no latent meaning to it, and that his older friend did not suspect him of treachery.

The "wave of relief" in question is surely to be scored *A:r*. Shortly after this imagined catastrophe the patient terminated his affair with his friend's wife. The anxiety he experienced is properly termed castration anxiety.

6. Stalin is supposed to have said, "Sweet is sleep after revenge." His remark could be scored *H:r*. We came across a similar state of affairs in the life of one of our patients, though her description of it does not have the epigrammatic quality of Stalin's. This woman cherished an open and long-standing hostility for her husband. Punishing him gave her pleasure. She said:

> [1]You know my husband isn't understanding about the children at all. [2]It makes me aggravated. [3]But I don't blame him too much because that's the way he was brought up. [4]But I feel he should have more understanding about them. [5]Last night we talked a little bit. [6]And I told him how I felt about his not showing the children enough affection, which I never thought I'd be able to do. [7]But I did. [8]I'm getting so brave!

The patient chuckled with satisfaction as she made the last statement. Her sadistic gratification (sentences 7 and 8) should be scored *H:r*.

V. DISCRIMINATIONS AND BORDERLINE CASES

At times *r* has to be inferred, since no direct expression of pleasure, comfort, or satisfaction is made. Some neurotic patients are afraid to confess to the therapist any satisfying honors which come to them; they feel, as it were, as if they would be boasting or "tempting fate."

1. A businessman patient reacted in this way:

¹I was sitting down in New York in the office minding my own business. ²And a fellow called me on the telephone. ³He thought I might be interested in a high-paying job at the Duplex Corporation. ⁴The fellow said I was the only one he could think of who could meet the requirements.

The patient does not declare his pride or satisfaction in being thus considered for an important job. It was undoubtedly a great feather in his cap and a great personal comfort. But one must infer, rather than know directly, that he was pleased with the offer. This inference should be made. The scoring of 3 and 4 should be *Mob:r*.

2. There are times when it is difficult to distinguish between *L* and *r*. Gratitude and simple satisfaction are so mixed that it is hard to tell them apart. A woman patient speaking of her childhood said:

¹I-I-uh I learned to read quite early. ²It was before I went to school. ³It must have been from Daddy reading to us. ⁴But when I got into first grade I knew something about it already. ⁵And it was wonderful. ⁶I'll tell you about something I read.

What was wonderful, one infers, was being able to read and to receive the notice and distinction in her first-grade class which reading skill brought her. There is in the quotation also evidence of appreciation for her father. Thus an *L* scoring would be possible; however, the major emphasis seems to be on the pleasure of reading and the distinction it brought her. The correct score for all units is *Mob:r*.

THE SIGN Reas

I. DEFINITION OF Reas

Reas is a shortened form of the word "reasoning" and is our "insight" sign. The process of *Reas* has to do with the manipulation of sentences, imageal responses, and emotions so that a mental solution of a problem is achieved. *Reas* covers the unbidden, impulsive emergence of a solution as well as the achievement of it by laborious formal reasoning. It is not combined with any other sign.

II. THEORY OF Reas

The sign *Reas* was invented in order to record the work of the patient in acquiring insights by himself. *Reas* reactions begin in a dilemma. The neurotic patient, in treatment, comes to be puzzled by his own mental life. He comes to realize that many of his descriptions of his feelings and of the world around him are inadequate, contradictory, or even misleading. He often experiences relief when he hits on a correct statement of his emotions or attitudes. As noxious neurotic tension is reduced, the patient acquires an "appetite" for the truth about himself.

Meantime, the therapist is standing by with support and aid in labeling and clarification. When the therapist provides a vital unit by interpretation and the patient borrows this unit and enlarges upon it significantly, we call this enlargement *Conf;* that is, the patient has confirmed an interpretation by presenting new material. If the connection between interpretation and confirmation is clear, the response is scored *Conf.* If the connection is unclear and if the patient's new unit appears more or less "by itself," we call the new unit *Reas.* When the patient, with however much prior help by the therapist, hits upon a novelty of labeling by himself, the new response is called *Reas.*

Obviously *Reas* occurs only in the context of a major therapeutic effort, and it tends to record the patient's ability to further the therapeutic work by his own powers. *Reas* is a part of what Freud (1914) called "working through," but is not identical with it.

There are some units from learning theory (Dollard and Miller, 1950, pp. 51–61, 110–15) which are useful in discussing the concept of *Reas.* We will deal swiftly with them.

1. *Anticipatory response. Reas* operations occur by means of anticipatory responses. These responses—verbal, emotional, imageal —have been evoked and connected in past learning dilemmas; when such responses recur in the attempt to solve a present problem they are used in an anticipatory way. Responses, such as the attempted descriptions of the goal or its hazards, which would ordinarily occur only at or near the goal point, are evoked in the reasoning situation. This is the situation which gives rise to planning and problem solving and also, in psychotherapy, to *Reas.*

2. *Anticipatory responses must be complete.* In order to solve a special problem at the mental level, one's repertory of anticipatory

responses must be complete. One can reason only with the responses which he already has. Furthermore, it is vital that these responses can be freely produced. In a military problem the soldier can use his past experience of logistic matters to solve the problem of supplying his unit. In a cooking dilemma a cook must be well supplied with a description of the cooking situation if she is to think adaptively. A cook cannot reason about military problems because she does not have the necessary anticipatory units at hand. Anticipatory units are often referred to as "experience." If, as in the neurotic patient, vital anticipatory units are prevented by repression from occurring at all, the mental solutions arrived at are bound to be inferior. Liberation from repression is thus an essential condition of improved reasoning in the neurotic.

3. *Learned generalization.* Tendencies to generalize response from one stimulus context to another are fortunately present in every neurotic patient. For example, a patient said:

> [1]I seem to feel guilty all the time. [2]If it's not one thing it's another. [3]I know that my wife takes advantage of my guiltiness to get me to do things which ordinarily I wouldn't do, and perhaps shouldn't do. [4]I wonder if the boss is using me the same way? [5]I always feel myself on the defensive with him.

The patient is here performing an act of generalization. He generalizes his inference that he is being managed from the situation with his wife to the situation with his boss. A common element in the two situations is that of feeling on the defensive. It is a great feat when the patient is naturally able or can learn thus to generalize.

4. *Learned discrimination.* Whereas generalization lumps together, discrimination separates and sorts out. Both are responses of which the mind is innately capable, as careful experimentation has shown. In the following quotation one sees a tortured man making a discrimination; in doing so he is using an interpretation already "loaned" to him by the therapist:

> [1]When she told me she had had intercourse with Bill I felt a terrible pain. [2]I felt utterly lonely and physically cold. [3]Somewhere in there I had a flash of anger. [4]But then I started blaming myself for what had happened. . . . [5]I thought that I must have offended her or neglected her, else she wouldn't have done this to me. . . . [6]Then I thought to myself, "Why get sore at your-

self; she's the one who injured you." ⁷Then I began to feel
lonely and cold again. ⁸Then I began to get sore again. ⁹But it
made me feel guilty. . . . ¹⁰Later I remembered what you told
me: "One doesn't have to feel guilty just for thinking; thinking
is not doing." ¹¹At this point I had a flood of hatred toward her.
¹²I thought of all sorts of ways of punishing her. ¹³I wanted to
beat up on her.

The history recited above does have a sequel but is too complex to
deal with at this point. Suffice it to say (units 6 and 10) that we have
seen an anguished patient using an interpretation in a novel situation
to permit himself to react fully to this situation. The consideration
that he need not feel guilty merely for thinking and acknowledging
inwardly what he was feeling enabled him to replace an unjustified
self-blame with a knowledge of the full extent of his angry feeling. In
childhood, action tends to follow, fluid and resistless, upon thought;
and punishment of action generalizes swiftly to preceding thoughts.
Resistance to rushing into action is one of the mental units crucial
to maturity; when such a mature habit is developed, however, it is
futile and unnecessary to inhibit thought—though such inhibitions
frequently remain. The formula is: Break the instant chain between thought and action; welcome every possible thought unit,
reprehensible or otherwise; be free with thought but cautious **with**
action because action, unlike thought, has consequences for others
and once performed it cannot be recalled.

5. *Planning.* The foregoing discussion on discrimination leads
naturally to the topic of planning. Planning involves the ordering of
anticipatory responses so that they can result in coherent, pointed
action. All responses relative to a problem must be evoked, including anticipatory goal reactions which produce drive reduction and,
so to say, cement the plan together. Planning may involve new com-
binations of old responses, as by a novel ordering of such responses.
In the course of the reasoning necessary to plan, novel or unusual responses may be evoked. An example of such an unusual response is
contained in the following true anecdote:

*A friend reported that his wife was one day driving him and
his children home from a hard day's work. While they were
driving along a storm broke out and a terrific downpour of rain
began. At this moment the car ran out of gas. The son of the
family volunteered to dash to a filling station and get gasoline.
This he did, returning with a two-gallon can of gas. Unfor-*

tunately, the can had no spout, so the gasoline could not be poured. A search was made of the car; there was no funnel at hand. The rain continued, the children were getting hungry, and the emotional climate was dank and dangerous. At this point the husband looked up and noticed that they were stalled in front of the chemistry laboratory. The flashing thought struck him, "Where there's a chem lab, there must be a funnel." This inspiration proved prophetic.

A unit such as that above, "Where there's a chem lab, etc.," is certainly based on experience, and yet its occurrence in a sequence such as is described above has the appearance, at least, of being a remarkable novelty. Perhaps the novelty exists in the fact that the unit appeared after many years of latency. At any rate, such units are vital in planning. Properly organized they can lead to actions which reduce painful tensions.

Plans are frequently "put on ice" when they cannot be usefully initiated at once. Some thinkers have a standard set of plans for various types of situations. Many cultural solutions of problems are taught to individuals and become integrated in their lives as plans —in many cases as plans designed to meet emergencies never as yet confronted. In this sense, childhood might be thought of as the period in which society teaches its best plans to its new members. Plans which have been tried out in action and have produced vital rewards should be best learned and most frequently evoked. It may even be that neurotic traits can be looked upon as maladaptive "plans" inadvertently taught in the course of socialization—but that is probably stretching the point too far.

6. *Insight.* "Insight" is a kind of over-all term for what has been discussed in this section. It includes new labeling of objects and emotions, new learned generalizations and discriminations, new connections made between stimuli, new plans prepared and tested. All of these activities could be scored *Reas*. Insight can be loaned, as by an analytic interpretation, but it must be rehearsed and tested by the patient if it is to have effect. Borrowed labels for repressed motives can be vitally important in developing the power to reason.

III. EXAMPLES OF Reas

The ability to *Reas* can be learned, but it is also partly a gift of nature. With gifted patients *Reas* or attempts to *Reas* will begin early in a therapy case; as the case progresses, and especially in the terminal stages, native ability plus learning will show forth as a splendid skill. As more and more units are released from repression and as vital habits of discrimination and generalization are acquired, examples of *Reas* begin to multiply. Unfortunately we have but little case material which is drawn from these terminal phases of therapy. Most of the examples that follow are derived from a single talented patient. Nevertheless, we remind the reader that all our examples are *real;* none are made up or composed for the occasion. They have all been found "in nature." As the reader can perhaps testify, our examples have the knobby properties of real events.

1. Our first example deals with a woman whose life was in dreadful confusion. She had been married and reluctantly divorced twice. Both husbands had exploited and abused her. Just before she said what is reported below, she had been working on severe feelings of rejection by her mother. She said:

> [1]And-uh . . . I think that-that with both Ralph and Jimmy I-I was repeating a pattern of behavior that I had developed with my mother of-of seeking love. [2]I-I would have done almost anything to get mother to love me. [3]And-uh . . . it's a-a pattern of uh-conciliation and-and trying to please . . . both. [4]I-I can see so many—so many similarities in the way I acted toward mother and both of my husbands. . . . [5]I think that I got married—I think I got married both times for the same reason.

The patient's relationship to her husband, which had been so mysterious, suddenly was illuminated when she saw it as similar in kind to her propitiatory reactions toward her mother. This generalization proved to be very useful. No husband should be asked to give what a mother failed to give her infant. The worst of the matter was that in picking husbands the patient also followed her older pattern; she picked men who, like her mother, had least capacity to gratify her yearning for love and care. Her insight should, of course, be scored *Reas*.

2. Later the woman just spoken of had another flash of insight. Her mother and both husbands had independently hit on a trick for managing her. It must have been an unconscious invention, after trial and error, in each case. The patient said:

> [1]And it-uh . . . the three of them—all had the same trick. [2]And oh it would floor me completely when they did it. [3]Uh

. . . any uh almost anyone can get me to do-uh almost anything they want me to do, with-uh within reason, by-by getting mad if I don't do it, and then stalking out. [4]And the minute they're gone, I feel that I must do it.

The patient's discovery is to note a similarity of tricks used by three important people in her life. As she first experienced it, she saw no similarity between the events. What her "managers" were doing was to dramatize abandonment, as if to say, "If you do not obey, you will be isolated and rejected forever." There was a time, in the patient's early childhood, when this threat had terrifying force, and she had never managed to outgrow her tendency to respond to it with compliance.

3. We can report a brilliant bit of insight by a professional writer who had come for treatment because of a prolonged inhibition of his ability to write. Early in the analysis he had reported his struggles as follows:

[1]I feel as if I am chained to my desk. [2]And I do the chaining myself. [3]I go to my desk at nine in the morning and plan to stay there until one. [4]I sit for the allotted time whether I am able to write or not. [5]When I am not able to write, the struggle is exhausting. [6]When I have a good day I experience a great sense of relief and elation. [7]But if unable to write, I am exhausted and depressed. [8]I am really afraid of my desk. [9]I used to call it desk-terror. [10]But I am proud to say that I drive myself to do it. [11]And eventually it gets done.

The foregoing report was made during the early months of analysis and would be scored as follows: units 1–5, 7–9, *A;* units 6, 10, 11, *A:r.* There was no further progress on the symptom for approximately two years. In the meantime a great deal of necessary work was done, and analysis was going on at deepest levels. One day the patient came in excitedly with what was for him a revelation. He said:

[1]I was sitting at my desk and not getting anywhere. [2]I began to feel more and more desperate. [3]I felt guilty and helpless. [4]I couldn't work. [5]And I couldn't see any way out. [6]Suddenly I thought, "This situation is just like the potty-chair situation when I was a child. [7]As a child, I was made to sit there until I produced. [8]My mother stood over me with threats just as my

conscience does now. ⁹I would sit there and strain till I exhausted myself, just as I do now." ¹⁰I ask you, Doctor, is this the only way to get writing done?

The patient had a right to be proud of his discovery. The source of the torturing obsessional conflict had become clear to him. He had suddenly seen important similarities between two apparently different situations. His insight (units 6 through 10) should be scored *Reas*. It was an interesting side light of this case that when he failed to "produce," that is, to write his assigned stint, he would console himself that he had at least suffered dreadfully while trying.

4. As the woman patient already mentioned learned better to bear her chronic feelings of rejection, new attitudes toward her rejecting mother began to come to the fore. On one occasion during the time of the treatment she had a birthday, and her mother gave her a string of beads. During the course of the birthday dinner the string holding the beads together was mysteriously broken, the beads scattered around the room, and some of them were lost. The patient accepted the accident with a strange light-heartedness. Later she spoke as follows:

> PATIENT   ¹. . . No, I felt more that the phrase that entered my head was that I was breaking, breaking up the past, that—
> THERAPIST   ²Mm-hmm.
> PATIENT   ³Uh . . . and I felt-felt that about the beads. ⁴I guess I deliberately broke those beads.

In the therapeutic work which had preceded the utterance given above, the patient had learned that events like the string-breaking are sometimes unconsciously caused. She used this knowledge to discover and label a formerly repressed motive, i.e. hostility toward her mother. In the string-breaking she sensed the latent meaning of revolt and rejection. It was as if she were saying to her mother, "It's too late now to show me love; keep your miserable beads!" By emotionally re-enacting her dependence, feelings of rejection, and resentment against her mother, she was at last able to free herself of these feelings. She could stop expecting childish things of adults and stop resenting them when childish demands were not met; when all this was worked through she made a marked advance in positive relations with other people.

5. The woman patient who has been mentioned several times in this section had a peculiar physical symptom. It was a kind of a skin eruption or rash, seemingly allergic in type. The ugly blotches were felt by the patient to be a disfigurement. For a time during her treatment these spots seemed to appear and disappear without rhyme or reason. One day in therapy the patient declared:

> [1]Yesterday it suddenly dawned on me, "I have the spots when I go home, and the minute I get back here it stops." [2]I remember now . . . I remember I used to have it on weekends because then I was going home for two days. [3]When I was working out of town I didn't have it. [4]And-and I would go out in the evening. [5]So I wasn't around too much. [6]But the minute Saturday and Sunday rolled around I . . . I'd start to have trouble. [7]And Monday it would stop. [8]And it would be all right until the next weekend.

It is highly pertinent to this discussion to know that when the patient went home she was also visiting her mother. In this flashing insight the patient connected the visits to the mother with the symptom. What is novel here is the new connection between events. It is, of course, scored *Reas.* It is not necessary to know the psychodynamics of the symptom in order to be able to allot this score. The knowledge that the symptom is some kind of a manifestation toward being at home with mother is sufficient to get the therapeutic work a step forward.

6. The writer already referred to had a marked fear of mental illness. If for any reason the probability of his being mentally ill seemed to him to be increased, he had an anxiety attack of panic strength; his heart would slam, his breathing would become shallow, and he would move about in restless anguish.

> *One day the patient came to therapy reporting that he had one of his attacks the day before. The apparent stimulus for the attack was that a friend of his had been hospitalized for a mental disorder. In the midst of his misery, the patient had tried to write out his thoughts to see whether he could hit on something that would help him. In point of fact, he did. His friend had always been fatalistic about mental illness; he had had a feeling that he was "cursed," and that such illness ran*

irresistibly in his family. In the course of his writing and think-
ing, the patient realized that he himself did not share this view;
he felt miserable but not accursed. This thought was quite
comforting to the patient, and a marked abatement of his
anxiety occurred. He seemed to be arguing, "If people have
different points of view, they can also have different fates."

It is clear that the patient made what was for him a valuable discrimination; it is not quite so clear why the distinction between
himself and the other man had such a great effect in reducing panic.
It suffices that his insight enabled him, for the moment, to escape
from the terrible reality of neurotic suffering. The proper scoring
is *Reas.*

7. A neurotic woman several times referred to had, among other
aspects of her personality, marked feelings of worthlessness. The
existence of these feelings was quite clear to the therapist but not
so to the patient. In the following citation she is struggling with the
problem of why she seems to prefer "peculiar" people like the two
ineffectual and disturbed husbands she had had:

> [1]Uh . . . the people that I've always gotten along with have
> been . . . the peculiar ones. [2]I . . . I feel at ease with them,
> I guess. [3]There's some things that . . . you know, like . . . I
> suppose that in some way I feel superior to these people. [4]I
> know I definitely do. [5]And . . . and . . . and then I . . .
> I'm not afraid of them. [6]And . . . and there's no problem at
> all. [7]. . . I don't think that they're so critical.

This was the first time that this idea had appeared in her therapy.
The patient is approaching the idea of her own feelings of unworthi-
ness and helplessness; one link in the approach is to know that she
selects weak people in order to get the benefit of feeling superior to
someone. In this case the patient labels a feeling which was formerly
inarticulate. The scoring is *Reas.*

8. This example has to do with an often-cited woman patient. In
the course of her treatment the patient reported that her father had
had a mistress to whom he gave expensive presents, even when she
and her mother lacked necessary things. In her childhood the patient
had felt this to be unfair but had smothered her resentment. It was
only during psychotherapy that she realized the true extent of her
hostility toward her father. She said:

[1]For a time in my life it was absolutely necessary to feel that my father loved me . . . well, more than anyone. [2]And up-up until all this started I thought he had. [3]And-uh-and then I thought he didn't. [4]And-and I made all kinds of excuses and tried to cover the thing up. [5]And I made myself think uh that I was bad to have resented him. [6]But I really wasn't.

Although the insight was based on prior work, the patient here achieved this remarkable insight by herself. She had only partial insight into her resentment of her father since, obviously, it was not merely the presents he gave the mistress but the fact of his having a mistress at all—and thus abandoning the patient—which was the cause of her resentment; but it is not necessary to have full insight to get credit for a *Reas* score.

IV. DISCRIMINATIONS AND BORDERLINE CASES

Herewith are a few discriminations and precautions concerning the use of *Reas:*

1. *Reas* is scored only the first time a new insight occurs. It is not scored when such an insight is repeated. On succeeding occasions the former insight is scored according to its content. Thus when repeated the behavior in example 8 above would be scored *H father.* Sentence 5 above (thinking herself bad) would be scored *H-A.*

2. *Distinction between* Reas *and* Conf. *Conf* is scored when the insight is a direct response to an interpretation. *Reas* is scored when the patient hits on it, to a certain degree, by himself. It is understood, however, that every response in a psychoanalysis or psychotherapy follows upon interpretation, near or remote; thus every *Reas* response is to some degree influenced by prior interpretative work. If the insightful response occurs apart from a direct reaction to interpretation we score it *Reas;* it is of great importance that the patient is able to make a familiar discrimination in a new situation, to generalize, to make connections, and to label. We use *Reas* to evaluate this innovative power of the patient.

3. In general it is our practice to use *Reas* conservatively, that is, only for the clearest examples. The patient should clearly earn his *Reas.*

The Sign Res

I. DEFINITION OF Res

Res is an abbreviation of "resistance," i.e. any response of the patient that operates against the therapeutic process (Knight, 1952). Resistance prevents the uncovering and dissolution of the neurotic conflict. We score as *Res* any such response for which there are identifying cues in the patient's speech or behavior. In addition, we score as *Res* 5 any silence of five seconds in length. In what follows we define various subtypes of *Res* in order to show the scorer the variety of responses classified as *Res;* however, all subtypes are given the same sign, i.e. *Res.* This is not combined with any other sign.

II. THEORY OF Res

Psychotherapy is, after all, a conversation between two crucial people, the patient and the therapist. Each is highly active in his own distinctive way. Everything that has to do with the relation between these two people plays a central role in a theory of psychotherapy. The therapist tries to uncover unconscious motives in the patient to the end that the patient may exert increasing conscious control of such motives and make better total plans; the patient cooperates toward this objective but with many hindrances, lapses, deviations, and falterings.

The neurotic patient is in conflict—impelled to approach certain goals and yet afraid to do so, urged to act on impulse and yet unable to act. The exposure of unconscious motives causes pain. The patient naturally resists such experience of pain and thus also *naturally* resists therapy itself. Thus the patient partly cooperates, perhaps one should say *mostly* cooperates, but also he partly resists. One must have some record of such resistant gestures.

In psychotherapy the therapist asks the patient to say freely whatever comes into his mind; this instruction to associate freely is the chief weapon used to revoke repression. As the patient tries to do what is asked of him, repression appears as resistance, i.e. as behavior designed to maintain repression and to ward off the anxiety that occurs when repression is weakened. Freud gives an excellent statement of this matter (1916–17, pp. 253–62).

Patients are infinitely ingenious in producing resistant gestures. They may dispute the utility of the rule of free association or express a wish to escape from the physical situation of therapy. Nothing may come to mind, even though the patient has a lifetime of experience to report on. Intellectual criticisms may be made of the theory or practice of therapy. Patients may simply deny the existence of unconscious motives while behavioral evidence steadily points to them. Patients may evade, or joke, or show resentment of the therapist—all in the service of the one aim, escaping the pain of therapeutic work. All of these forms of resisting or hindering the clarification of the patient's emotional status are scored with the sign *Res*. Of course, if the patient does not talk at all, repression cannot be undone. Therefore we call silence resistant, and we count one unit of resistance for each five seconds of silence (*Res 5*).

III. EXAMPLES OF Res

The reader is reminded that all the subtypes of resistance exemplified below are scored by the single sign *Res*. The various types of resistance are presented to enable the scorer to see the range of resistant response.

1. *Res (escape)*. *Res* is used when the patient shows a wish to escape from the therapeutic situation, as by imagining himself somewhere else, inquiring how long therapy takes or how soon it will be over, or stating that the therapist should be talking to someone else (e.g. the spouse) not to him. Early assertions that the patient feels well and has no further need of treatment frequently give evidence of the wish to escape therapy. Here follow some concrete examples of the wish to escape:

a. A severely neurotic man pointed the finger at his wife in the following exchange:

> PATIENT ¹But I don't know. ²I . . . as I say it's a matter of . . . petty little daily things that upset me. ³I mean as far as being emotionally stable, I feel—
> THERAPIST ⁴Pretty good—
> PATIENT —in pretty good condition, frankly.
> THERAPIST —condition, yeah.
> PATIENT ⁵I think I'm running at any rate. ⁶I've heard it said that . . . that you never know who needs treatment. ⁷I think

if, if anyone needs treatment, it's on the other side. [8]As a matter of fact—

THERAPIST   [9]Well, that is about what I understood from what you said.

PATIENT   —I suppose everyone feels that way.

If it is not the patient who needs treatment but, as alleged, his wife, it is a mistake for him to come. Unconsciously he wishes to escape from the labors and perils (as he sees them) of treatment. The hard fact remains, however, that he is neurotically ill, and however it may be with his wife, the patient himself needs help. His proposal to escape and to send a substitute is therefore scored *Res.*

b. A woman patient whose life was severely circumscribed by phobic fears nevertheless said the following:

[1]And-uh well, I wonder why myself these things can't be overcome just by keeping on doing the things you're afraid to do and getting confidence back. [2]I thought that was all you had to do.

In this quote the patient pictures herself as out of the therapeutic situation and trying again what she has failed in so often, i.e. extinguishing fear by doing what she's afraid to do. She knows that this solution, which would take her out of therapy, will not work. Her escape attempts should be labeled *Res.*

2. *Res (rule)*. Flouting the basic rule of free association is a direct challenge to therapeutic work. A patient may argue, for example, that the rule is impossible to follow, he has too many thoughts in his mind to speak any one of them, the mind doesn't work so as to permit free association, he has a poor memory and thus can't comply. Again, patients assert that the rule doesn't make any sense, reserve the right to judge whether thoughts are important or trivial and to speak only the important ones, and withhold thoughts or expressions out of supposed tact, in order to protect the therapist. Those of us who have had much experience in electronic recording of interviews can testify that objection to recording is frequently a resistance. One such objector wished to withhold direct expression of certain thoughts by claiming that they would offend the ears of psychiatric nurses who might sometime listen to the recording. A couple of examples of objections to the rule follow:

a. A schizoid patient had an ingenious proposal for avoiding the rule; although his talk is hazy, his meaning drifts through:

[1]Uh . . . how much if any of my problem um . . . can be uh . . . resolved by an application of uh . . . something along the lines of New Year's resolutions? [2]In other words, if uh my problem can be broken down into facets and facets of the problem . . . can be uh . . . can be isolated and recognized and then worked on, uh-it comes to my mind of what good or how much value would there be, or would it be worth an intent on my part to apply strict mental and emotional discipline on a facet of the problem at a time, hoping to build the facet into two and three, and then eventually kind of chip away at the problem that way.

The patient is proposing that free association be abandoned and that a more logical and better controlled (by him) method of working be tried out. His utterance should be scored *Res*.

b. A woman patient had been talking about her mother and finding it extremely stressful:

[1](*She sighs*) [2]And I-I don't want to talk about my mother any more.

Urging her distress as a good reason, the patient wants to stop following the rule. Evidently further thoughts about her mother are present, thoughts which she would find it painful to relate. Although the gesture is resistant, we are not urging that the best thing for the therapist to do in such a situation would be to demand that the patient immediately talk more about her mother.

3. *Res (disturbance)*. This variant of resistance shows plainly the effects of repression. We have no special sign for repression, although repression is plainly related to resistant disturbances of various kinds. Disturbances of free association are revealed when the patient reports a blank mind, when he plies the therapist with repeated questions, and when the patient claims not to know something which he could know. Memory gaps and confused and conflicting statements likewise reveal the working of repression. Here follow some examples of such resistant disturbances of thinking:

a. A neurotic war veteran has been describing some of his sexual experiences while in the army. In this connection he recalled that

there was an army slang expression for masturbation. His memory
failed him and he could not bring the term to mind. He said:

> [1]And-uh incidentally, it's the same word that's being used for a
> character in a TV show. [2]I can-can never for the life of me
> understand, I mean, why they permit the word on this TV
> children's program. [3]But my youngsters look at it, know the
> word but think nothing of it. [4]For the life of me, I can't think
> of the name of that character on the show.

The therapist happened to know that the name of the character
was Flub-a-Dub. Evidently the same word was used for masturbation among some soldiers. The operation of repression is shown by
the fact that the word the patient is seeking is blotted out by anxiety.
Presumably anxiety was first attached to the act of masturbation and
then generalized to the word in question. To recall it would be embarrassing. The patient's lapse should be scored as a resistant disturbance of association.

b. A wife began her hour as follows:

> [1]Bill has an invention on which he has been working for several
> years. [2]He started on it just about the time we got engaged.
> [3-7](25-sec. silence) [8]I've forgot what I started to say.

Something connected with the engagement interrupted and preoccupied the patient, as evidenced by the twenty-five-second silence
(which would be scored as five *Res 5* units). After the silence she
couldn't think of what she had intended to say. Repression has fallen
upon her original thought, and we score her last sentence, accordingly, as resistant.

c. A woman patient came to her hour in a somewhat flighty mood,
saying:

> PATIENT   [1]Well, let's see, where shall I start? . . . [2]My mind
> is a blank [3](*Laughing anxiously*) from all this running. Uh—
> THERAPIST   [4]Well, you just start when you're ready.
> PATIENT   [5]I don't even remember what we were talking
> about last time.

Sentences 1, 2, and 5 are all resistant.

d. A woman patient who suffered from sexual inadequacy spoke
about her situation as follows:

> [1]During the first years of our marriage I used to get satisfaction quite regularly. [2]I didn't get it all the time but most of the time. [3]But then it stopped. [4]I guess it was within the last year, I expect. [5]I just don't remember . . . roughly when it dropped out. [6]We've both been terribly irritable.

When a patient can't remember, it is likely that resistance is at work. One would think the sexual orgasm an event sufficiently memorable that the patient would recall at least roughly the time of its disappearance. Her failure to remember should be scored *Res.*

e. If the patient cannot remember behavior on a crucial occasion in the past and cites someone else's account of such behavior, we score it as resistance. The woman patient to be quoted had presumably repressed her feelings about such an important occasion:

> [1]And uh . . . somehow or other they start . . . they got talking about when I got married. [2]I don't know how that started. [3]And . . . and Mother said . . . "I'll never forget how . . . how terribly you looked. You used to cry all the time." [4]I don't remember that crying at all. [5]They told me that for about a month before I got married I cried constantly. [6]Four people told me it was so. [7]But I positively cannot remember it.

When the patient can't remember something as important as her wedding, repression is presumably operating. In addition, she recites what other people said instead of remembering her own feelings and behavior. Behavior of so dramatic a character as that reported, occurring in adult life, could not be so easily forgotten unless strong forces were in operation to produce forgetting. Score *Res.*

4. *Res (intellectual)*. When the patient produces thoughts or hypotheses which seem calculated to avoid free association, we suspect resistance. When a verbal account is given but appropriate emotional reactions are not experienced, we also feel that the patient is "intellectualizing." When the patient gives a facile explanation of a riddle and the explanation given tends to dismiss the need for therapeutic work, we suspect that an intellectual resistance is in operation. Here are some real-life examples of this type of resistance.

a. A woman patient with a severe marital problem had found herself more vulnerable to weeping as the therapeutic work had gone on. She said:

PATIENT   [1]One thing bothers me. [2]Why do people cry? [3]And why do I cry? [4]I don't want to cry. [5]And . . . [6](*She sighs*) . . . I don't know. [7]I seem to have lost my inhibitions about it or something. [8](*5-sec. silence*) [9]Ah . . . well maybe it's something like muscles. [10]Ah . . . I was always very much interested in what makes muscles work. [11]And I tried to find out. [12]And I found out that no one knows. [13]So . . . maybe crying is the same thing.

THERAPIST   [14]Well I don't think we've got quite a full understanding of that yet as to just what it is that makes you cry sometimes.

PATIENT   [15]Well I didn't mean that. [16]I meant the mechanism of crying.

The patient's crying is important; it is an emotional reaction partly produced by, and certainly related to, therapy. At this point the patient seems not to be concerned about why or when she cries. She tries to substitute an intellectualistic concern over the mechanisms of muscle action, apparently wishing to distract the therapist's attention from the pertinent therapeutic problem to an irrelevant one. This intellectualizing is properly scored as *Res*.

b. As every therapist finds, psychodynamic knowledge can be used in the service of resistance. Thus a sophisticated patient said:

[1]But I've really come to the conclusion that I want to do something about . . . ah these headaches I've been having, which I think is a . . . in . . . well, signifies [2](*Embarrassed laugh*) that I've internalized a great deal of aggression and things like that which I . . . I . . . have a very superficial understanding about. [3]And I think I want to know more about it.

We scored these statements *Res* because the patient gives a theory that is not related to anything that he presently feels. He is reciting a psychodynamic formulation of his case which he has heard, but this formulation is not a summary of real emotional events; indeed, it is an effort to replace such events by an empty formula.

c. The intellectualizing tendencies of obsessional patients—expressed by their hurling verbal units about without reference to the emotional reactions usually attached to them—are notorious. Here is an example from the case of one such patient:

¹And why—you have spoken to me about different things, and related them. ²But it hasn't made me feel any better. ³And I—like I think I mentioned to you before-uh if for instance, uh . . . after this has been thrashed out and we have talked it over, I mean, what then? ⁴Do you know what I mean? ⁵What then? ⁶Supposing-uh it happened that it was something, perhaps back in my childhood that had happened, that has brought on this fright. ⁷And you explain to me that, well, this is why it happened and this is how it happened, and uh this today is the result of what happened, and that's why you are like you are. ⁸I mean perhaps it goes along those lines. ⁹And then, all right, I know what has happened. ¹⁰I know it now. ¹¹This is it. ¹²This is what it was. ¹³This has brought on the fears and anxieties. ¹⁴Well, what then?

The patient does not experience in emotional terms any of the situations she speaks of. What she presents is a worthless check with none of the spaces filled in. She assumes that the therapist and the therapy have already had a fair chance with her, even though this is only the twelfth hour of her treatment. She fears treatment and tries to escape it with the intellectual assurance to herself that it could have no effect anyway. Score *Res*.

5. *Res (denial)*. Flat denial is a common defense mechanism. The patient contradicts what the therapist has recently asserted, or he denies the existence of a motive which has recently been evoked. Behavioral signs may show that an unconscious motive is active, but the patient denies its existence. Often the thing denied is a specific hypothesis of the therapist as to an unconscious motive. The existence of the unconscious motive is plain (to the therapist) from the patient's own behavior and associations; the patient, however, fearfully denies. We present herewith some examples which illustrate the denial mechanism:

a. A male patient, much confused about his sex role, gave a beautiful example of denial. He said:

PATIENT ¹Any-any-uh seduction, or whatever you want to call it, should be initiated, uh-continued, and followed through by the female. ²And *he* should bring the female to the point where she should more or less fall over the break and become a very erotic, sexual—

THERAPIST   [3]Just a second, you said "initiated by the female"?
PATIENT   [4]No.
THERAPIST   [5]Yes.
PATIENT   [6]Oh, I-I didn't mean that.

This passive patient expressed, by his slip, some such motive as his wish to be seduced or his need for the woman's permission to act in the sexual situation. Thanks to recording, the slip is undeniable, but nevertheless the patient denied it. Score units 4 and 6 *Res.*

b. A married woman patient with severe anxiety attacks tried to believe that she was not ill, saying:

[1]There is no reason why I should be sick. [2]I have everything that life can offer—a husband, children, a home, a car, friends. [3]So why should I be sick?

The patient implicitly denies that she is ill by stating she can see no reason why she should be. In the course of her argument she also denies the existence of inward sources of stress as a cause for illness; because she does not understand her obvious misery, she asserts that there can be no basis for it. The appropriate subtype of *Res* would seem to be denial, although intellectual resistance might also be appropriate. Score *Res.*

c. Denial is a frequent response to the attempt to investigate early sexual notions of a patient. Thus a woman with a severe sexual disturbance said:

PATIENT   [1]Uh-for instance, uh-masturbation, uh-I-uh I never did that until I was grown up I mean-uh—
THERAPIST   [2]Mm-hmm.
PATIENT   —consciously. [3]I-I've been thinking about it. [4]And I think that I did-uh do it in a concealed way. [5]But I didn't-uh have any idea what it was.

It is often hard for the therapist to know how sexual matters were presented to a patient in childhood. He does know, however, that thanks to childhood gossip and secretive communications between children, sexual ideas are extremely pervasive. It is hard to keep from acquiring a repertory of sexual notions and, in most cases, the specific words that go with them. Thus though there is some small risk in scoring these sentences as a denial, this risk should probably be taken. It is very likely that the patient did know what masturbation was and did have a name for it. Score *Res.*

d. A woman patient with a marital conflict reported on the confusion surrounding her wedding anniversary. She was at once pleased and reluctant to accept the fuss that people were making about it. The conversation goes:

> THERAPIST   [1]This is your tenth anniversary?
>
> PATIENT   [2]Yeah, yeah. [3]And normally we—or our group, will either take the couple out for dinner or have a party and buy them something and have the anniversary. [4]And that is it. [5]But this has been a constant going-on. [6]We have invitations for about a month ahead. [7]Instead of accepting them and feeling grateful, I say to myself, "Why should they do it for me?" [8]Instead of saying—feeling, "Well, thank you very much, this is real sweet," my mind is buzzing with, "Well, what am I going to do to repay them?" [9]I seem to want it such that I am not taking what I'm not giving back.
>
> THERAPIST   [10]It's something like saying, "Well, there was no occasion for making so much fuss anyway"?
>
> PATIENT   [11]Uh-I don't know if that is it. [12]No, I don't think that's it. [13]I think—I think that it's a question of—uh-I-I don't think it's a question of making a fuss over the occasion. [14]I think it's-uh—it's a question with me of reciprocity. [15]I-I think it's a question with me of obligation. [16]I don't want to be beholden to anybody.

As the patient senses, the therapist is approaching the following idea: "Maybe you don't like the wedding celebration because it makes you feel more committed to your marriage." If the patient were to return the presents given, or to give counterpresents, she would feel less that she was publicly consenting to her own entrapment. This idea the patient denies, and meanwhile claims protection of the moral principle that one shouldn't be beholden to anyone. The denial sentences should be scored *Res*.

6. *Res (misunderstanding)*. Patients often misunderstand or evade the meaning of an interpretation. They may go right on with their own train of thought, disregarding what the therapist has said. They may fail to react appropriately to an interpretation or fail to understand it when they might reasonably be expected to understand. Evasive utterances and *non sequiturs* would both appear under the subcategory *Res (misunderstanding)*.

a. The "pay-no-attention" or "go-on-as-if-nothing-had-happened" reaction is one of the commonest forms of evading interpretations. In the case at hand a male patient has been asked to associate to a dream in which several pairs of policemen were marching across a lawn. The transaction goes:

> THERAPIST   ¹Just why "a pair" of policemen?
> PATIENT   ²Mm-hmm, three pair of policemen.
> THERAPIST   ³Because you've emphasized this pair thing.
> PATIENT   ⁴Yeah, yeah, definitely. ⁵Almost in step.

The patient does not associate to the "pair" idea as asked but simply repeats the dream as he had told it before. He acts as if he hadn't heard the therapist and possibly, in the psychodynamic sense, he hasn't; in any case he evades the stimulus to give more information. The patient's sentences should be scored *Res.*

b. Any reference to "analysts in general" made by a patient in therapy should always be considered as possibly referring to the therapist himself. Such a reference is made by a woman patient as follows:

> PATIENT   ¹The magazine section had a couple of very good articles and one of which was one-uh how do psychoanalysts stand up under the strain? ²And-uh ³(*Anxious laugh*) apropos of nothing I thought of that. ⁴But I was reading through it this morning.
> THERAPIST   ⁵It wouldn't have any reference to me?
> PATIENT   ⁶Huh? ⁷(*Embarrassed laughing*)
> THERAPIST   ⁸It couldn't be a roundabout reference to me, by any chance?
> PATIENT   ⁹(*Embarrassed laughing*) ¹⁰But-uh it-it was written I-I don't know by whom. ¹¹I didn't even pay it any attention. ¹²But I was curious about it. ¹³And I read it through.

The patient's remark could have a number of different unconscious meanings. It could, for instance, be a kind of apology ("You must be exhausted trying to deal with a troublesome patient like me"). The patient's utterance could have a latent meaning of warning the therapist against her own unconscious angry feelings ("When you have to deal with my opposition as it really is, you will be tired enough"). At this point, all the therapist did was to try to test whether the patient was addressing her remark to him. In the course of her statement she twice denied any special interest in the matter, saying "apropos of nothing" and "I didn't even pay it any attention." Her method of response to the interpretation consists of simple evasion. She doesn't consider whether or not her thought could have roundabout reference to the therapist. While a denial is involved, the main force of the example is to illustrate evasion. Score patient's sentences 2, 6, 10, and 11 *Res*.

7. *Res (humor)*. All sorts of unsavory motives can appear, aerated and purified, in humorous disguise. The witty or humorful transformation must be appreciated in itself as one of the delightful human actions. We do not wish to train our patients out of a sense of humor. Yet it is also true that, with due care, the motive underlying humor must be pointed out. The limited time and energies of the psychotherapeutic transaction cannot be dissipated entirely in a sharing of the pleasures of humor. We are grateful to gracious humor for bringing the skulking motive upon the stage of mental life even when we have to "put the finger" on the motive under the disguise. Here are a few examples of the occurrence of humor in therapy.

a. A woman patient with marital difficulties had been discussing her sexual relations with her husband. She said that they had frequently had intercourse without contraception, the idea being that since her uterus was tipped, there was little danger of pregnancy. Even so, she went on:

> PATIENT   [1]Well, we talked about it a lot, that it doesn't . . . doesn't matter now if we get pregnant and particularly . . .
>
> THERAPIST   [2]You know you say that in an odd . . . slightly odd way: "if *we* get pregnant"—
>
> PATIENT   [3]Well, it—
>
> THERAPIST   —as if—
>
> PATIENT   [4](*Embarrassed laughing*)—takes two, you know.
>
> THERAPIST   (*Laughs*) [5]Yes.
>
> PATIENT   [6]Or as Bill says, "I've got news for you." [7](*Embarrassed laugh*)
>
> THERAPIST   [8]Who says that?
>
> PATIENT   [9]Bill. [10](*Embarrassed laugh*)
>
> THERAPIST   [11]"I have news for you"?
>
> PATIENT   [12](*Embarrassed laugh*) [13]Yeah.
>
> THERAPIST   [14]How do you mean?
>
> PATIENT   [15]Well, I was . . . I was just kidding you—

THERAPIST   [16]Yeah?

PATIENT   —about the fact that it takes two.

THERAPIST   [17]Yeah? [18]I don't understand.

PATIENT   [19]I just thought maybe you didn't know.

THERAPIST   [20]Oh (*Laughing*) you have news for me (*Mocking*) that it takes two.

PATIENT   [21](*Relaxed laugh*) [22]Yeah.

THERAPIST   [23]Thank you. [24]I did know. [25]But I appreciate your telling me.

PATIENT   [26](*Relaxed laughing*) [27]Yeah. [28]But it—just bong me on the head a coupla times when I do that.

THERAPIST   [29]Why?

PATIENT   [30]It must be infuriating to have to have so many . . . making snide remarks all the [31](*Embarrassed laugh*) time.

The warmth of the preceding episode may far overpass in therapeutic meaning anything that could be gained by pursuing the patient's peculiar statement. It is apparent that therapy is going on under very good conditions for the work. Nevertheless, what does she mean by saying "if *we* get pregnant"? When asked, she resorts to a humorous defense. The therapist does well to keep his eye on this sort of event. If the patient is certainly right when she says that it takes two people to make a baby, she is certainly wrong if she implies that it takes two people to carry it. Somewhere in this humorous scuffling there is a truth which the patient does not care to face (a wish to be the penis-bearer as well as receiver?). Whatever it was, the patient's fantasy was safe behind her sally. Score patient's units 3, 6, 9, 15, and 19 *Res.*

b. A woman patient, who had taken a job after a futile struggle with marriage, had been telling about the many new problems which she confronted: envy, unwelcome attentions, fatigue, etc. She ended her recital: "What shall I do, Dr. Anthony?"

In this jokelet the patient is comparing the therapist to the well-known "Dr. Anthony" who used to answer heart-rending questions on the radio. The joke permits her, as it were, both to ask for help and to pretend that she's not doing so. As other material in the case showed, the joke concealed an urgent dependent wish. If the therapist took her remark seriously, she could dismiss it as just a joke. Yet there is a plea in her statement which the therapist would be ill-advised to neglect—at least for any protracted period of time. Humor is used as the defensive wrapping of her plea. Her remark should be scored *Res*.

c. When one of our woman patients was a fourteen-year-old girl, the boy next door lured her over to his family apartment when the adults were away from home. When they arrived at the apartment Joe asked her to take off her clothes. She refused indignantly. He then chased her around the apartment, trying to undress her himself, and he did not desist until she went to an open window and threatened to scream. In describing the incident later, the patient said:

> [1]It was, in a way, very funny. [2]It was one of those things, "Now you're in my power." [3]It was something like a Keystone Comedy. [4]It was, I think, very funny.

Judging by the way the patient behaved at the time, the incident wasn't funny when it happened. Rather, she was by turns incredulous, indignant, and terrified. Only when time had mellowed the memory did the ludicrous aspects appear. A forceful attempt at seduction can hardly be funny to a young girl. In describing the event as funny, the patient is resisting and suppressing a full recountal of the fright she experienced. Humor and ridicule are made to serve a defensive function. Score *Res*.

8. *Res (H therapist)*. Hostility toward the therapist can serve as a gesture to discourage him from further interpretative work. Of course some rational ground for such hostility must be found and, if one is not too particular as to what constitutes rationality, usually can be found. If the therapist has wronged the patient, and is himself in the wrong, he does not deserve the patient's cooperation and should meekly cease his disturbing actions.

Herewith an example of resistance by hostility to therapist. A compulsive woman patient was in a defensive and litigious phase. She kept querying the therapist on various matters. Among other things she asked, "Did you grow up in New Haven?" The therapist answered, "Why do you wish to know?" The patient could not answer. But she returned the next week to the subject matter, saying:

> [1]Now, last week I asked you a perfectly uh normal question. [2]I mean, I was just uh asking you, for instance, uh-I mean, you seem sort of elusive, too. [3]Uh, I asked you if you came from New Haven. [4]And-and uh [5](*Embarrassed laugh*) you answer me-uh "well," or say, "Well, why?" [6]I mean, I was just being

curious. [7]I mean, you uh you seemed a little bit uh the way you answered me, uh as if you were a little suspicious of the fact that I was asking you where you came from.

The patient feels that she has caught the therapist in an unreasonable action, viz. failing to answer a proper question. She thereupon labels the therapist as "elusive" and "overly suspicious." It is not she, the patient, who out of her fright is attacking and harrying the therapist, but it is rather the therapist who, failing to cooperate in a reasonable human gesture, has caused the patient to be angry. In asking social and personal questions of the therapist, the patient is also making the implicit assumption that she, the patient, is not sick and is not the one on whom the major responsibility of therapy rests. This sort of behavior would be insufferable did not the therapist realize that it stems from the patient's terror; it is a maneuver which she has learned in order to prevent others from increasing that terror by directing attention to it. As will be plain to everyone, the patient's action is a resistance of the most obvious kind.

9. *Res (silence)*. We consider silence as resistance because it stops the work of therapy. The sign for a unit of silence is *Res 5*. The "5" refers to the fact that five seconds of silence are counted as a unit. Actually, a pause under five seconds is not counted at all; a pause of five to seven seconds is counted as one unit; seven to twelve seconds is counted as two units; thirteen to seventeen as three units; etc. Examples for this category have already been given. *Res 5* is not used for silence occurring before the patient addresses himself to the work of the hour (as by sitting in a chair or lying on the couch); nor is it used for silences occurring after the therapist has indicated that the hour is up, though other significant scores are possible in the "pre" and "post" periods. Thus a parting shot at the door could be scored, even though the hour was technically over.

IV. DISCRIMINATIONS AND BORDERLINE CASES

We will present two examples of borderline scorings in which the issue is a choice between *Res* and some other score.

1. Res *versus* h-a. A male patient, severely troubled by feelings of helplessness, has had a dream in which the painted sign, "Colt Revolvers," appeared. When asked to associate to this unit of the dream he responded:

¹I've never shot a gun of any size. ²I've shot a 20-caliber gun, and shot some carbines and revolvers in the war. ³But I've never done any hunting. ⁴I don't own a gun, don't plan to. ⁵I have no thought about getting one.

The patient does a lot of denying in this utterance. He is not, however, denying any hypothesis of the therapist. Thus calling this "denial" a defense against therapy does not seem to be suitable, and the utterance should not be scored *Res*. No one has intimated that he suspects the patient of harboring aggressive intentions, and yet his speech sounds as if they had. He is reacting as if someone had said, "I have an idea that you are about to do something dangerous to someone with a gun." The patient stresses that he can barely shoot a gun, that he doesn't own one and has no thought of getting one. The view which is urged upon us is that the patient does have unconscious aggressive intentions which cause him great terror; it is to this terror that he is responding in the utterance printed above. The terror, like the aggression, is unconscious. The appropriate score would seem to be *h-a*.

2. *Conscious withholding.* Once the patient has committed himself to the therapeutic enterprise and has accepted the basic rule, conscious withholding is rare; nevertheless it does appear, and when it does it should be scored *Res*. If, however, a patient says, "I didn't tell you, but I'm going to tell you now," we do not score *Res*. In the nature of things, resistance can occur only in present time. Therefore a report of past resistant behavior is not scored as *Res* provided the patient now communicates what he has formerly withheld.

THE SIGN S

1. DEFINITION OF S

S is our abbreviation for the word "sex." *S* is scored when the patient describes erotic feelings or motives in himself. Definite genital feelings or reactions are the clearest sign of *S*. *S* is also scored when the situation described is one in which erotic reactions are expected to occur, or when we know that the patient has had erotic feelings in similar situations. Libidinous fantasies are, of course, scored as *S*. When behavior is reported which can be understood only by positing an unconscious sexual motive, *s* can be scored. Planning for sexual satisfaction is scored as *S*. Courtship and dating frequently contain erotic elements which deserve the scoring *S*. Homosexual and masturbatory behavior are scored as *S;* similarly for "heavy" kissing and petting, and for various categories of perverse behavior. We have used the one sign, *S*, for all types of sexual arousal, but another investigator could, if his problem called for it, add to *S* such subscripts as would distinguish (for instance) heterosexual, homosexual, and masturbatory behavior.

II. THEORY OF S

For the four and a half years during which we have pursued our study we have been torn between two different though not necessarily incompatible theories of sexual development. The *libido theory* of Freud (see Freud, 1905) is immensely appealing. It shows the broad pleasure-seeking impulse as having a pregenital history, especially in the oral and anal phases of training of the child. Genital sexuality appears first in masturbatory form, with the inevitable incestuous fantasies adhering to it. Under the pressure of the incest taboo and castration fear these early incestuous strivings are abandoned, and the child sets forth, changed and chastened, in the pursuit of other-than-family sexual objects. Pregenital as well as genital motives and rewards are subsumed in the final genital position. From the Freudian standpoint, sex is an extremely complex matter. Much that at first glance does not appear sexual at all does nevertheless influence what everyone else calls sexual behavior; much of prior erotic history is concealed and condensed in the final genital sexual act. We firmly believe that Freud's libido theory is not an arbitrary construction but one that was forced upon him and was only slowly developed in response to the facts presented by neurotic patients. We cannot abandon Freud's facts, just as he himself could not escape them.

On the other hand, the viewpoint advanced by *learning theory* (Dollard and Miller, 1950) cannot be ridden down. Just why is it that some sexual acts which are essayed are confirmed and strengthened as habit, while others disappear without trace? Learning theory tells us that hunger, bowel pressure, bladder pressure, and sexual excitement can all be treated as drives whose reduction creates habits. From the viewpoint of learning theory, furthermore, there is no reason to split the infant's action in consuming food into two components, a metabolic and a pleasure component. If one could adopt the viewpoint of learning theory, the laws of learning could be applied to the history of all these drives; as a result, much valuable auxiliary theory would immediately become available—such as the principles of generalization, discrimination, and anticipation.

There is, however, a distressing circumstance in connection with the use of learning-theory principles to explain human sexual development: It is, in substance, that these principles have not been tried out in this area. Whereas Freud's theory is tailored to meet the known facts, learning theory is not because its theorists have not yet thoroughly confronted the facts of neurotic development. Thus, whereas learning theory gives us admirable general principles, it fails of the direct application and pertinence to neurotic problems which would be required of a usable theory.

It may well be that there are elements in Freud's theory, never yet clearly brought out, which if high-lighted would make it seem much more similar to learning theory. It may also very well be that learning theory can be both complicated and made specific in order to deal with the facts of human sex development. Learning theorists plainly need to know the facts of sexual development as they are revealed in psychoanalytic work. At the present time, learning theorists by and large have no true conception of the mysteries which become visible when one studies human motivation in the sexual sphere; until they do have such a conception, learning theory obviously cannot be appropriately elaborated, however good a candidate for such elaboration it may—in the abstract—seem to be.

Freudian theorists, on the other hand, having come so immensely far in developing a realistic view of sexual life, seem content with a theory which is far less rigorous than it can—possibly—be made. Perhaps the effects of primary reinforcement are present in psychoanalytic data (Fenichel, 1945, p. 15; Freud, 1950) but the significance of such reinforcement is not appreciated by psychoanalytic theorists. Certainly the teaching of discriminations is of primary importance to the work of the analyst, and yet the experimental knowledge on this subject is not a part of Freudian theory. Freudians, who understand so well the great role of anxiety in human sexual life and in other human affairs, might get pleasure from knowing what has been experimentally established in regard to fear and conflict.

Future scientists may be able to choose, as we now feel unable to do, between the two theories; but at the present time we find ourselves teased and pulled by two somewhat different views on the nature of sexual growth and adaptation. Our own data present evidence which often can be viewed from the standpoint of either the libido theory or learning theory. No real synthesis of these theories exists, and yet neither one can be wholly adopted or rejected. We admire the beauty and intricacy of Freud's realistic exploration of sexual development. We do agree that early growth phases play an important role in influencing genital sexual organization. We find Freud's powerful notion of regression indispensable in understanding neurotic symptoms. Nevertheless, for reasons already given, we have not been able to adapt our signs to a strict libido-theory form of description. Thus we use L for affiliative motives, whereas Freud might prefer to view them as libidinous. We use *Dep* for dependent reactions, not subsuming it under sex as a kind of libidinous relationship. As already said, we use S for specifically erotic feelings and motives. We treat aggression as a drive, H, and disregard its linkages with frustration in the oral and cleanliness-training situations. Perhaps others will see more clearly than we now can the dilemmas of our position, and perhaps these others will find a solution for them. Perhaps advance of theory will provide a better guide to a system of signs. For the moment, we can only explain our problem and proceed.

III. EXAMPLES OF S

1. A sexual fantasy, if untarnished by fear, should be scored S. In thinking back to his adolescence one of our male patients recalled the following incident:

> [1]Where I remember hearing stories of high school kids and their orgies . . . where they . . . ran around in the nude in an outside area, for instance, with headlights for illumination and not being uh . . . I wasn't revolted at the idea. [2]I think I kinda wished I could get next to something like that myself. [3]But I never did.

A problem arises in connection with these sentences: Should unconscious anxiety be supposed to be present whenever one finds a fantasy? It could be argued that, since the action indicated by the fantasy was not carried out, anxiety must have been present. We have rejected this view. We feel that the fantasy should be scored *S;* in the present instance the first two sentences should be so scored. The third sentence, however, which indicates some regret that he did not act out what was depicted in the fantasy, should be scored *S-a;* here, it would seem, an inhibition is clearly shown. This procedure illustrates another fact about our scoring; such a paragraph as that above should be scored not in general but in detail. Each sentence should be given the score appropriate to it. The evaluation of the third sentence should *not* be carried back to the first two. The correct scores would be: Sentences 1 and 2, *S;* sentence 3, *S-a.*

2. A woman patient, speaking of her adolescence, reported a form of masturbatory behavior in which she indulged:

> [1]I am ashamed to tell you. [2]I used to put my—pull my pants up as high as I could. [3]And-and-and I'd leave them like that. [4]In other words, I'd make them tight. [5]Uh-you know there's an elastic at the waist. [6]And-and you could pull up the sides under the elastic and roll them up so they were sorta like-uh well like one of those ads.

In the same connection the patient said that she had tried to bribe her brother to touch her genitals and play with her, but he wouldn't do it. Of course, all of the above statements should be scored *S,* except the first one. The first statement applies to a difficulty in communicating that occurs in present time. Thus it should be scored *S-A.* The latter scoring deserves a further word of comment. When talking to the therapist, the patient doesn't experience the obvious genital excitement that she had experienced at the time of the incident reported. We believe, nevertheless, that as she remembers the incident and prepares to tell the therapist about it she does experience some slight conscious sexual excitement—perhaps only a slight "buzz," but one strong enough to be recognizable. The emotional reaction of the "buzz" is attached to the thoughts of the sexual incident; however faint, it should be recognized as sexual. The correct scoring of sentence 1 is *S-A.* The rest are scored as *S.*

3. If an utterance of a patient describes a situation where sexual activity would be bound to occur, we will often score it *S.* A much-married woman patient had begun to pick up her courage again; she spoke as follows:

> [1]I often miss . . . miss the feel of a man around the house, even
> a bum like my first two husbands. [2]I would like to . . . to . . .
> I . . . I guess . . . guess I would like to marry someone again.

Since marriage by definition involves sexual activity, this utterance must be counted as an expression of a sexual wish. It could
be argued that the patient is just lonely, but the sentences give the
impression that something more than loneliness is involved. *S* is the
appropriate score.

4. An inhibited man patient had innocently dated a girl who
was at the time having sexual relations with other men. Upon hearing this news, the patient experienced the excitement which had
not occurred while he was with the girl. He spoke as follows:

> [1]Well, it was obviously true in her case as I found out . . .
> later. [2]She was . . . she really went to town after I left. [3]Well,
> she got into very bad company. [4]She went down to the low spots
> in Chicago and was hanging out with prostitutes and gangsters.

This belated erotic fantasy should be scored *S*. Although it was
too late for him to take advantage of the girl's vulnerability, the
patient could still indulge in lascivious thoughts.

IV. COMBINED SIGNS

The examples of *S* combined with other signs are quite numerous
compared with examples of unalloyed sexual emotion. Many different possibilities are actualized in our combined signs.

1. *S-A*. This sign represents the situation where conscious sexual
desire is opposed by conscious anxiety. It is the sign, so to say, for
temptation. Some examples follow:

a. A married patient reported a mystifying event:

> [1]We were in the middle of having intercouse. [2]And then she
> burst out weeping uncontrollably . . . which to put it mildly
> ain't exactly what you expect. [3]And she sobbed. [4]And I was
> puzzled naturally and uh kept asking her what was wrong, was
> there anything I could do, anything I was doing.

Since the action being carried out is one involving intense sexual
arousal, *S* is bound to be involved in the score; however, since the
wife's behavior did arouse conscious anxiety in the patient, *A* would

also be involved. After this incident, the contemplation of inter-course would be more likely to raise anxious anticipation. The correct score therefore represents a conflict. *S-A* seems appropriate.

b. A woman patient referred to her bashful adolescence in the following way:

> ¹Anyhow, those girls in high school used to have parties. ²And . . . uh . . . I think they had kissing games. ³And I remember the first one I ever went to. ⁴Uh . . . well I just felt like a fish out of water.

The patient was tempted. She was titillated by the kissing game but anxious because of prior sexual training. Even though the patient does not mention the fact, such a game would be expected to evoke sex excitement. Since the conflict situation prevailed throughout the party, we do not credit her with undisturbed sexual emotion; it was tainted by fear throughout. The correct scoring of all units is *S-A*.

c. A woman patient described her marital life in disparaging terms. She said:

> ¹It seems—it seems to me that-that whenever I embark on any sexual activity before I start I have-have an oppressive sort of feeling like-like you have before a thunderstorm. ²You know it —that-that something is going to happen. ³And it-it is un-pleasant.

In this case the involvement in sexual activity is obvious; however, it is attended by anxious foreboding which also is conscious. The correct score is *S-A*.

d. In the following quotation a woman patient was telling about a friend of her father who visited the house when she was a small girl. This friend played with the children, and the patient found him somehow stimulating but also repulsive. Here is how she described the incident:

> PATIENT   ¹He was the friendly type, you know, always grab-bing at you. ²And-and he used to sing a song to my brother and . . . ³You maybe know it . . . ⁴(*Embarrassed laugh*) . . . "There Was an Old Sow Who Had Nine Little Pigs," you know that?
>
> THERAPIST   ⁵Mm-hmm.

PATIENT ⁶Well, I think that's the most horrible song that was ever written. ⁷And he used to do that snorting business, snorting like a pig is supposed to. ⁸And-and I just felt sick to my stomach. ⁹(*6-sec. pause*) ¹⁰When I was—somehow or other this is connected with my sex life. ¹¹(*Embarassed laughing*) ¹²I'll get to that eventually. ¹³I lose the thread every once in a while.

The vulgar snorting may remind the patient of the noises of sexual intercourse. At any rate, she knows that the incident is somehow connected with her sexual life. We infer that a conscious sexual motive is involved. She also reports aversion for the man, sufficient to make her sick to her stomach, a plain indication of anxiety. All the patient's sentences except the last two should be scored *S-A*. The terminal sentences should be called *Res*.

2. *S-a.* This is a much used sign which commonly designates a symptom or an inhibition. We present herewith an example.

A married patient experienced a peculiar and disturbing difficulty in his relations with his wife. As he described it:

> ¹It's a funny thing. ²But-but I don't seem to be interested in my wife sexually. ³We haven't quarreled or anything. ⁴I can't understand it. ⁵When I am away from her the idea of her is exciting. ⁶But when I'm with her, no dice. ⁷I'll know that I want to or ought to. ⁸But I just don't do anything.

For some reason of which he was not aware, the patient's wife had suddenly become frightening to him; thus he had the peculiar experience of being sexually interested in her but unable to act. The "buzz," so to say, was there, but something interfered between motive and performance. What interfered, of course, was unconscious anxiety. Sentence 5 should be scored *S* but all the others *S-a*.

3. *s-A.* This sign depicts the situation where one can safely infer unconscious sexual motivation but the patient is aware only of the anxiety produced by the unconscious motive. Since one of the elements in the conflict is unconscious, the other element, the anxiety, seems—to the one experiencing it—to appear without adequate reason. This type of conflict is known, alike, to the black sheep and the white. We present some pertinent examples.

a. A male patient was explaining how he had acquired his negative attitudes toward masturbation. He described in the following way the only time that his father had discussed masturbation with him:

[1]He uh took down a book that he had uh in the bookcase and
—uh, it was an old book, I remember, a red-covered book—
and uh . . . started reading some things out of it. [2]And it was
evidently uh—some book that was written by a theologian.
[3]It had some Biblical phraseology and-and terms in it, or
sounded Biblical, let's say, religious.

Because the subject was masturbation, we infer that the patient
reacted with some kind of "sex buzz" (central excitation) when he
entered the discussion. Since the patient does not report sex excitement, we assume it to have been not noticed by him, therefore unconscious. Since the patient's father was quoting from a book discouraging (damning, denouncing?) masturbation, we assume that
the patient felt conscious anxiety; in fact, the recollection itself was
produced by the patient to illustrate how his adverse attitudes
toward masturbation were acquired. The net transaction, therefore,
would seem to be: an unconscious sex tendency to which additional
anxiety is attached. We offer the score *s-A* as appropriate.

b. A male patient was charged with the duty of seeing his nine-
year-old daughter through her bath. He found himself interested
yet strangely repelled at seeing the genital area. He said:

[1]Well, I can't say that-uh in viewing her nude body that I'm
not attracted by . . . the area of her body that is uh slightly
curved for instance and slightly protruding . . . and the folds
in it. [2]I've noticed all that. [3]In fact, I uh-I know I found myself
consciously avoiding . . . looking at that part of her, and
consciously trying to be casual about wiping her off with a towel
after a bath.

The patient felt that he was curious about the body of his little
daughter; behind this curiosity we sense an unconscious sex motive.
He is aware, however, of his aversion. The two reactions are undoubtedly linked. The proper score of unit 3 is *s-A*. It would seem
that the patient here is struggling with an old problem in his life,
i.e. the urgent wish that, despite all reason, the woman would be
found to have a penis.

c. The same patient showed a similar reaction to his little girl
when he was required to put some ointment on her genitals. He said:

PATIENT [1]And yet I have specifically made it a point to have
my daughter apply that—rather than myself.
THERAPIST [2]Mm-hmm.

PATIENT   ³It's a very pointed effort on my part. ⁴Why, I don't know.

When the patient recoiled from external viewing, it would be expected that he would, even more so, refuse to touch his daughter's genitals. Again, the sexual interest is unconscious but the anxiety and the avoidance response to the anxiety are manifest. Score *s-A*.

d. In reviewing her childhood a woman patient called to mind an uncle whom she found particularly offensive. The discussion came up in the context of talk about her erotic development. She said:

PATIENT   ¹And then I had an uncle who used to come to the house. ²And-uh he was very noisy. ³Uh-well, I would say, he was a vulgar sort of person. ⁴He-he struck me that way when I was a child.

THERAPIST   ⁵How do you mean "vulgar," why vulgar?

PATIENT   ⁶Oh well ⁷(*Embarrassed laugh*) uh-he was—he was noisy. ⁸And he laughed loud and-and-and-uh drank and-and told off-color stories. ⁹And-and-and he smoked cigars constantly. ¹⁰And I-I don't know whether that had anything to do with my dislike of him or not. ¹¹But I-I can't stand the smell of cigar smoke to this day. ¹²And that's funny because I smoke myself. ¹³He used to handle us.

It would seem that the uncle teased and titillated the little girl in such a way as to arouse erotic feelings. Evidently she was not aware of that feeling but was aware of a sense of threat or danger in connection with the uncle. The whole transaction of unconscious urge and conscious threat became cued to the odor of cigar smoke. Score *s-A*.

e. As has been seen, unconscious incestuous motives can occasionally be glimpsed under the protective coating of well-socialized habits. An incestuous motive seemed to underlie a curious claustrophobic reaction of one of our women patients. She reported her feeling toward her brother as follows:

¹And-and my-uh feelings about him now have-have only really uh developed recently, I would say since he's gotten out of the army which was about six years ago. ²Uh I-I've gotten to a point today where I-I uh I don't even like to be in the same room with him. ³He-he-well, this is a funny thing to say. ⁴It's hard to understand unless you feel the way I do. ⁵He-he-he looms.

⁶He-he-he's so big. ⁷And-and he-he stands up a lot. ⁸I would say that he looms and hovers. ⁹And-and he gives me a feeling of being hemmed in. ¹⁰I—he-he always is touching people, and-and handling them and-and hugging them.

There is no doubt that the patient feels something threatening about her brother. Why she feels "hemmed in," however, is mysterious. We read the passage in this way: The brother's pawing and hugging arouses a sex motive in the patient of which she is not conscious; this motive, in turn, arouses guilt of which she *is* conscious. Her sense of entrapment represents the internal conflict —attraction to and horrified avoidance of her brother. Were it not for the unconscious conflict the patient could easily have dealt with the situation. The correct scoring is *s-A*.

4. *s-a*. It turns out, remarkably enough, that there are mental conflicts which do not register at the conscious level at all; neither the thrusting nor the denying component is registered in conscious mental life. The patient is vaguely aware that he has a problem of some kind, but its elements are unclear. The onlooker is, however, aware of a mystery. The mystery lies in the fact that unmotivated behavior is inconceivable; the observer is impelled to set up a motivational hypothesis even though the owner of the behavior, so to say, is unable or unwilling to do so. When such a conflict is played out in the sexual sphere the appropriate sign is the one we are considering, *s-a*. We will approach the understanding of this singular sign with a number of examples.

a. A married male patient gives a typical example of the *s-a* state of affairs when, in ruminating about his sexual life, he said the following:

¹There's something . . . I don't understand. ²But . . . in this, well . . . pattern of mine is consistently this matter of staying away from my wife during her menstrual period.

A sexual motive is imputed to the patient because he has repeatedly had enjoyable sexual intercourse with his wife though, in the present instance, he is not aware of desire for her. There is a force, however, which stops him from carrying out the sexual act. This force is not disapproval or rejection by his wife; rather the contrary, since he has said that she would especially welcome sexual intercourse during the menstrual period. We suppose, therefore, that it must be a force within the patient. The logical candidate as inhibitory agent is anxiety. The patient, however, does not experience his inhibition as conscious fear. He notes his behavior simply as something he does not understand, a consistent avoidance of his wife. The description, "unconscious sex motive opposed by unconscious anxiety," would seem to cover the ground. Score *s-a*.

b. Occasionally the purposive character of an unconscious gesture becomes entirely plain—to the outside observer, that is. An overly modest woman patient, well along in therapy, reported the following embarrassing incident:

> [1]Well, uh-I-I was taking a bath last week . . . [2]And I got out. [3]And I started to dry myself. [4]And I dropped the towel in the water. [5]It was very annoying because I have a back hall and I keep-keep the towels out in the back hall. [6]And I had to go out and get another one. [7]And it was cold. [8]And I was—I haven't done any—I've never done such a thing. [9]So, and the next night I was taking my bath. [10]And I started to dry myself. [11]And I dropped a towel in the water. [12]It happened three nights, believe it or not.

To the patient this singular repetition had no meaning at all except, perhaps, vexation at having to report such silly behavior. It was just a matter of dropping a towel several times and getting chilled when she had to run for a new one. The therapist, however, found illumination in the fact that there lived near by a young man who had a fair-to-middling view of the back hall. When her curious action was interpreted to her the patient blushingly supplied abundant confirmatory detail as to romantic thoughts about the young man. Before interpretation the patient's behavior would be scored *s-a*. (After interpretation the patient was able to hit upon less primitive means of attracting the attention of her neighbor.)

c. A sexually inhibited patient was constantly pressed and challenged by his wife to cooperate more frequently in sexual intercourse. It seemed that her pressure had an effect opposite to that intended. The patient described one of her ruses as follows:

> [1]Though uh . . . last February when this business of ours came to a head, she decided on her own that she was going to experiment with wearing nightgowns. [2]They weren't particularly attractive nightgowns. [3]And—as far as I was concerned that . . . approach didn't work at all. [4]There was no teasing at all there.

We approach the scoring of this incident as follows: Evidently it is a sexual situation, so this element must be recognized. Sexual desire, however strong or weak, is not conscious. Some force, probably best described as anxiety, is inhibiting the patient. Nor is this force conscious, since the patient claims to feel only indifference with regard to the nightgown device. Indeed, this ruse seemed to increase the patient's indifference rather than lessen it. The patient experienced the attempt to tease as an attempt to coerce. The description "unconscious sexual motivation inhibited by unconscious fear" seems to fit. Score *s-a*.

d. Occasionally the *s-a* conflict will seem visible to the naked eye —to the eye of anyone, that is, except the one who experiences it. A father of an adolescent daughter spoke of his child as follows:

> [1]Uh . . . I was just thinking of my-my daughter . . . after not seeing her for four weeks and then picking her up at the station as I did yesterday. [2]It's-it's amazing how I'm becoming conscience—I mean, conscious—of her growing up. [3]And uh-she seems uh . . . oh, more of a young lady than ever before. [4]And I'm becoming aware of her long lanky legs, lithe figure . . . and uh, not thinking of her as a little girl any more but a person that's got more advanced emotions.

We will not make anything of the patient's slip, using "conscience" for "conscious," since we have no additional information from him on this matter. From the nature of his thoughts, and from the details that he gives, it is apparent that the patient feels a rising excitement about his daughter which is basically erotic in character; dread incest-fear keeps him from more explicit fantasies, let alone overt actions. The patient is having to take his daughter out of the "little-girl" category and put her in the "nascent-woman" category. His own emotions, all unconsciously, "advance" with her development. Score *s-a*.

e. Patients frequently speak with yearning and regret of periods of their lives when they were ruled by rigid inhibition. Thus a man patient spoke of a "best" girl friend of his early young manhood:

> [1]And uh, never got around to any necking or petting. [2]I doubt if I ever kissed her. [3]And-uh we struck up quite a correspondence while I was in the army. [4]And-uh, I got one letter from her that uh, in which she said that she-she regretted that I had spent so much time in a band that I was in, and in

athletics and outside activities that I never had time enough for her, which was actually the case. [5]Our dates would be very infrequent, maybe three or four times a year. [6]Yet I probably liked her as much as any other girl that I ever met. [7]It was, as you mentioned last week, that type of activity does fill up a young person's life to the exclusion of-of sex in some cases. [8]That's exactly what happened to me.

Apparently the patient not only didn't "do anything" with the girl but, at the time, didn't even know he wanted to. Repressing the whole problem, both sex motive and fear, he plunged into preoccupying activity. The girl, however, understood the situation more clearly and tried to recall him, by letter at least, to the ways of love. As of the time reported, the patient was not aware of either his sexual interest in the girl or his fear of sexual thoughts and gestures. Score *s-a*.

f. It can happen that the patient himself is aware of the mystery created by an unconscious conflict. The man patient already mentioned, whose father read to him from a religious book on the subject of masturbation, said:

[1]And for some reason or other that book stayed with me. [2]It was—stayed in—in, even reached—when I got married. [3]I had a lot of textbooks. [4]I moved them along with me from my bachelor quarters to our home. [5]I thought I might use them for reference in my work. [6]And that was one of the books that-uh stuck around.

What is noteworthy here is his curious way of referring to the book, saying that it "stuck around." He speaks of the book as if it had a will of its own. Rather than assume, with the patient, that his keeping the book was a meaningless item of behavior, we prefer to assume that unconscious motives are involved. Since the subject matter is masturbation we assume that the motive is sexual. The patient does not mention conscious fear, and so we judge that the motive that holds the masturbatory striving in check is unconscious. The one derivative of the original conflict is the preservation of the book. Our explanation is this: By keeping the book the patient is maintaining his "no-masturbation" pledge to his father. The book is the symbol of that pledge. Score *s-a*.

g. A woman patient described one boresome day of her adoles-

cence when she was poking around the house and looking for something to amuse her. She came across a book of what were (for adults)
somewhat "sexy" cartoons. She described her experience as follows:

> [1]Uh-there were some books around the house-uh a collection
> of Peter Arno cartoons. [2]And I-I remember looking at them.
> [3]And-and-uh-uh the—there-there's one of a man and a woman
> with an automobile seat tucked under their arms. [4]And-and
> they're-they're stopping a motorcycle cop and saying, "We want
> to report a stolen car." [5]And-uh-uh-I-I really pondered that.
> [6]I couldn't see the sense of it. [7]Recently I came across this book
> and was flipping through it. [8]I saw the picture and burst out
> laughing because it-it all came back to me how-how often I
> sat and wondered what it meant and that it must be something
> because adults wouldn't be interested in it otherwise.

It would seem that the patient was on the prowl for sexy materials
when she first ran across the book of cartoons. In other cartoons
than the one mentioned she could observe bosomy women and
leering men. In the case of the famous cartoon which stumped her,
however, she had to repress the episode of sexual intercourse that had
occurred before the couple reported the loss of the car. Involved in
this repression was a nascent excited response opposed by unconscious fear. The first six sentences are a record of that inhibition
and should be scored *s-a;* the last two sentences, where she got the
point, should be scored *S*.

h. It is inevitable that the repressive sexual training of children
will have many strange-seeming consequences in later life. In the
context of a discussion of masturbation a woman patient reported:

> [1]Uh I-I know when we were little, well, we used to take naps
> in the middle of the afternoon and, of course, go to bed at
> night. [2]And we'd get tucked in. [3]And the last thing that, well,
> Mother would say when she was leaving was to pu-put your
> hands over your head. [4]And-and for years and years I thought
> that you had to put your hands over your head to go to sleep.

The patient is here reporting the circumstances of her training
against masturbation. The last unit of this training was the injunc-
tion, "Keep your hands over your head." The preceding units, the
excitement and the fear which was attached to the excitement (and
perhaps the words which were once attached to the excitement and

the fear), have all been eliminated by repression. In their place remained the patient's mysterious habit of being anxious if she slept
with her hands under the sheet. The appropriate scoring of this
transaction is *s-a*. Once the patient had challenged her curious habit,
she was able to recover recollection of both the sexual tingling and
the intense anxiety which had been attached to it by punishment.

5. *S:r*. As stated heretofore, *r* is the sign for drive reduction. An
episode of reduction of sex drive not only reduces disturbing sexual
tension but also reinforces the responses, including thoughts, which
have preceded it. Of necessity, the report of a sexual orgasm is often
preceded by units which are scored as sexual excitement.

a. A man patient gave this description of conjugal intercourse:

> [1]My wife uh came to bed without a uh—well, we went to bed
> late again last night, for about the fourteenth straight day, I
> think. [2]And even though it was the first night after a period-
> ending, and usually the night when we have some sexual action,
> she didn't wear a diaphragm. [3]She didn't think I would be
> interested since I had had a headache all evening and thought
> I'd pop right off and go to sleep. [4]But I showed an interest and
> got an erection. [5]And I asked her to-to install the diaphragm,
> which she did. [6]After very little kissing and caressing, we started
> having intercourse. [7]And uh we both went to orgasm in pretty
> short order.

All sentences except the last should be scored as *S;* the last is, of
course, *S:r*. The patient gives a curious technical description of
intercourse, devoid of the passionate overtones which many would
be able to report after such an experience. We hold, nevertheless,
that orgasm is orgasm and should be scored as the reduction of a
drive.

b. Neurotic patients are not the ones from whom one would
expect the most vivacious reports of orgasm. There is among them
a good deal of silent spoiling of the orgastic response. A male
patient said:

> [1]And again . . . I didn't . . . go to any frenzy or have any
> all-out emotional exhibition on my part, except that I enjoyed
> it. [2]But it wasn't too obvious, I don't imagine. [3]I enjoyed it in
> a passive way, I guess you'd say.

Although the patient's orgasm was evidently hampered to some
degree by fear, we nevertheless think that the appropriate score for

this report is *S:r*. The rule is this: If the scorer believes that the orgasm as it occurred would strengthen subsequent sex habits, even though less than maximally possible, the event should be scored as a sexual reward. Such was our belief in this case.

6. *S:j*. This sign stands for sexual jealousy. It is an emotion frequently and painfully experienced, although but few examples of the sign happen to have turned up in our data.

Sexual jealousy arises from the deepest and oldest conflict of our lives. Powerfully represented in literature, as in the anguish of Othello, it frequently produces important social consequences and even mental illnesses. It is one of the most dreadful and devastating aspects of the human condition.

S:j, though unmistakable, is a nearly indescribable emotion involving sexual and aggressive motives and attendant anxious reactions. It usually precipitates a torturing inner conflict. The storm of emotional reactions is such that the situation seems to require a special sign.

An intelligent male patient reported as follows his reaction to the news from his wife that she had been unfaithful with a friend:

> ¹When she told me I felt sick all over. ²And yet . . . I couldn't help asking her the details. ³I had to know when, where, how many times . . . everything about it. ⁴I wanted to strangle her. ⁵And I did beat her up. ⁶I couldn't seem to get it off my mind. ⁷By turns I felt sick. ⁸And then I would get cold all over. ⁹I felt terribly alone as if no one could ever reach me. ¹⁰I made up my mind I was going to kill Bill. ¹¹But then I thought I shouldn't because she was as much to blame as he. ¹²I felt something you might call grief at being betrayed by both of them. ¹³It was a whirlpool, the most awful experience I have had.

This "whirlpool" cannot be described by any of the other signs in our repertory; it needs the special score *S:j*. In this case, as in many others of this kind, the therapist doubted the wisdom of the wife's confession; it seemed that silent reform on her part would have been preferable.

V. DISCRIMINATIONS AND BORDERLINE CASES

The *S* sign and the *Dep* sign are sometimes difficult to separate. *S* can also be confused with *L* and sometimes with *H*. In all of these cases the scorer, in considering S, should stick to demanding evidences of sexual excitement, actual or implicit.

Different variants of S can also be confused. It is the latter possibility which we shall illustrate again at this point.

1. S *versus* S-A. It is sometimes a marginal matter to decide whether S is or is not alloyed by, and opposed by, anxiety.

a. Our patient, who had a tolerant older brother, went through a phase of fascination with his brother's girl which he reported as follows:

> [1]My chum of the time had two sisters. [2]And my brother went with one of the sisters. [3]He was—well, they were all young. [4]We were only in eighth grade. [5]And I think my brother was in high school. [6]And we were very close friends for many years. [7]And I fell in love with the—my brother's girl, of course, the big sister of my chum. [8]I used to sleep with my pal over at his home every . . . Saturday night practically. [9]And . . . we were only kids. [10]We used to . . . pop out of bed in the morning and . . . dive into the girls' room and climb right into bed with them. [11]And it was . . . just all pals and friendship, you know, nothing— [12]But I was really gone on her, of course, very much in love. [13]I . . . I 'fessed up to my brother one night, uh . . . that I was in love with his girl. [14]He just laughed [15](*Embarrassed laughing*) in my face, thought that was funny. [16]But to me, it was a very . . . deep thing at the time, as I recall.

This report of an Oedipus-like relationship with brother's girl was at times plainly erotic in tone; at other times the erotic feeling was opposed by conscious anxiety. Each of these situations is recognized in the scoring as it occurs; thus sentences 1-8 are scored S; sentence 9 is scored S-A; sentence 10 is scored S; sentence 11 is scored S-A; sentence 12 is scored S; sentences 13 and 14 are scored S-A; sentence 15 is, of course, scored Lf—; and sentence 16 is again scored S. The scoring represents the alternation between enjoyment of a sexual fantasy and the feelings of guilt which were attached to that fantasy. This example brings out that the scorer must follow the material *in detail,* and score discriminatingly.

b. The same practice of close, detailed scoring should be followed in every example. One of our patients had recently returned from

military service and reported an experience he had had in the bosom
of a family near an army training camp:

> [1]When it came bedtime I was just casually invited to go to bed.
> [2]And . . . the mother didn't seem to have any objection to my
> sleeping with her daughter. [3]She tucked us in, for God's sake.
> [4]And I saw the girl on my next leave also, at which time I
> discovered that she was fifteen years old . . . of all things. [5]You
> wouldn't believe it. [6]She-she was working at a store and cer-
> tainly didn't look anything like that . . . rather maybe seven-
> teen. [7]That was a rather shocking experience.

Pathologically permissive as apparently this mother was, she
could not quite allay all of the patient's anxious reactions. Sentences
4 and 7 must be scored *S-A* while the rest are simply scored *S*.

2. S *and* S-a. A conscious sex reaction can exist briefly and then
trip off an inhibitory response. The following example is a record
of sequence.

In describing his adolescent years a male patient spoke of visiting
burlesque shows:

> [1]I'd go to the strippers. [2]It was always-ah on the sly. [3]My parents
> didn't have the foggiest idea where I was. [4]There wasn't—I
> don't think it became an obsession or anything, maybe three or
> four times a year.

The first sentence should be scored *S*, thus giving the patient
credit for sexual excitation while watching the burlesque show.
Even though he went on the sly, he went. The other sentences,
however, we would score *S-a* since the patient recorded that he
didn't go very often, in other words, not as often as he wanted to.
Some force kept him from attending more frequently.

3. *Somehow aware but unlabeled equals unconscious.* We have
taken the position, and we are sticking to it, that the unlabeled is
the unconscious. We agree, however, that this is a decision that sometimes makes for discomfort. Patients will show that they are aware of
"something," usually some motive, even while they are not able to
name it or to describe the goal toward which it is pressing. At the
time, the patient cannot say that he is aware of anything; it is only
later, when he learns the nature of his motive (that is, acquires a
name for it), that he realizes he was disturbed and activated. Here is
an example:

Years after the event, a woman patient realized that "something" was happening when she was playing post office:

> [1]It's hard for me to say now because I-I'm thinking of myself now. [2]And I can't—I can't uh . . . I can't really remember exactly how I felt. [3]It-it's a hard thing to do. [4]But I think that I got some feeling of-of sexual excitement from those games that we played. [5]I'm-I'm almost positive of it. [6]But it's hard to explain that because a-at the time I wasn't conscious that that's what it was. [7]I mean that's-that's something that-that comes later.

The patient describes the situation exactly as we see it. She distinguishes between becoming retrospectively aware and being conscious of the motive at the time. When an incident of the past is reported in present time, we always score it *as of* the time that it actually occurred. Since the patient could not identify and label her excitement when she went into the room to be kissed by a boy, we describe her as being, so to say, excited but inhibited. The correct scoring is *s-a*.

4. *Don't score unless strong presumption.* Two antagonistic tendencies have been working in the development of our scoring system. On the one hand we have tried to push ourselves to the utmost to identify and label the fugitive elements of psychic life; in the development of our system we have pondered, canvassed, and struggled to find a sign for everything. The general principle is that the more detailed a scoring system can be, while still being reliable, the more useful it should be. But there is an opposite tendency also operating: *Don't reach for it.* If after brooding and debate the evidence is not strong enough to permit the assignment of a known sign, resist giving any sign at all. In this case one would use our omnibus sign, *Unsc* (for unscorable). We'll give an example of a scoring dilemma.

A man patient was describing a time during his fourth or fifth year when his mother was taken to the hospital. He said:

> [1]We lived in a small house near Booneville. [2]It was one of a row of houses. [3]It was here that my mother got sick. [4]It was during this time that we were taken care of by an outsider.

At the time of scoring we had only the bare facts reported above to deal with. Probably everyone would join us in assuming that a small child whose mother was suddenly taken to the hospital for an operation would feel some anxiety; thus one might risk the score of *A* for these lines. However, one could consider going further and supposing that, since the event took place during the Oedipus phase, some *S* was also present. One could conceive of such a score as *s-A* which would be read "boy unconsciously sexually attracted to his mother, and falsely connecting her illness with his surreptitious feeling, might be frightened that his motive had created her illness." After considering this possibility, not at all ridiculous in itself, we rejected it. If unconscious sexual feeling is to be imputed to the patient, there must be some evidence for it; in scoring, at least, we would not *assume* that such feeling occurs because theory calls for it. We describe the rejection of such a possibility as "not reaching for it," by which we mean allotting a sign only on the basis of definite evidence or an assumption with which hardly anyone would disagree (i.e. that mother's sudden leaving causes anxiety in small child). Thus, evidence for the *S* scoring is inadequate but the anxiety is plain enough for an *A* score. *Unsc* would be inappropriate.

THE SIGN Sigh

I. DEFINITION AND THEORY OF Sigh

We do not define *Sigh* in any erudite way but assume that the recognition of a sigh is a capacity common to intelligent people in our culture. Since the persons transcribing therapy protocols are assumed to be intelligent, it will be understood that they can identify and record the behavior of sighing. If sighs are inaudible they will of course be missed.

Sighing is thought of as a brief form of behavior. One cannot imagine a sigh lasting for twenty-five seconds. Each sigh is counted as a separate unit. If a sigh occurs in the midst of a sentence it is counted as a unit apart from the sentence itself.

II. EXAMPLE OF Sigh

The following example is from a young married woman. Her father is dying, and she is deploring that she has never been able to give him a grandchild. She spoke as follows:

PATIENT [1]I . . . we . . . both of us, my brother and I, I guess have been disappointing children. [2](*She sighs*) [3]I . . . I

know they . . . they both . . . both wanted grandchildren.
[4]And there aren't any. [5](*Crying while talking*) . . . [6]I was not
going to do this.

    THERAPIST   [7]Well, just let it come out.

    PATIENT   [8]Well, my . . . it's . . . [9](*Weeping while talking*)
it's just an awful mess. [10](*She sniffles*) [11]I didn't bring any
Kleenex. [12](*She sighs*) [13]I think that's another reason that . . .
[14](*She sniffles*) . . . that I feel so . . . so upset about Daddy
because he . . . [15](*Audible crying*) can't make plans.

Units 2 and 12 are scored *Sigh;* the rest of the units are scored
either *W* (weeping) or according to content. Although sighing is
obviously allied to weeping, one cannot be sure that it is always
merely an alternative to weeping; thus we provide a separate sign
for it.

THE SIGN W

I. DEFINITION AND THEORY OF W

The sign *W* replaces the word "weeping." In the case at hand it
does not seem sensible to separate definition and theory of the sign.
As to definition, one could say with Gertrude Stein that weeping is
weeping is weeping. One could also have recourse to the complex
definition in a standard dictionary. For our part, we say that weeping is what the transcribing typist can identify and report as weeping; of course the typist has not only the sounds which she hears
but also the context to guide her. Obviously this is a common-sense
definition of weeping, a definition which depends on the general
social training of intelligent people. It must be granted that some
barely audible elements of weeping may be missed in a case record.
The typist does not have the facial gestures to guide her in identifying weeping. We argue, nevertheless, that where weeping is important in a case it will come through strongly enough so that the
transcribing person will identify it and report it.

II. RULES FOR SCORING W

Each instance of weeping, no matter how short, is to be designated
as one unit; if it lasts for more than seven seconds it is to be counted

as more than one unit, the number of units being the number of five-second intervals occupied by the behavior, to the nearest five seconds. Weeping is to be scored as behavior even when it occurs simultaneously with speech. When it does thus occur both speech and emotional behavior are to be unitized and scored. Weeping includes such responses as sobbing, sniffling, and talking through tears.

III. EXAMPLE OF W

In the following example the reader will notice the way in which weeping is counted as a separate unit when it occurs during speech:

> PATIENT   [1](*She sighs*) [2]I felt that I had killed the baby, which I had, I suppose. [3]And I used to think about it. [4]I . . . I thought about it . . . [5](*She sighs*) . . . for . . . for years. [6]I mean . . . ah . . . I knew for instance I knew that if I had a baby it would have been born in December. [7]And . . . ah . . . and . . . and I . . . I used to think about it quite frequently. [8]I mean I imagined what it would be like. [9-10](*12-sec. pause*) [11](*She cries audibly*)
>
> THERAPIST   [12]I know this is hard to talk about. [13]But you try and talk about it a little.
>
> PATIENT   [14](*Weeping while talking*) [15]I . . . I just think about it. How . . . how old it would be. [16](*She sobs quietly*) [17]Think . . . I . . . sort of follow [18](*Weeping while talking*) . . . followed it in my mind as time went along. [19](*She sniffles*) [20]Funny. [21](*Weeping while talking*) [22]I always thought of it being a boy for some reason. [23](*Weeps while talking*) [24]I don't know why. (*She blows her nose*) [25]Well, he'd be about ten years now.

Sighs (as in 1, 5) are counted as units of sighing. Starting to weep during a pause (11) is counted as a unit. Sobbing and sniffling (16 and 19) are counted as weeping units, but in this instance blowing nose was not because the patient had evidently stopped crying. Weeping during a verbal unit is counted as weeping (as in 14, 18, 21, and 23) and given a score for weeping in addition to the score given the sentence itself.

THE SIGN Y

I. DEFINITION OF Y

Any affirmation not expanded is scored *Y*. If the affirmative statement is expanded, it is scored by its content (such as *H, S, Mob*) rather than as *Y*. Any agreement to perform some act is scored *Y*, unless it should be scored *Unsc* (as having to do with the pleasantries at the beginning and end of the hour, with the administrative arrangements, etc.).

If the data immediately after an affirmation (in the same sentence) —explaining, defining, or expanding the affirmation—follow without final pause and without drop to intonational level 4, scoring should be by such supplemental content.

II. THEORY OF Y

The score *Y* will often be used when the patient answers "yes" to a direct question of fact. For example:

> THERAPIST   You were ten years old then?
> PATIENT   Yes.

Presumably the patient's reply cannot be scored by emotional dynamics because his response occurs not in a stream of free association, where we have the associative links that make its meaning clear, but in response to the intruding stimulus provided by the therapist's question.

III. EXAMPLES OF Y

We will use *Y*, rather than a content scoring, when there is bare assent to a statement of the therapist:

> THERAPIST   You were angry?
> PATIENT   Mm-hmm.

But in the following more elaborated example, we would score by content:

> THERAPIST   You were angry?
> PATIENT   Yes, I was furious.

THE SIGN Unsc

I. DEFINITION OF Unsc

Unsc is short for "unscorable," a category to which are assigned any units which cannot be allotted to any other of our categories.

II. THEORY OF Unsc

Our system of signs was developed empirically; that is, we started not with a set of signs but rather with case material, and we developed signs as the material seemed to require it. Although in developing our system of signs we were guided in a rough way by psychoanalytic and learning theories, we did not start with a set of signs which would represent every event thought to be important in psychoanalysis or learning theory. This way of proceeding has the great merit that all of the signs we offer are known to be useful; we do not have a "theoretically" complete system with many categories for which no practical use can be found. On the other hand, our procedure has a defect: The creation and definition of signs is odious and laborious work; thus the scorers tend to economize on the invention of new signs, and as a result tend to stretch existing categories as far as they will go—and, the reader may think, sometimes farther than that. In general, however, we defend our empirical approach; the maker of the code always has his feet on the ground, he always has a concrete problem to solve. This merit outweighs considerations of theoretical nicety.

Unsc is by no means entirely a wastebasket category. There are certain indications for its use. Thus we assign to *Unsc* unintelligible materials, as well as sentences for which no category can be found and which do not seem important enough to warrant the creation of a new category. Also in *Unsc* are the trivia of conversation before and after the session begins and ends, and legitimate questions put to the therapist by the patient. Each of these subcategories will be discussed. *Unsc* is not combined with any other signs.

III. EXAMPLES OF Unsc

Other scorers may find uses for *Unsc* that we have not thought of; it is certain that an omnibus category is needed in any kind of a system which proceeds empirically. The omnibus or *Unsc* category would contain the unsolved problems. When an appropriate new category is invented, materials formerly chucked into *Unsc* could be put into the new category. Here follow the four kinds of materials which we now put into *Unsc*.

1. *Unintelligible materials.* Some case materials are directly unintelligible. They do not make grammatical sense, or one may not be able to guess what is meant to any degree at all, as in the case of psychotic materials, or one may have a guess of such uncertainty that he does not wish to act upon it. Material that looks like the following would, of course, go directly into *Unsc:*

> THERAPIST   You see them?
>
> PATIENT   Yes.
>
> THERAPIST   What do they look like?
>
> PATIENT   I see them in . . . in . . . ah . . . imaginary people. They are imaginary. They are there, but they're in a different dimension, you might say.
>
> THERAPIST   How is that?
>
> PATIENT   I don't know. Some . . . some brilliant mind concocted this. You can see them, but they . . . and they can see you. But you can just about vision that.*

If one usually would be scoring normal and neurotic case materials one might wish to assign these sentences from a hallucinated patient to the *Unsc* category; however, our system could be adapted to deal with psychotic materials by the invention of new categories.

2. *Materials at beginning and end of hour.* In a psychotherapy hour there is frequently a certain amount of desultory conversation before the therapy situation is "turned on" and after it is "turned off." Such conversation consists of pleasantries, casual instructions, and, sometimes, significant remarks which cannot be understood from a motivational standpoint. We are accustomed to allot such remarks to the *Unsc* category. Examples of such remarks would include: "Good morning," "See you tomorrow," "OK," "See you later," and the like. But "Sorry I'm late" is not casual, since it is an apology—presumably a response to anxiety. If a remark is meaningfully related to the therapeutic transaction it should be scored according to motivational content.

---

* Quoted from Gill, Newman, and Redlich (1954) by permission of the authors and publisher. Copyright 1954 by International Universities Press, Inc.

3. *Legitimate questions.* Questions which do not seem dynamically related to the therapy transaction can be allotted to *Unsc.* A patient with a cold may say, "May I borrow a Kleenex?" This utterance would be assigned to *Unsc.* "Can you see me at six instead of five o'clock?" would be assigned to *Unsc* if the request is a reasonable one. "Are you able to meet me on Friday?" would be similarly considered a justified question and scored *Unsc.* We realize that realistic-seeming questions may conceal unconscious motives; where such implications are suspected, the scoring should be according to such content. When the patient says the equivalent of "When are you going to start abandoning me?" his utterance should not be treated as a realistic question, even though it may be asked in such a form as, "When are you going on your vacation?" Perhaps all transactions between the therapist and the patient are unconsciously loaded; however it is only when this loading is obvious and calls attention to itself that we tend to score according to unconscious motives.

4. *Unscorable utterances.* When we invented this subcategory we had much hope for it. We thought that we would agree that many utterances were unscorable in the sense that they could not be assigned to any of our existing categories. Our reliability of judgment, however, was not very good. When one of us thought an utterance unscorable the other would nevertheless "make the stretch" and assign it to one of our existing categories. Reliability problems discouraged us from using the *Unsc* category and encouraged us either to fit an utterance into the scheme we had or to devise a new category to take care of it. Ideally the unscorable-unit category should be a kind of limbo of the scoring system. It should contain the problems not solvable in terms of the current system and not as yet pressing enough to require development of a new sign; but it did not work out very well for us as such a storehouse of problems-on-the-doorstep.

Example: The word "oh" was regularly assigned to *Unsc* when one didn't know whether the patient was surprised, pleased, or disappointed.

IV. DISCRIMINATIONS AND BORDERLINE CASES

The nature of our system could be quite materially changed depending on the degree to which scorers decided to make use of *Unsc.* Some scorers might decide to use only our categories of the very highest reliability and classify everything else as *Unsc;* others will probably want to follow us in attempting the finest differentiation of material which is possible. There may be some problems where it would be highly desirable to make liberal use of *Unsc,* as when one is interested in measuring aggression or fear in a record but not much interested in coding other materials. Each user of our system will decide in terms of his own problem what is his most advantageous strategy.

PRIORITIES IN SCORING CATEGORIES

Our most general instruction about scoring is to score the main point of the unit or units. Thus, if a series of sentences represents conscious sexual desire and a conscious fear to act sexually, the unit should be scored *S-A* without regard to the fact that the units may have a secondary significance as resistant. The salient point should be scored.

It often appears, however, that a sentence or series of sentences have several elements in them of about equal weight; for example, there may be an element of self-criticism and an element of anxiety, and in addition the utterance may be resistant. If no one interpretation of the sentences seems strikingly apt and if all seem possible, the scorer is likely to fall into confusion. To meet the situation, we are tentatively suggesting a series of priorities among categories. These priorities require that among elements of equal emphasis, those features which are *theoretically* most important should be preserved. We proposed the following order of priority:

1. Anything concerning the therapist or the transference, be it love, hostility, or what not, should have first call.

2. Anything resistant should have next preference.

3. Anything confirmative of an interpretation or demonstrating reasoning would rank third in choice.

4. Score by motivational content as usual, making an arbitrary choice of one of the equally salient alternatives.

As for us, although we have made the rule above, we have not found much use for this priority system. The meaning in terms of motivational content is usually plain enough so that one does not have to choose between more or less equal patterns of stimuli. Even though used only infrequently, the rule above could be very valuable at some junctures in scoring.

CHAPTER 5

The Signs of the Content-Analysis System: Categories for Therapist

SCIENTIFIC VIEWPOINT

THE THERAPIST'S SIGNS, like the patient's, have as their frame of reference a Freudian-behavioral point of view. They also have an anchorage in the behavior of the therapist as preserved in our recordings; they were suggested by real examples in actual cases. While our system has its origin in a definite point of view, the signs can, we believe, be applied to any therapeutic transaction.

CONCERNING MEANING

The problem of meaning is a psychological one and not semantic or philosophical. Without attempting to be exhaustive, we will say a few words about our stance on this problem. Meaning is best used to refer to a pattern or, perhaps better said, a patterning. Stimulus and response, question and answer, interpretation and rejoinder are bound into a common pattern. Thus the meaning of the question portion of a dialogue lies in the answer portion. Question-and-answer patterns may lie in the same person, as when one queries oneself, or the questioner may utter one part of the pattern and the respondent the rest of it. In the latter case the questioner only evokes in the *other* the latent answer portion of the pattern which already exists in *himself*. Persons who are members of the same society share a large number of such meaning patterns.

Words and sentences play a principal role in meaningful patterns, but by no means an exclusive one. Facial gestures are also important. Furthermore, unless words have the appropriate (that is, common) emotional responses attached to them they may lack an important element which gives meaning. Inward imageal responses may also be critical in giving meaning. Stimulus-producing proprioceptive reactions may at times be important. All of these responses—emotional, imageal, proprioceptive—may be enchained to one another and to sentence responses. Thus the cue of the sentence may evoke the response of the image, and the cue of the image, in turn, the emotional reaction. Portions of the meaningful pattern may be central rather than peripheral—in the brain and not in the gut, for instance.

As the speaker ripples along with his sentences, his hearers rehearse the responses which he produces and stimulate themselves to the response patterns which give meaning to his utterances. In children this kind of meaningful training can occur so slowly as almost to be visible to the naked eye; in adults it goes very swiftly, so to say, unconsciously, because of enormous overlearning of the units involved. Novel meaningful patternings (say, the sentences of a foreign language) have to be slowly acquired by adults as conventional ones are slowly acquired by children. Meaningful patternings are frequently connected to gross actions, to the observable responses of the great muscles.

That which is said to be "meaningful" is closely connected to the concepts of "higher mental processes"—reasoning, foresight, and planning. The units of response are the same for these different processes. The notion of "meaning" simply stresses a common patterning and organization which has been impressed upon them.

THERAPIST'S ROLE CRUCIAL

In the most general sense the therapist's behavior must be the crucial factor in psychotherapy. If it were not for something the therapist does or refrains from doing, some systematic situation that he creates, some relationship in which he participates, some atmosphere which arises out of his attitudes and viewpoints, there would seem to be no point in his meeting the patient. At the present time we conceive that some or all of the following factors are efficient: that the patient is determined to be rid of neurotic suffering; that he understands and accepts his job of revealing his thoughts and feelings; that a comradely atmosphere of investigation is established between patient and therapist; that the patient's unconscious fears of communication are systematically reduced by the therapist; that the therapist makes correct interpretations. Of all aspects of the situation the last is the most important. Our signs attempt to indicate crucial activities; they attempt to catch the therapist motivating the patient to try the hopeful responses, rewardingly reducing both conscious and unconscious fears, naming unconscious motives, connecting and discriminating, as may be appropriate.

THERAPIST'S SIGNS

The therapist's utterances are unitized and numbered exactly as are the patient's. We have defined six signs for therapists, as follows:

D for drive. Any unit which is thought to raise motivation in the patient is labeled *D*. A question would likely be scored *D;* a comment raising anxiety would be scored *D*.

Interp is the sign which is used for naming an unconscious motive, for connecting motives or ideas not previously thought to be connected, for discriminating meanings falsely believed to be related. We have sometimes lumped naming, connecting, and discriminating under the single term, "labeling." The therapist's utterances leading up to an *Interp* are sometimes also scored *Interp*. *Interps* deal with unconscious motives or conflicts, but they are not judged from the standpoint of tension. *Interps* may raise or lower tension and this feature is not isolated by a score.

Many therapists make a sound such as "mm-hmmm." This sound would be scored *M*. Therapists may say "yes" or "no" when these words do not have the sense of affirmation or negation but only signify the therapist is listening; in this case "yes" or "yeah" would be scored *M*. Thus *M* means mild agreement, mild assent, social facilitation, the mooing and cooing of social interaction.

Pretni is the sign for a serious error by the therapist. Thus marked countertransference reactions, egregious failure to understand what the patient is saying and therefore failure to interpret at the right time, notably incorrect interpretations would all be scored *Pretni*. We use *Pretni* grudgingly; if there is any plausible way in which the therapist's utterances can be favorably interpreted, any reasonable point of view by which what he does can be defended, we do not use *Pretni*.

R means reward. It is the therapist's sign which indicates reduction of tension within the patient. In the case of this sign, drive reduction is presumed to have its usual effect in reinforcing what the patient has just done, said, or felt.

Unsc is used for unscorable utterances of the therapist. An utterance garbled in transcription might be scored *Unsc;* an unintelligible remark of therapist would be scored *Unsc;* in addition, the prattle of noises between therapist and patient which sometimes occurs at the beginning or end of an hour ("Hi," "So long," etc.) are scored *Unsc.*

Each of the therapist's signs is always used singly, and never in combination with any other.

Signs Note Only the Most Critical Variables

Obviously, a very elaborate set of signs for the therapist's activity could be devised and, it may well be, should and may yet be devised. For the moment we are trying to get along with as few signs as possible; our signs are, we think, few but crucial. We intend to test whether they will be adequate for a rude description of therapist activity. In the sign system we have, the three vital variables are represented: the case where therapist motivates patient (D); the case where therapist rewards patient (R); and the case where therapist labels—that is, names, connects, or discriminates (*Interp*). From our standpoint, for this moment, these are the vital principles.

Two Rules for Scoring Therapist's Utterances

Rule 1. The scorer should read the patient's and therapist's statements up to the unit being scored. He may read a sentence or two beyond, but his score should be allotted primarily on the data which is available up to the instant of scoring a particular unit. Thus a scorer would not be expected to revise unit 200 of an hour (when it happens to be a therapist's unit) if unit 550 gives new information on the subject being scored. The scorer uses the information up to the point of the utterance and allots his score in terms of the meaning which the utterance seems to have at that point.

Rule 2. Many utterances have a dual quality; thus they may be at once rewarding and demanding. The dominant element in the utterance is scored and the subdominant element neglected. For example, the therapist may say laughingly to the patient, "And what of it?" The context may be such as to show that the therapist is brushing aside an act which the patient thought wrong. In such a case, despite the interrogative form of the "what of it?" the utterance would be scored *R*. Naturally, where the scorer faces such problems there will always be an element of error in the scoring.

The Sign D

I. DEFINITION

D is the sign used for drive or demand. Any therapist unit which is thought to raise motivation in the patient is labeled *D*. Thus a question would likely be scored *D,* as would a comment raising anxiety.

II. THEORY OF D

The patient comes to the therapist with a general wish to cooperate; this general wish is converted into particular and suitable motives by the judicious use of interventions labeled as *D*. All the drives which are effective in psychotherapy are, of course, learned drives (Dollard and Miller, 1950, pp. 229–32).

The conditions of therapy themselves set up strong motivational stresses in the patient. Thus the instruction to say what comes into his mind arouses motives to speak (and not to speak). To have the therapist say, "What's your problem?" or "What brought you here?" arouses motivation in the patient. The silent expectation that the patient will carry the burden of conversation arouses motivation.

Some units will be both demanding and rewarding; in such a case whichever aspect seems dominant should be scored. Allotment of the signs *D* and *R* should be determined almost entirely by the information preceding the patient's response to the utterance. The formal properties of the speech unit should be considered; if one is in doubt as between *R* and *D,* the fact that the utterance ends with a question mark might throw the weight toward *D*. We are again relying upon an intuitive skill of the scorer, i.e. his ability in case of a tie to decide whether an utterance is more drive-arousing or more rewarding. The main sense of the utterance should always be followed and risky or "brilliant" versions rejected.

III. EXAMPLES OF D

    1. *The patient has been discussing racial and religious discriminations as they apply to admission to a certain college. The therapist asks, "Can a person of any color or religion be admitted to this school?" Patient responds affirmatively.*

A request for particular information should be scored *D*. In the case at hand it was, to be sure, flattering to the patient to have the therapist show a lively interest in matters of racial and social justice —and thus there was an element of *R* in the therapist's utterance. Its main meaning, however, was indubitably *D*.

    2. *The patient has been explaining that her husband is somewhat antisocial, as follows:*

PATIENT   [1]I . . . ah . . . he acts like somebody who had . . . was afraid somehow to . . . to get in too thick with people—

THERAPIST   [2]Hmm?

PATIENT   —or to get to know any one person too well for fear he'd be hurt some way.

The therapist's "Hmm?" seems to indicate that he is not entirely clear about what the patient means; his remark is scored *D* as an interrogation.

    3. *The patient explains that his wife is too busy with her outside interests to entertain his friends. The therapist responds dubiously, "Yeah?"*

By his "Yeah?" the therapist indicates mild disbelief in the validity of the reasons given by the patient's wife for not entertaining. This disbelief serves as a motive to the patient to explain further.

    4. *The patient is speaking of an unhappy administrative situation in which he is involved; his whole work group is up in arms against an inefficient woman supervisor, but no one seems to do anything to remove her.*

PATIENT   [1]I . . . I think it's a matter for some of these other chicken livers [2](*Anxious laugh*) to do somethin' too. [3]Ah . . . I think it's a problem which concerns all of us. [4]And while at times I feel quite certainly that we're all re-reacting against her—

THERAPIST ⁴Why yes.

The therapist's agreement seems to incite the patient to solo action against the supervisor and thus would be felt as motivating. Score *D*.

5. *The patient has indicated that many divinity students "carry a church" while they are in school, thus serving as both minister and student at the same time. The therapist asks, "That's a fairly common practice?"*

The therapist's remark expresses a doubt that the practice is common, and thus the remark is motivating; it would tend to excite the patient to explain the matter further.

6. *In the case of the divinity student just mentioned, the therapist also asked, "Do you have a church at all yet?" This not only asks for information but also raises the question whether the patient should have a church, but doesn't. Thus it is motivating on two grounds, and it should be scored D.*

IV. BORDERLINE CASES

D is most frequently confused with the sign *Interp*, but it sometimes is also hard to discriminate from *R*. Here follow some examples of such close decisions:

1. *The patient has said that while in college he followed a premedical course but after college switched to the theological course. The therapist asks, "First a premedical?"*

The therapist's remark could be construed in two senses: It could be a matter of asking the patient to tell more about his change from the premedical course to divinity study; the question also has, lurking in the background, the notion that the patient's interest in psychotherapy might be related to his original interest in a medical degree. We believe that the latter understanding of the question should be suppressed since it is risky to make such an inference. The utterance should be taken at its face value as a question and scored as *D*.

2. *The patient has carefully explained to the therapist the manner in which he and his wife have intercourse; in particular,
the patient has emphasized the amount of time they spend
in foreplay. Invariably they dedicate an hour to it. The
therapist asks, "Where'd you get that idea?"*

What the therapist has done by his question is to condemn the
practice of long foreplay. In doing so he raises the patient's anxiety
and sets up a motive against the practice of foreplay. Such an au-
thoritarian intervention is not an interpretation. The therapist does
not attempt to modify unconscious forces in the patient by his utterance; instead he forbids practices which are consciously undertaken. We take no position, at the moment, as to whether this type
of intervention is wise or unwise. We note only that it is demanding
and drive-arousing. The therapist's score is *D*.

3. *The patient has been disturbed about having his analysis
recorded and asks the therapist if he is the only patient who
is being recorded. The therapist replies, "You're the only one
right now. But it's a very common procedure."*

The first of these two therapist units should be scored *D* because
it makes the patient more anxious to be "the only one"; the second
unit should be scored *R* because it reassures the patient against the
feeling of being unique or peculiar in being thus recorded. The
first unit raises motivation (for the instant), and the second unit reduces it. Of course the therapist could have dealt with this matter
by investigating other and earlier sources of the feeling of being discriminated against; in the case at hand he did not choose to do so. If he
had, his remarks could probably have been scored as *Interp*.

4. *In a long discussion a woman patient described her husband's behavior in the sex act as "aggressive." The therapist
inquired in what manner her husband showed his aggression. The patient responded evasively. She had described as
aggressive what would not ordinarily be viewed as such, i.e.
as involving some threat of damage or actual harm to her.
The therapist then remarked that there was a paradox at
hand in that the patient spoke of aggressive behavior and yet
did not describe aggressive acts as occurring.*

Should the therapist's pointing up of the contradiction be described as *Interp*? We think it should not. The therapist is engaging

in a kind of pre-interpretative activity (according to us); he notes a contradiction and senses some kind of problem but does not say that an unconscious motive is involved, nor does he apparently have any theory of the nature of such a motive. This pointing out of contradiction should be scored as *D*.

> 5. *A woman patient refers to fears that she might injure a newborn child of hers, and further reports having anxiety attacks at night in the month following the birth of the child. It is the moment before the end of the hour. The therapist says, "There's something behind that all right."*

Should the therapist's statement be an *Interp?* We think not. Although the therapist indicates that he thinks an unconscious motive is present in causing the anxiety attacks, he does not in any way describe its nature. Therefore we would score his comment *D,* to describe the setting up of a motivational stress toward future explanation by the patient.

It will be seen from the above that we take a narrow view of interpretation. That is because we would like to get as clear and unambiguous a measure of the *Interp* variable as possible. It comes easy to emphasize at this time that these categories are not divinely given but are rather set up by men who are trying as best they can to identify consistent and important variables.

THE SIGN Interp

I. DEFINITION

Interp is the sign used when the therapist names an unconscious motive, connects such motives to the situation which evokes them, or discriminates unconscious meanings or situations which have been falsely believed to be related. We have sometimes lumped naming, connecting, and discriminating under the single term, "labeling."

II. THEORY OF Interp

1. Interp *is unique. Interp* is the uniquely efficient variable in therapy because it is the ego-creating variable. If neurotic misery is to be reduced and, concomitantly, if adaptive behavior changes are to occur, new ego (that is, higher mental) units must be tried out

and learned. Can the patient himself hit upon these new units? It would be most remarkable if he could, since he has already spent part of a lifetime trying and failing to do so. It is our belief that the patient cannot provide the necessary units and that the therapist must do so if therapeutic progress is to occur. When the patient is experiencing mysterious emotions the therapist provides the verbal labels which make them manageable. It is further true that the verbal units the therapist supplies cannot be any old units but must be exactly the right ones, fitting tightly to the emotional responses and feelings which the patient manifests. The patient's part in the task of therapy is to put himself in a position to suffer emotional reactions and feelings either by recounting past events (not necessarily far past) or by responding in the relationship to the therapist. Then, when emotion is active, the therapist must be ready with his *Interp*.

2. *Forms of interpretation*. We will list some forms of interpretation without pretending to be definitive or exhaustive. The idea is to clarify matters as far as we can see them now.

a. Naming an unconscious motive is certainly one form of *Interp*. A patient with a dreadful abulia may be asked by the therapist, "Are you on strike because I am leaving shortly for my vacation?" The therapist in this way identifies an unconscious rebellious motive. (In the case mentioned, the abulia lifted when the interpretation had been made.)

b. Another type of *Interp* is the evoking by the therapist of a motive to search for an unconscious conflict, that is, to identify a paradoxical situation. When behavior provides a paradox, unconscious motives are likely to be operating. The therapist may recognize that such a situation exists although the patient does not; if the therapist then motivates the patient to discover the situation for himself, such an intervention should be called an *Interp*.

c. Eliminating rationalizations is an interpretative activity. The patient often has explanations that do not properly explain his behavior. Eliminating any irrational explanation opens the way to the discovery of the role of unconscious factors.

d. Providing the verbal units that permit discrimination between past and present is interpretative. A fear appropriate to childhood and still unconsciously active may be extinguished when *differences* between the external situation of childhood and that of the present are highlighted.

e. Providing units for generalization of emotional response is also decisively interpretative. For a patient to know, for instance, that everyone feels certain basic emotions, often unconsciously, can reduce the painful sense of being isolated or odd.

3. *Minimum requirement for* Interp. As a minimum, a therapist's utterance which qualifies for the score *Interp* should point to some specific unconscious motive. For our purposes it is not enough for the therapist to assert that an unconscious motive exists; in addition the scorer should have some idea as to the nature of this motive. Similarly, it is not enough for the therapist to point out that the patient faces a problem, contradiction, or paradox; he should specify at least one of the motives operating to produce the paradox if his utterance is to qualify as *Interp*.

4. *Therapist's hypothesis re unconscious factors.* We have said that in order for a sentence of the therapist to be scored *Interp* he must identify a particular unconscious motive. How can one tell what his hypothesis about an unconscious motive is? The following considerations would seem to bear on this point:

a. That the therapist has a hypothesis at all may be inferred from the fact that he is known to be using some well-known theory. Thus, if the patient shows a depressive reaction at the news that the therapist will be out of town to attend a scientific meeting, the therapist might inquire if the patient feels the hiatus in treatment as a rebuff. Such a remark, which accords with psychoanalytic theory, would be an indubitable *Interp*.

b. If a mystery appears in the data preceding the therapist's utterance and his intervention is related to this mystery, his utterance would be called *Interp* if it refers to unconscious factors.

c. In order for a sentence of the therapist to qualify as *Interp,* it is not necessary that the patient immediately adopt the therapist's viewpoint. Correct *Interps* do dissolve resistance and lead to the production of new information, but it is not necessary that they should do so immediately in every instance. The patient may reject a correct *Interp* immediately but accept it eventually. Thus the decision to score *Interp,* while highly dependent on information prior to the sentence being scored, is rightly independent of behavior that immediately follows it. *Interp* is scored when the scorer has good reason to believe that the therapist is referring to a specific unconscious motive of the patient.

5. *Concerning relations of* Interp *and* R. Both *Interp* and *R* can

change the patient's behavior; it is believed, however, that different kinds of change occur in the two instances. R can strengthen response in the immediate therapeutic situation; it can reduce tension and thus bring immediate relief; it can help to keep the transference a positive and facilitating factor. What R cannot do is affect the patient's behavior in a more general way, especially as it is related to events outside of the therapeutic situation. R is believed to be a kind of local facilitating force aiding therapy but limited to the therapeutic situation itself; whereas *Interp* is believed to mediate drastic and general behavior changes. Unless unconscious forces are labeled, the occurrence of R within the therapeutic situation leads only to a temporary amelioration—but, perhaps, to a more remote and permanent disappointment. The true *Interp,* worked out well, can change the course of higher mental and emotional events throughout the patient's life.

In accord with the principle of getting an unambiguous measure of *Interp,* we are accustomed to exclude doubtful and marginal cases. If in serious doubt we decide against scoring *Interp.*

III. EXAMPLES OF Interp

1. *Labeling*

> *The therapist noticed that during the current hour a woman patient showed marked signs of disturbance in talking. There were more false starts, more promising trails that came to a sudden dead end, and much more silence than usual. At one point in the hour the therapist said: "I had the impression that you are somehow slowed down today—or is it depressed?"*

The patient was not in any way aware that there was anything different about her behavior on this day from that on any other. The therapist was therefore calling attention to an *unconscious* mood reaction and giving it a label, "depressed." The patient agreed, come to think of it, that she was feeling "low," and this agreement opened up the further question, why?

2. *Labeling*

> *The patient has told the therapist some things the disclosure of which might be a betrayal of confidence—and is suffering from the thought of his treachery.*

THERAPIST [1]Does that mean that you feel a bit ashamed of having talked as you have today?

PATIENT [2]No.

THERAPIST (*Quizzically*) [3]No?

The therapist's first remark would be scored as *Interp* since he is pointing to an unconscious motive of shame; however his second remark, the quizzical "No?" would not be called *Interp* even though it follows upon, and is in a sense a repetition of, the interpretative remark. By this example we mean to emphasize that we use *Interp* quite narrowly. The "No?" would be scored as *D*.

3. *Labeling*

The patient, a man, has been concerned about the fact that his interview was being recorded and especially about the possibility that people in his profession would have access to the recording. In opposition to his own feelings, he also expressed the somewhat defiant view that it didn't make any difference to him if people did hear his records; he really wanted, he said, to cooperate with the institution. The therapist, not quite accepting this declaration of loyalty, said: "Are you quite sure that you are not hiding some further feelings about this matter?"

The therapist evidently believed that the patient had not revealed the full extent of his negative feeling about recording. He realized that the patient had a wish to please the therapist and a fear of the consequences of not pleasing him, and knew that these wishes might lead the patient to restrain full expression of his negative attitude. The question is thus permissive of negative expression. It should be called *Interp*.

4. *Connecting two problems*

A man patient had been discussing his lack of initiative in regard to various life problems. He had bewailed his inability to start things, to make friends, to make prompt and reasonable decisions and, in general, bewailed his failure to "take over." In another and separate connection he had spoken of feelings of sexual inadequacy with his wife. At an appropriate point the therapist said, "You think, conceivably, that your lack of decisiveness colors your relationship with your wife also, and perhaps has something to do with the sexual problem?"

Here the therapist is pointing to a possible unconscious connection between two spheres in which the patient feels inadequate. Such an interpretation, if accepted, raises the question: What might the connection be? Score *Interp.*

5. *Preparatory to an* Interp

> *Early in the therapy sequence the patient came late for an interview. The therapist asked, "Was there some problem about the appointment time?"*

This kind of question is preparatory to an interpretation. The therapist has it in mind that the patient may have been detained by reasons beyond his control, but he also has it in mind that failure to come on time may represent an unconscious wish to avoid therapy. By his question the therapist is structuring the situation so that he can interpret such an unconscious wish to escape if it is present. Score *Interp.*

6. *Discrimination*

> *The patient had explained that his wife had recently had a baby and was still recuperating in a hospital. He continued as follows:*
>
> PATIENT   [1]I think I miss my wife also. [2]And I think I feel a little jealous that she's being able to rest in the hospital and have all this nice attention.
>
> THERAPIST   [3]Whereas?
>
> PATIENT   [4]Well, more or less—well, I've told you what I've been doing. [5]*(Embarrassed laugh)* Uh-it's obvious tha-that—
>
> THERAPIST   [6]You mean whereas you have your nose to the grindstone. That sort—
>
> PATIENT   [7]Yeah, yeah.

In his last remark about "nose to the grindstone" the therapist tries to express the patient's unconscious sense of resentment that his wife is resting softly in the hospital whereas for him the cares of life have been increased. The child within the patient is registering its voice as though to say, "What about me? I need care, too. She has it soft, and I have it all too hard." The therapist here makes a discrimination between the patient's official attitude toward his wife and his actual unconscious feeling toward her; the unit is scored *Interp.*

IV. BORDERLINE CASES BETWEEN Interp AND OTHER SIGNS

1. *Borderline between* Interp *and* D

a. *A man patient had just explained to the therapist that he had been accustomed to masturbate throughout his married life. The therapist asked him, "What do you think about while you masturbate?"*

By implication the therapist has given the patient some new information, i.e. that fantasies occurring during masturbation have some importance for the treatment; however, the therapist did not deal with unconscious motives or attitudes. Therefore this comment should be scored *D*.

b. *In the first hour of therapy the following exchange took place:*

PATIENT ¹I've told all this before to the admitting officer. ²Do I have to tell it again?

THERAPIST ³I know a bit about it. ⁴But I would rather hear it as you would put it yourself.

This unit might be considered a part of the instructions which set up the therapy situation; it should not be viewed as *Interp* because the therapist is not directly labeling nor is he pointing to an unconscious motive. Therapist unit 4 should be scored *D*.

c. *The patient explained that his wife is a somewhat dependent person and that he thinks of himself as overactive, possibly a little overbearing. When he feels rising within him tendencies to coerce his wife, he tries to restrain himself. The therapist asks, "So you have to watch out for her against yourself, is that it?"*

The therapist is here repeating and reflecting what the patient has already said; nothing new is added, no attempt to indicate an unconscious motive is made. The unit should be scored *D*, since it tends to emphasize the subject matter and to require the patient to elaborate it.

d. *Of the same patient who complained that his wife lacked ability to make ordinary decisions the therapist asked, "Did the fact that your wife lacked initiative strike you before you were married?"*

If this statement of the therapist had been followed up by another, to wit, that a person may unconsciously pick his wife for the very traits he later objects to, the statement would have been viewed as initiating an interpretation. Since it was not followed up by a direct statement of the hypothesis about the unconscious, it is viewed as an ordinary question and is scored *D*. This is one of those cases where, in order to judge a statement of the therapist, one has to look forward and see how he develops his theme.

> e. *Again, this is the man who has so frequently expressed the fear that a supervisor is destroying the morale of his department. The patient was debating whether he should go over the head of the supervisor and express his misgivings to a higher authority.*

> PATIENT   [1]I'm afraid to go upstairs because it might drive the supervisor off his rocker.
> THERAPIST   [2]Do you really believe things are organized in such a way—that one person saying something to another can be the thing that's responsible for a breakdown which otherwise wouldn't have occurred?

We view the therapist's sentence here as *D* rather than as *Interp;* it is scored *D* because the therapist discusses the reality issue but not the patient's unconscious conviction that one gesture by him could destroy another human being. If the therapist had made the point that the patient felt his own thoughts could be dangerously causative, we would have scored the units as *Interp*.

2. *Borderline of* Interp *with* R

> a. *A woman had shown some fear about having her conversation recorded and, in the very same hour when this fear was expressed, had mentioned a frightening dream in which intruders were breaking into her room. These intruders were provided, strangely enough, with microphones.*

> THERAPIST   [1]Maybe the intruder in your dream is somehow allied to my recording your words in this situation. [2]Is that possible?
> PATIENT   [3]But if it is, it's all unconscious.
> THERAPIST   [4]Even if unconscious, the idea is still yours. [5]It's a force that causes action within you. [6]However I don't mean to

imply that you have been withholding information. ⁷It is really something that you haven't been aware of.

The therapist's units 1, 2, 4, and 5 quoted above would be scored *Interp;* they attempt to identify unconscious attitudes and fears. Units 6 and 7, however, are not scored as *Interp;* rather they should be designated as *R.* They are reassurances rather than means of identifying unconscious attitudes.

> b. *The patient had been annoyed about being recorded but then reproached himself with the thought that he was probably being resistant by complaining about the recording. The therapist asked, "Why should this be resistant?"*

The therapist evidently felt that the patient translated the word "resistant" as "bad." The therapist wanted to encourage the patient to bring out doubts and misgivings about any aspect of therapy; he therefore reassured the patient by this query that it was not "bad" to do so. Viewed casually, the therapist's question might be thought of as interpretative, but under closer scrutiny it appears to be a form of reassurance which operates at the conscious level, and probably at the unconscious level as well. Score *R.*

THE SIGN M

I. DEFINITION

M means mild agreement, mild assent, social facilitation on the part of the therapist—a part of supportive social interaction.

II. THEORY OF M

Many therapists have a sound such as "Mm-hmm" which signifies that they are listening to what the patient is saying. It is a mildly reinforcing utterance. It certainly indicates that the therapist is not objecting to what the patient is saying, even if it also indicates that he is not "heavily" accepting what the patient is saying.

The sense of being heard and understood is valuable to the patient in carrying on his work; this sense is conveyed, to a mild degree, by *M.* The therapist's alert though relaxed attention is one of his important contributions to the therapeutic situation. The utterance of "Mm-hmm" indicates that this useful attention is being accorded to the patient.

The utterance of M does not necessarily commit the therapist to belief in all that he hears. As he listens he reserves the right to accord belief to some of what he hears and to doubt other parts of it. This delay in judgmental reaction is not compromised by his use of M.

M is the score for all ordinary cases of "yeah," "mm-hmm," "I see," "yes," and other evidences of mild agreement. "No" could be scored M if it is an answer to a question like, "Do you mind if I smoke?"—where the question itself is a mere form of politeness and the questioner has no doubt that the answer will be affirmative. What is important is that the verbal response be a token of mild social affirmation.

III. EXAMPLE OF M

In answer to several questions from the therapist the patient was explaining the kinds of degrees that were available to social workers in the school she attended. She finally said that a Ph.D. was not available, but a master's degree could be earned. The therapist replied, "I see."

The issue as to social-work degrees seemed of no great importance in this case. Nothing vital for the therapy seemed to hang upon it. The therapist was in a very mild way exploring the patient's professional background. When he said "I see" he was registering understanding and mild reward.

IV. BORDERLINE CASES

There is only one borderline case of any importance: the occasion when a "yes" or "no" has a much sharper meaning than ordinarily. In such a case "yes" or "no" might be scored R. We believe that such a coding should be very rare. If a patient, worried about the outcome of a study by the Cancer Clinic, asks "Do I have cancer?" and the therapist answers "No," his utterance could not be viewed as mildly supportive; it would necessarily have sharp anxiety-reducing value. Therefore it should be scored R. If a patient in a psychiatric hospital asks his therapist, "May I leave the closed ward and go to an open one?" and the therapist is able to answer "Yes," this utterance of the therapist should be scored *R*—granted of course that the scorer knows that the patient has an intense wish to escape from the closed ward. Thus "yes" and "no" would occasionally, but only very occasionally, be scored *R*.

PRETNI

I. DEFINITION

Pretni is the sign for an error by the therapist. The reader will notice that the scheme for the name has been borrowed from Samuel Butler: *Pretni* is *Interp* spelled backward.

II. THEORY OF Pretni

If the *Interp* sign says, by inference, that the therapist is doing something useful and correct, there should be an opposite sign that indicates an error or "boner" by the therapist.

Two such signs can exist only in a consistent theory of therapy. Thus it should be immediately granted that *Pretni* would be defined differently according to different theories of how therapy occurs and of how the therapist's intervention brings it about. In the common-sense theory of therapy which is so widely in fashion it might be viewed as an error if the therapist failed to instruct the patient to forget his neurotic problems and be like other people. In the "uncovering" theory of therapy it might be scored as a *Pretni* if the therapist failed to call attention to unconscious emotions and assumptions displayed by the patient. In an old-fashioned military theory of therapy it would be a mistake if the therapist failed to try to make the consequences of not fighting seem worse than those of fighting. In a Jungian theory of therapy the therapist would err if he failed to detect and note the presence of inherited, archetypal images in the productions of his patient. Similarly a Rankian therapist could be imagined who would be mistaken if he failed to relate the anxieties of the patient to the birth experience. Thus every theory of therapy would have its rights and wrongs, its obligatory gestures and its alleged errors. It follows that scorers, following different therapeutic theories, would score *Pretni* at different points in a case transcript.

We have invented the *Pretni* sign because we conceive that to locate such points, as they would be viewed by different theorists, could lead to detailed, objective discussion of theoretical differences. It seems possible that setting up the problem in this way—that is, by identifying the therapist's responses as correct or incorrect—could help reduce theoretical differences to testable form. Instead of saying, for example, "One theorist believes the matter should be approached by analysis of the relationship," one could say, "In the face of such-and-such data, theorist A believes that the therapist should say or convey so-and-so."

Pretni should be scored only for what are believed to be big and important errors of the therapist. If an error is viewed as trivial, mincing, or finespun *Pretni* is not used.

Using as context a Freudian-behavioral theory of therapy, and possibly from any other kind, we would suppose that no therapist can follow perfectly the behavior and emotions of the patient. Often such emotions are unconscious and the cues revealing them are doubtful. The therapist will make errors inevitably. Nevertheless, these considerations should not prevent one from scoring *Pretni* when it is deserved. If the therapist recoups himself, rapidly orients himself, and repairs his *Pretni* his new gesture should simply be scored *Interp*. We assume that no therapist can ever carry out a case as well in the fact as later study of the record would indicate was possible. At one time or another he is bound to be "behind" his patient, confused or temporarily lost. Thus we estimate that *Pretni* scores would always be present in the work of any therapist.

Types of Pretni. Viewed from a Freudian-behavioral frame of reference, there are four types of therapist errors which we can now identify. They might be described as the *countertransference error,* the *failure-to-interpret error,* the *incorrect interpretation,* and the *technical error.*

In the first type, the countertransference error, the therapist's own needs are allowed to enter into the therapeutic transaction. Instead of helping the patient to solve his problem, the therapist unwittingly attempts to solve a problem of his own. In doing so the therapist withdraws that benign, absorptive attention which is what the patient pays for, and begins to attend to his own needs and motives. The least that can happen in such a case is that the patient feels bewildered. It can also occur that the patient will feel severely rejected.

The second type of error, failure to interpret, is a sin of omission.

As such it is hard to catch. The error occurs when the therapist fails to understand, in an emotional sense, what the patient is saying or acting. When the data cry out for a particular interpretation and the therapist fails to make it, we score this as *Pretni*.

The third kind of *Pretni,* incorrect interpretation, occurs when a particular interpretation is called for by the data that the patient produces—but the therapist makes a different interpretation. This type of *Pretni* can cause only bafflement and confusion in the therapy. We expect that it will prove to be the most common, since the therapist often may feel that something is called for from him but be uncertain what to say; reacting to the motive to "say something," he will say what is actually irrelevant. Of course in this case, as in all others, unless such errors can be reliably detected by at least two people, no *Pretni* exists.

The fourth or technical error occurs when the therapist breaks the rules of his particular technique of therapeutic action.

There may be other types of therapist's errors which we have not yet learned to identify. We will now exemplify from actual case material those types of errors that we have learned to notice.

III. EXAMPLES OF FOUR TYPES OF Pretni

1. *Countertransference error.* A patient remembered in the course of her thoughts that she had recently been reading a book by Dr. Otto Rank.

> PATIENT [1]I got a great deal out of the book by Rank. [2]Of course, it was all at the rational and not at the emotional level. [3]But still it was very enlightening. [4]I wondered if you would suggest something perhaps along the same line, maybe with a slightly different viewpoint?
>
> THERAPIST [5]I think Rank's work has some valuable emphases. [6]But I have certain differences of opinion with him in regard to some major principles. [7]You know he was trained first as a Freudian analyst . . .
>
> *Thereupon therapist gave a discussion of Rank's defection from the Freudian movement and his subsequent history.*

The patient has shown by her utterances that the issue of Rank versus Freud means little to her. As far as she is concerned Rank's views are a variant of Freudian views and not in competition with them. To the therapist, however, the Rankian schism is a matter of great emotional importance; thereupon, driven by his own need, he gives the patient a kind of lecture on a matter on which she has little interest. In the case at hand, the therapist's needs have taken the center of the stage and the patient is an uneasy witness as he responds to them.

2. *Failure to interpret*

a. *We trust the reader will believe that the woman patient reported on here had shown many dependent tendencies and had reacted with anger when they were frustrated. In the case at hand, however, she was reacting in a different way. She stressed how much she enjoyed being a free-lance writer despite the hardships of her profession. She emphasized that she would not return to editorial work on a magazine in any conceivable case. She described the advantages of free-lance work: keeping her own hours, meeting new people, and enjoying the exciting change of tasks. She added that she felt better and had actually gained weight after making the change from a fixed job to free-lance work. To all this therapist said nothing. At the end of her discussion the patient changed the subject, saying, "Now let's see what's been on my mind."*

Since the patient was constantly victimized by her dependent needs, it is a grave error for the therapist to fail to understand these. In the material just cited the patient is emphasizing her joy at finding that she can live an independent economic life. She presents facts which emphasize that she is not dependent, but she fails to notice that there remains the problem of why she gets such extraordinary satisfaction from the free-lance work, which is feared and avoided by so many. The therapist might have moved in on the subject by saying, "It seems to give you unusual satisfaction to know that you can be economically independent. How does it happen that independence means so much to you?" It does not matter too much whether or not the reader agrees with us as to what the therapist *should have* said; what matters is that he understand the structure of this kind of error. If the reader is a therapist, and if he studies therapy protocols, he will rapidly find for himself instances where he thinks the therapist should have talked instead of remaining silent.

b. *Patient recounted that she was playing cards with her mother and her two aunts when her sister-in-law entered the room. The sister-in-law selfishly wanted to get into the game and, since she was a guest, patient's mother deferred to her. The mother made a half-hearted gesture as if to withdraw from the game herself. The mother's gesture stimulated the patient to offer to quit. The others accepted patient's offer. Patient got up from the table but was suddenly so outraged that her sacrifice was accepted that she stamped out of the room and slammed the door. She told the therapist:*

[1]I was mad, I guess. [2]It embarrasses me to tell you that. [3]And I felt rejected. [4](*Anxious laugh*) [5]I felt they didn't want me. [6]And I was going to show 'em I can get along without them.

Therapist made no interpretation at the end of this discussion.

As is often the case, the therapist could have taken up this passage in a number of interpretative ways. He might have said that the problem of rejection is an important one for the patient—that the incident is not trivial but central. He might have inquired why she meekly offered to leave the card game at a sign from her mother. He might have suggested that the incident was patterned on a sibling-rivalry model, i.e. the mother prefers sister-in-law to patient. He might have also inquired whence stemmed the patient's willingness to retire and put the other person forward. In short, the incident offered the therapist a dramatic opportunity to investigate the area of rejection, feelings of abandonment, of being despised while others are preferred, and acceptance of one's fate as a secondary kind of person. It is plain from the record that the therapist did not do any of these things because he did not, despite the plainest evidence, react to the feature that the patient felt rejected and abandoned.

3. *Incorrect interpretation*

a. *There is more to the state of affairs just described. After explicating the card-playing incident, patient went on to say that she was ashamed of her anger. It was true, she continued, that her mother apologized to her later, but patient could not rid herself of a sense of guilt at having flared up in wrath.*

THERAPIST [1]Just one thing more before you go on. [2]The point is that you seem to have a tendency that if you don't get your own way you will just—in the past have felt very hopeless

and cried. ³Or else . . . you have a temper outburst like this
. . . like this.

In effect the therapist, by his utterance, criticizes the patient for
her angry outburst and implies that she should have complied ("if
you don't get your own way"). What the therapist says would tend
to lead the patient to suppress her anger and fail to notice her
intense feelings of rejection. Feelings of abandonment cause great
suffering and distortions of behavior; when the therapist fails to
react to them he is, in effect, condemning the patient to continued
suffering. Such an intervention is bound to confuse the patient and
disturb the course of therapy.

> b. *The younger brother of a woman patient was a dissolute and
> disordered person. He hated his parents and was a cause of
> suffering to them and especially to his father who was dying
> of cancer. He exploited members of the family, including
> patient. As an adult he seemed to be more or less on his own.
> Nevertheless the patient felt guilty.*
>
> PATIENT   ¹I feel that I have some sort of a responsibility. ²But
> I can't see what it is. ³It's just an awful thing to—to watch
> someone go on headlong into disaster and . . . and not be able
> to stop him. ⁴But I feel absolutely helpless.
>
> THERAPIST   ⁵Well, there are some things in life that we are
> powerless to change.

The therapist utters a bromide at a point when the patient is
blaming herself excessively for her brother's psychopathic behavior.
It would seem better for him to inquire why she feels so great a
sense of responsibility. This example and others that could be offered show that the patient is suffering from an irrational degree of
guilt. This unconscious sense of guilt shows itself now by means of
one example, now by another. The therapist muffed the chance to
call attention to the patient's irrational guilt reaction. The practical
effect of this error is to leave the patient suffering needlessly.

> c. *A woman patient in her seventh hour of treatment said:*
>
> PATIENT   ¹Nothing much has been going on. ²I mean . . . I
> haven't hit any lows or highs . . . ³I have no real ups, no real
> downs except that I have been distressed about pressure of
> time—as far as these hours are concerned. (*Tempo of speech has*

slowed markedly, she hesitates) [4]I was wondering specifically
. . . what happens . . . where am I gonna be in this work at
the time we are supposed to stop?

THERAPIST   [5]Do I understand you? [6]I'm a little puzzled . . .
by the implication that you wonder if your marriage will go
on after we finish working. [7]Is that what you're saying?

It seems to us that the therapist has failed to notice an important
implication of the patient's utterance. She is speaking with considerable feeling about the approaching end of her short period of
psychotherapy. In the recent past she had discussed, among other
things, her marriage, and she had wondered how permanent it
would be. At the moment, however, she seems not to be concerned
about the marriage but rather about her relationship with the
therapist. She fears a premature end to therapy. At the unconscious
level it seems also probable that she is wondering how shocking it
will be not to have her relationship with the therapist, whether she
should understand the end of therapy as a rebuff from the therapist;
she is explaining, at a minimum, that she will miss her therapeutic
hours. The therapist completely misunderstands and asks her if she
is talking about the end of her marriage. She vigorously responds
that she has not been.

It would seem that the therapist has failed to notice the strength
of the transferred dependent reactions which the patient has attached to his person. Perhaps there is some force in him which works
against such notice, since he seriously misconstrues what the patient
has said. Having done so, the therapist is unable to give the patient
what little help he could in enabling her to accept the termination
of treatment calmly. It seems likely that leaving treatment falls into
a series of experiences which have happened to the patient in which
someone has left her, rejected her, or abandoned her. If she knew
this emotionally, it would probably help her. The therapist's error
deserves the *Pretni* score.

d. *This obsessional male patient, knowing a little psychoanalytic theory, had been discussing the circumstances of his
cleanliness training. He described a family nurse who was in
charge of his training:*

[1]Uh-uh-she's-uh-she's a very unforgettable character. [2]I think
she had her influence in my formative years. [3]At that time

people were very rigid about things. ⁴And-uh you-uh sat 'em on the potty. ⁵And they produced or else. ⁶And they-uh gave-gave off with something or ⁷(*Embarrassed laugh*) they didn't get off the potty kind of thing. ⁸⁻¹⁹ (*Patient stops for sixty seconds as if waiting for therapist to say something. When therapist does not do so patient continues*) ²⁰I—you had mentioned that you would be interested in-in hearing about some of the dreams that I've had. ²¹I don't know whether you want to get into this at th-this time.

To this offer the therapist responded, "Oh, surely."

As we see the above behavior it goes as follows: The patient *dutifully* describes his cleanliness training as he thinks he is supposed to do. He waits for the therapist to reward him, perhaps by asking further questions (i.e. putting further pressure on him). When the therapist does not respond the patient unconsciously tries to provoke the therapist to put pressure on him by saying, "Didn't you tell me that you wanted dreams?" The therapist by assenting falls into the trap. The patient now has the therapist in a familiar role, i.e. that of one who puts heat on him to "produce."

If this reasoning is correct, the therapist should have called attention to the patient's expectation of pressure in the immediate situation of therapy. Naturally the therapist does not want to be cast in the police-like role of the childhood nurse; nevertheless he lets himself be typed in this way: With a policeman, so to say, the patient knows how to deal. It would certainly seem better if the therapist had explained the patient's unconscious expectation of pressure and thus refused to comply. The therapist might have said, "Of course, dreams are often useful in furthering psychotherapy. But at this moment it is more important for you to notice that you are frightened of me and are trying to offer me something (the dream) in order to placate me." Each therapist would pick his own phrasing of such a point, but we believe that the main idea is clear. Score *Pretni*.

4. *The technical error*

A woman patient was rambling along:

PATIENT ¹I was thinking about coming here. ²Some days when I come here I just don't know what to say. ³So I try if I have a . . . [4](*She sighs*) . . . if I have time . . . to think about it. [5]I mean to . . . to try and think what am I doing. [6]What . . . ah . . . what direction am I trying . . . ah . . . to go in? [7]And . . . ah . . . it's happened several times that I've done this—like I did last night.

THERAPIST   [8]It's quite true that you would be expected to make some progress . . . ah . . . on your own. [9]But . . . ah . . . I think it probably does help. . . to report in on some of these things that you have been thinking about too.

In the Freudian system of therapy the patient is supposed to speak spontaneously what comes to his mind during the interview hour. It is viewed as resistant for him to prepare a story and recite it when he comes to the therapy session. The patient here gives evidence of having, so to say, prefabricated her analytic report to the therapist. Not to call the patient's attention to the fact that pre-preparation may be a sign of resistance is thus a technical error. The therapist *might* have said: "By all means, tell me what you were thinking yesterday, but I must remind you that to prepare a story in advance is often a sign that you are afraid of what you might spontaneously think if you 'let yourself go' in this situation." Again, each therapist can find his own phrasing but ours would convey the main idea. The appropriate score for the therapist's error is *Pretni*.

THE SIGN R

I. DEFINITION OF R

R means reward or, in our system, tension reduction. It is used for a therapist's utterance which causes relaxation and reduction of motivation in the patient.

II. THEORY OF R

Drive reduction is believed to have, in the therapeutic situation, the same effect that it has in other life situations, namely, it reinforces whatever responses have just preceded the drive reduction. *R* strengthens whatever the patient has just done, said, or felt.

The patient's reactions to *R* are of course all learned responses. Although *R* is not the force which moves therapy forward—that force resides in interpretation only—it is undoubtedly of great importance in the practical relations between patient and therapeutic situation, and patient and therapist. From the patient's standpoint the setting for psychotherapy is in many ways strange, angular, and even menacing. *R* reactions on the part of the therapist help to reduce this strangeness. Such reactions make the therapist seem near and friendly rather than remote and hostile. *R* reactions make it seem that the therapist is on the patient's side (and indeed he is, so far as the patient's interests permit). Irrational fear of the therapist can be partly reduced. Positive transference is strengthened by the occurrence of *R* reactions.

In general it may be said that *R* reactions help to make the patient more comfortable so that he can bear the work of "uncovering." They tend to make it likely that the patient will not suffer from irrelevant irritations in the course of therapy, from misunderstandings and misestimates of the situation or of the therapist. As has been said, they cannot substitute for the vital interpretative work of the therapist. Unless unconscious motives and forces are discovered, experienced, and labeled, the best results cannot be obtained from the psychotherapeutic situation. Nor, we believe, can the patient hit upon these necessary interpretations for himself—at least not many and certainly not all of them. The most fundamental insights must be provided by the therapist. However, the occurrence of *R* can be a help in setting the situation up so that interpretative work can go forward.

III. EXAMPLES OF *R*

1. *The patient had been worrying that in some accidental way friends of his from the law school would see the transcript of his therapy hours.*

PATIENT [1]I know that some law students are studying psychiatry here in this building. [2]I wonder if they have the chance to see this material?

THERAPIST [3]You may be certain that they have no access to your material.

To the extent that the patient believes the therapist, his anxiety about exposure to his schoolmates is reduced. Score *R*.

2. *The patient had been late for an appointment and the following transaction occurred:*

THERAPIST ¹Was there some misunderstanding about the appointment time?

PATIENT ²No. ³It's my own fault, though I did sss . . . I came in the door just about two-thirty on the nose which was wrong. ⁴I got tied up in the traffic. ⁵And then . . . ah . . . I sat down there about ten minutes not knowing that I need not bother with the appointment slip when the girl wasn't there.

THERAPIST ⁶Oh!

The therapist first motivates the patient to explain why she is late, and when she has explained he responds by saying, "Oh." The "Oh" has the effect of saying that he understands why the patient was late and does not blame her. Thus the utterance is tension-reducing and should be scored *R*.

3. *Patient had been saying that both she and her husband were at times depressed; that on some occasions one would be up and the other down, but that there have been times where they both hit bottom at the same time. The therapist remarked, "That's bad!"*

The therapist offers sympathy, always an important matter to a patient with a high level of general anxiety. His comment reduces tension and should be scored *R*.

4. *Patient, a law student, had hesitated to enter upon a long and technical explanation of a legal problem; he seemed to assume the therapist would understand without being informed. The therapist replied, "Thanks indeed for the compliment. But I don't know everything."*

In rejecting the trappings of omniscience the therapist is probably reducing an anxiety of the patient at the conscious level, and he is probably also reducing unconscious fears of the patient. The anxiety at speaking before the remote, all-wise therapist is reduced by such a remark. Score *R*.

5. *Therapist had misunderstood something that was plainly said by the patient. Patient repeated his utterance, and the therapist said, "I'm sorry."*

An apology from the therapist is a form of deference to the patient. The anxiety that all patients have of being a mere guinea pig or a boy-before-teacher is reduced by having the therapist honestly follow the patterned ways of human deference; thus his confessing an error is anxiety-reducing and should be scored *R*.

> 6. *Patient had been complaining that many of his friendships had an unfortunate outcome. He stated that friendship, for him, was likely to begin by feeling close to the other person, and then having the other person disappoint him. Thereupon, patient stated, he withdrew and felt hurt. The therapist said, "And stop getting close to people, huh?"*

The therapist's statement is partly a paraphrase, but it is also a completion of the patient's utterance—it produces closure. Such a statement gives the patient the feeling that the therapist is listening closely and sympathetically. It reduces an anxiety, ever present in neurotic people, that the patient will not be cared for and attended to; as such, it deserves to be scored *R*.

> 7. *Patient, a forest ranger, explained that he is qualified for a civil service post and has chosen a certain park in a certain state. The therapist replied, "Oh, you may select the state?"*

Although the therapist's comment is put in the form of a question, it is essentially an item of "social iteration." It is not really necessary to communication, but it assures the patient that the therapist understands and is following the discussion.

> 8. *Patient explained that a supervisor on his job had been causing a great disorder in his department. The supervisor had been foolishly impulsive in his praise and destructive in his excessive condemnation of faults of others. Patient did not see how the department could continue if this supervisor held his place. The therapist said, "He could really wreck the place, huh?"*

The therapist's comment indicates that he understands, has been following the discourse, and has entered into the mood-picture created by the patient. The utterance makes him seem near and friendly to the patient, on the patient's side, and taking the patient's point of view. The ever present anxiety before the remote or critical therapist is thereby reduced. Score *R*.

IV. BORDERLINE CASES

R is somewhat confused with the sign *M*, again with the sign *Interp*, and sometimes even with the sign *D*. Some of these problems will be exemplified here.

> 1. *Patient asked when the building in which patient and therapist are working was built. The therapist replied, "About ten years ago."*

Since this utterance occurred as a part of the byplay which accompanied terminating an hour, it might have been scored *Unsc*; but the proper scoring is *R*. The therapist shows by his answer that he takes the patient seriously and that he answers normal questions sensibly. Nevertheless, since there is always a reason why such questions are asked the therapist might well have kept it in mind to inquire later why the patient wanted to have this question answered. Unconscious fears and other meanings often lurk behind innocent-seeming questions.

> 2. *A patient had complained that at times his wife seemed too compliant, too considerate of his wishes.*
>
> THERAPIST   [1]You don't think that that's the sort of thing that you should hardly complain about?
> PATIENT   [2]*(Anxious laugh)* [3]Yes. It doesn't seem quite—
> THERAPIST   [4]Well, why not?

Auld first scored unit 4 *Interp* and Dollard scored it *D*. On second thought we both agreed that the preferred scoring was *R*. *Interp* was rejected because the therapist's utterance does not refer directly to an unconscious force or factor; *D* was rejected because, despite its interrogative form, the utterance seems to be tension-reducing. Evidently the patient had some anxiety about having complained; the therapist reduces this anxiety by his question.

> 3. *A woman patient was explaining a chronic conflict which she had with her husband. Patient's husband claimed that his wife makes all the decisions. Patient admitted she might have a tendency to take over but also claimed that her husband was extremely slow in assuming the initiative. She gave examples where she waited and waited, husband did not*

act, and she was forced to decide. The therapist commented,
"Well, then how does he justify the complaint that he doesn't
have a chance to make decisions?"

Although the therapist's comment is in interrogative form, actually
he is siding with the wife against her husband, thus reducing anxiety
she might have about her active role toward her husband. This
should be scored *R*.

>   4. *Patient had explained to therapist that his friendships with*
>   *other men seemed to be fleeting, that they began with warm*
>   *feeling on both sides, that patient gave too much and then*
>   *was hurt when the other did not respond. After being re-*
>   *jected patient suffered a miserable ambivalent period toward*
>   *his friend. The therapist said, "Oh, you mean you can't get*
>   *over it?"*

The therapist's statement is put in interrogative form, but on
balance it would seem that the rewarding elements are prepon-
derant. The therapist gives a kind of iterative summary of what the
patient has said, showing that he is following closely and sympathetically. He doesn't really need the answer to his question to
understand the patient's feeling. Though the case is marginal, it
should probably be scored *R*.

>   5. *Therapist had asked a woman patient how she happened to*
>   *be in the town where she sought therapy. She explained that*
>   *she had finished college in June, that her husband was*
>   *coming to the university in the fall, that she and her husband*
>   *were married in September. The therapist said, "And then*
>   *you came."*

The therapist's remark again shows that he is following the patient
closely. His statement has the effect of summarizing or even antici-
pating what she is going to say. There is a slight element of tension-
raising interrogation, but this is believed to be secondary to the
rewarding evidence of the therapist's interest in the patient.

THE SIGN Unsc

I. DEFINITION OF Unsc

Unsc is used for unscorable utterances of the therapist. There are
three subcategories of *Unsc*. The first might be called "unintel-

ligible." Because of garbled transcriptions or deleted words, the utterance cannot be deciphered. A second variety might be called "not evaluatable." Some things that the therapist says are enigmatic; the patient might respond to them in any erratic way. Thus the scorer cannot evaluate therapist's statement. A third kind might be called "slush"—the introductory and terminal greetings, talk about arrangements or about changes in arrangements, when these do not seem to have dynamic value, and other casual speakings before and aft.

II. THEORY OF Unsc

We assume that what the therapist says makes sense, and in the overwhelming majority of cases this assumption is borne out. If the transcription is mutilated, however, and the scorer does not have access to the original data, it seems sensible to take such a mutilated utterance out of the counts concerning significant behavior. In yet other cases the therapist's remarks are enigmatic. They might mean any one of a number of different things. If the scorer is hard pressed to decide which among a number of meanings an utterance has, he is justified in using *Unsc*. Various ways of dealing with preliminary and terminal utterances of a casual character could be found; we preferred not to score them.

In point of fact, we use *Unsc* quite sparingly. The scorer must be in real conflict to have recourse to it. The usual thing is for the scorer to struggle to assign the therapist's utterances to one of the other categories; if this struggle proves in vain, the "out" is *Unsc*.

III. EXAMPLES OF Unsc

1. *Unintelligible utterances*

   a. *Patient has been talking about whether or not he is bothered by having his material recorded, and asks therapist if his previously recorded material is being used at the time of therapy.*

   PATIENT   [1]I mean are you using 'em now?
   THERAPIST   [2]Mmm.
   PATIENT   [3]God!
   THERAPIST   [4]Does it bother you?
   PATIENT   [5]*(Anxious laugh)* [6]I think it's going to.

THERAPIST   [7]Well—
PATIENT   [8]But I'll get over it.
THERAPIST   —going through that.

The therapist's statement "Well . . . going through that" was unintelligible and was therefore scored *Unsc*. It will be noted that the scoring *Unsc* calls into play an unanalyzed ability of the scorer to tell when statements do and do not make sense. This wonderful and exclusive human skill could doubtless be more closely described, but we will forbear the attempt to do so at this point.

> b. *Patient had been talking about whether or not he would prefer to be treated by a physician.*
>
> PATIENT   [1]—enough to-to bring it up.
> THERAPIST   [2]Of course. [3]Surely.
> PATIENT   But-uh—
> THERAPIST   [4]Well, this probably rational part—it is that-that
> I can deal with quite similarly.

The therapist's last remark is plainly unintelligible. It is hard to tell whether it was originally intelligible or not. This kind of garbling and hiccoughing in human speech does occur, as every therapy record will reveal; on the other hand, it is most likely that the material was incorrectly transcribed.

> c. *Patient was concerned about the effect which being recorded might have on his life and was arguing the matter pro and con.*
>
> THERAPIST   And that's-uh anything that hampers what you do, if you—is bad, anything that you—well, if you don't want to do anything that nothing can happen.

Presumably this utterance of the therapist was garbled in transcription. Transcription is likely to be carried on by people who are not familiar with the vocabulary of therapy. Sometimes, also, the transcriber will lack knowledge of the higher levels of English speech. Thus what is plainly on the record for the experienced ear may be inscrutable to the typist. If the episode seems vitally important one can always go back and listen to the original record.

2. *Material not evaluatable*

a. *In connection with this example the reader must know that the interviewing room had facilities for face-to-face interviewing as well as a couch for therapists who wish the patient to lie down. Patient was talking facing therapist and asked:*

PATIENT [1]I'd just like to know who uses this sack over here. [2]*(Embarrassed laugh)* [3]Who's lacking for an afternoon snooze? THERAPIST [4]I dunno.

The therapist does not know the motive behind the patient's request for information about the couch; he answers noncommittally, and hence one cannot evaluate this response. The patient may be annoyed at the therapist's uninformative response, or the whole incident may be some kind of resistant plot. In any case it is difficult to say what the therapist's response means to the patient; it could be motivating or rewarding for all the scorer knows.

b. *Patient had explained to therapist that his wife had been masturbating as a solace.*

THERAPIST [1]You haven't felt any impulse to masturbate yourself during this period? PATIENT [2]Oh yes. [3]And I have. THERAPIST [4]Oh!

The therapist's "Oh" is hard to evaluate. On the one hand it might be permissive, or on the other hand the patient might perceive it—the "Oh"—as threatening. There is no evidence available to permit the scorer to decide which of these two alternatives is correct. In a case like this—usually after considerable conflict—the scorer should use *Unsc.*

IV. BORDERLINE CASES

1. *This patient had been talking about what therapist does with the recorded materials of the therapy hour and had asked the therapist whether he is writing a book or using the material in his teaching or what. The therapist replied, "Yes."*

The therapist's brief utterance might not seem to give us enough information for scoring, and thus we tend to consign his utterance to the *Unsc* category. On second thought, however, since the patient has shown some concern about recording it may be fairly presumed that the knowledge that his material is being currently used would frighten him. Thus the preferred scoring in this case is *D*—for demand or drive. The fact that an utterance is brief should not influence the scorer to consign it to *Unsc*. Where the surrounding atmosphere shows anxiety about a matter like recording, the news that it is being used for current purposes could safely be understood as stressful.

CHAPTER 6

An Illustrative Interview

THE BEST WAY to learn our system is to use it, i.e. to take pencil in hand and score some psychotherapy interviews. To enable the reader to do scoring with the opportunity of comparing his scores with ours, we have printed in this book two interviews that we have scored. For the first of these interviews—which is included in the present chapter—the text of the interview is printed on the left-hand pages and the authors' scoring on the facing right-hand pages. We hope that the reader will follow the scoring as he reads the interview and by doing this become familiar with the system as applied to real and continuous case material.

The second illustrative interview—which appears in Appendix D—is intended as a practice exercise. The reader is advised to score that interview completely before turning to the end of the appendix to see how we scored it. As equipment for the scoring he needs only the following: some sheets of paper, having numbers running from 1 to 785, on which to write his scores; a pencil; an agile mind.

Because the illustrative interviews are, in each instance, from the midst of therapy, we have provided some orienting information about each case. The reader should read the orienting matter on Mrs. Davidson before he reads the interview transcript in this chapter, and should read the orienting remarks about Mrs. Smith before he attempts to score the interview printed in Appendix D. Such familiarity with what happened earlier in the cases is necessary for adequate scoring, since our principle is that the scorer should know whatever the therapist knew about the case up to the sentence being scored.

The Case of Mrs. Davidson

SUMMARY OF HOURS 1-4

The patient is a twenty-five-year-old woman who has been married for two years to a student now in his last year at law school. The Davidsons went to their pastor for marriage counseling. After several interviews the pastor decided that they needed more intensive treatment than he could give. Mrs. Davidson then started the series of interviews that we shall report on here. Mr. Davidson took steps to begin psychotherapy with another therapist.

The pastor reported that Mrs. Davidson had not been able to obtain satisfaction in sexual intercourse. The Davidsons have intercourse about once a week. Mrs. Davidson is depressed. She says that she is never able to let herself go and have a good cry. Her parents, she says, were old-fashioned about sex. Mrs. Davidson's mother was a college graduate, but her father, who works for the telephone company, never went to college. She has one sibling, a brother who is younger than she is. Mrs. Davidson's mother was "nervous," especially during menopause, but this nervousness receded into the background when one of her brothers fell ill of a heart ailment and she had to devote herself to caring for him. The pastor believed that Mr. Davidson is somewhat insensitive to his wife's needs. The pastor's over-all impression of Mrs. Davidson was of a "shy, apologetic, restrained person" who was a little afraid to ask for help but "probably willing to cooperate with a therapist in working on her problem."

First interview. The therapist—apparently to put the patient at ease—inquired about her part-time job, about her educational background, and about her husband's studies. The patient brought out that she is a college graduate; she got to know her husband at college, but they had known each other casually before that. Then the therapist inquired, "What brings you here?" Mrs. D. replied that she doesn't get the orgasm; she remarked that she has been depressed several times. Her sex life with her husband has been getting worse rather than better. At first she had hoped it would improve with time; now she doesn't know whether it will ever change. She can achieve an orgasm through masturbation. She said she would like to have a baby, but her husband—more cautious than she—doesn't want one until he has established himself in law practice.

The therapist explained the sound recording and asked, "How do you feel about these interviews being recorded?" Mrs. D. agreed to the recordings but inquired whether the therapist was writing a book or using the recordings in his teaching. He replied that he wanted the recordings for both research and teaching, then asked, "You're quite sure that you're not hiding some feelings?" She answered that some law school faculty members collaborated with psychiatrists on medicolegal research; she wouldn't want them to hear her interviews. The therapist assured Mrs. D. that no one connected with the law school would have any access to the tape recordings. At the end of the session the therapist arranged to see Mrs. D. regularly once a week for several months.

Second interview. Mrs. D. commented on the table lamp in the therapist's office. "This lamp! This intrigues me . . . It's just cork blocks, isn't it?" The therapist replied, "Yeah. For us it has a more utilitarian purpose. See, the microphone is in here." (He pointed out the concealed microphone.) Mrs. D. remarked that her husband would be interested in the recording because he is a hi-fi fan; but he wouldn't want his own interviews to be recorded. Mr. D. had an appointment to see his therapist on Friday.

Mrs. Davidson said her husband felt that his sex attitudes had contributed to their problem. Mr. D. says that he is sometimes as attacted to men as to women, and he fears that he is effeminate. Mrs. D. believes that their sexual troubles don't stem from anything her husband does during intercourse; but she does wish that he would take more initiative than he does, not only in sexual matters but in a lot of things. Mr. D. doesn't take an interest in extending social invitations to their friends, doesn't remember friends' birthdays, and doesn't have many friends.

Mr. D. scolded the patient for telling friends that she was having psychotherapy. He is afraid to have family and friends know that he or his wife are in therapy, also afraid that knowledge of it might damage him professionally. Mrs. D. reported that he felt ambivalent about starting therapy himself.

After speaking again of their sexual problem—and complaining that sometimes her husband is "too considerate"—Mrs. D. said that she's afraid she's become "too domineering" toward her husband. She would like to see the ballet; because her husband isn't much interested, she thinks she'll have to order the tickets. The therapist remarked that Mrs. D. is justified in taking over, if her husband dillydallies, failing to take effective action. Mrs. D. retorted, "Give him a chance to tell his side of it."

Mrs. D. said her husband is reluctant to reveal his feelings to others; he seems afraid he might get hurt. Mrs. D. feels she is more trusting—and gets hurt. She fears that she and her husband will grow farther and farther apart, and that she'll become more domineering. Bill is so thoughtful, she said, that she's ashamed to make a fuss about his not taking initiative. Bill often brings her flowers or candy.

As the hour drew to a close Mrs. D. asked, "Are you going to be more directive?" She expressed disappointment that she hadn't been able to "probe below any depths" that she and Bill had been able to reach in their discussions. The therapist answered, "Of course you and I are going to have to go over some of the ground you've already gone over. Maybe we can plow a little deeper." Mrs. D. and the therapist said good-by and parted.

Third interview. Mrs. Davidson reported that her husband had seen Dr. Smith, who talked with him for an hour but had too crowded a schedule to accept him for treatment. Dr. Smith arranged for another doctor to take Bill. Bill is very upset; he hadn't realized till now that their marital problems were so serious. He is burdened by many demands on his time and feels that therapy would be just one more demand. He's also afraid that therapy would upset him and hinder his studies.

Mrs. D. said she thought Bill's knowledge of law was too theoretical, not practical enough to help him in his work as an attorney. Bill's parents would have liked him to become a college professor; they think that law is a cynical, crass profession.

Mrs. D.'s brother, she said, is gregarious and athletic—different from Bill, who is shy and bookish. She said she is dissatisfied with Bill's dillydallying during intercourse. Sometimes she's eager to have him "get to the matter at hand" instead of spending so much time in foreplay; but he seems "insensitive" to her wishes. At times, too, it's just that she'd like to get it over with. Although she's so dissatisfied, Mrs. D. feels it is selfish to complain about sex. Before they got married Mrs. D. was in conflict about whether she should marry Bill.

The therapist asked, "Does he talk to you when you're making love?" Mrs. D. replied that Bill does talk to her while making love, but he isn't sincerely expressive. Sometimes he kids her about her "fees" for intercourse, as though she were a prostitute. Mrs. D. is used to kidding, though; indeed, it was more common in her family than in Bill's.

The therapist brought the patient back to her conflict before marriage over whether she should marry Bill. Mrs. D. launched into a recital of her troubled feelings at that time. She had gone steady with her husband during their senior year in college. Toward the end of the year she began having "a dreadful time." She couldn't sleep at night; her menstrual periods became agonizing. She was nagged by a constant fear that Bill wasn't sincere, that he was going to drop her "flatter than a pancake" when they graduated. The next year, when he went away to law school, she invited him to a Christmas dance in their home town. She never heard from him until the day of the dance, and she felt as though she'd been stabbed—she felt that he was letting her down. The day Bill gave her his fraternity pin she felt terrible, had stomach pains. She was unable to trust him, always expecting that he would reject her.

The therapist announced, "I'm sorry, we just have to stop now, but I think there's a great deal more." Mrs. D. replied, "It's just more background." The therapist asked, "You think it's just more background, therefore wasted time perhaps?" Mrs. D. denied feeling the time was wasted; but she appealed to the therapist, "I wish you'd say, 'Listen here, I know what your case is.' "

She expressed the feeling that therapy was going too slowly. The therapist countered, "You're doing pretty well!" Then therapist and patient exchanged good-bys.

Fourth interview. Mrs. Davidson reported that her husband had had his first therapy session. "I just didn't know that he would be so afraid about it," she said. "He's so afraid of the effect it will have on his work, and he seems to be completely insecure as far as I am concerned, which is the worst." Mrs. D. regrets that she told her husband the marital situation was so bad that it had to be changed, that she couldn't take it any longer.

The patient said she is different from Bill. He is slow, she is fast. They went to a concert last week; Bill was maddeningly slow in eating supper, so they barely got there in time. Bill is always late. Bill, she said, is insensitive to other people. One of his friends got engaged to a nice girl, thereby solving his "security problems," and Bill wasn't interested and didn't understand how important the engagement was to his friend.

Mrs. D. doesn't think that Bill can change; any change will have to be on her side. She will have to suppress her needs and not complain.

The patient and her husband had intercourse at noontime a week ago. Afterward the idea of intercourse repelled the patient and she felt "antagonistic" toward Bill. She can't stand the thought of having intercourse, and yet she needs satisfaction. She never gets the orgasm.

Mrs. D. wondered whether she'd made a mistake in getting married when she did. At the time of their engagement Bill blew hot and cold and she went through a period of emotional turmoil.

"If I hadn't come here for help," Mrs. D. lamented, "Bill wouldn't be going through these things now." Bill is very upset emotionally, she said, and she feels guilty at his being upset. "Until last week I had begun to really see some dim rays of hope," Mrs. D. explained; ". . . until last time I was here. And now I don't know whether it was what was said then or . . . or that particular . . . sex experience that happened the same day that made me very antagonistic toward him."

It makes Mrs. D. very guilty to realize she is selfishly expressing her dissatisfactions to Bill. A good woman should show forbearance. Should she express herself to Bill and "talk it out," or should she hold it all in, she wondered. The therapist commented, "We don't have any solution, but we see the puzzle a little more clearly, don't you think?"

Fifth Interview

Davidson Case

Transcript, Scoring and Comments

TRANSCRIPT

PATIENT   [1]I think I'll have to buy some Air-Wick and ss . . . put it in the corridor outside your office. [2]Have you noticed that odor?

THERAPIST   [3]Smells bad, does it?

PATIENT   [4]Ooohh—[5](*Embarrassed laugh*)—understatement. [6]Each week I keep trying to see how long I can hold my breath going along there. [7](*Laughing anxiously*) [8]And I can never quite get through it.

THERAPIST   [9]Mmm.

PATIENT   [10]But . . . very . . . nasty atmosphere. [11]I . . . um . . . have wished this week, as I did last, that . . . the interviews were at a different time . . . in the week because it seems like . . . [12](*Embarrassed laugh*) . . . such strain and stress comes in between and then by the time I get here I'm kinda calm and collected again and . . . and it's . . . [13]It doesn't seem useless. [14]But it's . . . in these more trying periods I've . . . wished that I could . . . get things . . . [15](*Laughing anxiously*) . . . out of my system then.

Scoring and Comments

1. *H therapist.*

Comment: In this example and also in some of the following scores we have included the object of the reaction; that is, in this case, "therapist." However when we make counts of scoring categories (such as *H*) we do not specify the objects. We do not count *"H therapist"* as separate from *"H mother"* or *"H husband,"* etc. Other scorers may wish to indicate the object of reactions and to make separate counts for designated objects, but we did not see fit to do this.

2. *H therapist*

Comment: These hostile statements about the situation surrounding therapy were, of course, scored *H therapist.* Another somewhat reasonable score would be *Res,* since one could argue that the resistance is taking the form of an attack on the therapist. However, we thought it best merely to notice the most obvious feature, the hostile feeling.

3. *R*
4. *H therapist*
5. *Lf—*
6. *H therapist*
7. *Lf—*
8. *H therapist*
9. *M*
10. *H therapist*
11. *Dep therapist*
12. *Lf—*
13. *Dep therapist*
14. *Dep therapist*
15. *Lf—*

Comment: It seemed to us that the main burden of these communications (11, 13, 14) was that the patient wanted more from the therapist. However, there are other aspects that invite attention: the patient's description of her stressful feeling, her statement that she feels calm and collected when she gets to the therapy, and her statement that the therapy isn't useless even if it doesn't happen when she needs it most. These statements of the patient invite scoring such as *A, A:r, L,* or *H-A;* we decided, however, that these features should be ignored and only the main point of the paragraph should be scored.

THERAPIST   [16]How would it be different if it were at a different time?

PATIENT   [17]I d . . . I don't know whether it . . . it's just that it's *bound* to coincide like that, that . . . that during the week after an interview, things'll happen, or . . . or whether it's just happened that way . . . so far, but . . .

THERAPIST   [18]Mmm.

PATIENT   [19]. . . seems like both times I get here when I'm, oh, over most of it. [20]And it's kind of a false security . . .

THERAPIST *(Softly)*   [21]Mm-hmm.

PATIENT   . . . 'cause I . . . I thought I'd hit the . . . the lowest depths last week. [22]But I—

THERAPIST   [23]But there were still lower ones, hunh?

PATIENT   —guess I haven't. [24]Yeah, [25]*(Embarrassed laugh)* a few other untried places.

THERAPIST   [26]What happened this week?

PATIENT   [27]I'm afraid now there're gonna be quite a few. It's . . . oh, just . .

THERAPIST   [28]You mean you have a feeling that it's going to get *worse?*

PATIENT   [29]Well, I just don't know. [30]I thi . . . I think that it gets worse so that it seems to involve Bill more. [31]And as he gets into his, then we both seem to be . . . in it together, and . . . [32]And while we . . . we knew there'd be bad moments, just the fact

16. *D*

17. *Res*
   Comment: One might be tempted to continue with *Dep therapist,* since the patient has not given up her plea for something more from him. But the main point of this sentence seems to be that she is neglecting to react to the therapist's question about how it would be different if the therapeutic sessions were at a different time and is offering confused and obfuscating comment about the time of the interviews.

18. *M*

19. *A:r*
   Comment: The problem here is whether to consider this sentence in the context of her plea for more help from the therapist or to score it in terms of what it tells about her feelings as she relaxes during the psychotherapy session. We decided that the score recognizing this latter aspect was better.

20. *A*

21. *M*

22. *A*

23. *R*
   Comment: The therapist's sympathetic completion of the patient's thought is rewarding to the patient.

24. *A*
   Comment: This is not scored *Y* because the patient goes on to amplify.

25. *Lf—*

26. *D*

27. *A*

28. *D*

29. *Res*

30. *A*

31. *A*

32. *A*

that they *are* seeming to coincide isn't . . . good. [33]And yet I think that's probably natural. [34]And if we can just get through 'em it . . . ah [35](*7-sec. pause*) I think he is probably going to . . . cancel the rest of his . . . partly because of time and partly because he thinks it's too disturbing now.

THERAPIST (*Softly*)   [36]Hmmm!

PATIENT   [37]It . . . and I can see that part of it. But—

THERAPIST   [38]How many did he have?

PATIENT   [39]He just had one.

THERAPIST (*Softly*)   [40]That's enough.

PATIENT   [41]And . . . uh . . . he was to have one yesterday. [42]And the doctor wasn't able to meet him. [43]And I thi . . . there will be one next week. [44]But he wants to . . . ah . . . call it off. [45]Both . . . all the people that he has seen, except Dr. Smith, have been completely directive. [46]And it's just antagonized him . . . so.

THERAPIST   [47]Who's the doctor who saw him over there?

PATIENT   [48]I'm not certain. [49]His office is in the Medical Arts Building. [50]And . . . uh . . . he said he was floored when he saw him because he looked so much like Doctor O'Neill. [51](*5-sec. pause*) [52]Manning!

THERAPIST   [53]Hmm.

PATIENT   [54]I think that's . . . it's over . . . lives close to us there and . . . [55]Bill was going to go into his office. [56]But . . . he's in a . . . awful position . . . [57] (*Embarrassed laugh*) . . . real-

33. *A:r*

Comment: It is moot whether this reflection, "that's probably natural," really reassures the patient. If it doesn't, the sentence should be scored merely *A*.

34. *H-a Bill*

Comment: Unit 34 includes, of course, both what precedes the pause and what follows. It would be reasonable to score 34 *L Bill* on the ground that the patient here is expressing sympathetic concern for her husband's welfare. But the more important thing seems to be that his quitting therapy disturbs and frustrates her; she is inclined to attack him for this decision, as is seen later in sentence 73, but since there are elements of reasonableness in his position she is inhibited from openly criticizing him.

35. *Res 5*
36. *M*

37. *H-a Bill*

38. *D*

39. *H-a Bill*

40. *R*

41. *H-a Bill*
42. *H-a Bill*
43. *H-a Bill*
44. *H-a Bill*
45. *H doctor*
46. *H doctor*
47. *D*

48. *Res*
49. *Unsc*
50. *Unsc*
51. *Res 5*
52. *Unsc*
53. *M*

54. *Unsc*
55. *Unsc*
56. *H-a Bill*
57. *Lf—*

izing that he's got to study so much for the bar exam. [58]And . . .
uh . . . he just feels like . . . any emotional letdown will completely scuttle him as far as preparing for the exam—if he can just
kinda bury it under the surface 'til he gets through. [59]And maybe
that is wisest— [60]I'm beginning to see that.

THERAPIST   [61]He talked that over with you before he decided?

PATIENT   [62]Well . . . no, not exactly. [63]I think he had decided first
and never wanted to go in the first place and then . . . just felt
like he . . . he wasn't going to get any place or that it . . . that
it would be so disturbing. [64]And . . . uh . . . when I realize
how just little things have thrown him off—

THERAPIST   (*Softly*) [65]Mm-hmm.

PATIENT   —in the last few weeks, then I can see that it is a choice
between passing the bar or not—or just . . . just qualifying.
[66]And he's got so many other . . . commitments.

THERAPIST   [67]This disappointing to you?

PATIENT   [68](*5-sec. pause*) [69]Ah . . . in a way, yes. [70]In a way I think
I . . . have foreseen all along what was probably going to happen.
[71]But . . . uh . . . well I don't know for now I . . . it does seem
the wisest thing to do.

THERAPIST (*Softly*)   [72]Mm-hmm.

PATIENT   [73]It isn't exactly what I'd choose.

THERAPIST (*Softly*)   [74]Yeah.

PATIENT   [75]But it . . . if the disturbances that come about are . . .
wou . . . would be due to that only, then I can see that it . . .
[76](*Embarrassed laugh*) . . . it's pro . . . it's probably a good
thing, 'cause I don't think we can stand much more of it . . . [77]I
don't think they *are* due entirely to that, but it's kinda precipitated things.

THERAPIST   [78]Mm-hmm.

PATIENT   So [79-81](*14-sec. pause*) it seems like [82](*6-sec. pause*) it . . .
uh . . . (*Very softly*) [83]I can't quite express what I think. [84]In any
li . . . any decisions . . . on which he may be neutral or hasn't

58. *H-a Bill*
59. *H-a Bill*
60. *H-a Bill*

61. *D*

62. *N*
63. *H-a Bill*
64. *H-a Bill*

65. *M*

66. *H-a Bill*

67. *Interp*

68. *Res 5*
69. *H Bill*
70. *H Bill*
71. *H-a Bill*

72. *M*

73. *H Bill*

74. *M*

75. *H-a Bill*
76. *Lf—*
77. *H-a Bill*
78. *M*

79. *Res 5*
80. *Res 5*
81. *Res 5*
82. *Res 5*
83. *Res*
84. *H Bill*

made up his mind, it . . . it doesn't . . . it takes him so long to
figure out where *I* stand on it . . . or even things that aren't
actually decisions . . . but . . . ⁸⁵It seems like . . . I have to
about go off my nut before he finally figures out that something
disturbs me, and . . . uh—

THERAPIST ⁸⁶You have something in mind?

PATIENT ⁸⁷Yeah, only it seems kinda . . . odd. ⁸⁸But . . . uh . . .
well I had a birthday Monday. ⁸⁹I probably . . . uh . . . aged
ten years . . . ⁹⁰(*Embarrassed laugh*) . . . sss . . . not . . . just
one. And . . . ah . . .

THERAPIST ⁹¹A birth— . . . you aged ten years?

PATIENT ⁹²Yes, I've aged ten years since last week (*Light tone*). ⁹³But
it was just one year according to birthday. ⁹⁴(*Embarrassed laugh*)

THERAPIST ⁹⁵This week was *so* bad?

PATIENT ⁹⁶(*Embarrassed laugh*) ⁹⁷Well it . . . really was.

THERAPIST (*Softly*) ⁹⁸Tell me about it.

PATIENT Well . . .

THERAPIST ⁹⁹We'll finish first with this.

PATIENT Well it's . . . ah . . .

THERAPIST ¹⁰⁰It's part of your psychotherapy.

PATIENT ¹⁰¹But . . . what was it? ¹⁰²Why . . . ah . . . birthdays
are kind of a delicate subject anyway. ¹⁰³(*Embarrassed laugh*) . . .
¹⁰⁴It was . . . his family has always made so much of 'em. ¹⁰⁵And
. . . and our family never *have* . . . that . . . ¹⁰⁶In a way . . .
they seem to be more practical minded, though they're almost
identical income-bracket and—and everything. ¹⁰⁷You'd think
they'd be alike. ¹⁰⁸But anyway . . . uh . . . Bill's always been
used to gettin' just stacks of stuff that he . . . ah . . . it would
seem to me sometimes almost unnecessary, like getting another
electric razor when he already had a perfectly good one, and—
and stuff like that. ¹⁰⁹And . . . ah . . . but . . . ah . . . it's
. . . it's a different way of . . . showing your affection. ¹¹⁰And . . .

85. *H Bill*

86. *D*

87. *Res*
88. *Dep Bill*
89. *Dep Bill*
90. *Lf—*

91. *D*

92. *Dep Bill*
93. *Dep Bill*
94. *Lf—*
95. *D*

96. *Lf—*
97. *Dep Bill*
98. *D*

99. *D*

100. *D*

101. *Res*
102. *Dep Bill*
103. *Lf—*
104. *Dep Bill*
105. *Dep Bill*
106. *Dep Bill*
107. *Dep Bill*
108. *Dep Bill*

109. *Dep Bill*
110. *Dep Bill*

and I've fallen in with that, just like all the rest, and . . . uh . . . have gotten . . . him much better things, and things that I know he likes, than I have for my own family. [111]But . . . that's . . . that's natural too I think. [112]We . . . love each other. [113]But he never seems to feel that way. [114]And . . . ah . . . and I always have the feeling that he never has put much thought into anybody else's gift, not just mine, but any other people. [115]They go around. [116]And if I didn't just hound him and say, "Well now, in two weeks it's Mother's birthday, what are we going to get?" eventually I'd get it anyway. [117]But he just . . . it just doesn't mean as much. [118]And I've just felt that he kinda takes it for granted. [119]Well . . . ah . . . we had *hoped* to go down to see the ballet last night. And . . . uh . . .

THERAPIST   [120]That was a kind of a birthday present you mean?

PATIENT   [121]Yeah, that was to be the birthday thing. [122]And . . .

THERAPIST   [123]Yes.

PATIENT   . . . gosh, nothing could've pleased me more, even if we had sat in the last row of the top balcony . . . [124](*Embarrassed laugh*) [125]But . . . uh . . . and we got the letter . . . in. [126]We knew the tickets were going fast. [127]And evidently it-it was there the first day they were sold. [128]But anyway we didn't get the tickets. [129]And Saturday noon when I got home from work, the first thing there was this letter. [130]And . . . and he didn't . . . it didn't seem to grieve or bother him at all—particularly that I was just crushed. [131](*Embarrassed laugh*) [132]And . . . then . . . I threw this big fit about how everybody else seems to get stuff for their birthday that they want, [133](*Embarrassed laugh*) but I never—— And . . . oh! . . . I . . .

111. *Dep Bill*
112. *Dep Bill*
113. *Dep Bill*
114. *Dep Bill*
115. *Dep Bill*
116. *Dep Bill*
117. *Dep Bill*
118. *Dep Bill*
119. *Dep Bill*

120. *D*

121. *Dep Bill*
122. *Dep Bill*
123. *M*

124. *Lf—*
125. *Dep Bill*
126. *Dep Bill*
127. *Dep Bill*
128. *Dep Bill*
129. *Dep Bill*
130. *Dep Bill*
131. *Lf—*
132. *Dep Bill*
133. *Lf—*

Comment: This whole story, from sentence 88 on, hangs together and should be scored the same way. It was our decision that it ought to be scored as showing the patient's dependent motives. She wanted to receive love from her husband; he disappointed her by not giving it. An alternative scoring which we considered is *H Bill.* We rejected this because the patient's disappointment, rather than her anger, is in the foreground. In sentences 111 and 112 one is tempted to score the patient's avowal of affection for her husband as *L Bill.* Here, as elsewhere, we believe it best to subordinate a minor feature of the communication to the main theme of the story: the patient's disappointment at not receiving love from her husband.

THERAPIST   [134]What do you mean "a big fit"? [135]How did you behave there?

PATIENT   [136]Oh, I just started to cry.

THERAPIST   [137]Oh, you *did* start to cry.

PATIENT   [138]I don't very often cry. [139]And that was a good thing actually . . . to get *that* out of my system.

THERAPIST   [140]Mm-hmm.

PATIENT   [141]But . . . ah . . . he slammed out the door, which he *hardly ever* does, and left. [142]And then I was really worried. [143]I didn't know where he went or why he went, exactly whether he was mad or, or whether his feelings were hurt or what.

THERAPIST   [144]You mean when you began to cry—

PATIENT   [145]Yeah.

THERAPIST   —he slammed out the door?

PATIENT   [146]He just left. [147]He said that he was tired of the . . . this whole business of . . . of having things coming to an issue at all, or any . . . anything like that. [148]He just said he was tired of it all. [149]And *I* didn't know where he went.

THERAPIST   [150]You'll . . . excuse me, who had planned this . . . ah . . . outing?

PATIENT   [151]Well, I had suggested that . . . w . . . i . . . it . . . if we could possibly do something like that it would be nice because they might not come to America again ever.

THERAPIST   [152]Yeah.

PATIENT   [153]And . . . uh . . . this was a program that kinda interested us both.

THERAPIST   [154]Mmm.

PATIENT   [155]He doesn't care for ballet as much as I do. [156]But it seems that that would be more interesting than . . .

134. *D*

135. *D*

136. *Dep Bill*

137. *D*

138. *Dep Bill*
139. *Dep Bill*

140. *M*

141. *Dep-A Bill*
142. *Dep-A Bill*
143. *Dep-A Bill*

Comment: In 141–3 the patient shows that her husband's behavior made her anxious. This anxiety followed her demands on him and thus would be expected to become attached to her dependent feelings.

144. *D*

145. *Y*

146. *Dep-A Bill*
147. *Dep-A Bill*
148. *Dep-A Bill*
149. *Dep-A Bill*

150. *D*

151. *Dep Bill*

152. *M*

153. *Dep Bill*

154. *M*

155. *Dep Bill*
156. *Dep Bill*

THERAPIST   [157]So, who took the initiative, and who sent away for the tickets and all?

PATIENT   [158]Well he . . . ah . . . he started to. [159]Actually I . . . ah . . . finished the letter . . . ah . . . because we had then thought that it would be fun to do it with several kids and we had asked two fellows that we know and—and their girls. [160]And . . . ah . . . so I actually *sent* it. [161]But that didn't matter because . . . if I can do details like that—after all it was already decided.

THERAPIST   [162]Yeah.

PATIENT   [163]And . . . ah . . . he w . . . he wanted to go, I know. [164]But just . . . it just didn't matter so much. [165]He's . . . he just doesn't react hurt . . . and he'd-uh . . . uh . . . especially about the ballet, that . . . [166](*Embarrassed laugh*) . . . he wouldn't be as enthusiastic as *I* would be.

THERAPIST (*Very softly*)   [167]Yeah.

PATIENT   [168]And then I di . . . I worried about it that afternoon, and—and [169]I couldn't figure out . . . I kn . . . I knew then that I never should've said anything, that . . . whether his feelings were hurt, or whether he was just angry, that it . . . just that it wasn't helping the situation any. [170]So I finally . . . got . . . went up to school. [171]I . . . have . . . uh . . . the . . . helped with the typing at the law journal . . . once in a while. [172]And it was a good job to do . . . to just have something to do and not think. [173]So I went up and did that for a couple hours in the afternoon, and got home about the same time he did. [174]I guess he'd . . . he'd decided after he got out of the house that that'd be a good time to go for a haircut. [175]So he went. [176]And . . . and then after that we . . . talked about it quite a bit . . . an' . . . and just the seeming hopelessness of the situation, that he couldn't go on having an afternoon that was intended for work ruined that way, and . . . and that I couldn't go on just *feeling* these things that seemed t' have to come out, and . . . not doing it, that . . . we were just going to crack up . . . [177](*Embarrassed laugh*) . . . pretty soon. And—

THERAPIST   [178]How did he evaluate *your* behavior? [179]What did he say about it?

157. *D*

158. *Dep Bill*
159. *Dep Bill*
160. *Dep Bill*
161. *Dep Bill*

162. *M*

163. *Dep Bill*
164. *Dep Bill*
165. *Dep Bill*

Comment: Further discussion of the episode (sentences 151 ff.) should be scored as the episode was scored on first telling, in sentences 88–132, i.e. as an expression of dependent wishes.

166. *Lf—*
167. *M*

168. *Dep-A Bill*
169. *Dep-A Bill*
170. *Dep-A Bill*
171. *Dep-A Bill*
172. *Dep-A Bill*
173. *Dep-A Bill*
174. *Dep-A Bill*
175. *Dep-A Bill*
176. *Dep-A Bill*
177. *Lf—*

Comment: These sentences express the patient's conflict about making known to her husband her dependent needs. She would like to let him know what she wants, but she is deterred by the conscious fear that her demands will only make the situation worse. An alternative scoring with some plausibility is *H-A*. But we believe that her conflict is not so much one of expressing or not expressing aggression toward her husband as one of making known or not making known her dependent needs.

178. *D*
179. *D*

PATIENT   [180]Well, then . . . he said his feelings had been hurt, and he was sorry . . .

THERAPIST   [181]His feelings.

PATIENT   [182]Yes. [183]And then he went out, even later, just about supper time and . . . and got this very, very pretty dress.

THERAPIST   [184]For your birthday.

PATIENT   [185]For a birthday thing.

THERAPIST   [186]How had his feelings been hurt?

PATIENT   [187]Well, he said he just . . . ah . . . felt that . . . about . . . that he'd . . . he hadn't realized that . . . uh . . . I had wanted it so much, and that it hadn't meant anything to him, and that he realized that he'd taken a lot for granted.

THERAPIST   [188]But how had his *feelings* been hurt?

PATIENT   [189]Well, he just felt very guilty.

THERAPIST   [190]Oh!!

PATIENT   [191]We *both* felt . . . that way.

THERAPIST   [192]Yeah. [193]I didn't understand, because usually when someone says—

PATIENT   [194]Yeah!

THERAPIST   —your feelings are hurt, you mean that somebody . . . that . . .

PATIENT   [195]Yeah!

THERAPIST   . . . you feel that somebody else has been unkind.

PATIENT   [196]Oh, oh yeah. I . . .

THERAPIST   [197]Did he feel that in some way you had been unkind to *him?*

180. *Dep-A:r*

181. *D*

182. *Y*

183. *Dep-A:r*

184. *D*

185. *Dep-A:r*

186. *D*

187. *Dep-A:r*

188. *D*

189. *Dep-A:r*
Comment: When the patient's husband apologized and made a peace offering of the dress, the patient's fear about having expressed her dependent wishes was reduced.

190. *R*

191. *Dep-A*
Comment: The scorer's conflict here is between plain *A* and *Dep-A*. Should guilt be represented simply by the *A*, or should the apparent source of the guilt be recognized? We decided in favor of indicating the presumed source as well as the guilty reaction itself.

192. *M*

193. *D*

194. *Y*

195. *Y*

196. *Y*

197. *D*

PATIENT   [198]Well, I'm sure he did. [199]He didn't say anything . . . then. [200]But from . . . —what night was it? I guess just night before last, it seems longer than that—nothing particular . . . came up. [201]We . . . since Sunday we have hardly . . . had a . . . a chance to even see each other. [202]He's been gone almost every night. [203]And I have too. [204]And I don't think we've even had fifteen minutes together at—at any one meal. [205]It's just been a . . . a *hectic* week. [206]And . . . ah . . . we finally got to bed about ten o'clock that night. [207]And then neither one of us could sleep. [208]And we lay there kinda alternately blaming the other person and hating them for that, and then feeling these . . . waves of guilt, and both of us feeling the same . . . same way, I mean just . . . [209](*Embarrassed laugh*) not knowing which wa-way to go, and you know this—maybe you don't know—the hopeless [210](*Embarrassed laugh*) feeling of . . . lying awake at night when you're just dog-tired and stewing about whether you get to sleep. [211](*6-sec. pause*)

THERAPIST   [212]What was *your* feeling about *his* behavior?

PATIENT   [213]Well . . . while I could see that he had nothing to do with the fact that we didn't have the tickets . . .

THERAPIST   [214]Mm-hmm.

PATIENT   . . . I felt that in some way that . . . that he just . . . he just doesn't *feel* things like I do. And . . .

THERAPIST   [215]You feel that it would be reasonable for you to expect him to be more sensitive to your disappointment?

PATIENT   [216]Yes, bu . . . I . . . I re . . . I am too much that way!

THERAPIST   [217]But he isn't enough.

198. *Dep-A*
199. *Dep-A*
200. *Dep-A*
201. *Dep-A*
202. *Dep-A*
203. *Dep-A*
204. *Dep-A*
205. *Dep-A*
206. *H-A*
207. *H-A*
208. *H-A*
209. *Lf—*
210. *Lf—*
211. *Res 5*

Comment: Here the scorer is asked to slice things pretty thin. We have decided to call units 198 through 205 *Dep-A,* on the ground that they refer to the aftereffects of the Saturday incident. It is perfectly plain, however, that the patient on Wednesday night was in conflict between hostile impulses and guilt—she even labeled her feelings as "hate"—although it is true that a whole tangle of other feelings such as despair, frustration, dependence were also present. We can only say that the scoring presented represents our best judgment on the matter, and we admit that it would be perfectly reasonable to call the earlier sentences *H-A* also or to recognize in the later sentences other aspects of the welter of motives that were present.

212. *D*

213. *Dep*

214. *M*

215. *D*

216. *H/self*

217. *D*

PATIENT   [218]Yeah, if we could just . . . both of us . . . get into it, 'cause I know I'm . . .

THERAPIST   [219]Yeah.

PATIENT   . . . so damn sensitive to everything. (*Therapist clears throat*) [220]But I can't . . . just by saying it doesn't correct it.

THERAPIST (*Softly*)   [221]Mmm.

PATIENT   [222]And you can try to let things slide off your back. [223]And they don't.

THERAPIST (*Softly*)   [224]Mm-hmm.

PATIENT   [225]And [226-7](*9-sec. pause*) it all seems so hopeless. [228]That night we just didn't know what to do. [229]And then . . . today things are better 'cause we—

THERAPIST   [230]Were there any very cross words exchanged?

PATIENT   [231]Not very many, no.

THERAPIST (*Very softly*)   [232]Mm-hmm.

PATIENT   [233]We never come right out and—and tell each other what we think or what we think's wrong, or anything like that. [234]It . . . we k . . . we sorta *suggest at* it. [235]And as we each think over what the other has said then . . . [236](*Laughing anxiously*) . . . we get the full implication. But we—

THERAPIST   [237]Then when you said, "We were lying there hating each other," you didn't mean that that was *expressed*?

PATIENT   [238]No . . . well, he did say once he . . . he didn't know whether he was hating or loving any more.

THERAPIST (*Softly*)   [239]I see.

PATIENT   [240]And I certainly know what m . . . that feeling is. And that—

THERAPIST   [241]Because you have it too?

218. *H/self*

219. *M*

220. *H/self*

221. *M*

222. *Dep Bill*
223. *Dep Bill*

224. *M*

225. *Dep-A Bill*
226. *Res 5*
227. *Res 5*
228. *Dep-A Bill*
229. *Dep-A:r Bill*
230. *D*

231. *H-a Bill*

232. *M*

233. *H-a Bill*
234. *H-a Bill*
235. *H-a Bill*
236. *Lf—*

237. *D*

238. *H-A Bill*

239. *M*

240. *H-A Bill*

Comment: The earlier sentences, 231–5, were scored *H-a* because the patient is describing an inhibition of aggression. The later ones, 238 and 240, describe the patient's conscious conflict between aggression and fear, thus are scored *H-A*.

241. *D*

PATIENT (*Softly*)   [242]Sure.

THERAPIST (*Very softly*)   [243]Yeah.

PATIENT   [244]But I . . . it seems to me that it . . . it's just because all of these *extreme* feelings were . . . are concentrated into a—a short period, and in . . . the fact that the . . . the first . . . year and a half or two years were just so completely smooth and harmonious, with the exception of this . . . sexual business, and then it . . . and then all this other stuff when you . . . it just seems like every *little* difference between you is . . . as you'd expect there'd be between people, seem to be so heightened. [245]And you . . . while we . . . are constantly aware that there's something more than these things that bother us, and that there is a . . . a deep and abiding affection there to build on, it's sometimes it's so far down . . . you can't seem to get *at* it, or to remember it. [246](*7-sec. pause*) [247]Not . . . and I don't think *it's* going to change. [248]But I just don't want to . . . [249](*Anxious laugh*) . . . lose sight of it . . .

THERAPIST   [250]Mmm.

PATIENT   . . . because I think otherwise . . . well we wouldn't . . . we wouldn't bother about *any* of this . . .

THERAPIST   [251]Mm-hmm.

PATIENT   . . . if it wasn't there. But I—

THERAPIST   [252]Just quit then?

PATIENT (*Softly*)   [253]Yeah. And yet . . . that's—

THERAPIST   [254]Is divorce readily accepted, by the way, among lawyers?

PATIENT   [255]What?

THERAPIST   [256]Divorce?

PATIENT (*Softly*)   [257]Oh heavens, yes.

THERAPIST   [258]Mmm.

242. *Y*

243. *M*

244. *Res*
Comment: In this sentence the patient essentially denies that she has for a long time had an important problem in the relationship with her husband.
245. *L Bill*
246. *Res 5*
247. *L Bill*
248. *L Bill*
249. *Lf—*

250. *M*

251. *M*

252. *D*

253. *Y*

254. *D*

255. *Res*

256. *D*

257. *Unsc*
Comment: Unsc or *Y?* The rule is that *Y* should be used only for a simple agreement, not amplified. Since "Oh heavens" does seem to amplify this statement, the sentence can't be *Y*. Yet one doesn't know quite how to evaluate it, therefore the score *Unsc*.
258. *M*

PATIENT   259But . . . well I think it depends on . . . the law firm. 260It . . . it certainly wouldn't be . . . wouldn't help you at all in your career.

THERAPIST   261Wouldn't ruin it though?

PATIENT   262Some small towns it would. 263And other places it wouldn't. 264I think in most cases, unless it's something extreme or . . . or a case where the husband is so obviously at fault and the wife isn't . . . why . . . people realize that. 265I think it's . . . I think it's more the common thing that you have these . . . estranged . . . partners who stay together for . . . for the looks of the situation . . .

THERAPIST   266Mm-hmm.

PATIENT   . . . when it probably would be more helpful not to. 267But . . . it's . . . it's more and more prevalent. 268And I think there . . . are possibly a number of cases in our circle where it might be better if . . . if they were separated . . . though 269-70(*8-sec. pause*) 271It always seems, unless there. . . it's just . . . a complete . . . incompatibility that . . . that it's . . . just running away, and you don't really improve much. But 272-4(*17-sec. pause*) 275So I don't know what to do. 276I mean not about that, but—

THERAPIST (*Softly*)   277But about what?

PATIENT   Well I 278-9(*8-sec. pause*) 280If there's much more of this emotional strain and stress—and I think that possibly there might be—just in going on with these, that it's . . . it's going to be a very difficult end . . . 281(*Embarrassed laugh*) . . . of the year. And I'm—

THERAPIST   282I didn't quite understand. 283Have you asked yourself whether you should stop too . . . the therapy?

PATIENT   284No, not really seriously considering it, 'cause I've . . . I feel like now I'm just in the middle of it, that . . . that bad . . . it'd . . . t . . . you can't go either direction. 285I mean I can't back up by myself . . .

259. *H-A Bill*
260. *H-A Bill*

261. *D*

262. *H-A Bill*
263. *H-A Bill*
264. *H-A Bill*
265. *H-A Bill*
Comment: The patient's conflict about getting a divorce, which would be a hostile act toward her husband, is scored *H-A* because both elements of this conflict are conscious, are represented in her thoughts.
266. *M*

267. *H Bill*
268. *H Bill*
269. *Res 5*
270. *Res 5*
271. *H-A Bill*
272. *Res 5*
273. *Res 5*
274. *Res 5*
275. *Res*
276. *Res*
277. *D*

278. *Res 5*
279. *Res 5*
280. *Res*
281. *Lf—*
Comment: Sentences 275, 276, and 280 are scored as resistant because the patient is expressing the wish to escape from therapy.
282. *Interp*
283. *Interp*

284. *Res*
285. *Res*
Comment: This is a resistant denial of the interpretation.

THERAPIST   [286]Mm-hmm.

PATIENT   . . . and that if I can just hang on . . . [287](*Embarrassed
laugh*) . . . [288]And . . . I have . . . I have gotten so *much* out
of it, particularly the last . . . couple of times . . . stuff that
broadened . . . [289]I'm very grateful that you were nondirective . . .

THERAPIST   [290]Mmm.

PATIENT   . . . 'cause I'd . . . if you'd told me some of this stuff,
naturally I'd . . . I can build up my defenses so fast. [291](*Embarrassed laugh*)

THERAPIST   [292]Mm-hmm.

PATIENT   [293]But I have some of it . . . when it sinks in under my
own thought processes.

THERAPIST   [294]Can you point to anything that you mean especially
that seemed—

PATIENT   [295]Well just . . . just that . . . the general fact that . . .
that I thought I saw myself and—and knew myself, but I . . . I
didn't. [296]I w . . . if . . . I mean we analyze so much ourselves
. . . (*Alarm clock ticks loudly*) . . . [297]And I thought I could
. . . could pretty well size up the kind of person I was and everything. [298]But I don't think I was able to do that, I'm beginning to
get a little idea. [299]But [300-1](*10-sec. pause*) [302](*Laughing anxiously*)
that's a ghastly experience— (*Therapist interrupts*)

THERAPIST   I just wondered . . . [303]That's a ghastly . . . hunh?

PATIENT   [304]I'm gettin' to . . . getting to see yourself as others see
yuh is kinda demoralizing.

THERAPIST   [305]Really! What—

PATIENT   [306]Some of it.

THERAPIST   [307]What have you seen that you don't like the looks of?

PATIENT   [308]Well, in general terms it's the same thing that I said

286. *M*

287. *Lf—*
288. *L therapist*
289. *L therapist*

290. *M*

291. *Lf—*

292. *M*

293. *L therapist*
    Comment: Other scores that were considered for the last few units were *Dep therapist, A:r therapist* (because of the expression of relief at his not pushing her around), and *H therapist* (because of the imagined coercion from therapist). On the whole, however, *L* seems the best score.

294. *D*

295. *Reas*
296. *Reas*
297. *Reas*
298. *Reas*
299. *A*
300. *Res 5*
301. *Res 5*
302. *Lf—*

303. *D*

304. *A*

305. *D*

306. *A*

307. *D*

308. *H/self*

before, this selfishness. ³⁰⁹Only it's . . . I see it in a different way. ³¹⁰And I . . . I'm not sure that I can explain that.

THERAPIST   ³¹¹I wish you would try, because I think that's one of the unclear areas in your thinking. ³¹²(*6-sec. pause*) ³¹³It might get a little clearer if you'd try to—

PATIENT   ³¹⁴Mm-hmm, probably.

THERAPIST   —state it.

PATIENT   ³¹⁵⁻¹⁷(*16-sec. pause*) ³¹⁸Well, the thing that amaze—well it doesn't amaze me—but the thing that I really can't figure out is . . . is which is right of . . . ah . . . of my thinking . . . ³¹⁹(*Laughing anxiously*) . . . the way it was before, the way it is . . . now or is beginning to be. And . . . ah . . .

THERAPIST   ³²⁰Can you tell me what change you think has occurred?

PATIENT   ³²¹Well I think . . . well the . . . the idea of . . . of say . . . ah . . . in a given situation, well as . . . as last Saturday afternoon, whether to express . . . myself . . . and . . . give way to my feelings, or whether *not* to, my . . . I mean in terms of whether . . . ah . . . when other people are involved in that . . . and . . . ah ³²²⁻³(*9-sec. pause*) I used to think that there just wasn't any . . . ah . . . question that it was *always* better to . . . if it was . . . ³²⁴(*Laughing anxiously*) . . . within your control . . . t' . . . t' not say anything that would in any way hurt somebody else, and if ever in doubt, to make sure you didn't. ³²⁵And . . . uh . . . at that time I was beginning to realize that that was a good theory, but not always practical . . . ³²⁶(*Laughing anxiously*)

THERAPIST   ³²⁷Yes.

PATIENT   ³²⁸I mean not always possible. ³²⁹And now . . .

THERAPIST   ³³⁰Mmm.

PATIENT   . . . I . . . I'm beginning to think that if . . . if I could've tempered that a little bit . . . ah . . . not just left

309. *H/self*

Comment: The scoring should be *A* for the earlier sentences of this series from 299 on, because at first the patient mentions only the discomfort of self-revelation and does not blame herself. When she switches to self-blame the score should become *H/self*.

310. *Res*
311. *D*
312. *Res 5*
313. *D*

314. *Y*

315. *Res 5*
316. *Res 5*
317. *Res 5*
318. *Reas*
319. *Lf—*

320. *D*

321. *H-A Bill*
322. *Res 5*
323. *Res 5*
324. *Lf—*
325. *Reas*
326. *Lf—*

327. *M*

328. *Reas*
329. *Reas*
330. *M*

everything unexpressed, but get some of these things out of my system . . . ah ³³¹(*6-sec. pause*) trying to temper it with consideration too . . .

THERAPIST (*Softly*)   ³³²Mm-hmm.

PATIENT   ³³³And I . . . I still am not sure about that because it's . . . I . . . I'm not . . . the thing I haven't figured out is . . . is whether I . . . I am essentially liable to be as . . . as expressive and outspoken and . . . and get all of these things out as I have the last few weeks, or whether that's just letting the cork out and that's the first—

THERAPIST   ³³⁴You're scared to speak—

PATIENT   —burst of steam, and that the rest isn't gonna *be* like that . . .

THERAPIST   ³³⁵Mm-hmm.

PATIENT   . . . and that it's . . . it's gonna be more easily . . . controlled, not that it's always a . . . a thing that you can decide at . . . at every . . . point of decision, that you're going to have time.

THERAPIST   ³³⁶No.

PATIENT   ³³⁷But . . . and that's what I'm not certain about. ³³⁸I have . . . keep having a feeling that . . . if once I could *completely* get everything out, then I would have a . . . ³³⁹(*Embarrassed laugh*) . . . more controllable spray and could adjust the nozzle or whatever . . .

THERAPIST   ³⁴⁰Yeah.

PATIENT   . . . might come out. ³⁴¹What do you think?

THERAPIST   ³⁴²You're under a special handicap now, really.

PATIENT   But . . .

THERAPIST   ³⁴³I mean your husband's having to cram for the bar is really sort of making it almost essential that you inhibit some of it, isn't it?

331. *Res 5*

332. *M*

333. *Reas.*

334. *R*

335. *M*

336. *M*

337. *Reas*

338. *Reas*

339. *Lf—*

340. *M*

341. *Dep therapist*

342. *D*

343. *D*

Comment: Sentences 342 and 343 might superficially seem to be interpretive. However, no unconscious motive is made conscious; this is pure advice. Since the likely effect of the advice is to strengthen the patient's fear of self-expression, we score it *D*.

PATIENT   [344]Mmm . . . yeah. I . . .

THERAPIST   [345]And I think in a way that has something to do with the . . . ah . . . question you asked.

PATIENT   [346]Oh I kn . . . I know it does. [347]I've . . . ah . . . I've thought that just for the time being it would be . . . be better almost if we didn't *see* as *much* of each other, and—I don't enjoy separation 'cause he's . . . he's such a good friend and we have . . . we have so many things to talk over that aren't in an emotional sphere, and things that we enjoy discussing . . .

THERAPIST   [348]Mm-hmm.

PATIENT   . . . but that . . . if I could keep all of this outburst, or most of it, away from *him* . . .

THERAPIST   [349]Mmm.

PATIENT . . . and he could go along . . . ah . . . I think possibly if most of this were diverted from him, he could . . . gather himself . . . [350](*Laughing anxiously*) . . . together and master the torts and misdemeanors. But . . .

THERAPIST   [351]Mm-hmm.

PATIENT   . . . I just . . .

THERAPIST   [352]Has he done much studying yet?

PATIENT   [353]Hardly any.

THERAPIST (*Softly*)   [354]Oh, Lord.

PATIENT   [355]And the worst of it . . . well it isn't so much *that*—he can . . . he can buckle down to the law books because it's so purely theoretical. [356]But he's confronted with a series of talks to the Young Republicans that he was kinda bulldozed into. [357]And

344. *Y*

345. *D*

346. *H-A Bill*
347. *H-A Bill*

348. *M*

349. *M*

350. *Lf—*

351. *M*

352. *D*

353. *H-A Bill*

Comment: These sentences (346, 347, 353) are scored *H-A* because they represent the patient's conflict over asserting herself against her husband. Her concern that her husband be able to finish law school and pass the bar exam might of course be considered *L*, but the better scoring—*H-A*—recognizes the opposition between her wish to express aggression toward him and the fear that holds this in check. Incidentally, the anxious laughter probably has its origin in the fear side of this conflict.

354. *R*

355. *L Bill*
356. *L Bill*
357. *L Bill*

he, besides this domestic business, he is . . . constantly . . . buffeted back and forth in his thinking between the . . . ah . . . the feeling of wanting to . . . make people understand the . . . have a better understanding of the Bill of Rights and the freedoms that they have under the Constitution, and on the other side the . . . the practical type of thing which the ward politics . . . crowd down there just— [358]There isn't any room for any other . . . any other interest than winning the next election as far as they're concerned. And . . . if . . . they . . .

THERAPIST   [359]This is a kind of controversy among the Young Republicans or . . . ?

PATIENT   [360]Yeah. [361]Well, it isn't . . . it isn't that outright. [362]But . . . ah . . . this certain bunch who control the town committee and know all the political hacks up at the capital, and are so active in local affairs, while we . . . ah . . . go very much for political action, Bill is much more at home in the . . . in the kind of just pure political theory . . .

THERAPIST   [363]Yeah.

PATIENT   . . . and . . . the philosophical background. [364]And it . . . there does seem to be quite a chasm between the two . . .

THERAPIST   [365]Mm-hmm.

PATIENT   . . . that, as long as you're in law school . . . I think you feel more than when you actually get into practice and meet people and . . . [366]And then you're compelled to be realistic. [367]But he doesn't know whether to give them pointers on organizing for door-to-door campaigning or whether, you know, to give something of a more basic kind, not sentimental . . . [368]But . . . so he's . . . he's got this talk. [369]And he's written . . . I think he's beginning now the fourth time on the darn thing. [370]And that's the place where . . . ah . . . where his feelings are involved in it too, that is when any . . . any emotional thing really gets him. [371]But he's just . . . he's got too much this year and . . . in the legal-aid office he was doing more than anyone else. [372]And he's also got the coaching of the freshman tennis team and sings in the church choir and practices once a week and just a few little things like that . . . that. [373]So when a . . . when something scuttles . . . ah . . . an afternoon . . . or three or four

358. *L Bill*

Comment: Here the emphasis seems to swing over to her loving concern for Bill.

359. *D*

360. *Y*
361. *L Bill*
362. *L Bill*

363. *M*

364. *L Bill*

365. *M*

366. *L Bill*
367. *L Bill*
368. *L Bill*
369. *L Bill*
370. *L Bill*
371. *L Bill*
372. *L Bill*
373. *L Bill*

hours of time for him, he . . . [374](*Embarrassed laugh*) . . . it really means something.

THERAPIST   [375]Mm-hmm.

PATIENT   But . . . so that's why . . .

THERAPIST   [376]That's all very true, but it makes it harder for you doesn't it?

PATIENT   (*Softly; hard to tell whether she said "Yeah" or "No"*) [377]Yeah.

THERAPIST   [378]What?

PATIENT   . . . [379]And in the long run I think it makes it harder for him because . . . he . . . needs this kind of thing too. [380]He feels very much . . .

THERAPIST   [381]Unn.

PATIENT   . . . as though he still needs it. But he . . . he was—

THERAPIST   [382]He's quite definitely going to give it up?

PATIENT   [383]Why . . . he . . . he said last night that he was.

THERAPIST   (*Softly*)   [384]Yeah.

PATIENT   [385]He wa . . . he did want to have one more talk with the doctor. [386]Or the doctor told him that—actually, Bill had . . . had . . . uh . . . mentioned this sex business as the chief reason . . . for . . . for needing the help—and . . . the doctor said that wasn't in his sphere, that he handled only more seriously disturbed people. (*Softly*) [387]So . . . I don't know.

THERAPIST   [388]What *do* you think is . . . ah . . . responsible for your taking a little different attitude towards . . . this problem of expressing or not expressing?

PATIENT   [389]I'm not *sure*. [390](*6-sec. pause*) [391]It's decidedly self-conscious . . . I mean to . . . be . . . even concerned about it. [392](*Embarrassed laugh*) [393]It just . . . I don' . . . I can't explain

374. *Lf—*

375. *M*

376. *Interp*

377. *Y*
378. *D*
379. *L Bill*
380. *L Bill*

381. *M*

382. *D*
383. *L Bill*
384. *M*
385. *L Bill*
386. *L Bill*
387. *L Bill*

388. *D*

389. *Res*
390. *Res 5*
391. *Res*

   Comment: Sentence 391 is troublesome. Its main effect is resistant, since she hasn't yet answered the therapist's question but is evading it. Yet there is a self-critical note here, tempting the scorer toward *H/self.*

392. *Lf—*
393. *Res*

any specific thing, but it [394-7](*19-sec. pause*) [398]Maybe the fact that
. . . I, at times, and seemingly more frequently, I find it almost
. . . well it is *impossible* not to.

THERAPIST   [399]Mm-hmm. [400]And you think it emerges in any way
from the talks we've been having?

PATIENT   [401]Well, I . . . I . . . it *must* in some ways. [402]I'm not
sure just how much of it just . . . inevitably under the . . . just
the pressure . . .

THERAPIST   [403]Mm-hmm.

PATIENT   . . . that we've both been under might of come up.

THERAPIST   [404]Mm-hmm.

PATIENT   I don't—

THERAPIST   [405]I wondered if you felt that I had taken any position
on it though.

PATIENT   [406]No, [407](*Embarrassed laugh*) I never—

THERAPIST   You don't think—

PATIENT   —I never know. [408](*Embarrassed laugh*)

THERAPIST   [409]Mm-hmm.

PATIENT   [410]And . . . ah . . . while I'm curious th . . . I . . . it
seems to me better if—if I don't know. [411]I mean I don't . . . I
don't really in some ways care, other ways—

394. *Res 5*
395. *Res 5*
396. *Res 5*
397. *Res 5*
398. *Res*
399. *M*
400. *Interp*

401. *Res*
402. *Res*

Comment: In sentence 398 the patient doesn't really answer the therapist's question about *why* her attitude has changed. Thus 398 is scored *Res* rather than *H-A*. In sentences 401 and 402 the patient doesn't really consider whether her changed attitude might have come from her experience in the therapy: In 401 she mostly brushes the query aside; in 402 she offers an alternative explanation—her attitude would have changed anyhow because of external events in her life, not because of internal changes. The therapist's remark at 400 was called *Interp* because he linked her changed attitude to the therapeutic process, thus calling her attention to a connection she had not previously been aware of.

403. *M*

404. *M*

405. *Interp*

406. *Dep therapist*
407. *Lf—*

408. *Lf—*

409. *M*

410. *Res*
411. *Res*

Comment: The patient seems to let slip in 406 ("No, I never—I never know.") her wish to have the therapist tell her what to do. Then in 410 and 411 she denies that she really feels this wish. It would also be plausible, though, to consider sentence 406 resistant on the ground that the patient does have some feeling about what the therapist's opinion is, but is unwilling to admit this.

THERAPIST (*Softly*)   412Mm-hmm.

PATIENT   413Yet I don't know . . . well . . . ah . . . for instance if you . . . if you said, "Well, you gotta stop this and keep your mouth shut and . . ." ah . . . I'd say, "Fine, I'll try it . . . 414(*With embarrassed laugh*) (*Therapist laughs*) . . . but I don't think it's going to work." 415(*Embarrassed laugh*)

THERAPIST   416Yes?

PATIENT   But it—

THERAPIST   417And if I said, "Go ahead and blow your top"—

PATIENT   418Then I'd say—

THERAPIST   —you'd say, "I *can't,* I *can't,* I've got to help my husband," huh?

PATIENT   —"You don't know what a sweet husband I have."

THERAPIST   419"You don't know what a sweet husband I have"?

PATIENT   420Yeah.

THERAPIST   421Yeah.

PATIENT   422So 423(*5-sec. pause*) there is the unanswered question.

THERAPIST   424Namely?

PATIENT   425Of how to be able to . . . to achieve what you would like to, to be the kind of person you would like to be. 426You can *never* quite make it.

THERAPIST   427You think a really good person would inhibit any expression of feeling that would hurt somebody else?

412. *M*

413. *H therapist*

   Comment: We score this sentence as hostile toward the therapist because the patient imagines him doing something to which she aggressively takes exception. A somewhat less satisfactory score would be *Dep therapist,* to represent the patient's wish that the therapist would give her advice as she here imagines him doing.

414. *Lf—*

415. *Lf—*

416. *D*

417. *D*

418. *Res*

419. *D*

420. *Y*

421. *M*

422. *Res*

423. *Res 5*

424. *D*

425. *Res*

426. *Res*

427. *D*

PATIENT   428No, I . . . it's just that I see the kind of person I want to be, and see that I'm not that. 429And I still can't say to myself that . . . that I . . . I will be that . . . other kind of person. 430I can *try*. 431And I can get a little closer to it maybe. But I never—

THERAPIST   432Well what kind of person do you *want* to be?

PATIENT   433Well, I'm not s . . . 434(*Embarrassed laugh*) . . . sure yet. 435I bu . . . I *would* choose, I think if I could, to *be* less expressive . . . just . . . ah . . . by reason of the fact that a . . . a professional man's wife just . . . ah shouldn't be too pushy. 436The ones who are, or who seem to be . . . get their husbands into trouble.

THERAPIST (*Softly*)   437Mmm.

PATIENT   438And I'd rather fit into the expected pattern a little easier if I could.

THERAPIST   439Well, would that lead you to a position like . . . ah . . . if you have some dissatisfaction in the sexual relationship you should simply stifle that?

PATIENT   440Well, no, not particularly . . . unless it uh . . . influences other things, because, ordinarily, that would be . . . just between two people.

THERAPIST   441But let's say that—

PATIENT   It would just be—

THERAPIST   —that if you stifled it your husband would be more comfortable. 442He would go on feeling, as I think you expressed it last time, mmmm . . . pr . . . reasonably good. 443He was satisfied.

PATIENT   444Mm-hmm. That—

THERAPIST   445Whereas if you bring it up he suffers discomfort.

428. *Res*
429. *Res*
430. *Res*
431. *Res*
   Comment: The patient is talking in generalities, not about her own feelings and conflicts. This is an intellectual resistance, scored *Res*.
432. *D*

433. *H-A Bill*
434. *Lf—*
435. *H-A Bill*
436. *H-A Bill*

437. *M*

438. *H-A Bill*

439. *D*

440. *Res*
   Comment: Another possibility would be to call this sentence simply *N*, because she answers rather reasonably that expressing herself outside isn't the same as expressing herself within the family. Yet on the whole it seems that the patient isn't really answering the therapist directly; her problem about self-expression *is* to a considerable degree centered around the question of sexual satisfaction, and this answer doesn't come to grips with that point.
441. *D*

442. *D*
443. *D*

444. *Y*

445. *D*

PATIENT   [446]Mm-hmm.

THERAPIST   [447]What shall you do?

PATIENT   [448]Well, if there's a . . . a chance of changing it, then I think it's better to bring it out, because . . . ah . . . the improvement . . . is going to benefit him too . . .

THERAPIST   [449]I see.

PATIENT   . . . 'cause I don't doubt for a minute he hasn't been fully satisfied either even if . . . he has physically.

THERAPIST (*Softly*)   [450]Mm-hmm.

PATIENT   [451]If he were . . . completely self-centered, which he isn't . . . even then I'm not certain. [452]Things that . . . that couldn't be changed, if a person could—could stifle them, it . . . it would be better. [453]I'm just never quite sure how you meet frustration best, 'cause you . . . you have to learn to accept it in *some* phases eventually . . .

THERAPIST (*Softly*)   [454]Mmm.

PATIENT   . . . and if you . . . go all to pieces every time, that—

THERAPIST   [455]Do you notice, by the way, that it seems that . . . ah . . . that the kinds of things we've been saying would almost lead to the conclusion that you *can't* really make any kind of abso-

446. *Y*

447. *D*

448. *Obs*

449. *M*

450. *M*

451. *Obs*

452. *Obs*

453. *Obs*

Comment: Sentences 448 and 451–3 are very difficult to score. On the one hand the patient's utterance seems resistant because she focuses attention on the external situation, saying that the problem is in the situation between herself and her husband, not in her. This diversion of attention from inward conflicts that have produced her frigidity is of course resistant. Then there is a certain slight reasonableness in her comment in 448 that if something can be done about the conflict between herself and her husband it would be better to bring it into the open; so one is tempted to score *Reas.* Finally, it is clear that the patient is ambivalent about her husband, torn between expressing aggression toward him and restraining herself. It is tempting to designate this by a score such as *H-A Bill.* While these alternative scorings have a certain attractiveness, it is our judgment that the patient's ambivalence—rapidly alternating feelings of love and hate—is the most striking feature of these sentences. Moreover, her indecision is very clearly shown later on in sentences 468, 470, 472, 474. Taking a look at these later sentences helps us to decide what is going on in the earlier ones.

454. *M*

455. *D*

lute statement about whether it's better to express or not to express . . .

PATIENT   [456]Yeah.

THERAPIST   . . . that it *depends* on the context . . .

PATIENT (*Softly*)   [457]Mm-hmm. [458]Sure!

THERAPIST   . . . just like you now said, "Well, if it's something that *can't* be helped, . . . then to try to express it would only be painful. It might be better to stifle it."

PATIENT (*Softly*)   [459]Mm-hmm.

THERAPIST   [460]Or like another example . . .

PATIENT   [461]Yeah.

THERAPIST   . . . would be if in the present context for you to express yourself, let's say, would lead to your husband's not passing the bar, and if that's something that's paramount in your . . . in the immediate life of *both* of you, it has to take precedence . . .

PATIENT   [462]Mm-hmm.

THERAPIST   . . . then to some extent *that* will regulate what you do. [463]So . . . it depends on a number of things, as against some . . .

PATIENT   [464]Yeah.

THERAPIST   . . . sort of an absolute . . .

PATIENT   [465]Mm-hmm.

THERAPIST   . . . rigid decision about how one lives.

PATIENT   [466-7](*9-sec. pause*) [468]In the second way, I'm not so sure what . . . (*Therapist clears throat*) . . . I'd decide . . . but—

THERAPIST   [469]I—I didn't hear what you said.

PATIENT   [470]In the . . . in the second instance I'm not . . . sure *what* I'd decide.

THERAPIST   [471]About . . . ?

456. *Y*

457. *Y*
458. *Y*

459. *Y*
460. *D*
461. *Y*

462. *Y*

463. *D*
   Comment: Sentences 455, 460, and 463 are on the borderline of *Interp*. It almost seems that the therapist is helping the patient to make a discrimination; but one cannot point to any unconscious motive that he is labeling, hence *Interp* must be rejected.
464. *Y*

465. *Y*

466. *Res 5*
467. *Res 5*
468. *Obs*
469. *D*

470. *Obs*

471. *D*

PATIENT   [472]Well I can see the importance . . .

THERAPIST   [473]Yeah?

PATIENT   . . . to *him* of . . . of passing the bar exam. [474]And . . . I may say I . . . ah . . . the . . . the ah bar exam ah . . . doesn't mean as much to me as it does to him . . .

THERAPIST   [475]That's right.

PATIENT   . . . any more than . . .

THERAPIST   [476]Mm-hmm.

PATIENT   . . . than ah—

THERAPIST   [477]Then in practical terms that would lead to . . . some questioning on your part maybe whether he should drop out of treatment, hmm?

PATIENT   [478]Oh yes.

THERAPIST   [479]Oh, I thought you had accepted that.

PATIENT   [480]Well, in a way I have 'cause it seems like there's—

THERAPIST   [481]But . . . there's nothing you can do about it. (*Laughs*)

PATIENT   —not much I can do about it one way or the other. [482](*Embarrassed laugh*)

THERAPIST   [483]Yes.

PATIENT   [484]But . . . ah . . . he had . . . has brought out other things that . . . that seem to distress *him* just as much at times as . . . as this other thing distresses me.

THERAPIST   [485]Yes, what are they?

PATIENT   [486]Well that . . . this idea that he feels as though he's effeminate, and . . .

THERAPIST   [487]Oh you mean that . . . that there are enough reasons within *himself* . . .

472. *Obs*

473. *D*

474. *Obs*

475. *R*

476. *M*

477. *D*

478. *Y*

479. *D*

480. *Unsc*

481. *R*

482. *Lf—*

483. *M*

484. *L Bill*

485. *D*

486. *L Bill*

487. *D*

Comment: This sentence is not quite an *Interp* because the therapist does not label for the patient something she previously had no words for. He does strengthen her tendency to accept the thought that her husband has neurotic problems of his own; and since this thought could play an important role in the patient's reasoning

PATIENT   [488]Yeah.

THERAPIST . . . which might make it desirable for him to go on with treatment.

PATIENT   [489]Mm-hmm.

THERAPIST   [490]Yeah.

PATIENT   [491]So then it's a question of . . . of between the two things—cramming for the bar exam or getting psychotherapy— which is most important. And [492-3](*8-sec. pause*) [494]But . . . but actually . . . my . . . even if I . . . ah . . . followed what would appear to be the more *selfish* course, just going right along and . . . letting off steam when *I* felt like it, it isn't going to decide him either way. [495]I mean, it just may . . . [496](*Embarrassed laugh*) . . . ruin everything.

THERAPIST   [497]Yeah. [498]You realize, don't you, that one of the things which is really troubling you . . . is the feeling that he . . . is not . . . sufficiently concerned with your feelings and your needs.

PATIENT (*Softly*)   [499]Mm-hmm.

THERAPIST   [500]You know that?

PATIENT   [501]Yes, I'm very aware of that.

THERAPIST   [502]This is what happened about the birthday.

PATIENT (*Softly*)   [503]Mm-hmm.

THERAPIST   [504]You might have wept a little in disappointment. [505]But it wouldn't have become so crucial . . .

PATIENT (*Softly*)   [506]Mm-hmm.

THERAPIST . . . if he hadn't seemed so disinterested, because that meant to you . . .

PATIENT   [507]Yeah.

THERAPIST . . . that "he doesn't care if I get what I want or not."

PATIENT   [508]It seems like a . . . so many things that aren't neces-

activities, the therapist has done something to help her master her problems. Thus the sentence comes close to being an *Interp,* yet the strengthening of one of her feelings makes *D* a more apt scoring.
488. *Y*

489. *Y*

490. *M*

491. *L Bill*
492. *Res 5*
493. *Res 5*
494. *H-A Bill*
495. *H-A Bill*
496. *Lf—*

497. *M*
498. *Interp*

499. *Y*

500. *Interp*

501. *Dep Bill*

502. *Interp*

503. *Y*

504. *Interp*
505. *Interp*

506. *Y*

507. *Y*

508. *H Bill*

sarily . . . my . . . way, but . . . well actually it . . . it would be, but that . . . ah . . . it has t' come to some kind of strain or stress, actually touch him *emotionally* before it means *anything* to him. [509]And yet it's . . . it's so *hard* to do that. He just—

THERAPIST   [510]You mean you have to be hit pretty hard and—

PATIENT   [511]Yeah, I—

THERAPIST   —let out a squeal . . . [512](*Patient laughs*) . . . before he knows something's going on, hunh?

PATIENT   [513]Just be rocked or . . .

THERAPIST   [514]Yeah.

PATIENT   . . . about ready to cave in before he realizes that there's anything there.

THERAPIST   [515]You think that has anything to do with the problems for which you first came?

PATIENT   [516]Sure!

THERAPIST   [517]In what way?

PATIENT   [518]Well I don't know exactly what way. [519]But uh . . . ah . . . he *still* says that he doesn't believe that it could be quite so crucial, that it would mean so much.

THERAPIST   [520]That what could be "quite so crucial"?

PATIENT   [521]Well, just this matter of . . . sexual satisfaction or not, that it means something, but that it may be just something that we'll have to adjust to.

THERAPIST   [522]Yeah.

PATIENT   [523]His whole pattern is of adjusting to a situation—in everything.

THERAPIST   [524]Rather than . . . ?

PATIENT   [525]Than doing something about it—if something can be done . . .

THERAPIST   [526]Yeah.

PATIENT   . . . or maybe . . . maybe doing something even if . . . it can't make any improvement.

509. *H Bill*

510. *R*

511. *Y*

512. *Lf+*

513. *H Bill*

514. *M*

515. *Interp*

516. *Y*

517. *D*

518. *Res*

519. *H Bill*

520. *D*

521. *H Bill*

522. *M*

523. *H Bill*

524. *D*

525. *H Bill*

526. *M*

THERAPIST [527]Yes, I wondered if you felt that your feeling that he isn't sufficiently aware of your needs has something to do with your . . . dissatisfaction in intercourse?

PATIENT [528]Ah . . . I feel quite certainly it is, 'cause it . . . in li . . . little ways it was a thing that . . . bothered me even before we were married.

THERAPIST (*Softly*) [529]Mm-hmm.

PATIENT [530]Then I . . . just thought that . . . possibly it . . . it might change a little bit, that as we grew together, we would both . . . come in [531](*Embarrassed laugh*) from our opposite extremes. [532]And perhaps . . .

THERAPIST [533]Mmm.

PATIENT . . . I should've known that—even then when I knew him so well—that if it wasn't that way, then . . .

THERAPIST [534]Mmm.

PATIENT . . . it might never be. [535]And yet he is a . . . a very sensitive person, and . . . it . . . [536]Once . . . he is aroused it's just as . . . it seems like there's a kind of concrete on top of his feelings . . .

THERAPIST [537]Mmm.

PATIENT . . . that they're there and just as . . . as turbulent as mine are . . .

THERAPIST [538]Mmm.

PATIENT . . . only . . . because then when he finally *does* get them out—

THERAPIST [539]They're quite strong.

PATIENT . . . It just . . .

THERAPIST [540]Yeah. [541]And this, of course, is related to the question that you asked about expressing yourself . . .

PATIENT [542]Mm-hmm.

527. *Interp*

528. *Dep Bill*

529. *M*

530. *Dep Bill*
531. *Lf—*
532. *Dep Bill*

533. *M*

534. *M*

535. *L Bill*
536. *L Bill*

Comment: The patient's evident identification with Bill in sentences 535–6 deserves the name of "love." The mention of arousal in sentence 536 apparently is not intended as a sexual allusion; if it were, one would be inclined to consider this sentence as a candidate for *S*.

537. *M*

538. *M*

539. *R*

540. *M*
541. *Interp*

542. *Y*

THERAPIST . . . because that almost amounts to saying, "When I have the feeling that *he* doesn't realize what my need is, shall I . . .

PATIENT 543Mm-hmm.

THERAPIST . . . *make* him see it?"

PATIENT 544Those are the times when I . . . I just can't seem to help myself.

THERAPIST 545Yes. 546And his reaction initially apparently is . . . uh . . . sort of to be angry, and offended, and hurt—"*She* is complaining that I don't do enough . . .

PATIENT 547Yeah.

THERAPIST . . . for her," is what it amounts to, hunh?

PATIENT 548Mm-hmm.

THERAPIST 549But later he sees that there's some justice in it, you feel . . . and goes and buys a new dress, hunh?

PATIENT 550He always . . . he *always* then has these . . . guilt feelings. 551And that's what makes us *both* feel so terrible because . . .

THERAPIST 552Yeah.

PATIENT . . . we'd drift into the guilt feelings at exactly the same time.

THERAPIST 553Yeah. 554How did the week go after . . . that? 555The real disturbance was Saturday, wasn't it?

PATIENT 556Mm-hmm.

THERAPIST 557And then what happened?

PATIENT 558Well we . . . we hardly . . . had a chance to . . . to be together as I s—

THERAPIST 559Mmm.

543. *Y*

544. *Dep Bill*
Comment: Is this an aggression-fear conflict or a conflict concerned with expressing dependent needs? We believe that the question of dependence is far more important in the situation described by the patient in sentence 544, therefore the correct score is *Dep*.
545. *M*
546. *D*

547. *Y*

548. *Y*
549. *D*

550. *A*
551. *A*
Comment: The debate here (550–1) is between plain *A* and *H-A*. Since it is somewhat debatable what the source of the guilt is, we prefer *A*.
552. *M*

553. *M*
554. *D*
555. *D*
556. *Y*

557. *D*

558. *H-A Bill*

559. *M*

PATIENT   [560]We had an overnight guest Monday, though Bill was gone . . . ah . . . all the evening. [561]He's been gone every evening. [562]And . . . ah . . . it's . . . it's been *much* smoother . . . [563]Ah . . . wi . . . ah . . . Wednesday night, there wasn't anything actually to . . . to set things off, no particular thing. [564]I think it was that we were just both at . . . had been living off nerve for—

THERAPIST   [565]What happened Wednesday night?

PATIENT   [566]Well that . . . we couldn't sleep that night.

THERAPIST   [567]That was the night you couldn't sleep.

PATIENT   [568]And we . . . we just seem to *never* get enough sleep.

THERAPIST (*Softly*)   [569]Yeah.

PATIENT   [570]And we . . . we haven't had an intercourse since . . . [571](*5-sec. pause*) well, I guess a week ago Sunday, or some time like that. [572]And it . . . w . . . the idea of it still just is . . . completely repulsive to *me*.

THERAPIST   [573]Mm-hmm. [574](*7-sec. pause*) [575]I guess we have to recognize that your having come into treatment *has* in some sense stirred these things up.

PATIENT   [576](*Embarrassed laugh*) [577]Yeah.

THERAPIST   [578]Hmmm?

PATIENT   [579](*Embarrassed laugh*) I uh—

THERAPIST   [580]I mean before you said you just weren't interested. [581]And now . . .

PATIENT   [582]Yeah.

THERAPIST   . . . it's actually a little repulsive—

PATIENT   [583]Mm-hmm.

560. *H-A Bill*
561. *H-A Bill*
562. *H-A:r Bill*
563. *Res*
564. *Res*

Comment: The whole context is considered in scoring 560–1 *H-A Bill.* Presumably the patient's conflict about her husband was continuing throughout these days. Her mention of the somewhat reduced tension earns an *r* in 562. We consider 563 and 564 to be resistant, particularly 564, because the patient belittles the psychological stimuli which produced the distress Wednesday night and advances a countertheory, the "living-off-nerve" theory.

565. *D*

566. *H-A Bill*

567. *D*

568. *Res*

569. *M*

570. *S-A Bill*
571. *Res 5*
572. *S-A Bill*

573. *M*
574. *Res 5*
575. *Interp*

576. *Lf—*
577. *Y*
578. *D*

579. *Lf—*

580. *Interp*
581. *Interp*

582. *Y*

583. *Y*

THERAPIST   [584]But I don't think that should alarm you.

PATIENT   [585]I have a feeling that . . . that . . . it just may go to the very depths . . .

THERAPIST (*Softly*)   [586]Mm-hmm.

PATIENT   . . . before [587](*Embarrassed laugh*) we get out of it. [588]But I want to know how far I am from the bottom. [589](*Laughing anxiously*)

THERAPIST (*Softly*)   [590]Yeah.

PATIENT   [591]Is there any way of . . . telling how long this goes on?

THERAPIST   [592]No. [593]No, I don't think so.

PATIENT   [594]I feel in some small way as though . . . there's *some* [595](*Sighing*) progress. But . . .

THERAPIST   [596]I certainly sympathize with your feeling that . . . it might be better if you could have more frequent interviews. [597]Unfortunately we can't.

PATIENT   [598]Yeah, well that . . . actually I . . . I couldn't either . . . [599](*Embarrassed laugh*) . . . from a time standpoint.

THERAPIST   [600]I see.

PATIENT   [601]I think . . . well I don't know. [602]I used to think that . . . when I'd . . . these things would bother me if I were home an afternoon, like I usually am on Friday, that . . . I could . . . could sorta get them out of my system by myself.

584. *R*

585. *A therapy*

586. *M*

587. *Lf—*
588. *A therapy*
589. *Lf—*

590. *M*

591. *Res*
Comment: Sentence 591 is scored *Res* because it expresses a wish by the patient to escape the treatment. After all, this is only the fifth hour; she shouldn't expect to be cured by now.
592. *D*
593. *D*
Comment: Since these sentences would be expected to increase the patient's motivation, they are scored *D*.
594. *L therapist*
Comment: The other possibility for 594 is *A therapy,* on the ground that the patient's predominant feeling is anxiety about the therapy. We believed that there was some slight edge for positive feeling; therefore *L* is more appropriate.
595. *Sigh*
596. *R*
597. *D*

598. *Res*
Comment: One is torn between *Res* and *H therapist*. *Res* has in its favor that the patient is denying that she ever had any wish to get more time from the therapist; *H therapist* has in its favor that the patient is saying in effect, "Well, I'll reject you, too, just as you rejected me."
599. *Lf—*
600. *M*

601. *Res*
602. *A*

THERAPIST (*Softly*)   [603]Oh yeah.

PATIENT   [604]But I never could. [605]And I just got into a . . .

THERAPIST   [606]Just fretted and stewed about it. [607]Yeah.

PATIENT   . . . depressed morbid kind of thinking which I don't think was healthful.

THERAPIST   [608]Yeah. [609]But I think our attitude should be that we'll accomplish what we can—

PATIENT   [610]Mmm.

THERAPIST   —in the time that we have, hmmm?

PATIENT   [611]I just . . . ah . . . I was so concerned about the depression, never—and I had been about his too—never knowing how far . . . a person can go on, how much of that you can take before you *do* just crack.

THERAPIST   [612]Mmm.

PATIENT   [613]And . . . ah . . . I still don't know. But I—

THERAPIST   [614]I don't think you should be concerned about your basic stability.

PATIENT   [615]I . . . well I . . . I *have* been very concerned about it.

THERAPIST   [616]About *yours?*

PATIENT   [617]Yes.

THERAPIST (*Softly*)   [618]What do you mean?

PATIENT   Well I just—

THERAPIST   [619]You've been scared?

PATIENT   [620]Yeah, I've really been awfully scared. [621](*Embarrassed laugh*)

THERAPIST   [622]What do you think by that?

603. *M*

604. *A*
605. *A*
     Comment: The scoring conflict about sentences 602, 604, and 605 is between *A* and *Dep therapist*. In a way, the patient's utterance here is a plea to the therapist to help her since she can't help herself. Yet this is not explicit, nor is it very clear, so *A* is probably the better score.
606. *R*
607. *M*
608. *M*
609. *D*

610. *Y*

611. *A*

612. *M*

613. *A*

614. *R*

615. *A*

616. *D*

617. *Y*

618. *D*

619. *D*

620. *A*
621. *Lf—*

622. *D*

PATIENT   623Well I . . . well I know for one thing that I, at least as I am now, unless something would just completely go off, that I . . . I could *never* take my own life. 624Goodness knows, I . . . I'd . . . ah . . . I just am not made that way.

THERAPIST   625Mm-hmm.

PATIENT   626And that's the pity of it, 627(*Embarrassed laugh*) 'cause I'm sure I'd have done it fifty times by now.

THERAPIST   628Really!

PATIENT   629Not . . . I . . . I can't ever think . . . specifically in terms of . . . suicide. 630I can just feel awful sorry for myself and wish I were dead. But—

THERAPIST   631Does that mean that during this past week or two you have, on occasion, had feelings that were so painful that it seemed to you—

PATIENT   632Yeah, I just . . . as I lay awake that night and couldn't . . . just couldn't see *any* direction out of it, and . . . then I wished that there would be some way that I could go to sleep and never wake up in the morning.

THERAPIST (*Very softly*)   633Oh yeah.

PATIENT   634But it didn't occur to me to go out and turn the gas on. 635(*Embarrassed laugh*)

THERAPIST   636Mm-hmm.

PATIENT   637I mean . . . ah . . . if I ever am faced with a realistic possibility like that, then I . . .

THERAPIST   638Yeah.

PATIENT   . . . know what the decision is.

THERAPIST   639I don't think you should be alarmed.

623. *A*
624. *A*

625. *M*

626. *A*
Comment: Sentence 626 is also a candidate for a *Res* scoring, since it might be considered a humorous way of defending herself against these painful feelings.
627. *Lf—*
628. *D*

629. *A*
630. *A*

631. *D*

632. *A*

633. *M*

634. *A*
635. *Lf—*

636. *M*

637. *A*
Comment: The scorer's dilemma about 634 and 637 is: Is there a real reduction in the patient's anxiety, stemming from her self-reassurance that she wouldn't really kill herself? This is plausible but didn't seem convincing enough to make us decide for the score *A:r.*
638. *M*

639. *R*

PATIENT   [640]Thanks! [641]*(Anxious laugh)* *(Therapist laughs; he rises to go)* [642]I consider you an authority. [643]*(Laughing anxiously; she rises)*

THERAPIST *(Laughing)*   [644]A hot potato. *(Opening doors)* [645]I'll see you next week.

PATIENT   [646]All right.

THERAPIST   [647]Good-by.

PATIENT   [648]Good-by.

640. *L therapist*
641. *Lf—*
642. *L therapist*
643. *Lf—*
644. *R*
645. *Unsc*

646. *Unsc*

647. *Unsc*

648. *Unsc*

CHAPTER 7

Reliability of the Scoring

A SURVEY of current research on psychotherapy reveals a curious state of affairs: A good many therapists are reporting their experiences, and some of them claim considerable therapeutic success, but there is little agreement among therapists about what makes for therapeutic success or, indeed, about what happens in psychotherapy. Thoughtful consideration of this paradox leads to the conclusion that the confusion stems from lack of attention to the development of reliable measures.* In general, reliable measures of the behavior of the patient and the therapist during psychotherapy interviews do not exist. There are no adequate measures of the success of the therapeutic process taken as a whole. There are no adequate measures of the strength of resistances, transference, cathartic experiences, loosening of repression, or development of insight.

It is not surprising that therapists cannot agree whether a transference neurosis is a necessary development in successful psychotherapy, when they cannot agree what should be designated as transference or how one can evaluate success. Nor is it surprising that they cannot agree on the best method for dealing with resistances of the patient, when there is no reliable way to designate a resistance. It should be apparent therefore that developing reliable measures of the events in psychotherapy is no pious and empty exercise, nor is it a compulsive absorption in minutiae. It is, instead, a necessary step in the development of a science of psychotherapy.

We considered it therefore a necessity of our work to devote much attention to the reliability of our measures. Much of our work, in fact, could best be described as the devising of reliable

---

* In this discussion we will say that a method of measurement is *reliable* if it gives consistent results, i.e. if any scientist using the method on a particular body of data gets the same result as any other scientist.

measures for concepts such as resistance, conflict, anxiety, and hostility, which have hitherto been poorly defined.

DEFINITION OF "MEASURE"

By "measurement" we mean any designation of an event as belonging to one class rather than another. To be sure, this is the most general definition of measurement, a definition that places even bare classification—the most primitive type of quantification—in the domain of measure. The more advanced kinds of measurement involve an ordering of the classes (e.g. Class A is said to be "higher" than Class B—as when we say that diamond is harder than topaz), a measurement of the distances between classes (e.g. between things two inches long and things three inches long), or a comparison of the size of the things within the various classes (e.g. a quart of milk is twice as much as a pint of milk). Though these more advanced types of measurement have advantages over the crudest type of classification, it is useful to remember that precise measurement can always be considered as a refined form of classification (Wilson, 1952, p. 166; Stevens, 1951).

The fundamental operation of our content-analysis system is the classification of each of the sentences in an interview. We start, then, with the most primitive kind of measurement. By taking this first step we have tried to lay a foundation for the quantitative study of psychotherapy.

ACCURACY OF THE MEASUREMENT SYSTEM

Professor Wilson (p. 232) cogently points out: "A measurement whose accuracy is completely unknown has no use whatever. It is therefore necessary to know how to estimate the reliability of experimental data and how to convey this information to others."

What we are interested in is the accuracy of the whole measurement system. For example, the Smith family buys a new bathroom scale. Is the measurement system accurate? That depends on the built-in accuracy of the scale's mechanism; on its proper use (the scale must not be put on a bath mat, lest its readings be thrown off; the adjusting screw must be set to zero each time); and on the ability of the observer to read the dial numbers accurately (he must stand directly over the dial marker to avoid errors of parallax; he must estimate the weight accurately when it falls between scale divisions). The reliability of the measurement thus depends on much more than the accuracy of the instrument itself; it depends on the accuracy of the whole measurement system.

Our complete content-analysis measurement system includes: the scoring rules, the scorer, some particular material to be scored, the processing of the raw classifications, and the testing of hypotheses with the resulting data. In determining reliability of measurement we must take into account the functioning of this whole measurement system. The reliability will surely differ somewhat with different scorers, with different cases, and with different methods of processing the data and using it to test hypotheses. Accordingly, one should show the reliability of the method in a particular application—so that one can know that the whole measurement system is reliable. Just as the best bathroom scale would be of no use to a chemist performing a semimicroquantitative analysis, so a content-analysis system that is appropriate for cruder tests of general hypotheses may be quite inadequate for sensitive tests of special hypotheses. Conversely, a system that is inadequate for very refined purposes, or that could not be applied to certain kinds of material, may be appropriate for other uses.

EXAMPLE OF A SPECIFIC TEST OF RELIABILITY

Ideally, therefore, the statement of the reliability of the content analysis should specify the kinds of comparisons that are to be made. We may illustrate this by showing the way in which reliability could be demonstrated for the test of this hypothesis: Resistant statements show more of a downward trend, in the course of therapy, in the O'Connell case than in the Davidson case. Two psychologists independently scored these cases. The amount of resistant talk which they found in the average hour of early and late portions of the two cases is shown in Table 2.

TABLE 2. NUMBER OF UNITS OF RESISTANT TALK AS
JUDGED BY TWO SCORERS

	SCORER A		SCORER B	
	Early hours	Late hours	Early hours	Late hours
Davidson case	47	92	57	65
O'Connell case	169	107	193	138

Now we may take the difference between the average number of resistant sentences in an early hour and the average number in a late hour as a measure of the trend. Subtracting the late hours from the early, we obtain the data shown in Table 3.

TABLE 3. DIFFERENCE BETWEEN NUMBER OF UNITS OF
RESISTANT TALK IN EARLY AND LATE HOURS

	Scorer A	*Scorer B*
Davidson case	−45	−8
O'Connell case	62	55

We see that, whether the scores of psychologist A or of B are used, one reaches the conclusion that there were more resistant sentences in late hours of the Davidson case than in early hours but more resistant sentences in early hours of the O'Connell case than in late hours. However, one does not know whether still another scorer would get the same result. Can one estimate the variability in result caused by differences between scorers, and can one say how likely it would be that the Davidson and O'Connell cases would be found to be different, if other psychologists should score these cases? Yes, one can, by using the variation between A's and B's scores as an estimate of the variation among scorers and performing a *t*-test. In this example $t = 4.51$, which is significant at the 5% level. It can be concluded that other scorers like A and B would get similar results.

In this example the measure of reliability is exactly pertinent to the use made of the scores. Frequently, however, one cannot foresee just what comparisons will be made. Under such circumstances one needs some general measure of the agreement between the scorers. Either a product-moment correlation coefficient or a percentage-of-agreement figure is ordinarily used to measure such agreement.

HOW GOOD MUST THE RELIABILITY BE?

When, as in the preceding example, one knows exactly what comparison is to be made, one can determine whether the reliability of scoring is adequate to permit measurement of the difference one is interested in studying. The question is simply this: Is the measurement system precise enough to detect differences of the size one expects to find? When one does not know beforehand what comparisons will be made, it is more difficult to decide how precise the measurement must be. Hence it is hard to decide whether a particular reliability coefficient is good or bad.

If we look at common practice we discover that most behavioral scientists have considered their scoring reliability to be satisfactory if the product-moment correlation coefficients were about .85 or higher. Berelson (1952) states that reliabilities reported in the literature on content analysis have ranged between .78 and .99, with a concentration at about .90. He notes, however, that in only 15 to 20% of the content-analysis studies have investigators reported the reliability of classification. One suspects that the more careful workers reported reliabilities; thus the reliabilities are probably poorer in the studies where they were not reported. Bales, whose Interaction Process Analysis system is generally well regarded, was satisfied with reliability coefficients ranging from .74 to .97, with a median of .90 (Heinicke and Bales, 1953). Murray (1956) considered coefficients averaging about .80 to be satisfactory. Saul and Sheppard (1956) considered reliabilities of .83, .84, and .85 to be adequate.

These judgments about the minimum size for a satisfactory reliability coefficient seem to have been carried over into content analysis from testing. In testing, unless there is very high scoring reliability and great consistency of individual differences, one cannot hope to use the test to predict various outcomes. When content-analysis scores are to be similarly used for predicting outcome by means of individual differences in scores, the same high standards should be brought to bear. It is possible, however, that for other uses—for example, for testing quite broad hypotheses—cruder measures will suffice, so that lower product-moment coefficients will be adequate. Whether or not this is true can only be determined by research.

THREE WAYS OF USING THE CONTENT SCORES

The data of our content-analysis system can be put to use in a number of ways. The scores for a whole case can be added up to give a picture of the case, perhaps to contrast it with other cases. The scores for a particular category can be studied over the whole series of interviews, to examine trends in this category or variations related to those in some other category. Finally, the score for a single sentence can be considered. One may ask, for instance, whether a sentence scored as indicating anxiety is likely to be accompanied by a change in the patient's skin resistance. Each of these uses of the system brings distinct problems of reliability of scoring.

RELIABILITY OF THE PROFILE FOR A WHOLE CASE

If the use of the scores is to construct a profile of the whole case, the appropriate measure of reliability is the degree of correspondence between the profiles of two persons who independently score

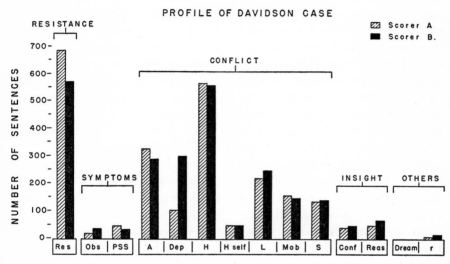

Fig. 1. Number of sentences assigned to each category by two scorers for the case of Mrs. Davidson.

the case. Such scoring, it must be emphasized, has to be completely independent, without any consultation between the scorers until after all of the scoring has been completed. We have scored the Davidson case in this way. In Figure 1 we compare the profile of the patient's categories constructed from the scores of psychologist A with that of psychologist B. The product-moment correlation between these profiles is .95. A similar comparison for the therapist's categories yielded a correlation of .99. One can conclude that the two scorers arrived at essentially the same over-all picture of this case.

RELIABILITY OF A CATEGORY OVER A SERIES
OF INTERVIEWS

If we are interested in studying the changes in the categories during a series of interviews—for example, in finding out whether resistant sentences decline and insight sentences increase during psychotherapy—it is appropriate to consider whether scorers agree on the relative frequency of occurrence of each category in various hours. After we had given the patient's categories of the content-analysis system essentially their present shape, we scored 18 hours in two cases. Table 4 summarizes the reliability coefficients for the patient's categories in these two cases. We scored 8383 sentences of these two patients. The table reports the results on 8133 sentences —97% of the material—omitting data from any category or sub-category that had less than 1% of the total sentences of the case. (For example, one scorer used *L-A* 11 times, the other used it 8 times, in the Smith case. The average frequency of *L-A* is therefore 9.5, or about .2 of 1% of the total number of sentences scored. Any coefficient based on such meager evidence is bound to be quite unstable.) There was no other basis for omission of data; all categories meeting the 1% standard are reported, regardless of whether they make us look good or bad.

At the time these cases were scored, our work on developing the therapist's categories had not been completed. Thus we do not have similar data from these cases on reliability of therapist categories. In order to evaluate the reliability of the revised therapist categories, however, we later scored six hours from two cases, and the results of this test are shown in Table 5.

To give the reader an intuitive grasp of how good or bad these product-moment correlations are, we show in Figure 2 a typical correlation from the Smith case—that for the *Dep* category. Note that there is a strong but far from perfect tendency for the two scorers to agree about the relative frequency of sentences expressing dependence. It may be noted that the scorers agree in their description of the general trend of *Dep* in the case, even though their correlation coefficient of .62 doesn't sound like a very good level of agreement. We illustrate one of the "excellent" correlations in Figure 3, so that the reader can form an impression of how much agreement is involved in these very high correlations. This graph

PRODUCT-MOMENT CORRELATIONS

Category	Davidson case	Smith case
A (broad) *†	.68	.70
A (narrow) *	.62	.60
A:r *	.80	.67
Conf *	.63	.88
Dep (broad) *	.54	.62
Dep (narrow) *	.75	.78
dep-a *	—	.67
H (broad) *	.65	.77
H (narrow) *	.70	.79
H-A	.63	—.07
H-a	.54	.00
H/self *	.74	.37
L (broad) *	.36	.76
L (narrow) *	.56	.80
Mob (broad) *	.94	.97
Mob (narrow) *	.97	.00
Mob-A *	—	.81
N *	.74	—
PSS *	.91	.97
Reas *	.32	.73
Res talk *	.59	.44
S (broad) *	.96	.67
S (narrow) *	.67	.89
S-a *	.97	—
s-A	—	.53
Unsc	—.09	.81
Y *	.95	.95

* Indicates that the category is statistically significant at the .05 level or better, when the coefficients for the two cases are considered jointly (according to the procedure suggested by Stouffer).

† "Broad" means the inclusive category; e.g. A (broad) includes A, a, and A:r, whereas A (narrow) includes only A.

TABLE 5. RELIABILITY OF THERAPIST'S CATEGORIES OVER A
SERIES OF INTERVIEWS

	PRODUCT-MOMENT CORRELATIONS	
Category	Davidson case	Foote case
D	.96	.93
Interp	.55	.90
M	.36	.996
R	.82	.98
Unsc	.998	—

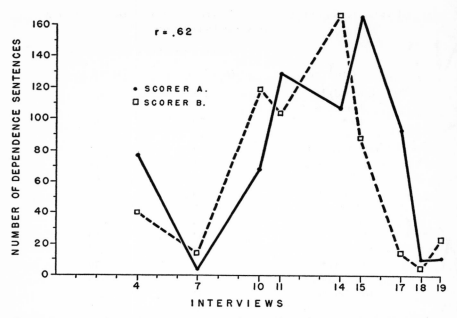

Fig. 2. Agreement between two scorers on the number of sentences expressing dependence in each hour of the Smith case.

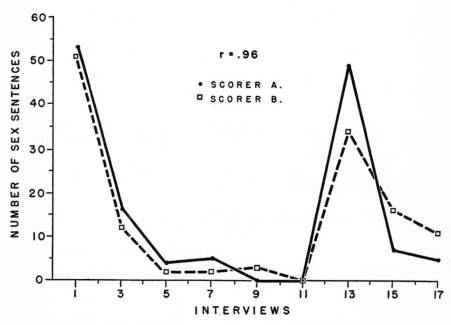

Fig. 3. Agreement between two scorers on the number of sentences expressing sexual motivation in each hour of the Davidson case.

shows how many sentences each of the scorers classified as S in each of the hours of the Davidson case.

Lest the reader be bedazzled by the array of coefficients in Table 4, we hasten to summarize. The weighted average of the correlation coefficients for the main categories of the Davidson case is .75; the weighted average for the subcategories of that case is .75. The weighted average for the main categories of the Smith case is .71; for the subcategories .72. We have used weighted averages in order to let each category influence the result in proportion to its frequency of occurrence; to have counted each category equally would have let little-used categories have as much effect as the more common ones, which might have been misleading. These weighted averages are slightly larger than the coefficient illustrated in Figure 2.

Three-quarters of the sentences we scored were assigned to categories having a reliability coefficient of .60 or higher, the other quarter went into the less reliable categories. A seventh of the sentences were assigned to categories having coefficients of .85 or higher. All of the main categories except *Unsc* have coefficients that are statistically significant when both cases are considered.* Three of the subcategories—*H-A, H-a, s-A*—have coefficients that are not statistically significant; although these categories have more than the minimum 1% of total sentences that we set as a requirement for inclusion in the table, they are nevertheless rather infrequent. *H-A* in the Davidson case had 5% of the sentences scored; in the Smith case it had 2%. *H-a* had 1% in the Davidson case, 2% in the Smith case. *s-A* had 2% of the sentences in the Smith case. Since these categories haven't been given much of a trial, we believe that final judgment on their reliability should be suspended until more extensive evidence is available.

It is obvious that whether the scoring is reliable enough to permit a study of the hour-to-hour variation in these cases depends very much on the category considered. Some categories are sufficiently reliable for this, others are not. It should also be said that the reliabilities of some categories are low not so much because the scorers disagreed in their judgments of the sentences as because there was little variation in the frequency of the category over the series of hours. Statisticians have pointed out that the size of the correlation coefficient is affected by homogeneity or heterogeneity of the vari-

* We have used Stouffer's method of combining probabilities to throw both cases into a single test of significance (Mosteller and Bush, 1954).

ables; where there is little variation in the scores the coefficient shrinks, where there is greater variability it expands. It is quite likely, therefore, that for many of the categories having low coefficients, satisfactory reliability could be demonstrated in any case that had considerably greater hour-to-hour variation in these categories.

A study of Table 5 drives home the point that high product-moment correlations between the scorers are unlikely for those categories that show little variation from hour to hour. The category M in the Davidson case had practically no hour-to-hour variation: Dollard found 55, 43, and 45 M's in the three hours that were scored; Auld found 48, 48, and 41. Thus it is not surprising that the r between their hour totals is quite low—a distressing .36—despite excellent agreement between the scorers on single sentences (τ of .90). The relatively low coefficient for *Interp* in the Davidson case is also partly attributable to low hour-to-hour variability (but the single-sentence reliability of *Interp* is not so high as that of M, showing that lack of variation between hours is not the sole cause of the relatively low r).

The reader is reminded that the coefficients shown in Table 5 are based on only six hours, three for each case. They are therefore much less dependable, as estimates of the coefficients that will be obtained over the long run, than the coefficients in Table 4.

Taking the hour-by-hour coefficients as a whole, we consider them to be good. Nevertheless it is clear that there is room for further clarification of the rules for some of the categories. We believe that such clarification may have to wait for theoretical advances, since it has been our experience that inability to agree on scoring finally gives way when the principles involved in the behavior to be scored are understood. The imperfections in the system ought not to obscure the fact that most of the categories are sufficiently reliable to permit one to study trends within a psychotherapy case.

RELIABILITY OF CLASSIFICATION OF SINGLE SENTENCES

In testing many hypotheses about therapy one needs to be able to score individual sentences reliably. For example, if one asks whether an interpretation by the therapist is likely to evoke an immediate welling up of resistance, one can answer the question by noticing whether resistant sentences occur more frequently after interpretations.* To do this one has to be able to identify *single* interpretations and *single* resistant sentences; it is not sufficient to identify the hours in which interpretations and resistances are frequent and those in which they occur less frequently, since the scorers could agree that an hour had 231 (or some other number of) resistant sentences but fail to agree about which particular sentences were resistant.

Traditional ways of measuring agreement on single sentences. A straightforward measure of how well different scorers agree is the percentage of the units that they code the same way. The percentage-of-agreement measure has the great advantage that it is easily understood. It has the disadvantage, however, that this index is not always zero when the scorers do not perceive the material in the same way. If there are only a few categories in the system, the scorers can get a percentage of agreement appreciably above zero despite differing perceptions, simply because when they are in doubt they have only a limited choice of categories in which to place the items. Similarly, when the scorers' judgments on the variable are in only modest accord, the percentage-of-agreement figure for a system having only a few categories can make it seem that the scorers are agreeing marvelously.

Table 6 illustrates these generalizations with some data from the

TABLE 6. PERCENTAGES OF AGREEMENT ON D.R.Q. JUDGMENTS

		SCORER B		
		+	0	−
	+	44	8	7
SCORER A	0	6	54	12
	−	3	36	157

D.R.Q. scoring of an interview. The D.R.Q. method is a content-analysis procedure utilizing only three categories, + for positive statements, − for negative statements, 0 for neutral statements.†

* Auld and White (1959) have presented data bearing on this point. They found that interpretations did not produce immediate, large increases in resistance.

† For further information about the D.R.Q. method see Dollard and Mowrer (1947).

From the table one can see that the two scorers agreed on 44, 54, and 157 units out of 327, or on 78% of the units. Now let us suppose that the scorers had been required only to distinguish between sentences that are either positive or neutral and sentences that are negative. In this case they would have agreed on 269 of the units, or 82%. If, instead, the 0 and — categories had been combined and this inclusive category contrasted with the + category, the scorers would have been found to agree on 303 units (on 44 which they both called +, and on 259 which they both assigned to the other category), for an agreement index of 93%. So, without changing the scorers' behavior at all one might find a percentage of agreement ranging from 78 to 93, depending on the number of categories used and on the way in which categories were condensed.

It seems to us that, in view of the tendency of the percentage-of-agreement index to rise with fewer categories and whenever some few categories get a lion's share of the classified units, one cannot use percentage-of-agreement to compare the reliabilities of content-analysis systems having different numbers of categories or differing in the degree to which units are concentrated in a few of the categories. To compare the reliabilities of systems that differ in these ways, it would be more appropriate to use an index that was not affected by the number of categories in the system and that took into account the boost to apparent agreement given by a concentration of the units in one or in a few of the categories.

The percentage-of-agreement index has still another flaw: In a system having more than two categories, it tells us only the over-all level of agreement, failing to give any indication of which categories are well discriminated and which are poorly discriminated.

Kendall's tau as a measure of reliability. The index of reliability that we prefer is Kendall's *tau*. This coefficient, as we use it, is based on a set of 2×2 tables, one table for each category; and so we avoid the bias of increased index when there are fewer categories in the whole system. *Tau* corrects for concentration of the units, because the computation of *tau* in effect subtracts the chance agreements from the total agreements (as will be explained later on), thereby preventing high concentration, which raises chance agreement, from raising the coefficient. Finally, *tau* is computed for each category separately, so that deficiencies of individual categories are not masked by the excellencies of other categories within a summary index for the system as a whole.

In using *tau* we consider the scorer's classification of each sentence to be an assignment of the sentence to one of two ranks, Rank 1 (more of the quality indicated by the category) or Rank 2 (less of the quality indicated by the category). When the scorers agree, they are ranking the sentences in the same way, for example:

	Scorer A's ranking	*Scorer B's ranking*
Sentence a	*Res talk* (1)	*Res talk* (1)
Sentence b	Not *Res talk* (2)	Not *Res talk* (2)

For these two sentences the scorers are in agreement that Sentence a has more of the quality indicated by *Res talk* than Sentence b does. When the scorers disagree, they are ranking the sentences differently, for example:

	Scorer A's ranking	*Scorer B's ranking*
Sentence c	*Res talk* (1)	Not *Res talk* (2)
Sentence d	Not *Res talk* (2)	*Res talk* (1)

If, for the whole body of material that is scored, we take each pair of sentences and notice whether the scorers agree on their rankings and if we count each agreement as $+1$ and each disagreement as -1, then we can form a coefficient by algebraically summing all of these agreement and disagreement scores and dividing the result by the maximum possible number of agreement scores. This coefficient is Kendall's *tau*. In his book on rank correlation methods Kendall (1948) has given a thorough exposition of the theory of rank correlation, derived his *tau* coefficient, and shown that when there are only two grades in each ranking this coefficient is algebraically equivalent to the better-known *phi* coefficient.

To compute the *tau* coefficient we take each category separately and construct tables like Table 7, which shows the reliability of the *Res talk* category for the Smith case. The table is read as follows:

TABLE 7. RELIABILITY OF THE *Res talk* CATEGORY FOR THE SMITH CASE

		SCORER B	
		Res talk	Not *Res talk*
SCORER A	*Res talk*	453	346
	Not *Res talk*	335	4195

The scorers agreed on 453 sentences as belonging to the *Res talk* category. They agreed on 4195 other sentences as not belonging to this category. Scorer A classified as *Res talk* 346 sentences which Scorer B did not put in this category; and Scorer B classified as *Res talk* 335 sentences which Scorer A did not call resistant.

Studying the table, we see that the scorers agreed on the assignment of 87% of the sentences. One feels, however, that the percentage-of-agreement figure gives too favorable a picture of the reliability attained, since 4195 of the agreements were just that sentences did *not* belong in the resistance category. With both scorers having relatively little disposition to put a sentence into *Res talk* (they so classified only 15% of the sentences), sentences were very likely to be put into the "not *Res talk*" bin. This high proportion for the "not *Res talk*" marginal frequencies raises the probability of agreeing that sentences aren't *Res talk*, even in the absence of any ability by the scorers to distinguish consistently between resistant and non-resistant sentences. Thus the percentage of agreement for such a 2×2 table is, in a sense, inflated. The *tau* coefficient is not inflated; it measures the improvement of the scorers' agreement over the chance level. The value of *tau* for this table is .50, which is statistically significant at the .001 level.

Tau *as an index of improvement above chance level.* It can be shown that, if the marginal totals of the two scorers are the same, *tau* is equivalent to an index of agreement computed from the formula:

$$I = \frac{\text{observed agreements} - \text{chance agreements}}{\text{total items} - \text{chance agreements}}$$

The index, *I*, expresses the improvement of the observed agreements above the chance level, compared to the total possible improvement above the chance level. When the observed agreement is at the chance level, *I* is zero; when the observed agreement is perfect, *I* is 1.* If the marginal totals in the 2×2 table are different—i.e. if one scorer has assigned more sentences to the category than the other scorer has—*tau* is slightly larger than *I*.

In our reliability studies we have found that for most of the categories, in most of the cases studied, the marginal totals of the two scorers are very close. The correlation of .95 between the total-case

---

* This index of agreement is formed according to the model suggested by Goodman and Kruskal (1954, pp. 759–60).

profiles of the two scorers of the Davidson case shows how nearly alike the scorers have been in their tendency to use the various categories much or little. It seems feasible, therefore, to use Kendall's *tau* as a measure of the agreement between the scorers on single sentences, with the interpretation that this coefficient indicates, approximately, how much better the scorers agree than they would be expected to do if only chance contributed to their agreements.

Warning: Don't interpret tau *as you would* r. The reader must be warned that one cannot interpret *tau* in the same way that one would interpret the product-moment *r*. *Tau* has a scale that is different from that of *r*. We quote the analogy chosen by Kendall (p. 11) in his discussion of the difference between his *tau* and Spearman's *rho*: "The coefficients have, in fact, different scales, like the different scales of centigrade and Fahrenheit thermometers. This will give rise to no difficulty in practice, for in a particular investigation we shall always work with the same kind of coefficient. The differences emphasize nevertheless the importance of not attributing too much importance to the actual magnitude of a rank correlation. If we find a value of *tau* equal to 0.67 we can only say that there is 'two-thirds agreement' if we recall clearly the nature of the coefficient and the scale of measurement which sets it up." The reader is therefore warned *not* to look up significance levels for *tau* in the tables appropriate for product-moment *r, not* to square *tau* in order to determine the per cent of the variance accounted for by the correlation, and in general *not* to transfer to *tau* all of his well-established habits for judging what the meaning of a correlation of a particular size is.

Indeed, we fear this ignorant transfer of habits so much that we have gone to the trouble of computing tetrachoric *r*'s (the interpretation of which can proceed much more by the habits appropriate for *r*) in order to demonstrate the vast difference between *tau* and *r*. In the reliability tables that follow throughout this chapter both *tau* and tetrachoric *r* are given side by side.

Despite the danger of misinterpretation of *tau*, we have retained *tau* and have placed our chief reliance on it because it has certain advantages over tetrachoric *r*. In the first place, *tau* has an interpretation as an improvement of the observed agreement over chance level, as indicated above, an interpretation that we believe to be quite valuable. Secondly, in using *tau* one need make no metric assumptions, no guesses even as to the shape of the underlying variable one is measuring; whereas with the tetrachoric coefficient one must assume that the dichotomized variables are normally distributed. Finally, with *tau* one avoids the troublesome sampling problems of tetrachoric r. These problems include the difficulty of estimating r with any reliability if the split of the dichotomy is extreme, for instance, if fewer than 5% of the items in the sample are in one category, more than 95% in the other.

Agreement on single sentences: results. Table 8 shows the *tau*

TABLE 8. RELIABILITY OF SINGLE-SENTENCE SCORES, PATIENT'S CATEGORIES *

Category	Davidson case		Smith Case	
	τ	r	τ	r
A (broad)	.44	.74	.40	.64
A (narrow)	.41	.78	.42	.68
A:r	.08	.70	.39	.93
Conf	.52	.97	.32	.91
Dep (broad)	.28	.78	.35	.62
Dep (narrow)	.33	.73	.36	.72
dep-a	—	—	.12	.62
H (broad)	.47	.73	.52	.76
H (narrow)	.48	.76	.58	.82
H-A	.33	.71	.24	.85
H-a	.01	.72	.10	.71
H/self	.55	.98	.42	.92
L (broad)	.44	.76	.27	.58
L (narrow)	.46	.77	.26	.56
Mob (broad)	.66	.96	.83	.997
Mob (narrow)	.68	.97	—	—
Mob-A	—	—	.47	.97
N	.56	.98	—	—
PSS	.75	.996	.70	.99
Reas	.22	.85	.21	.85
Res talk	.50	.76	.50	.75
S (broad)	.67	.97	.43	.74
S (narrow)	.51	.98	.57	.99
S-a	.56	.97	—	—
s-A	—	—	.42	.96
Unsc	.32	.73	.59	.93
Y	.89	.99	.74	.99

* Any *tau* larger than .03 is significant at the .01 level. All tetrachoric r's in the table are significant at the .05 level. "Broad" means the inclusive category, e.g. *H* (broad) includes *H, H-A, H-a, h-A,* and *h-a.* "Narrow" means the restricted category, e.g. *H* (narrow) includes only *H.*

coefficients and tetrachoric r's of patient's categories for the two recent cases that were scored with complete independence of the two
scorers. Table 9 shows the *tau* coefficients and tetrachoric r's for the
therapist's categories, in the two cases in which therapist's utterances
were scored, again with complete independence, after the therapist's
categories had been developed in their final form.

TABLE 9. RELIABILITY OF SINGLE-SENTENCE SCORES,
THERAPIST'S CATEGORIES *

Category	Davidson case		Foote case	
	τ	r	τ	r
D	.72	.92	.65	.86
Interp	.57	.85	.73	.90
M	.90	.998	.93	.997
R	.65	.91	.55	.78
Unsc	.64	.97	.42	.91

* All the correlations in this table are significant at or beyond the .01 level.

The weighted averages of the *tau* coefficients for the main categories in Table 8 (each category weighted according to the frequency of sentences assigned to it) are .54 for the Davidson case
and .45 for the Smith case. The average *tau*'s for the subcategories
are a little lower, .43 for the Davidson case and .43 for the Smith
case. The weighted averages for tetrachoric r for the main categories
are .89 for the Davidson case, .78 for the Smith case; the averages
for the subcategories are .82 for the Davidson case, .81 for the Smith
case.

It is obvious as one studies Table 8 that some categories are more
reliable than others. Those having *tau*'s of .50 or better (correspond-
ing roughly to r's of .85 and higher) are: *Y, PSS, Mob* and its subcategories, *N, S* and most of its subcategories, *H/self, Unsc, H* (both
broad and narrow), and *Res talk*. The reliability of these categories
can, we believe, appropriately be called "good." It is especially
gratifying to discover that the scorers were able to agree on the
designation of psychosomatic reactions, because we know that scoring
PSS involves a discrimination between somatogenic and psychogenic symptoms, with a judgment whether unconscious conflict has
led to the formation of the symptoms. It is also of considerable importance that the scorers agreed so well on *Res talk*, for such con-
currence means that they had a similar understanding of uncon-

scious motivation; resistance, obviously, is largely an unconscious process.

The categories that fall in a middle ground, with *tau*'s between .40 and .50 (*r*'s usually between .70 and .85) are: *Conf, A* and its subcategories, and *s-A*. The poorest categories, with *tau*'s of less than .40, are: *L, H-A, Dep, Reas, H-a,* and *dep-a*. We are not much concerned about the low coefficient of most of these "poor" categories, since sentences that were assigned to these categories were quite infrequent in the cases that we have scored. We are, however, troubled by the low reliability of the *dep-a* category, which did occur with fair frequency.

Though we have disparaged the lowest coefficients as "poor," we wish to point out that they still represent substantial agreement between the scorers. In Figure 4 we have represented graphically how well the scorers agreed on a "good" category (*PSS*), a "middling" one (*Conf*), and a "poor" one (*Dep*). The chart should be interpreted in the following way: If Scorer A decided that a particular sentence was *Dep,* the likelihood was 34 in 100 that Scorer B independently made the same decision. If A decided that a sentence was not *Dep,* the likelihood was only 4 in 100 that Scorer B called it *Dep.* The concordance in judgments is indeed very substantial, even for a "poor" category—and is highly significant statistically. If the scorers had not agreed at all on *Dep,* the two bars for *Dep* in the figure would be the same length. The agreement does, however, fall short of our hopes.

The therapist's categories—for which the reliability coefficients are shown in Table 9—all have good reliability. *M* apparently is as easy to score as rolling off a log. When the therapist said "Mm-hmm" or "Yeah" the scorers automatically wrote *M,* and borderline cases of this category were few and far between. *D, Interp,* and *R* all have coefficients in the .6 to .7 range—the region of struggle-with-achievement. While it was not so easy to determine whether an interpretation was made as to tell whether the therapist had said something like "Mm-hmm," nor so easy to tell whether non-interpretive sentences were motivating or rewarding as to detect a "Yeah," the reliability attained is in our opinion quite satisfactory.

It is difficult to summarize the reliability of scoring single sentences, even more difficult to say whether the reliability attained is good enough. We can only say on the first point that we believe the reliability to be better than that ever attained before by researchers studying variables of comparable complexity. As to usefulness of the scores, it is pertinent that Auld and White (1959) used this content-analysis method to study sequential dependencies in psycho-

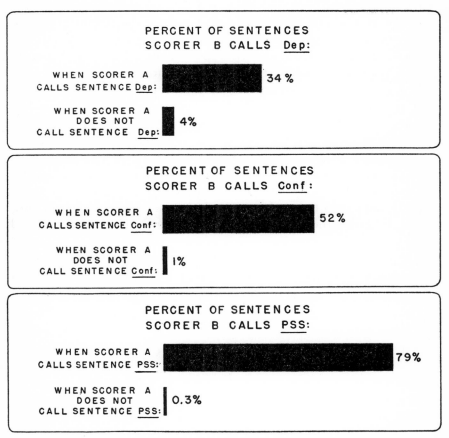

Fig. 4. Agreement between two scorers on assignment of single sentences to categories, for the Davidson case. A relatively unreliable category, *Dep*, a category of moderate reliability, *Conf*, and a category of excellent reliability, *PSS*, are used as illustrations. If the two scorers had not agreed at all, the two lines for each category would be of the same length.

therapy. Their scoring reliability was about the same as that reported in this chapter. With such a level of agreement they were able to demonstrate the effects of variables like "interpretation" and "resistance." Their success encourages us to believe that we have attained a useful level of reliability of scoring single sentences.

SUMMARY

Much of the current lack of agreement about the dynamics of psychotherapy can be traced back to a lack of agreement about the basic observations of psychotherapy. To settle the disputes and increase our knowledge of psychotherapy we need to develop reliable measures. In this chapter we have reported the reliability of scoring for our content-analysis system. We have shown that there is very high agreement between scorers in their evaluation of an entire case; that there is fairly good agreement between scorers on the number of sentences they assigned to a category in each hour of a series of hours (the average correlation coefficient was .66); and that there is fairly good agreement between scorers on the assignment of single sentences to categories. The reliability of some categories is much better than that of others; therefore it might be possible to study some hypotheses, but not others, with the system as it now stands. Whether the measurements we have developed are refined enough depends too on how small or large the effects to be studied are. In the applications of the system that we have made, we have found our measures to be precise enough to detect the workings of the variables we were studying.

CHAPTER 8

Validity of the System

SINCE the development of reliable measures was our primary aim, we concentrated our energies on that task and gave relatively little attention to application of our content-analysis method. Such a concentration of effort can be justified by the importance of reliability, we believe. Nevertheless it is obvious that no one would have any interest in a reliable but useless system. The fact that we were guided in a general way by psychoanalytic and behavioral notions in selecting and defining the categories gives some ground for hoping that the categories may be scientifically useful. Beyond this, however, what direct evidence is there that the categories are indeed valid? We present the available evidence in this chapter.

APPLICATION OF SYSTEM TO VARIOUS CASES

In the course of developing the content-analysis system we have scored some sixty-eight interviews by six different therapists with eight patients and one normal person. We experienced a few problems but no major difficulties in turning from one case to another in our scoring. Thus we know that the system is not limited in its usefulness to one or two patients but is applicable to a variety of patients treated by a number of therapists, who are quite different in their style of work.

One would expect that the two interviews with psychotic patients that we have scored would differ from the other interviews, which were with neurotic patients and a normal man. We have compared the scores on twelve of the first neurotic interviews that we scored with the scores of two interviews with psychotic patients. The results are shown in Table 10. If these samples of statements from neurotic and psychotic patients are generally representative of their respective populations, it would seem that direct aggressive statements are more characteristic of psychotic hours, whereas expressions of anxiety do not differ much between the two types of cases. Psychotics would seem to be much gabbier than neurotics, since they make little use of *Res 5*. On the other hand, psychotics present much

TABLE 10. COMPARISON OF SENTENCE COUNTS IN INTERVIEWS
WITH NEUROTICS AND PSYCHOTICS *

| | PER CENT OF TOTAL STATEMENTS SCORED | |
SCORE GIVEN TO STATEMENT	*Neurotic*	*Psychotic*
H	8	27
A	6	8
S	11	3
Res talk	10	11
Res 5	23	2
Unsc	5	42

* Total statements scored for neurotic hours: 9407 (12 hours)
Total statements scored for psychotic hours: 1607 (2 hours)

more unintelligible material, as is shown by their high count for *Unsc*. The way in which these data fall out encourages a small amount of hope that the sentence counts can be useful in the analysis of neurotic and psychotic case material.

CORRELATIONS BETWEEN VARIABLES

If the content-analysis system is valid, variables which theory says are related should prove to be correlated. Of course this need not always be so, since theories can be wrong. Yet theories are the best current approximations to the truth; and theories which have been found by other kinds of studies to have explanatory power should make some right predictions about which of our categories will be related to each other.

We have done correlational studies on three cases. Before looking at the data we made predictions about the relationships we expected to find among variables in these cases.

In studying the case of Mr. Carlson we used data from the first ten interviews. We made predictions concerning the relationships between ten pairs of categories. Three of the ten correlations are statistically significant at the .05 level, and two others are significant at the .25 level. We report here only those correlations involving categories that have not changed much as we developed the system:

1. We had the hypothesis that the motivational categories would be negatively correlated with the amount of silence in the interview, over a series of interviews. This hypothesis was not confirmed in the Carlson case; the correlation between anxiety plus hostility plus sex (the motivational categories) and silence is only —.01.

2. We believed that sexual material and anxious statements would tend not to occur in the same hour, since anxiety would have to be extinguished before sexual thoughts could appear. We found a correlation of —.42 between A and S. Although this correlation is significant only at the .25 level, the direction of the relationship is as predicted.

3. We believed that talk about sex and about hostility would not occur in the same hour. A correlation of —.72 between S and H was found, confirming this hypothesis. The correlation is significant at the .02 level. Perhaps the sexual motive is incompatible with hostility; or it may be that sex is the cue for the evocation of anxiety and that after sexual material has been brought out the patient is motivated by anxiety to stage a temporary retreat in subsequent hours to other topics, with the result that we see a seesawing between S and other motives.

4. The motivational categories—i.e. A, Dep, S, etc.—and Res should be negatively correlated. We found a correlation of —.21. This is not statistically significant.

5. We believed that hostility and anxiety would be negatively correlated because at times when the patient was anxious he would also be damping down his hostile feelings. The correlation between A and H was found to be —.66, which is significant at the .05 level. See Figure 5.

6. The comparison of paragraph 4 was repeated, with this change: Silences were excluded from the totals of Res, i.e. Res $talk$ was correlated with the motivational categories, rather than all Res. The correlation obtained is —.21, which is not statistically significant, although in the expected direction.

7. We believed that the patient's obsessional symptom served as a defense against his hostile wishes. Accordingly, in those interviews in which mildly hostile feelings were expressed and more violent hostile impulses threatened to break through, the obsessional symptom should occur also. The correlation between H and Obs was

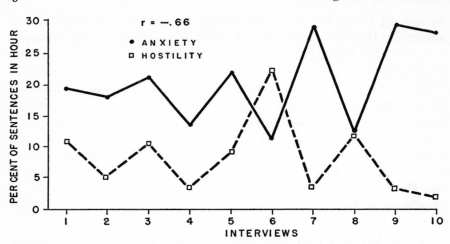

Fig. 5. Hour-by-hour trends of anxiety and hostility scores for the case of Mr. Carlson.

found to be +.75, which is significant at the .02 level. See Figure 6.

In studying the Chelovek case we made two predictions:

1. We predicted that *H* (hostility) would be negatively correlated with *Res* (resistant talk and resistant silence combined). In other words, we expected that in hours when he was resistant the patient would not express his hostile feelings; in hours when he expressed his hostile feelings he would not be resistant. The prediction is derived from psychoanalytic hypotheses about the function

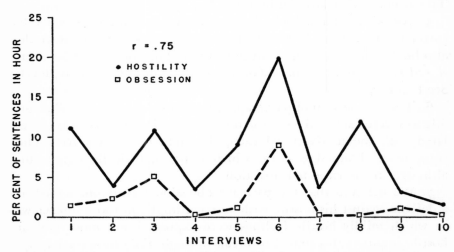

Fig. 6. Hour-by-hour trends of hostility and obsession scores for the Carlson case.

of resistance. The idea is that resistance serves to defend the patient against painful awareness of impulses. There is a very slight negative correlation between H and Res ($r = -.12$).

2. We predicted that Res would be negatively correlated with S. The reasoning is similar to that presented for the preceding prediction; resistance and expression of impulse are believed to be incompatible. The correlation actually found was $-.34$. Thus the prediction was confirmed.

In studying the O'Connell case we made three predictions:

1. We predicted that Res and H would be negatively correlated, for reasons discussed in connection with the Chelovek case above. The correlation is $-.91$, a striking confirmation of the prediction.

2. We predicted that Res and S would be negatively correlated, for reasons identical with those given above in connection with the Chelovek case. However, when making this prediction we recognized that Mrs. O'Connell seldom discussed sex at all, and so we believed that the findings on this point, whether favorable or unfavorable, should be given little weight. With S scores seldom occurring, it was likely that freakish chance factors would interfere with the discovery of any general relationship between S and Res, whatever that relationship is. We found the correlation to be $+.34$. This is in the opposite direction from our prediction.

3. We predicted that H and Obs would be negatively correlated. In other words, hours that had a high count of obsessional sentences would have a low count of hostile sentences, and vice versa. Such a result was expected because obsessional reactions are believed to be defenses against anxiety evoked by hostile impulses. Those hours in which the obsessional defense was working effectively would be expected not to have hostile expressions in them. (The predicted direction of the correlation for this case is opposite to what was predicted for the Carlson case above. This prediction is based on the assumption that the obsessional sentences serve a defensive function; the prediction in the other case was based on the assumption that the obsessional sentences not only defend against hostility but also are a compromise formation, partly expressing the impulse. Obviously, neither prediction can be made with much confidence unless one is aware of other factors—for example, extent of displacement of hostile impulses—that may influence the formation of the obsessional symptom, and unless one can somehow take these into

account.) The correlation is $-.24$, which was in the predicted direction but not statistically significant.

One may summarize these explorations of how variables correlate with each other by saying that predicted relationships sometimes did indeed occur. Our troubles, such as we had, seemed to stem more from difficulty in saying what relationships should be expected than from inadequacies of the content-analysis system. These troubles are most strikingly illustrated in the instance of the correlation between H and Obs, where in one case we predicted a positive relationship and in another case a negative one. It happens that we were right in both cases, but that is little comfort when the principles leading to our predictions were in conflict.

OCCURRENCE OF VARIABLES

One would expect that L (love, affection) would occur infrequently in the beginnings of cases, since neurotics find it difficult to relate themselves in a loving way to other people. And, since neurotic persons are bearing high drives because they have failed to achieve many gratifications and thus are seething with emotional conflict, we might expect them to feel hostile toward others. Putting these two expectations together, we predicted that a count of L sentences in the early hours of cases would show this category to be less than one-third as frequent as H. In the first five hours of the Chelovek case there are 80 L units and 258 H units; L is thus less than a third of H. In the first five hours of the O'Connell case there are 57 L units and 346 H units. Again, L is less than a third of H. Our expectation was borne out in these two cases.

We would like to point out also that it is sometimes illuminating to notice that a particular category doesn't occur when it might be expected to. For example, the S category occurred hardly at all in the O'Connell case, although it has appeared with considerable frequency in most of the other neurotic cases we have scored. This means, we believe, that Mrs. O'Connell, a frightened, suspicious patient, did not trust the therapist enough to reveal much about her sex life. As it turned out, the case was a therapeutic failure; Mrs. O'Connell left without gaining any appreciable insight. Could this result have been predicted from the absence of S scores in early interviews?

STUDIES OF WHAT FOLLOWS WHAT

To try out the content-analysis system in yet another way, we made some studies of the sequences of categories during psychotherapy. One might call these studies explorations of "what follows what." We shall only summarize here material that has been presented in detail by Auld and White (1959).

Four hypotheses were investigated:

1. The patient's speech hangs together, i.e. he is likely to continue with another unit belonging to the same category as the preceding sentence.

2. Various forms of resistance are equivalent as shown in their occurrence in units that follow one another. In particular, resistant talk is equivalent to resistant silence. If the patient is resistant at a particular time it will be shown at one moment by silence and at another moment by resistant talk; therefore resistant talk should be likely to follow silence, and silence to follow resistant talk.

3. The patient's activity affects the likelihood that the therapist will intervene and that, if he does intervene, he will make an interpretation.

4. Interpretive interventions of the therapist are no more likely to evoke immediate resistance by the patient than are noninterpretive interventions.

Four psychotherapy cases, carried by four different therapists, were studied. Two of the therapists had been fully trained in psychoanalysis and had had considerable experience; the other two, having taken an introductory course in psychotherapy, were having their first experiences as psychotherapists.

The method, in general, was to observe whether the kind of score assigned to unit n would enable one to predict the likelihoods of various scores being assigned unit $n + 1$. For example, if one knows that the patient has spoken a sentence classified as resistant, does that help to predict what kind of unit will come next? The results of the study may be summarized as follows:

1. It was discovered that the categories do indeed persist. For instance, the likelihood of a sentence scored *S* is greater after *S* sentences than after other sentences. Such a result was obtained for all the categories studied: *A, Dep, H, L, Mob, Res talk, Res 5,* and *S*. A typical finding is that for the *H* category. The chances are 71 out of

100 that sentence $n + 1$ was scored H if sentence n was scored H. However, if sentence n was not scored H, chances are only 3 out of 100 that sentence $n + 1$ was scored H. This finding is shown graphically in Figure 7.

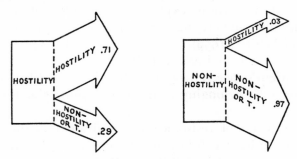

Fig. 7. Events following hostile and nonhostile sentences of the patient.

2. Silence does indeed occur more often after resistant talk than after nonresistant talk (see Figure 8). The probability is .24 that a silence of at least 5 seconds will occur after a sentence scored as resistant; it

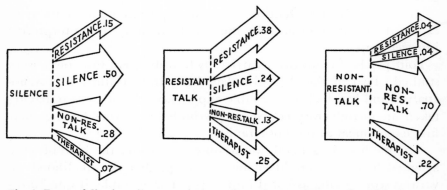

Fig. 8. Events following silence, resistant talk, and nonresistant talk. (This figure is reproduced from the paper by Auld and White [1959], by permission of the American Psychological Association. Copyright 1959 by the American Psychological Association, Inc.)

is only .04 that a silence will occur after a nonresistant sentence. Furthermore, silences are likely to be followed by resistant talk. These findings are what would be expected if silences are equivalent to resistant speech.

3. The two apprentice therapists were not more likely to intervene after resistant talk than after nonresistant talk of the patient. If they did intervene, they were as likely to make a noninterpretive remark as to make an interpretation. The experienced therapists, however, were more likely to interpret resistance, as can be seen in Figure 9.

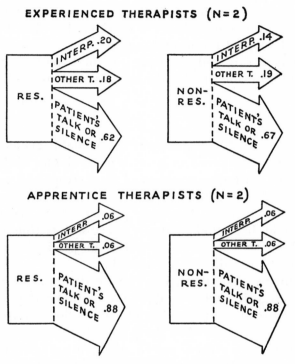

Fig. 9. Therapists' response to resistant and nonresistant talk of the patient. (This figure is reproduced from the paper by Auld and White [1959], by permission of the American Psychological Association. Copyright 1959 by the American Psychological Association, Inc.)

One of the experenced therapists was more likely to intervene after resistant talk than after nonresistant talk; the other was about equally likely to intervene after resistant or nonresistant talk but in intervening after resistance was more likely to make an interpretation than when intervening after nonresistant talk. Thus the experienced therapists were better able than the inexperienced ones to identify resistance quickly and to deal with it directly.

4. If one may judge by what the patient says immediately afterward, interpretation does not produce a great increase in resistance. The probability of the patient's saying "Mm-hmm" or "Yeah" is, however, very much greater after an interpretation than after some other kind of intervention. This happens probably because most interpretations call for some answer from the patient. We do not suppose, however, that the patient's agreement indicates more than "I heard you"; his reply cannot be considered evidence that he has accepted and adopted the interpretation.

The results of this study, bearing out the hypotheses which were proposed, afford evidence that the content analysis is valid.

SUMMARY

We have presented in this chapter the available evidence concerning the validity of our content-analysis method. Our ability to apply our method of scoring to a variety of cases treated by a number of therapists, the striking difference between neurotic and psychotic cases, the demonstration that some predicted correlations between variables could be found, and the successful testing of four hypotheses about sequences of categories in psychotherapy all give evidence for the validity of the method.

Much remains to be done, however, to demonstrate the validity of all the categories. One would want to prove that unconscious motives are correctly designated by our scores, for example, by showing that later in the case when the patient becomes aware of unconscious motives, they correspond to those earlier identified by the scorer. One would like to have evidence that the patient is relatively relaxed while resistant sentences are occurring, because these sentences protect him from frightening thoughts and feelings. Perhaps physiological measures can give such evidence. We hope that many co-workers will be interested enough to make additional tests of validity.

Previous Studies Bearing on Content Analysis of Psychotherapy*

CONTENT ANALYSIS

RESEARCH in psychotherapy, like behavioral research in general, acknowledges two masters: the stern disciplinarian, scientific rigor, and the solicitous parent, depth of meaning. Scientific rigor demands that theories be subjected to tests of objectivity, careful definition of terms, validity of methods. Depth of meaning requires one to study things that are important; this solicitous parent wants his child to amount to something. Research in psychotherapy has almost always served one of these masters better than the other.

Proponents of scientific rigor warn us that the requirements of science are not matters of taste nor symptoms of compulsively precise investigators but are painfully evolved, necessary rules. If scientific methods are ignored or only casually acknowledged, conclusions that are announced as true may easily be false, and no one can tell the difference. If scientific method is ignored there can be no way to describe human behavior and its regularities in such a way that others—even others with very different biases—can similarly describe these regularities. Without any way of achieving objectivity one is forced to rely for one's data on unknown powers of the observer, and these unknowns are just as mysterious as the behavior the observer is trying to understand.

The case for studying important things nevertheless cannot be brushed aside. Unless research is aimed at the vital aspects of human behavior, one may know a great deal and know it precisely without making any contribution toward the understanding of psychotherapy.

* This appendix was written by James E. Dittes.

   To meet demands for both rigor and meaning has been almost
impossible for the student of psychotherapy. Even investigators who
acknowledged the importance of both demands have been forced
to decide which would command greater loyalty. Some chose to study
what they could see, count, and measure easily; some even resorted
to conducting psychotherapy with cats, for the sake of the greater
control of conditions possible in animal experimentation (Masserman, 1943); and the writer does not at all despise the contribution
that such studies can make. It must be noted, however, that it is
difficult to relate the solid, objective measures obtained in these
studies to the more vital, more abstract, more meaningful concepts
of psychological theory. Other investigators chose the other road;
trying to penetrate the darkness with flashes of insight or clinical
intuition, they have sensed some important events in the therapeutic
transaction and have striven to record them so that others could also
sense them. But their communications are imprecise.

   There are still other investigators who tried to achieve some better
balance between rigor and meaning, and some of these scientists
turned to the method of content analysis. Content analysis was developed by social scientists as a way of studying the content of newspapers, personal letters, and other communications (Berelson, 1952).
This procedure is particularly appropriate for psychotherapy, since
it is a way of studying what is actually said and in its natural setting.
In using content-analysis methods the investigator does not limit or
interfere with the natural flow of behavior, as he would with a
questionnaire or an experiment; he does not come on the scene until
after the behavior under study has ticked itself off naturally and
spontaneously. Therefore the full verbal material of psychotherapy
comprises, in its natural form, the basic material of the content
analysis; and it follows that whatever aspects of behavior can be
clinically intuited, or otherwise perceived, can be sensed by the
content analyst. Content analysis thus is potentially prepared to
serve the master, Meaning, though it must be admitted that it is
difficult actually to use the full richness of the verbal material.

   Behavior is reliably identified when it can be placed in particular
categories according to explicit definitions. This reliable sorting is
the means of introducing the requisite scientific rigor into the study
of the verbal give-and-take of therapy. Such rigor should not damage
the meaningfulness of the investigation. If, for instance, the clinician
intuits that a person is showing resistance, anger, oral strivings, or
anything else, and if this perception is connected to anything actually

within the behavior of the patient, then the cues that led to the intuition can in due course be pointed out, named, and taught to others. Such designation, naming, and teaching is the core of content analysis.

Systems with easily defined categories. In the content-analysis studies of psychotherapy done so far, priority has been given to establishing objectivity, and greatest success has been achieved in this aim. Investigators have been less successful in comprehending the full height and depth of the material, its full meaning (see, for instance, the criticisms by Auld and Murray, 1955). What can be most readily and most reliably identified in the transcript of a therapeutic hour? Answer: "objective" features at a descriptive level, such as whether the patient is talking or is silent. Many of the earlier and some of the recent attempts to use content analysis have taken such obvious, easily identified aspects of behavior as their raw material. These obvious behaviors have been considered to be *indicators* of an important characteristic or of its strength. The important characteristic —we might call it a "theoretical construct"—is not measured directly; rather, it is said to be "indicated" by the behavior that can be identified.

When an easily identified behavior item is used as a sign of a theoretical construct, it is important to know what warrants such a usage. To illustrate: Lasswell (1935) classified clients' utterances according to the readily defined characteristic of whether the utterance explicitly referred to the interviewer or not. Lasswell proposed that reference to interviewer was a sign of "conscious affect." Similarly, he noted instances of slow speech and the occurrence of pauses, and proposed that these be taken as indicators of "unconscious tension." He justified the choice of these indicators for these constructs by showing their relevance to psychoanalytic theory and by demonstrating a correlation between these particular cues from verbal behavior and certain physiological measures, which he assumed were already established as indicators of the respective constructs. The present writer believes, however, that Lasswell should have given equal attention to justifying the selection of the physiological measures as indicants.*

---

* Physiological measures are easy to define, as are the simple content measures just mentioned; and like these simple content measures, they are often taken as indicators of important theoretical variables. One is justified, however, in demanding evidence that these physiological responses are, indeed, related to the theoretical variables they are taken to represent.

The structural properties of language provide easily defined characteristics that may be linked to theoretically important constructs. The variety of words a patient uses has been taken as a measure of adjustment (Johnson, 1944; Roshal, 1953); the frequency of future-tense verbs and of pronouns other than "I" has been taken as an indicator, respectively, of planfulness and socialization (Zimmerman and Langdon, 1949; Lazowick and Young, 1950). Time is also easy to measure reliably. Thus one group of researchers (Matarazzo *et al.,* 1956) has devised twelve different indicators of theoretical constructs, based on various time measures; for instance, a measure of "adjustment" consisting of the "average duration during which [the client] interrupted [the therapist] minus the duration during which [he] failed to interrupt." Other workers have followed up Lasswell's suggestion that pauses may be particularly revealing; see, for example, Gillespie (1953), Mahl (1956), and Dittes (1957). A variety of speech disturbances have been identified and scored by Mahl (1956), who has also presented evidence that they are related to psychological disturbances (as determined by clinical observation).

Turning now from measures that consider only the structural properties of language, we find that the simplest semantic aspects have been processed into a measure by Dollard and Mowrer (1947) and by Raimy (1948). The Discomfort-Relief Quotient, or D.R.Q., invented by Dollard and Mowrer, is computed by dividing the number of words indicating discomfort or tension by the number of words indicating discomfort *plus* the number of words indicating relief or tension reduction. Dollard and Mowrer allow the "common sense of intelligent people" to be the guide for deciding which words represent discomfort and which represent relief. Raimy's PNAvQ is a similar measure, in which the scorer classifies sentences as representative of positive, negative, or ambivalent feelings.

In the studies just described, much emphasis was put on reliability of scoring, and in general high reliability has been demonstrated. Good reliability was possible, it would seem, because the categories chosen are easily recognized. With such categories, scoring is in effect a simple matching procedure, requiring no inference, no self-debate by which a scorer arrives at the conclusion, "These cues in the record mean such-and-such." Rather, the scorer immediately recognizes that the item before him belongs in a certain category because it is like the other items in the category. No special training in scoring is required; "the common sense of intelligent people" is sufficient. The relative ease of scoring and the good reliability might lead one to conclude that such scoring systems do not require much inference. With respect to the scoring operation itself this is true; but it must be remembered that the investigator who draws conclusions from the scores must make bold inferences.

The inference in these simple systems brings up, in a painful way, the problem of *validity*. Do these counts of easily identified items really represent the theoretical constructs that the investigator believes they do? Thus the difference between the content systems just described and those soon to be described is not in amount of inference needed but in where the inferring is done—at the point of scoring or at the point of interpretation of simple scores. In general, the authors of these simple systems have all tended to slight the problem of demonstrating a valid relation between the indicator and that which it is asserted to indicate.

Systems with theoretically based categories. The content-analysis systems so far mentioned made use of only very limited aspects of the verbal material. Such narrowing of attention does not, of course, make these systems dangerous or useless; or it may well be that important characteristics of behavior "show through" the narrow window, that broad and deep aspects of the therapeutic transaction are visible in these fragments of the total situation. But it is also possible that human behavior reflects theoretical variables in such diverse ways that any single, partial measure cannot tell us much about these variables; and that one must examine the full scope of what is said, in its full context, to understand the transaction. Recognizing this possibility, some researchers have tried to develop content categories that are defined so as to permit the scorer such a broader view; and these researchers have hoped, by careful definition of their categories, to achieve reliability of scoring as good as that obtained for more easily defined categories.

Characteristically, the categories of such systems look like the theoretical constructs themselves, rather than like the cues from which such constructs may be inferred. The scorer, instead of picking out pauses or discomfort words or interruptions—from which someone else will infer resistance, psychological tension, or adjustment—now directly scores resistance, tension, and adjustment. The definitions of these categories include, of course, many examples of cues on which the scorer should base his judgment. Even so, it is very difficult to write down all of the pertinent cues; some will be missed. There-

fore the scorer must be not only intelligent but also familiar with
the theoretical basis of the categories. The need for the scorer to
understand the basis on which the category system was built does
not necessarily make the system less objective or more mysterious.
Training in the theoretical basis of the system can itself be made
a well-specified operation; indeed, the theoretical discussions in
this manual exemplify an attempt to make such a theory teachable.
Any intelligent person could, if he took the trouble to learn what
is required, become a scorer. Scoring would not have to depend on
wild surmises and on whatever peculiar meaning a lifetime of experience had given the concepts to be scored. There would be rules
for inference, orderly and controlled and repeatable operations for
arriving at the scores.

This survey of content systems that permit the scorer more inference should be prefaced by one more remark. Any set of categories
for content analysis is chosen not only because the categories seem
interesting and worth while themselves but also because they lend
themselves to the testing of certain hypotheses (Auld and Murray,
1955). The content analyst measures certain things because he wants
to relate these things to something else. If he chooses to score the
directiveness and nondirectiveness of the therapist, it is because he
has a theoretical interest in showing the relationship of these variables
to something else, for instance to the outcome of therapy.

The influence of theory on choice of categories is, of course, clearer
for construct-type categories than for easily defined, behavior-bound
categories. A good behavior-bound measure—such as number of
long pauses—chosen as much because it is available as because it
is meaningful, can be related to a great variety of theoretical formula-
tions and may, in fact, represent a common ground among them;
the investigator may use such a measure without much thought of
how he is going to relate it to important variables of the therapeutic
transaction. On the other hand, where the category *is* the construct,
or close to it, the researcher will customarily measure exactly what
he thinks it is theoretically important to know. Thus whether or not
the content categories prove useful in research will depend in great
part on whether or not the theoretical understanding that generated
them was of a high order. One can claim for the system presented
in this manual, at least, that the authors were aware that the system
could be no better than the theory which guided its construction.

Throughout the volume the theoretical considerations that led to the selection of categories are set forth.

Major efforts to develop comprehensive construct-related category systems for studying psychotherapy have been based on diverse theories; and each system asserts, by implication, that particular things are most important to know about psychotherapy. In the paragraphs that follow, several representative systems are described.

Bales carefully developed a twelve-category system for rating the behavior and remarks of persons toward each other during a group discussion. Some typical Bales categories are: "agrees," "gives opinion," "asks for suggestions," "shows antagonism." As Bales has said (1950, p. i), these categories represent some of the "formal dimensions of behavior of small groups." Bales has used these categories to test such hypotheses as: In problem-solving groups, discussion tends to proceed through various stages from orientation in the earliest period, through evaluation, suggestions, agreements and disagreements, to tension release, and finally to indications of group cohesiveness (pp. 131 ff.). Roberts and Strodtbeck (1953) have used these same categories in observing groups of psychotic patients in order to define how various kinds of patients differ from each other and from normal persons during group discussion. These authors suggest that the system could be used to study group psychotherapy.

An adaptation of the Bales categories to the dyadic therapist-patient group has been made by Richard W. Boyd and his collaborators (1956). Using the Bales system to study therapy implies, however, that psychotherapy is largely a rational problem-solving process —for the categories were originally developed to describe rational problem-solving and have been found useful in describing groups engaged in such tasks. The discussion sessions of top-level social scientists and clinicians meeting in a "diagnostic council" were Bales's original source of material; the activities of college students working out a group solution to some task, such as a chess problem, furnished further material for the system. The psychotherapeutic situation seems different from these tasks in some critical ways, and it is not surprising that when the Bales categories are applied to it the result is not very informative. One finds, typically, that a large part of the patient's remarks are scored as "giving information" or "evaluation"—which is to be expected, since in psychotherapy the patient is required to talk about himself. Yet much is concealed by this scoring: calling everything information or evaluation obscures the diversity of communications covered by these labels. Some evaluations may have a very different dynamic meaning from others.

Boyd (1956) has recently proposed a modification of Bales's system, introducing a complete new dimension of categories which he calls "content targets" in order to "get more clinical information" in the scores. Boyd's innovations make the system more like the one described in this manual. However, he has not yet worked these changes out in detail, and so one cannot judge how successfully he has overcome the defects of the original Bales system as a method of studying psychotherapy.

Strupp (1955) has used the Bales system in some studies but has abandoned it as unsuitable for most purposes of research in psychotherapy (1957a).

A system that, like Bales's, is intended for scoring the interactions of persons in groups has been devised by a group of researchers associated with the Kaiser Foundation (Freedman *et al.*, 1951; La Forge *et al.*, 1954; Leary and Coffey, 1954; Leary, 1957). Unlike Bales, however, these investigators have had as a primary aim the description of the behavior of *therapeutic* groups. They have been interested, moreover, in the personality characteristics represented by each interaction rather than in the contribution of such an interaction to group solution of a problem. The Leary system has sixteen categories, which Leary displays on a circular diagram. These categories are essentially trait names, for example, "autocratic," "aggressive," "self-effacing," "overagreeable." According to the theory that led to the selection of these categories, there are two primary dimensions of interaction between people: *love-hate* and *dominance-submission*. Any particular interaction is compounded of a specifiable quantity of love and a specifiable quantity of dominance. If one knows how much love and how much dominance, one can specify the kind of interaction between people; and if one knows what kind of interaction there is, one can tell how much love and how much dominance went into it. It is not clear just how the status of a patient on the love-hate and dominance-submission axes would affect the transactions of psychotherapy. Perhaps therapy should move the patient from hate to love and from submission to a reasonable degree of self-assertion. If so, it is hard to see how the dynamics which make such a change possible could be expressed in terms of this content system. One suspects, also, that human character structure is so complex a matter that this two-dimensional model cannot represent it very well.

The theoretical interests of nondirective therapists have, of course, influenced the kinds of categories used in their content-analysis studies. For example—perhaps paradoxically for a client-centered school—these investigators have been particularly concerned with assessing the therapist's personality and behavior (see Anderson, 1946; Aronson, 1953; Seeman, 1949) and have put great stress on comparing different therapeutic techniques. The first content system reported by a nondirective therapist (Porter, 1943a, 1943b) was devoted exclusively to categories for the therapist's behavior and ignored the client's activities. The most influential nondirective content-analysis system, Snyder's (1945, 1953), has in its latest form twenty-one categories for the therapist's utterances (with eight pages given over to definitions of scoring instructions for these) but only sixteen categories for the patient's speech (with two pages of definitions and instructions).

As would be expected in view of the interest of nondirective therapists in showing what is unique in their kind of therapy, and in keeping with their wish to compare its success with that of other methods, Snyder's system when it classifies the therapist's activities pays attention to whether the therapist takes initiative in the interview (interprets, forces the topic), or whether he follows methods believed by nondirective therapists to be more likely to produce therapeutic progress (restates content, clarifies feeling).

Snyder's categories for the client are of three main types, covering simple responses, problems, and attitudes. Simple responses include asking or answering a question, agreeing or disagreeing. Problem statements include seven stages of problem-solving, ranging from statement of problem to plans for future action. The attitude categories require judgments as to whether the patient's attitude is positive, negative, or ambivalent, and as to whether it is expressed toward himself, the counselor, or others. The simple-response and problem categories are reminiscent of Bales's categories (indeed, Bales says he borrowed from the nondirectivists when devising his system) and seem to imply that therapy is an intellectual, problem-solving process. The attitude categories express the interest of nondirective therapists in how the client, during therapy, gets changed perceptions and attitudes, which are of course a principal goal of client-centered therapy.

Investigators using Snyder's system have reported findings such as these: During the course of therapy counselors tend to use clarification of feeling less and less frequently. Patients whose therapy is judged to be successful tend, in the course of therapy, to decrease their statements of problem and to increase their utterances classified as discussion and planning (Snyder, Blau, Seeman). Certain personality traits of the therapist are associated with use of directive techniques (Aronson, 1953). Insight and planning increase when discomfort is reduced and when problems are resolved (Rakusin, 1953).

Influenced by the non-directivists and by the Bales system which he had used earlier (Strupp, 1955), Strupp has devised a set of five scales on which any statement by the therapist can be rated (1957a). He has demonstrated the use of the system in two subsequent studies (1957b, 1958). The scales are not concerned with the actual content of the therapist's remarks, but rather with those characteristics of the therapist's behavior which non-directive theory regards as important: 1) degree of therapeutic activity, ranging from simple exploratory questions to direct guidance; 2) degree of depth or inference which the therapist employs, indicating how far his remark is from the conscious thoughts of the patient; 3) a two-point scale of "Dynamic Focus," specifying whether the therapist works within the patient's frame of reference; 4) degree of initiative taken by therapist; and 5) therapeutic climate, ranging from "cold" to "warm."

Systems expressing psychoanalytic constructs. Has psychoanalytic theory—which, of all efforts to understand psychotherapy, provides the most conceptual illumination and the richest fund of research hypotheses—has psychoanalytic theory influenced content-analysis studies of psychotherapy? Not much, so far. Any content system based on psychoanalytic insights must somehow deal with the behavioral events, including unconscious processes, that psychoanalytic theory is concerned with. To deal with these events by content analysis one must painstakingly define concepts and develop rules of inference. Only in this way can the verbal exchanges of patient and therapist be made to yield reliable data. It is toward this goal —of getting such reliable data based on analytic theory—that the system proposed in this manual is directed. I wish to note here some attempts by other workers to develop content systems grounded on analytic theory.

The research of Leopold Bellak (Bellak and Smith, 1956) represents a far-reaching effort to capture reliably and objectively the trained intuition of psychoanalysts. His judges, for instance, rate the intensity of more than thirty variables in each hour or set of hours studied. The variables include transference, guilt, oral strivings, defenses. Although Bellak's work, involving ratings of whole hours, would not ordinarily be called content analysis, his aims are similar to those of Dollard and Auld and his variables somewhat resemble theirs.

Another ingenious attempt to capture and code expert clinical judgments has been reported by Leary and Gill (in Rubinstein and Parloff, 1959). They ask psychoanalytically trained experts to make a running written commentary on an hour of therapy, providing a set of interpretations paralleling the transcript of patient-therapist dialogue. Technicians then classify the experts' statements according to an elaborate set of categories. In this two-stage content analysis, all the inference is in the first stage, the clinical judgments. The second stage is a mechanical matching procedure, "like mail clerks trained to recognize addresses" Leary has characterized it (Rubinstein and Parloff, 1959, p. 118). Leary and Gill have demonstrated high reliability in this second-stage sorting but have not demonstrated reliability of the clinical judgments themselves, although they acknowledge that this is essential if this two-stage method of content analysis is to be trusted. That is, once an expert characterizes a patient's behavior as defensive, for example, technicians can reliably sort such a statement into a category with other statements describing patient's behavior as defensive. But there is no assurance available of the reliability or validity of the expert's judgment.

Leary and Gill do not undertake what Dollard and Auld have regarded as their principal task, namely to probe the clinical judgments themselves in order to discover and specify the cues, definitions, and criteria on which they are based and the processes of inferences by which they are made. They are therefore in a difficult position when they attempt, as they also do, to apply their same categories of content analysis to the raw material, the verbalizations of the patient and therapist in the therapy itself. The "clinical" categories—such as those concerned with defensiveness, lifting of repression, and other dynamic characteristics—can be scored only when these are the explicit subject of patient or therapist verbalization, i.e. when patient or therapist talks like a clinician making inferences. Since this happens relatively seldom in therapy, a major portion of the patient and therapist verbalizations must be scored in

"special" and "non-clinical" categories, which are essentially a list-
ing of possible topics, such as symptoms, financial matters, and religion. These categories do not in themselves reveal anything of
clinical or dynamic importance; discussion of symptoms or of religion, for example, could represent defensiveness or could represent
insight; such clinically important distinctions are lumped and ob-
scured in these topic categories. The limitation of this procedure is
emphasized when it is recalled that it is precisely from such "non-
clinical" conversation that Leary and Gill's experts are making their
clinical inferences. The Leary and Gill system—at least to date—is
without those definitions and rules of inference by which any statement in psychotherapy can be coded for its dynamic significance.

Whereas many of the content systems discussed in the previous
section treat all of the problems discussed by the patient as equal,
analytic theory suggests that different kinds of problems differ in
significance. It is of some importance, then, to know whether a
patient is talking about hostility, or sense of sin, or troubles with
school work. Thus it is appropriate to mention an attempt to classify
the problems discussed by the patient. Curran (1945), in the study
of a single case, identified fourteen distinct categories of problems.
It must be noted, however, that Curran's system was relatively
uninfluenced by analytic theory.

The previous work that has had a great and direct influence on
the Dollard-Auld content system is that of Murray (1954, 1955,
1956). Influenced by psychoanalytic theory, Murray emphasized in
his content system motivation and conflict, selecting four needs or
drives for scoring: sex, affection, dependence, and independence.
His system requires the scorer to judge, when one of these drives is
present, whether the patient is simply expressing or discussing
gratification of the drive, describing a blocking of the drive by internal factors (anxiety, fear, or guilt), or complaining about the
frustration of the need by external factors. Murray also included in
his system a number of other categories, such as "disturbance of
free association," "intellectual defenses," and "generalized anxiety."

The system described in this manual follows Murray in noting
the drives and conflicts believed to be expressed in the patient's
speech, but it diverges by using a considerably modified list of
drives. The drive for independence, less well defined than others
and perhaps less important theoretically, is not included in the
Dollard-Auld list; at the same time, Dollard and Auld have added

a number of new drives. The Dollard-Auld system employs Murray's device for indicating with convenient symbols that drives may conflict one with the other. It includes a number of categories, based on theoretical considerations, that were absent from Murray's system; especially important is the indication for drive reduction, r.

Murray was the first researcher to use content analysis to distinguish between conflict-related and resistant utterances. In his earliest study (1954) he identified two types of resistance, intellectual resistance and discussion of physical symptoms. Later (1955, 1956) he also scored disturbances of free association, which may be considered a further kind of resistance.

Earlier, Hogan (1952) and Haigh (1949) had attempted to measure resistance (they called it "defensiveness"), but they did not specify subtypes of resistance. Gillespie (1953) scored thirteen different forms of resistance, basing his categories on client-centered views. He defined resistance as any negative reaction by the patient that retards counseling and is attributable to poor counseling techniques. His system, accordingly, includes categories for various forms of criticism of and antagonism toward the counselor and counseling, as well as five categories for "resistance within the client." These latter categories are: long pauses; short answers, monosyllables, or reduced speech production; repetition of the problem in a stereotyped manner; changing the subject; and excessive verbalization or intellectualization. The Dollard-Auld system employs similar categories of resistance, but it also includes additional subtypes and gives much fuller definitions. In particular, it clearly defines a long pause by relying on timing of pauses by stop watch; thus the content analyst is not left at the mercy of a typist's estimate of what is a long pause.

In scoring the therapist's utterances Murray retained the distinction made by Snyder between relatively active and relatively passive interventions. Murray distinguished, for example, between "demands" and "mild probes." But, unlike the nondirectivists who assembled an array of descriptive categories, he limited himself to a few categories representing the chief roles of the therapist. Murray's analysis of the therapist's activities provided the starting point for the scores for therapist set forth in this manual. Important developments in the present system, wherein it diverges from Murray's, include the following: Whereas Murray distinguished various types of interpretation (labeling, teaching discriminations, showing similarities), all interpretive activities are here combined in a single category. Murray's "mild approval" and "unh-hunh" categories have been telescoped. The distinction between demands and mild probes has been abandoned, and the demand category has been redefined so that it is based not on whether the utterance is in the form of a question but on whether the utterance is motivating. The "disapproval" category has been dropped; presumably most utterances formerly scored as disapproval would now come under the redefined demand category (*D*). The possibility of incorrect interpretation has been recognized by establishing a new category, *Pretni*. Finally —and quite importantly—each sentence of the therapist's utterance is taken by itself and scored in itself, whereas Murray scored the utterance as a whole, attempting to represent the most important feature of it, neglecting the subdominant aspects.

In spite of the fundamental importance that psychoanalytic theory has attached to unconscious reactions, and in spite of the frequency with which diagnosticians and therapists intuitively identify unconscious reactions, no previous content system has attempted to provide rules for designating these. The attempt in this manual to do so represents, I believe, a decided advance, even though this system can be considered only a rough first try.

Influence of previous systems on the Dollard-Auld system. Taking stock now of the influence of previous content systems on the one presented here, the present writer would summarize matters as follows: The D.R.Q. showed that the emotions expressed by a patient can be scored, in at least a rough way, and that the scoring system can be tied to theoretical variables (such as motivation and reward). The Bales system and those developed by nondirective therapists had little influence on the present one. Murray had a great influence on the present system, and indeed constituted the starting point for it. The ways in which Dollard and Auld changed the system since this beginning make it, however, essentially new. In particular they confronted the problem of unconscious reactions, which Murray did not deal with; they have different and more detailed content categories for the patient; they have bound the therapist categories closer to a theoretical analysis of his activity; and they have sought to provide, in the form of this manual, more adequate definitions, closer linkage of the categories to pertinent theory, careful discussion of scoring problems, and extensive teaching material.

UNITIZING

Since content analysis is the sorting of units of communication into various categories, it requires definition of the units to be sorted. Moreover, investigators almost always use content analysis to compare the contents of different communications; to make such a comparison one must know that the units in the different communications are, in some meaningful sense, comparable. Finally, it is evident that the reliability of content analysis usually is no better than the reliability of dividing the communication into units. Undefined and unreliable unitizing would open the way to a radical distortion or obscuring of results, particularly if unitizing were done in conjunction with categorizing.*

That unitizing and categorizing are distinct acts, even when performed simultaneously by the same person, has been recognized by most content analysts who have studied psychotherapy. But the importance of care in unitizing and of evaluating reliability of unitizing has not been widely recognized. Clear definitions of units and full reports on reliability of unitizing are rare. Statements like the following are more common: "One very significant question that has faced every person who has attempted to objectify spoken or subjective statements has been the question of determining the boundaries of the units of material . . . The present writer felt that to interject the question of reliability of breakdown into this material would complicate the problems under study. It was, therefore, decided that the breaks between ideas should be arbitrarily decided by the classifier" (Snyder, 1945, pp. 201–2). Another typical statement: "Variations between observers in unitizing will affect all [subsequent] operations. In practice these points are not too important; we find that observers who perform one operation reliably

---

* For example, if in scoring category X a judge tended to include a larger amount of material per unit than when he scored category Y, we could not believe him when he subsequently reported that category Y appeared more frequently; the bias in unitizing could account for the greater frequency of Y units. Such a bias could occur either because the scorer had some tendency to include more material when X was present than when Y was present, or because the definitions of the categories made bias inevitable (e.g. one category might be so defined that it would be scored only for a lengthy, comprehensive speech, whereas other categories could be scored for either long or short speeches).

also tend to perform the other operations reliably" (Bales, 1950, p. 114). But the last statement is not accompanied by any report of an actual test of the reliability of the unitizing.

Covner is reported (by Snyder, 1945) to have found "rather high consistency" in the unitizing of "ideas"—defined as any change in subject matter or attitude; but no reference to unitizing is made in Covner's published report of his dissertation research. Dollard and Mowrer (1947) assessed the "accuracy of clause identification" by comparing the number of "thought units" found per page by different judges. In view of the scant attention previously given to unitizing, it is clear that Murray (1955, 1956) pioneered in drawing attention to its importance, in making the unitizing task distinct from categorizing, in formulating definitions of the unit, and in making an adequate appraisal of reliability of unitizing.

Quite apart from the problem of reliability, one is faced with the question: How large should the unit be? This question involves, to some extent, a conflict between objectivity and meaningfulness. The chief possible units are (in order of increasing size) the word, the sentence, the theme (a single idea or point, sometimes consisting of a sentence, sometimes of several sentences), the utterance (what one person says after the other person stops and before the other person begins again), and the entire therapy hour. Each of these units has been used by one or another of the authors mentioned previously. For most purposes some unit larger than the word and smaller than the hour is appropriate. Presumably the theme or episode (see Dollard, Auld, and White, 1953) would be most internally consistent as regards meaning, and so one might have an episode of confirmation, or one of denial of interpretation, or one of recital of a dream. However, the reliability of marking off such episodes would most likely not be as good as the reliability of designating sentences or utterances. Furthermore, it might not do justice to the material to count as equal, episodes that ran on for several minutes and those that lasted only several seconds. To make the episode unit better reflect what went on, one might wish to weight various episodes according to either their judged importance or the amount of time devoted to them. (The present system roughly weights each kind of communication by the amount of time spent on it, because each sentence in an episode or theme counts as one unit.) It is of course undeniable that someone may appear with a satisfactory solution on reliability of episodes or themes.

A line or page of typescript is readily identified, but such a unit seems quite unrelated to the sense of what the patient or therapist is communicating. The designation of a line or page of typescript depends largely on events that are unrelated to the patient's or the therapist's behavior; unit marks do not come when the topic changes, when an intervention is made, or when anything else theoretically important happens. In employing line or page or period of time as a unit, one gets reliability at too high a price—i.e. loss of connection to the patient's and therapist's behavior.

One can use the utterance as a unit with less loss of connection, since after all it is defined in terms of something that the therapist and patient do. But in psychoanalytic therapy utterances are apt to differ greatly in length, some of them being very short as therapist and patient engage in a quick give-and-take, some being extremely long as the patient rambles on without interruption. Such wide variation in length makes the utterance a somewhat unwieldy unit. Furthermore, it sometimes happens during a long ramble by the patient that his conversation turns in new and unexpected directions. One might be loath, therefore, to score all of such an utterance the same way; one would wish to recognize the changes within it.

The sentence has much to commend it if one wishes a very small unit (Auld and White, 1956). It is, after all, by definition the smallest piece of speech that can be understood in itself. In determining what constitutes a sentence the unitizer is guided by the behavior of the speaker; hence connection to the speaker's behavior is built in. It is true that the sentence is a structural block of language, not one that is determined by lexical meaning; but since structure signals a part of the total meaning of any communication, one should not dismiss structural features out of hand as meaningless. The reader should be warned, moreover, that attempts to define small units on a lexical basis nearly always come to grief on the rock of poor reliability. Dollard and Mowrer (1947), for instance, got only poor reliability when they tried to divide interviews into "thought units." Leary and Gill (in Rubinstein and Parloff, 1959) have used a "statement"—defined as the shortest verbalization which can be understood to consist of a subject and a characteristic—which is usually shorter than a sentence, generally a clause or a phrase. They report good reliability in unitizing expert clinical judgments, which tend to be written in clipped phrases, but do not indicate the reliability of detecting such units in the transcripts of therapy hours. Dollard and Auld's decision has been to use structural features as criteria for unitizing. The structure is, so to speak, a frame for the lexical cues of language. The lexical cues could not be conveyed unless there were a frame for them to ride in; nor could the complete meaning of the communication be carried without support from *both* its structural and lexical features. In Chapter 2 of this book instructions for dividing interviews into sentences are given (with examples of such unitizing in Appendix B), and the very satisfactory degree of reliability attained is reported.

MEASURING RELIABILITY OF SCORING

A content-analysis system like that in this manual involves such a complex set of judgments that it is not easy to find appropriate ways of measuring reliability of scoring. This difficulty may explain why almost every content analyst seems to have chosen a different way of assessing reliability. Some of these reliability checks have been more completely reported than others; the absence of an adequate report by some workers increases the difficulty of finding out what would be the best way to test reliability. Finally, one is at a loss to know—even after one has computed some coefficient or other statistic—how large the coefficient has to be before it can be considered satisfactory. Decisions about this matter have varied, and few authors have given the problem explicit attention. One is probably justified in assuming, however, that if an author published a study he believed that the reliability statistics he got were high enough.

Percentage-of-agreement is a straightforward and easily understood measure of reliability. Freedman *et al.* (1951), Seeman (1949), and Snyder (1953) have used it. Percentage-of-agreement means, simply, the ratio of the number of agreed-on units to the total number of units scored, times 100. Percentages reported in the literature range from 31 to 95. Whereas percentage-of-agreement seems appropriate, in some respects, for measuring over-all reliability of the content system, it cannot be used to measure the reliability of the separate categories in the system. It does not give an adequate measure of reliability on separate categories because collapsing the content system into two categories, A and Not-A, raises the possibility of purely chance agreement to an unacceptably high level.

At best, when there are only two categories two scorers cannot disagree more than 50% of the time, even when they are utterly in-
competent. If percentage-of-agreement is to be used as a reliability
index in such circumstances, therefore, it must be corrected for
chance agreement.

A correlation coefficient might be used to assess reliability of a
single category. For instance, one can record the frequency of selection of the category by each judge for each of a series of hours, then
correlate these counts for different judges. The resulting coefficient
tells us whether the judges agree in finding proportionately more
units of category A in some hours than in others. Such coefficients,
based on total-hour counts, have been used by Murray (1956) and
by Dollard and Auld. High reliability on hour counts does not, it
should be noted, indicate that the judges are scoring the same units
in the same way but only that they get relatively the same totals. If
the conclusions to be drawn from the content analysis are going
to be based on hour totals, then this index of reliability is entirely
appropriate; but if the investigator is going to make use of the
categorization of individual units within hours, then some other
index, which shows that the judges agree on the scoring of individual
units, is needed. Such an index is also used in this manual.

The measure of agreement on each and every sentence used by
Dollard and Auld is the *tau* coefficient. Like the percentage-of-
agreement index, *tau* counts as "agreement" only the concordance
of scorers on individual items; compensating errors do not boost
tau as they do the product-moment correlation of hour totals. But
tau, unlike the percentage-of-agreement measure, is not inflated by
the possibility of hitting on similar categorizations by chance. With
tau this chance level of agreement has, so to speak, been subtracted
out. A full discussion of this coefficient and how it is used to measure
reliability is given in the chapter on reliability.

A reliability index, like any statistic, is more satisfactory if it is
unbiased (which means that the index in the sample is a good estimate, neither systematically too high or too low, of what one would
find in an infinite number of such samples). Percentage-of-agreement
is an unbiased statistic, and the product-moment correlation coefficient is very nearly so. A statistic proposed by Strodtbeck (Bales,
1950, ch. 4), however, is seriously biased. Strodtbeck proposed that
one decide whether the reliability of scoring is high enough by
looking at the probability figure associated with the value of chi-

square, chi-square being computed by comparing the frequency of assignment of units to various categories by the two scorers. The reliability is satisfactory, Strodtbeck advised, if the probability value is .50 or more. It is easy to show that this probability figure is, in general, smaller as the sample size increases. With a sample of infinite size this figure would diminish to zero. Obviously, such an index is a risky one to use in deciding how well the scorers agree; for the smaller the sample, the more likely one would be to suppose that they were agreeing well—but one's trust in the result would most likely be shattered if one had a larger sample.

It may be well, now, to mention certain precautions in the use of reliability checks:

1. Reliability should be tested on the kind of judgment that is to be used in the research. It was pointed out above, for example, that if scores on individual units are to be used, it is not sufficient to show that hour totals can be reliably arrived at. Another problem arises when reliability is checked on broad categories, but subcategories are used in the processing of the data. Bales, for instance, used all twelve of his categories in reporting research results, yet in testing reliability collapsed six of them into a single category.

2. The reliability test should be based on a random sample of the material, and the sample should be sufficiently large. The amount of material used in reliability checks, when reported by the investigator, has ranged from twelve minutes (Bales) to six hours out of 218 which were scored (Snyder, 1953).

3. Since the reliability coefficient is essentially an index of the teachability of the definitions of the content system, these definitions should be the only basis on which the various judges assign the material to categories. Other cues for sorting, such as consultation between judges, recollection of how the material was previously scored (where a test-retest correlation is used to assess reliability), cues in the material extraneous to the definitions but helpful as hints of how the other judges will score the material—all these should be ruled out when reliability of the content system is being tested. Unfortunately these factors have not always been controlled in the reliability studies reported in the literature.

SOUND RECORDING OF INTERVIEWS

Content analysis of psychotherapy has become feasible only in the last quarter century, as technical developments have enabled us to capture an accurate, word-for-word record of the therapeutic transaction.* The idea of getting complete records of therapy hours by using a sound recorder probably occurred at about the same time to many people. In this section a few of those who began to make sound recordings will be acknowledged.

The world's pioneer in the recording of the psychoanalytic transaction was *Earl F. Zinn,* M.A., now resident in Miami, Florida. Zinn began his work in 1925 and pursued his purpose inflexibly for twenty years. His work was widely though informally noticed by other investigators and many, including Dollard and Auld, took courage and example from him. Zinn had become interested in psychoanalysis both as a theory of human behavior and as a research method while serving as executive secretary of the National Research Council's Committee for Research in Problems of Sex. In 1925–26, while in Europe on committee business, Zinn discussed with Ernest Jones and Freud the ways in which psychoanalytic theory could be tested within the framework of the committee's work. The committee, having little enthusiasm for psychoanalysis, ignored Jones' and Freud's suggestions. Zinn, however, got the sponsorship of the Social Science Research Council and the financial backing of George Coe Graves for a program to make recordings of analytic interviews. With the help of the Dictaphone Corporation, a system for recording analytic interviews on wax cylinders was developed. When Zinn could not get any analyst to record a patient in his laboratory, Zinn's sponsors decided to send him to Berlin for thorough analytic training which would prepare him to record psychoanalyses that he himself would conduct. Zinn had begun experimentation on the recording of interviews in 1929; he began his analytic training in Berlin in the fall of 1931, and upon his return from Berlin in 1932 he began recording analytic interviews.

Zinn's experiences in recording psychoanalytic data are best told in his own words:

> On my return to New York I continued training, attending the lectures and seminars offered by the Psychoanalytic Institute and carrying a control case with Dr. A. Kardiner. This case

* Recordings are useful, of course, not only for research but also for teaching and even as an adjuvant to the usual therapeutic procedures. (Bierer and Ström-Olsen [1948] found that patients would record material when alone that they could not express in the presence of the therapist, and these authors also experimented with playing back to the patient portions of his previous interview to show him his hesitations and parataxes and to release his associations.)

had been referred to me by Dr. A. A. Brill. The New York Society still disapproved of the recording of analysis and I was told that if I wished to continue my training in that Institute I would have to refrain from recording. Our sponsor and the Committee for the Study of Personality allowed me to stop recording until the time came that no question as to the adequacy of my training and competence could be raised; thus, I was permitted to continue training in the New York Institute.

In all fairness, however, it should be stated that the Society had some grounds at the time for objecting to my recording analytic data. First, it was considered unethical to record the data without the analysand's knowledge and consent. Furthermore, it was assumed that if the analysand knew he was being recorded it would affect his associations in such a way that a valid account of analytic procedure could not be obtained. I was subsequently able to disprove this assumption. Secondly, I was not very well known by many members of the Society . . .

The following summer . . . our sponsor, Mr. George Coe Graves, died suddenly. He left no provision in his will for the continued support of this project. . . . While in Berlin I had met Dr. John Dollard, who was also training in the Berlin Institute. We became fast friends and discussed this recording project at great length. When he learned of our difficulty he introduced me to Dr. William Bryan, then superintendent of the Worcester State Hospital . . . who invited me to come to Worcester and continue the recording experiment. He extended to me the facilities of the hospital and the privilege of selecting any patient or patients as subjects for recorded analysis. After careful screening I chose a nineteen-year-old man, who was accessible and on whom a most complete case history was available. The patient's parents were most co-operative and gave their consent to the analysis being recorded. This patient had been diagnosed as hebephrenic shizophrenic by both the hospital and research staffs. The analysis was begun and continued in the Worcester State Hospital for approximately two years.

In the fall of 1935 I was invited to join the faculty of the Yale Medical School with the rank of assistant professor of psychiatry (psychoanalysis) with the privilege of continuing my research. It was agreed that I could bring my research subject to New Haven and house him in the Psychiatric Institute. There

I was able to continue his analysis until June 1937 when, with the consent of the psychiatric staff, I discharged him. . . . A transcript of this analysis, consisting of 425 hours, plus other material about the patient, has been prepared and is edited to protect the patient's anonymity and is available to qualified researchers.

In addition to this recording, I made several partial recordings of neurotic patients at Worcester and three complete recordings of graduate students while at Yale. . . . The recordings of the three mentioned above were not edited and the complete records were turned over to the students thus recorded to do with what they chose. These recordings, incidentally, were made with the subjects' knowledge. The analysis of my schizophrenic patient . . . was recorded without his knowledge in Worcester but with his parents' consent, and with his knowledge when I brought him to New Haven. The record reveals that this knowledge made no discernible difference in his behavior or associations, other than that for the first few hours he endeavored to seduce my secretary via the microphone. She was transcribing the records and I had introduced him to her.*

Harold D. Lasswell became interested in psychoanalysis because he believed psychoanalytic therapy to represent the most intimate kind of human interaction. The social scientist, Lasswell reasoned, if he wanted to understand the whole range of human behavior from most intimate (psychoanalysis) to most impersonal (mass communication), must know something about psychoanalysis. Lasswell went to Europe in 1928–29 on an SSRC fellowship to study psychoanalysis. Before he left for Europe plans had been started to establish a recording laboratory at the University of Chicago in the Social Science Research Building soon to be built there. While in Europe, therefore, Lasswell consulted the leading analysts about his plan to record analytic interviews. Lasswell's path crossed Zinn's in at least one place: Lasswell recalls that Zinn had already talked with Ferenczi, who was upset at the idea of recording psychoanalysis. (No other analyst was so opposed to the idea.)

Upon returning to Chicago Lasswell set up a recording laboratory and, using special Dictaphone equipment, began—apparently

* Letter from Earl F. Zinn to Granville Fisher, May 22. 1958.

in 1930—to make sound recordings of analytic interviews. He also recorded skin resistance, heart rate, breathing, and bodily movements of the patient (see Lasswell, 1935, 1936, 1937). He continued this research until World War II when he went into government service.*

Percival M. Symonds was one of the first to make recordings of counseling interviews. Some of his experiences were reported in an article published in 1939. In answer to a query by the authors, Symonds wrote:

> Yes, so far as I know, I am the first person to have used sound recording of counseling interviews somewhere around 1938. . . . At that time I had some equipment which today would seem very antiquated, consisting of two very heavy cases weighing about 40 pounds each. I remember lugging these by car out to Hastings High School where I recorded some interviews between the school counselor and pupils. On that occasion I had the recording instrument in a little anteroom which was between the classroom in which the interviewing took place and the auditorium. The microphone was concealed, and being somewhat naive in those days, I was in trepidation during the whole process that the subject being interviewed or someone else would discover what was going on. Actually, of course, the subject being interviewed had too much else on his mind and it never occurred to him. I remember, however, that a whole troop of kids rushed from the auditorium through the anteroom where the turntables were in full view, but they also were concerned with other matters and did not stop to pay attention to what we were doing. . . .
>
> I made an analysis of the amount of time spent by the counselor and the student during the interview, and to my amazement the counselor used over 70 per cent of the time. Of course, since that time Rogers has given this older approach a thorough airing and I believe that this would be considered poor practice today, although I imagine that one could find it rather readily.†

* This account of Lasswell's experiences in recording psychoanalytic sessions is based on a conversation between Lasswell and Frank Auld, Jr., on June 7, 1958.

† Letter from Percival M. Symonds to Frank Auld, Jr., November 12, 1957.

Carl R. Rogers is deservedly famous for his pioneering work in recording counseling interviews. Since the recording procedures of Rogers and his colleagues were first described by Bernard J. Covner (1942), the authors asked Covner about the early days of recording at Ohio State University. He replied as follows:

> I came in September of 1939, Rogers in January of 1940. In one of Rogers' courses the question of the desirability of recording came up. I was a radio ham and said that recorders were available even though I hadn't ever seen one. I covered the market and found adequate equipment made right in Columbus. But no one showed much of an interest in my great discovery.
>
> Then one day Rogers called me at home, saying that the department's budget had $150 left that had to be spent that day, and since I knew of purchasable equipment he would like to see it. We drove over to Bell Sound Systems . . . bought a recorder, an extra turntable for doubling capacity (about 3-min. limit per 10-in. disk), and a supply of disks and styli.
>
> The University installed microphone cable lines from several interviewing rooms into a central (and secret) recording room . . . I designed a switching arrangement to enable a single amplifier to serve two recording heads and turntables. My father supplied rugs and drapes from his store for sound-absorption treatment of the interviewing rooms. . . .
>
> I did most of the recording until I left in April of 1942. . . .
>
> The desirability of recording was stressed by Rogers. Prior to coming to Ohio State he had tried the conventional mandrel-type Dictaphone without success, and gave it up. My role was essentially that of a mechanic. And my thesis, which compared phonograph typescripts with interviewers' reports, showed that the discrepancies were great enough to show the superiority of the former for research purposes.
>
> Robinson, as I recall, got into recording research a little later, and probably was most active after I left.[*]

At *Yale University* the first recordings were those made by Earl F. Zinn (see above). With the development of magnetic recording, and taking his lead from Zinn, John Dollard began making magnetic

[*] Letter from Bernard J. Covner to Frank Auld, Jr., November 18, 1957.

tape recordings of his own psychotherapy interviews, and Richard
Newman began to use a wire recorder for the same purpose. Also
F. C. Redlich, chairman of the Department of Psychiatry, began
to tape-record his own interviews for use in teaching; and Dollard,
beginning to teach a course in psychotherapy, had his students
record all their interviews. It became apparent that better facilities
for recording were needed, and with the aid of grants from the
Markle Foundation and the Social Research Foundation interviewing rooms were constructed and high-fidelity recording equipment
was obtained. These facilities have been described in two papers,
by Redlich *et al.* (1950) and by Mahl *et al.* (1954).

This quick review of some of the origins of sound-recording
of psychotherapy brings out that those who pioneered recording
had to overcome not only equipment problems, not only prejudices
against recording of interviews, but also their own doubts about
the feasibility of capturing the therapeutic transaction on disk,
cylinder, wire, or tape. Would the patient be disturbed? Would the
therapy be so changed that no scientific value could accrue from a
study of the records? Could the patient be told that the recording
was being made? These scientists did not know what the answers
would be, but they went ahead and recorded. Now we know—thanks
to the courage of these researchers—that the patient is seldom disturbed by the recording (and if he is, it is a problem to be dealt
with like any other problem arising in the therapy), that the essential
features of the therapy are not changed, and that one can risk telling
the patient that one would like to record his sessions.

The experience of Dollard and Auld in working with recordings
has given them the conviction that a researcher ought to get the
best possible sound-recording to use as raw material for his scientific
work. At the present stage of technical development he does not
need to suffer with unintelligible or garbled records. Magnetic tape
can capture the sounds of the therapeutic transaction with breath-
by-breath clarity. Every sigh, every pause, every slightest inflection
can be preserved.

It is their conviction also that one should not take too seriously
the laments of some commentators that the sound recording misses
part of the therapeutic transaction. Of course it misses something,
because it preserves only auditory stimuli and none of the visual
or olfactory stimuli. But is the loss really so great that one can learn
nothing from the sound record, as some of these mourners imply?

And would not the disturbance of the therapeutic situation that seems necessary for movie-making detract more from the usefulness of the sound movie than the addition of visual stimuli to the record would add? No one can doubt that visual stimuli will add an important dimension to the data, when it is possible to make a visual record without too great a disturbance of the therapy. It is doubtful, however, that it is a service to science to deprecate the enterprise of sound recording on the ground that someday it will be possible to study still other events which sound records do not capture. The important issue is: Does a sound record preserve enough of the cues of the therapy transaction to permit the observer to detect major variables in action? The authors of this book believe that it does.

Examples of Unitizing

Rule 1. A noun or noun substitute tied to a verb comprises an actor-action construction (here italicized).

Statements:

All of a sudden *something clicked*

I hardly ever *took* my brother's advice on anything

I graduated in June

Questions:

Do *you feel* like doing that

Am I following you there

Was there some *misunderstanding* about the appointment time *

Have you been trained as a teacher

Was that a major in English

An actor-action construction is sufficient for a complete sentence except in the following cases:

a. A transitive verb (italicized) lacks direct object.

You want to *use* the ummh

But I've *had* enough satis—

Well I *think*
_____

For one thing I *have*
_____

The last summer I was I was there I *had* this
_____

---

* For discussion of the function word *there,* see Fries, pp. 160–2.

And we *found* that *

b. The verb is from the list headed by the forms of *be* (italicized) and predicate nominative or predicate adjective is missing.

   Is it . . .

I haven't *been* . . .

But you*'re* not . . .

   And the minute I went back to working and had some sort of
      income I-ah I *felt* ah
c. The verb (italicized) is incompletely modified. The function words in the examples are: *through, to, with, about,* and *about.*

   It all *goes* through ah the

   I think I *objected* to the ummh

   I *consulted* with uh

   I *was wondering* about

   So often the-the usual marriage-counseling books uh *talk* about
d. The verb is an auxiliary (italicized), and the main verb is lacking.

   Then they*'ll*
e. Subordinating conjunction (italicized) signals a dependent clause.

   that I could not bother with the appointment slip *when* the
      girl wasn't there

   when the time wore on

   because there is no reason for it

   if that's all right.

   after I got married

   until I just happened to read through the whole lot of them

---

   * The intonational pattern shows that *that* is a function word (which should introduce a dependent clause) rather than a substantive.

that you felt somewhat guilty *because* he was masturbating you
   in order to help you toward a climax
how certain things were put
whether I told you about that
who was weaker than myself in some way
why I had picked out that type of person
what I really want
which I appreciated immensely
as I was driving down this morning

Dependent clause with elision of *that:*

   I didn't think I could begin to do that in the time (*I could begin to do that in the time* is the dependent clause.)

Rule 2. Two actor-action constructions linked by what most grammarians call a coordinating conjunction (italicized) should be treated as separate units, not a compound sentence. (The vertical lines mark off the sentence units.)

   I never thought about it for years| *and* then it all came back to me after I was married|
   You may have been perhaps a little more aroused than the average sort of person| *but* nevertheless it is a normal expression of the normal sort of desire|
   I mean he tried as he knows how| *and* I've felt that I should be grateful to him|
   I loved him like he was my own child| he was a little fellow| *and* she took him away to Florida| *and* I tried to forget about it|
   We can't say thank you for the time you've put in this 'cause it well just can't| *but* we appreciate the fact that if I'd been paying fifty dollars an hour we couldn't 've had better help|
   I started seeing her| *and* I was going out of my way to find time to-to be with her and asking her out and so forth| *and* uh there was a conflict here for a while within the family of

some doubts upon the part of the various members of the
family|

She had traveled| *and* she liked the arts| *and* she was familiar
with the sciences and all these various things| *and* it put her
on a different level than that which we were accustomed to
and which our relatives and parents and so forth recognized
as a level for us|

Oh I just love clothes in general| *and* so many times I'd like
to go and buy|

I don't think I stand alone in thinking about things like that|
but still it doesn't alter the fact and doesn't help me to even
think about somebody else|

Rule 3. Intonation determines whether a group of words belongs
with the preceding or with the following sentence.

And of course there was no room for conflict in the eyes of the

law you had to be either one way or the other

(The final pitch on *law,* and the pattern signaling continuation
on *conflict,* indicate that *in the eyes of the law* belongs with
the earlier unit. The sentence division comes after *law.*)

I mean you made the best of it as best you could you went on and

accepted being competent as the next best thing

(The final pitch on *it,* and the 2–3 signal of continuation in
best you could, indicate that *as best you could* belongs with the
second unit.)

Well in this case not too much// more likely she would uh say all

right

(*More* could conceivably go with *much*. But the intonational pattern shows that it does not; there is a final pitch on much.)

Rule 4. Certain conventional expressions may lack an actor-action construction and yet be sentences. (See page 16.)

Rule 5. Questions signaled by repetition, with rising intonation, of preceding statements may be treated as complete sentences, though lacking an actor-action construction.

PATIENT   My major was in English of all things

THERAPIST   English

PATIENT   But it sounds like a parasite existence

THERAPIST   Parasite

PATIENT   All the boy friends I've ever had have been older than myself at least ten years I would say

THERAPIST   All of them have been at least ten years

Rule 6. Certain function words (italicized) operate as a signal of supplement questions that are complete sentences though sometimes lacking actor-action construction.
Supplement questions having actor-action construction:
How much do they ask you to pay
What are you going to do now
Which one was that
Why did you change
How did that interest arise
Where'd you get that idea

What were you afraid of
With whom was this
What does that mean
Where had you studied sociology

Supplement questions lacking actor-action construction:

Hmm

How so

Because *what*

Yeah

Like *what*

Yes

Well *why* not

For instance
Social pressure in *what* direction
Why
But *what*

Rule 7. Answers to questions may be complete sentences, though lacking an actor-action construction.

    a. *Yes, no,* or an equivalent (italicized) is a complete sentence.

    PATIENT   Is there a scrap basket around

    THERAPIST   *Yes*

THERAPIST   Well I think that what you're worrying about is whether or not you'll have to go for just a few weeks and then have to change to somebody else

PATIENT   *Yes*

THERAPIST   What you are saying is that you did love him then but as you see it now you don't love him at all now

PATIENT   *No, no*

PATIENT   And I can pay afterwards I take it

THERAPIST   *Sure*

THERAPIST   You were studying science

PATIENT   *Mhm*

Yes or *no* supplemented by a statement utterance is a single complete sentence.

THERAPIST   I guess what you're wondering is how this may affect your treatment| is that the point|

PATIENT   Uh *yes* I was wondering how long it'd take

PATIENT   You're German aren't you

THERAPIST   *No* Dutch

PATIENT   I don't know whether I told you about that

THERAPIST   *No* I don't think so

THERAPIST   You were intending to become married

PATIENT   *Yes* we were engaged that year

THERAPIST   Have you been trained as a teacher

PATIENT   *No* not exactly

THERAPIST   This is one of the leading schools

PATIENT   *Yes* it's one of the top five in the country

If there is a final pitch after the *yes* or *no* the material following is
not supplemental but is considered a separate unit:

THERAPIST   Was that where you met

PATIENT   Oh yes| we-we met when we were a few months old

THERAPIST   You do want to have a baby|

PATIENT   Oh yes| I ah think now it would be difficult finan-
cially to have one|

PATIENT   I had a Jewish friend who was very much insulted
when I said that|

THERAPIST   Yes| well I think that what you're worrying about is

whether I'm touchy about unintended slights|

THERAPIST   And you don't understand what it was that made
you do it|

PATIENT   No| and it's been I guess you might say it's been on

my conscience because I very ah frequently have thoughts of
those incidents

PATIENT   And I didn't tell him all that ha—I didn't tell him
what had happened I just told him that I'd done it

THERAPIST   Yes| this was the occasion which was unsuccessful

wasn't it|

(The *yes* in this last example is not an answer to a question but rather a signal of continued attention. However, the example bears on the same issue: whether to assimilate the *yes* with a supplemental utterance or to consider it as separate from what follows.)

b. A completive sentence (italicized) may be of any form called for by the question it completes.

THERAPIST   How much do they ask you to pay
PATIENT   *A dollar and a half*

THERAPIST   Which school was that
PATIENT   *Horace Mann*

THERAPIST   What did you teach
PATIENT   *English*

THERAPIST   To children of what grade
PATIENT   *Fourth and fifth grades*

THERAPIST   Are you still doing anything with your French
PATIENT   *Not very often*

THERAPIST   How large is Lincoln School
PATIENT   *About four hundred*

THERAPIST   That's a fairly common practice
PATIENT   *Quite common I think*

THERAPIST   How long have you been there
PATIENT   *Three years*

THERAPIST   Well but do you get excited when you're stimulated sexually by your husband
PATIENT   *Sometimes*

THERAPIST   But you know Minnesota
PATIENT   *Pretty well*

> THERAPIST   What was this you brought up
> PATIENT   *Well the question of why I why the family hadn't been able to help me to go to college*

Rule 8. The completion of a sentence (italicized) by another speaker is to be considered a sentence even when lacking an actor-action construction if it is complete when considered within the frame of the speech that it finishes.

> PATIENT   There's this very close family relationship that has reduced a great deal getting into the community into the social things that you find outside of your
> THERAPIST   *And centered more around the religious group hmm*
>
> PATIENT   No not necessarily religious group just the family
> THERAPIST   *Just the family huh*

Rule 9. A signal of continued attention (italicized) constitutes a complete sentence.

> PATIENT   Dick was stationed in Alabama for two years in the service
> THERAPIST   *Oh*
>
> PATIENT   It's hard to figure out how things do happen so luckily with such inauspicious beginnings
> THERAPIST   *Hhm*
>
> PATIENT   We were engaged that year
> THERAPIST   *I see*
>
> PATIENT   It's not required at Columbia
> THERAPIST   *Hhm*
>
> PATIENT   Fortunately I didn't break any bones so everything was all right
> THERAPIST   *Yeah*
>
> PATIENT   That was the Polish boy
> THERAPIST   *I see yes*

PATIENT   But uncle was so small that when we danced he could
lean his head on my shoulder

THERAPIST   *Yes*

Rule 10. False starts (italicized) are not counted as sentences.

What the why do why do you ask this question

It seems as there's some thing that it it's not I haven't any reti-
cence about telling you anything

I've been I worked very hard the last week

I just it should make me relax

I want I-I-I don't I think that that I want someone that's
stronger than I am

And we I was just as glad

I've I'm reasonably certain that as a doctor's wife I'll never have
to work again

Well I don't know | *what* | *I'm* I am | looking for | something

(This could have been unitized "Well, I don't know. What I'm—
I am looking for something" if the intonational pattern had
been different. However, there is no final pitch on *know;* therefore the first part is a false start, not a separate sentence.)

And I that I ah I can't quite swallow that

And I I can't say that right now

Well I was very I'm very conscious of this burning sensation

But actually I think I fee I felt somewhat dubious about therapeutic endeavors by people because I haven't clearly been
able to understand it until now

For one thing I have Dick is very considerate about it

Rule 11. No words are to be "understood" or "supplied"; the noun
or noun substitute and verb must be explicitly stated.

He was able to see factors on both sides and often would not make a decision (Only one sentence.)

We found out more about it and are ashamed of ourselves that our first reaction wasn't more positive (Only one sentence.)

In a thing like this when two people are involved one seems not to be able to do anything about it and just suffers while the other person calls the signals (Only one sentence.)

But she's adjusted and reconciled herself to the fact that these fancy clothes and stuff that she had so much before are secondary to her children (Only one sentence.)

Rule 12. A paratactic word or phrase (italicized) is to be included in the adjoining sentence.

Goodness this is a maze to find

Won't you come in *please*

THERAPIST   That's a fairly common practice

PATIENT   Quite common *I think*

But their ideas *I guess* of art instruction were a little different from mine

Oh within the last year *I expect* (I don't quite remember roughly when it began) it seemed like it was so unsatisfactory

But *I mean* if you wanted something that would that I could be a part of it would be all right

This sounds sort of peculiar *I guess*

It was a *you know* a feeling as if I well like when you commit a faux pas in public

The only difference was in locale in setting *I guess*

Rule 13. Parenthetic clauses (italicized) are to be included with the sentence that they interrupt.

Oh within the last year I expect *I don't quite remember roughly when it began* it seemed like it was so unsatisfactory

I don't think truthfully uh *and this again is another thing that I never bring up with anyone I have never discussed it with anyone* but truthfully I don't think I'm really a happy person

So this time you know when I checked with the girl *and I have a job now though it's hardly anything that you get rich quick on* it amazed me that the fee was lower now

We first ah ah *I don't know if Miss Ruppert told you or not* had gone to see Dr. Schlitz

I guess I ah felt at that time *maybe I still do* I felt that any therapy would be ah something that would bring me face-to-face with things that I perhaps had uh would be frightened by

Well I think this with a great deal of emphasis *I guess this fits in with the pattern* that uh if I miss an appointment or if I'm a couple of minutes late somebody's going to say aha resistance

Rule 14. Greetings, farewells, and calls are treated as complete sentences.

Hello

Good afternoon

Good-by

See you next week

Rule 15. Requests and commands signaled by an infinitive verb (italicized) are considered sentences.

Won't you *come* in please

Perhaps you want to take your coat off| *put* it over here|

Even if there should happen to be a line *forget* it and come over here

Go ahead (said in response to patient's beginning to talk at the same time as therapist.)

So if you'd just take the lead from whatever you are⌐talking

about| just⌐*let* it⌐flow|

Rule 16. Quotations (italicized) are included in the surrounding sentence.

You can pick it up from the point *yes something must have happened to me and that is why I am impelled to aid others who are miserable and deprived* but just what the extent of that

thing was for you is uh a great deal more difficult apparently a more difficult problem|

I think *oh golly gee if only this if only I hadn't had another child*

She was as blue as ever| and she didn't eat when we were there| and this immediately caused some concern *well what's wrong with her*| and my mother observed this|

I said *is anything wrong*

I can look back and say *this is very humorous* because now he'll come into the house without any difficulty

Even Thursday when I'm out there he says *be sure to come out Sunday*

So many times I think to myself *well just what is what is a happy person are we ever really quite happy*

One part of you says *you're supposed to behave according to the Christian ideal*| but another part of you says *no I don't want to do it that way*|

Rule 17. Weeping, laughter, and sighing are to be designated as separate units.

THERAPIST   And what does the address label say New Jersey

PATIENT   I should let you guess| but I won't| (*Laughs*)|

THERAPIST   (*Laughs*)

PATIENT   Yeah|

PATIENT   I had perfectly normal sexual desires up to possibly a year after I got married| and (*Sighs*)| uh I don't know what happened then|

PATIENT   For instance like if I see a new dress or oh like I love shoes and|*(Sighs)*| oh I just love clothes in general

PATIENT   I discovered I never should have gotten married when I did| *(Sighs)*|

PATIENT   I haven't told you too much about my father| I find it very difficult to talk about him because of his illness| uh but uh oh we we read together| and and and uh *(Weeps)*| see I can't talk about it| *(Sobs 11 secs.)*| this is ridiculous| *(Sobs)*| well anyhow my brother when he came home started to act bad|

Practice Exercises in Unitizing

To ENABLE the reader to practice unitizing we present here several extracts from interviews. They are given entirely without punctuation or capitalization, but with intonational contour or pause pattern shown whenever it provides the distinctive contrast between sentence and nonsentence. A final pause is indicated by the symbol //, a tentative pause by the symbol /. Where there is a false start which can be identified only if one hears the recording and not if one merely reads the words, the false start is bracketed in the transcript. The correct unitizing is given on the facing page for the first excerpt, and at the end of the appendix for the other two excerpts.

EXTRACT FROM INTERVIEW WITH MR. A

PATIENT   well from the book uh which prompts me to think more and of my feelings I think I was conflicted in-in-in the sexual area uh-uh in adolescence uh-and-and I think I may have given you a clue or me a clue when I remarked my moth— er's attitude about kissing girls uh when she expressed this . . . now this could take me into a number of fields-uh areas of feelings uh-uh which I think might be important but aren't— don't come back to me too strongly . . . uh-um particularly I suppose uh as to how I satisfied I suppose I masturbated-uh with some-uh some-uh feelings of guilt during adolescence and I would try to stop this// although I never really got any advice on this from anybody until I was much older that this is a harmless-uh device I still felt that at that time I think I was quite guilt-ridden about it uh I can remember indulging when I was about fourteen or thirteen in the-uh grammar school grades uh-the-uh the in-in some sex play with another fellow-uh and feeling-uh years after it uh somewhat strange about it guilty about it uh
THERAPIST   you were trying to comfort yourself
PATIENT   yeah// it was something that I was trying to do I'm not I'm not sure I exactly know what I was doing but-but-uh these are the thoughts that I had (*14-sec. pause*) uh (*7-sec. pause*) I wanted to achieve [but if I thought I wasn't going to achieve . . .] well we've been over this material I

UNITIZED EXTRACT FROM INTERVIEW WITH MR. A

PATIENT ¹well from the book uh which prompts me to think more and of my feelings I think I was conflicted in-in-in the sexual area uh-uh in adolescence| ²uh-and-and I think I may have given you a clue or me a clue when I remarked my mother's attitude about kissing girls uh when she expressed this . . .| ³now this could take me into a number of fields-uh areas of feelings uh-uh which I think might be important but aren't— don't come back to me too strongly . . . uh-um particularly I suppose uh as to how I satisfied| ⁴I suppose I masturbated-uh with some-uh some-uh feelings of guilt during adolescence| ⁵and I would try to stop this//| ⁶although I never really got any advice on this from anybody until I was much older that this is a harmless-uh device I still felt that at that time I think I was quite guilt-ridden about it| ⁷uh I can remember indulging when I was about fourteen or thirteen in the-uh grammar school grades uh-the-uh the in-in some sex play with another fellow-uh and feeling-uh years after it uh somewhat strange about it guilty about it uh|

THERAPIST ⁸you were trying to comfort yourself|

PATIENT ⁹yeah//| ¹⁰it was something that I was trying to do| ¹¹I'm not I'm not sure I exactly know what I was doing| ¹²but-but-uh these are the thoughts that I had| ¹³⁻¹⁵(*14-sec. pause*) uh ¹⁶(*7-sec. pause*) ¹⁷I wanted to achieve| ¹⁸[but if I thought I wasn't going to achieve . . .] well we've been over this material| ¹⁹I

can go over it and expand on it again I-I do feel that I wanted
to achieve and be successful and be recognized [and-uh I did
it] I couldn't do it in-in studying so I did it in athletics
(*5-sec. pause*) but I got myself in a in a funny position because I
was really more-uh-uh tuned uh to the sensitive fellow-uh who
wasn't the strong athlete yet I was the stronger athlete-uh
than many of the-uh-the so-called athletic uh individuals which
I never really fitted into that crowd that was more uh coarse-uh
in-in terms of-uh their-uh language and their sexual habits
of-uh talk the way they talked about how they conducted
their social life uh-uh for that I would I would turn back and
somewhat with feelings of-of mixed regret that I couldn't be
with these other fellows but I would go back to these other
uh-uh meeker milder folk uh-and with somewhat a feeling of
degradation [it's that I wasn't uh] I was in betwixt and be—
tween

can go over it and expand on it again| [20]I-I do feel that I wanted
to achieve and be successful and be recognized| [21][and-uh I did
it] I couldn't do it in-in studying| [22]so I did it in athletics|
[23](*5-sec. pause*) [24]but I got myself in a in a funny position because I
was really more-uh-uh tuned uh to the sensitive fellow-uh who
wasn't the strong athlete| [25]yet I was the stronger athlete-uh
than many of the-uh-the so-called athletic uh individuals which
I never really fitted into that crowd that was more uh coarse-uh
in-in terms of-uh their-uh language and their sexual habits
of-uh talk the way they talked about how they conducted
their social life| [26]uh-uh for that I would I would turn back and
somewhat with feelings of-of mixed regret that I couldn't be
with these other fellows| [27]but I would go back to these other
uh-uh meeker milder folk uh-and with somewhat a feeling of
degradation| [28][it's that I wasn't uh] I was in betwixt and be-
tween|

EXTRACT FROM INTERVIEW WITH MRS. B

PATIENT   I guess this is all right to put it on I guess it's all soiled I think I'll put it over a chair (*29-sec. pause*) (*She lies down*) (*7-sec. pause*) I was going to ask you-uh . . . (*She sighs*) in the-the few or very few talks that we had-uh do you feel yourself now as though you-you're beginning to uh sort of know me a little bit more// uh I mean from the talks that we've been having// I mean do you feel as though-uh you're able to sort of work out or surmise a little bit more of what this thing is that-that uh bothers me// I mean uh (or shall I say or put it in another way) uh do you think we are making progress at all

THERAPIST   you're wondering if the treatment is uh

PATIENT   well yes//

THERAPIST   working out

PATIENT   uh I-you know I just wondered about it on coming down in the car tonight I was thinking "I think I've been here now I guess this is about the fifth or sixth time" and-uh I wondered you know if-if-uh some of the things that I have told you uh bring forth any light upon you know upon which we are trying to delve into uh the reason I ask is because-uh you know I-I-I know these things take a long time but I just wondered-uh like from your standpoint if-uh progress is being made uh with these talks that we are having

THERAPIST   well how do you feel about this

PATIENT   uh (*She sighs*) well I-I mean it's sort of mixed the-the feelings I have are sort of mixed uh-uh-one time I feel that-uh well I know this is to take time and-and then other times I feel as though . . . well I'm apt to be a little bit impatient and I'm wondering if that is sort of the reaction of most anyone that-that comes for treatment uh such as I have or the-this in the same (shall we put it as a category) or-or the same thing that I have I was wondering if uh you know through the-the talks that I have been having with you-uh if it did or has progressed// uh the thing that-that-uh you asked me you know about the feelings about this or how I felt uh I think I am always uh sort of waiting for you I'm sort of apprehensive as to the feelings that you have about this-uh you know like you said in the beginning that-that most of the-the talking will be on my part but-uh you know I am always looking for perhaps-uh maybe a little bit of encouragement or-uh something to go home with (do you know what I mean) sort of-uh well not like a reward but sort of uh well not like a reward but sort of in the sense to that I would be making progress or "you are coming along fine" as the doctor would say or-or uh something like that and uh so far uh you know the uh different subjects that I have been talking about you have asked me uh perhaps a few questions about it but (I mean) uh nothing that would-uh sort of encourage me// I mean am I making myself clear uh I hope I am

THERAPIST well I wonder why these thoughts are coming to your mind now because I noticed last week-uh too you were uh wondering about the treatment-uh whether it would help you and if it was working and now it seems to me again uh you are looking for uh reassurance and uh some active uh things on my part and uh uh I'd like to point out to you again that uh as these thoughts come to your mind they are-uh-uh last week and now again uh preventing the-uh treatment from continuing that is while you are thinking about these thoughts uh other thoughts are not coming to your mind uh that would be-uh in the treatment uh situation and I was wondering why uh these thoughts have been coming

PATIENT well it just-uh occurs to me uh this that . . . uh-uh I feel that-that-uh "fine" I mean I agree certainly with-with the type of treatment that there is because I know subconsciously it is something that's deep-rooted and inside [but all the while I think that uh . . . I mean I think like anyone else— I think-uh perhaps-uh] I don't know how many other patients you do see a day but I think perhaps (I don't know) that they are apt or liable to ask questions too uh [I only] I think it's only natural-uh to ask certain things like that I mean I don't see anything-uh too wrong about uh asking things I mean they bother me and uh seeing that this is part of the treatment I would think that-uh anything being on my mind like that-uh I'd like to ask you

THERAPIST   well what I meant was I wonder why these things are bothering you

PATIENT   I don't know

THERAPIST   and what-what-what

PATIENT   [uh]

THERAPIST   this means about your-uh feelings towards the treatment because they do-uh seem to me to be-uh in some way uh-uh-uh discussion of the treatment again

PATIENT   mmmhm

THERAPIST   and uh-uh reflect some lack of-uh confidence or unsureness on your part

PATIENT   well I think it is yes uh definitely there// [uh-uh for instance now-uh I think-uh I keep thinking now uh] you well . . . like you told me like in the beginning that the treatment was going to take uh well you didn't name any time at all but I mean it's always in my mind as to how long// or uh after uh these discussions I mean what then I mean is it-uh in a way asking too much to-uh assume that later on uh we could discuss this [I mean of-of uh] well it does it come down to like after I have told you over and over these things that come to mind uh is it that uh we decide well or you decide or in the treatment that well I shall come once a week or-or uh well "this is it" uh like for instance uh "we have done all we can for you and uh the rest will have to be done yourself" I mean-uh

I'm sort of thinking and looking forward to-uh an indefinite period where I don't know exactly what's going to happen-uh later on as along with the treatment too I mean it-it makes me think of uh well how long how far along it will be how-how long how uh mm-when it will ever you know come to being that-that-uh this will all end uh and I don't think that-uh I'm being too inquisitive about that I think anyone that has any type of ailment is liable to ask-uh even a physician that// don't you// uh I mean I'm trying not to-uh be too inquisitive and-and curious about-about it but uh I don't know// it just sort of makes me feel a little bit uh-uh unsure just a little bit and-uh I think as long as uh this is part of the treatment that uh (I mean) I'd rather discuss it with you than keep it to myself uh I don't talk to anyone else about it// [therefore uh I think . . .] uh I don't know// maybe it isn't right that I do this but I don't certainly know who else to speak to about it

THERAPIST well uh let's not worry for the moment about whether it's right or not I just uh would like to point out to you that uh as I said before uh uh there are forces working within you that are opposed to the treatment and uh it seems to me that a lo-uh these-uh worries and concerns that come up in your mind about-uh the treatment the length of the treatment-uh are you making progress and so on are thoughts that come to your mind because uh-uh there is something else that is uh troubling you or uh that should be coming out that for some reason is difficult for you to express and so uh instead these other thoughts come to your mind

PATIENT oh

EXTRACT FROM INTERVIEW WITH MR. C

PATIENT that's a fact// when-uh we were first brought together

I just couldn't see her for beans and she just couldn't under-

stand who this-uh creep was sitting across from her when we

went to dinner somewhere I think and-uh this was not a date
by the way I met her as merely just getting together with

THERAPIST   yeah

PATIENT   a small group

THERAPIST   uh hmm

PATIENT   well this thing just started to grow and I began seeing
more of her// [however all through this I knew all along what
her] she very frequently expressed what she wanted in a man—

THERAPIST   uh hmm

PATIENT   in a husband and-uh well there were many times I'm
sure when I had to reflect and consider well do I fill these expectations of hers and if I don't how can I convince her that-uh
I should be considered

THERAPIST   yeah yeah

PATIENT   and be given the opportunity to develop these things

THERAPIST   yeah yeah

PATIENT   perhaps today there is a thought in my mind that I
haven't filled these—

THERAPIST   well when did you know—

PATIENT   these expectations

THERAPIST   you wanted to marry her

PATIENT   well I began seeing more of her all the time of course
and being together and-uh several trips up to her house and I
just found myself-uh very much in love with her [and this
was-uh . . . I'm afraid it developed over] let's put it this way
after our first meeting I-I would say perhaps nothing material-
ized outside just a general friendship through an organization
that occurred for about a year

THERAPIST   uh hmm

PATIENT   and then the thing became more pronounced after
that

THERAPIST   uh hmm

PATIENT   uh-I started seeing her and I was going out of my

way to find time to-to be with her and asking her out and so
forth and-uh there was a conflict here for a while within the
family of some doubts upon the part of the various members
of the family not my-my own immediate family plus other relatives whether or not she was the right gal for me because she
had been she was of course initially very independent having
been away from home at that time for about four or five years
THERAPIST   hmm
PATIENT   on her own down here and-uh I think perhaps more
adjusted to the realities of life by being independent and so
forth than many of my own relatives were or ever expected any
of their children could ever be
THERAPIST   ['cause they were—]
PATIENT   well we've led this not sheltered life but there's this
very close family relationship that has reduced a great deal
getting into the community into the social thing that you
find outside of your family

UNITIZED EXTRACT FROM INTERVIEW WITH MRS. B

PATIENT   ¹I guess this is all right to put it on| ²I guess it's all|

soiled| ³I think I'll put it over a chair| ⁴⁻⁹(*29-sec. pause*) (*She*

lies down) ¹⁰(*7-sec. pause*) ¹¹I was going to ask you-uh . . .

¹²(*She sighs*) in the-the few or very few talks that we had-uh do

you feel yourself now as though you-you're beginning to uh

sort of know me a little bit more//| ¹³uh I mean from the talks

that we've been having//| ¹⁴I mean do you feel as though-uh
you're able to sort of work out or surmise a little bit more of
what this thing is that-that uh bothers me//| ¹⁵I mean uh (or

shall I say or put it in another way) uh do you think we are making progress at all|

THERAPIST ¹⁶you're wondering if the treatment is uh

PATIENT ¹⁷well yes//|

THERAPIST working out|

PATIENT ¹⁸uh I you know I just wondered about it| ¹⁹on coming down in the car tonight I was thinking "I think I've been here now I guess this is about the fifth or sixth time"| ²⁰and-uh I wondered you know if-if-uh some of the things that I have told you uh bring forth any light upon you know upon which we are trying to delve into| ²¹uh the reason I ask is because-uh you know I-I-I know these things take a long time| ²²but I just wondered-uh like from your standpoint if-uh progress is being made uh with these talks that we are having|

THERAPIST ²³well how do you feel about this|

PATIENT uh ²⁴(*She sighs*) ²⁵well I-I mean it's sort of mixed| ²⁶the-the feelings I have are sort of mixed| ²⁷uh-uh-one time I feel that-uh well I know this is to take time| ²⁸and-and then other times I feel as though . . . well I'm apt to be a little bit impatient| ²⁹and I'm wondering if that is sort of the reaction of most anyone that-that comes for treatment uh such as I have or the-this in the same (shall we put it as a category) or-or the same thing that I have| ³⁰I was wondering if uh you know through the-the talks that I have been having with you-uh if it did or has progressed//| ³¹uh the thing that-that-uh you asked me you know about the feelings about this or how I felt uh I think I am always uh sort of waiting for you| ³²I'm sort of apprehensive as to the feelings that you have about this-uh you know like you said in the beginning that-that most of the-the talking will be on my part| ³³but-uh you know I am always looking for perhaps-uh maybe a little bit of encouragement or-uh something to go home with (do you know what I mean) sort of-uh well not like a reward but sort of uh well not like a reward but sort of in the sense to that I would be making progress or "you are coming along fine" as the doctor would say or-or uh something like that| ³⁴and uh so far uh you know the uh different subjects that I have been talking about you have asked me uh perhaps a few questions about it but (mean) uh nothing that would-uh sort of encourage me//| ³⁵I mean am I making myself clear| ³⁶uh I hope I am|

THERAPIST ³⁷well I wonder why these thoughts are coming to your mind now because I noticed last week-uh too you were uh wondering about the treatment-uh whether it would help you and if it was working| ³⁸and now it seems to me again uh you are looking for uh reassurance and uh some active uh things on my part| ³⁹ and uh uh I'd like to point out to you again that uh as these thoughts come to your mind they are-uh-uh last week and now again uh preventing the-uh treatment from continuing| ⁴⁰that is while you are thinking about these thoughts uh other thoughts are not coming to your mind uh that would be-uh in the treatment uh situation| ⁴¹and I was wondering why uh these thoughts have been coming|

PATIENT ⁴²well it just-uh occurs to me uh this that . . . uh-uh I feel that-that-uh "fine"| ⁴³I mean I agree certainly with-with the type of treatment that there is because I know subconsciously it is something that's deep-rooted and inside| ⁴⁴[but all the while I think that uh . . . I mean I think like anyone else—I think-uh perhaps-uh] I don't know how many other patients you do see a day| ⁴⁵but I think perhaps (I don't know) that they are apt or liable to ask questions too| ⁴⁶uh [I only] I think it's only natural-uh to ask certain thinks like that| ⁴⁷I mean I don't see anything-uh too wrong about uh asking things| ⁴⁸I mean they bother me| ⁴⁹and uh seeing that this is part of the treatment I would think that-uh anything being on my mind like that-uh I'd like to ask you|

THERAPIST   ⁵⁰well what I meant was I wonder why these things are bothering you

PATIENT   ⁵¹I don't know|

THERAPIST   and what-what-what

PATIENT   [uh]

THERAPIST   this means about your-uh feelings towards the treatment because they do-uh seem to me to be-uh in some way uh-uh-uh discussion of the treatment again

PATIENT   ⁵²mmmhm|

THERAPIST   and uh-uh reflect some lack of-uh confidence or unsureness on your part|

PATIENT   ⁵³well I think it is yes uh definitely there//| ⁵⁴[uh-uh for instance now-uh I think-uh I keep thinking now uh] you well . . . like you told me like in the beginning that the treatment was going to take uh well you didn't name any time at all| ⁵⁵but I mean it's always in my mind as to how long//| ⁵⁶or uh after uh these discussions I mean what then| ⁵⁷I mean is it-uh in a way asking too much to-uh assume that later on uh we could discuss this| ⁵⁸[I mean of-of uh] well it does it come down to like after I have told you over and over these things that come to mind uh is it that uh we decide well or you decide or in the treatment that well I shall come once a week or-or uh well "this is it" uh like for instance uh "we have done all we can for you and uh the rest will have to be done yourself"| ⁵⁹I mean-uh I'm sort of thinking and looking forward to-uh an indefinite period where I don't know exactly what's going to happen-uh later on as along with the treatment too| ⁶⁰I mean it-it makes me think of uh well how long how far along it will be how-how long how uh mm-when it will ever you know come to being that-that-uh this will all end| ⁶¹uh and I don't think that-uh I'm being too inquisitive about that| ⁶²I think anyone that has any type of ailment is liable to ask-uh even a physician that//| ⁶³don't you//| ⁶⁴uh I mean I'm trying not to-uh be too inquisi-

tive and-and curious about-about it| ⁶⁵but uh I don't know//|
⁶⁶it just sort of makes me feel a little bit uh-uh unsure just
a little bit| ⁶⁷and-uh I think as long as uh this is part of
the treatment that uh (I mean) I'd rather discuss it with
you than keep it to myself| ⁶⁸uh I don't talk to anyone else
about it//| ⁶⁹[therefore uh I think . . .] uh I don't know//|
⁷⁰maybe it isn't right that I do this| ⁷¹but I don't certainly know
who else to speak to about it|

THERAPIST ⁷²well uh let's not worry for the moment about
whether it's right or not| ⁷³I just uh would like to point out to
you that uh as I said before uh uh there are forces working
within you that are opposed to the treatment|⁷⁴and uh it seems
to me that a lo-uh these-uh worries and concerns that come up
in your mind about-uh the treatment the length of the treatment-uh are you making progress and so on are thoughts that
come to your mind because uh-uh there is something else that is
uh troubling you or uh that should be coming out that for
some reason is difficult for you to express| ⁷⁵and so uh instead
these other thoughts come to your mind|

PATIENT ⁷⁶oh|

Unitized Extract from Interview with Mr. C

PATIENT ¹that's a fact//| ²when-uh we were first brought to-
gether I just couldn't see her for beans| ³and she just couldn't
understand who this-uh creep was sitting across from her
when we went to dinner somewhere I think| ⁴and-uh this was
not a date by the way| I met her as merely just getting to-
gether with

THERAPIST ⁶yeah|

PATIENT a small group|

THERAPIST   ⁷uh hmm|

PATIENT   ⁸well this thing just started to grow| ⁹and I began seeing more of her//| ¹⁰[however all through this I knew all along what her] she very frequently expressed what she wanted in a man—

THERAPIST   ¹¹uh hmm|

PATIENT   in a husband| ¹²and-uh well there were many times I'm sure when I had to reflect and consider well do I fill these expectations of hers and if I don't how can I convince her that-uh I should be considered

THERAPIST   ¹³yeah yeah|

PATIENT   and be given the opportunity to develop these things|

THERAPIST   ¹⁴yeah yeah|

PATIENT   ¹⁵perhaps today there is a thought in my mind that I haven't filled these—

THERAPIST   ¹⁶well when did you know—

PATIENT   these expectations|

THERAPIST   you wanted to marry her|

PATIENT   ¹⁷well I began seeing more of her all the time of course and being together and-uh several trips up to her house| ¹⁸and I just found myself-uh very much in love with her| ¹⁹[and this was-uh . . . I'm afraid it developed over] let's put it this way| ²⁰after our first meeting I-I would say perhaps nothing materialized outside just a general friendship through an organization that occurred for about a year|

THERAPIST   ²¹uh hmm|

PATIENT   ²²and then the thing became more pronounced after that|

THERAPIST   ²³uh hmm|

PATIENT   ²⁴uh-I started seeing her| ²⁵and I was going out of my way to find time to-to be with her and asking her out and so forth| ²⁶and-uh there was a conflict here for a while within the family of some doubts upon the part of the various members of the family not my-my own immediate family plus other relatives whether or not she was the right gal for me because she had been she was of course initially very independent having been away from home at that time for about four or five years

THERAPIST   [27]hmm|

PATIENT   on her own down here and-uh I think perhaps more adjusted to the realities of life by being independent and so forth than many of my own relatives were or ever expected any of their children could ever be|

THERAPIST   ['cause they were—]

PATIENT   [28]well we've led this not sheltered life| [29]but there's this very close family relationship that has reduced a great deal getting into the community into the social things that you find outside of your family|

The Case of Mrs. Smith: a Practice Exercise in Scoring

A FULL interview for scoring practice is presented here. First there is a summary of what had happened to the patient before the interview; then the interview—the third hour of the case—is printed, exactly as recorded except for changes in proper names. The reader may score the interview himself, then compare his scoring with the authors' scores which are given beginning on p. 411.

THE CASE OF MRS. SMITH

Mrs. Elizabeth Smith, age 35, was referred by a private psychiatrist to the psychiatric clinic of a hospital in a very large city. She explained to the intake interviewer that she was separated from her husband—her second husband, because she divorced the first—and she was disturbed because she believed her marital troubles were her own fault. She now felt, she said, that she should never have married either of these men in the first place. Then Mrs. Smith started to cry. Her father, she explained, was dying of cancer. She didn't know what to do; the future seemed a blank.

Mrs. Smith went on to describe her husband—who from her description appeared psychotic—and told how she finally came to break off from him. Then, returning to her father's illness, she expressed concern that her mother might come and live with her after her father died.

Mrs. Smith asserted that she wouldn't kill herself, even though she had thought about doing it. She had felt a need for her husband now that her father was so sick, and she vacillated between seeing her husband and refusing to see him.

At the end of the interview Mrs. Smith confessed that she had been having an affair with a man in his sixties.

NOVEMBER 21: FIRST HOUR OF THERAPY

After explaining the administrative arrangements of the clinic, the therapist instructed Mrs. Smith in the free-association method and asked her to begin. She asked the therapist, "Do you ever tell me anything?" He answered that he would say something when appropriate.

"I don't see how you can stand it, just listening to people just talk," said Mrs. Smith. "Well," she continued, "I thought of something this morning I wanted to tell you. For the past day or so I've been doing something peculiar—counting out loud . . . I just wanted to tell you about it. I don't know what it means."

Then, turning to thoughts of her husband, Mrs. Smith said that he visits her occasionally and wants to come back and live with her. She feels sometimes that she never wants to see him again, but nevertheless she still feels sorry for him. She feels responsible for "the mess he's in."

"I think I should tell you the things I've never told anyone, right off the bat," Mrs. Smith exclaimed, "because if I get to know you, I might not want to."

The therapist replied, "Well, you should feel in this situation that there is nothing you should withhold at any time."

Mrs. Smith went on: "Well, when we got married, I don't believe I was in love with him. I don't know why I married him." She told how she came to know Smitty (her current husband). He seduced her, and they began to sleep together regularly. She was scared and didn't enjoy intercourse. Finally, to end the need for deception and secrecy, she married Smitty. They lived with her parents.

One Christmas Day, just before a big family dinner, Mrs. Smith's mother got sick, and Mrs. Smith had to contend with her mother's illness and the preparation of the dinner at the same time. Smitty came into the kitchen and began to offer unwanted advice. Mrs. Smith snapped at him, "Go away!" Smitty took offense and stalked out of the house; the patient didn't hear from him for two days. She finally called him up, went to see him, and begged him to come back.

After a time, she and Smitty went to Maine, where he had got a factory job. They lived in an apartment that had two very small rooms. "I felt that eventually we would have a home," Mrs. Smith said. "I mean sort of settle down; we'd be there for a year or so . . . and maybe have children. He—he is very fond of children." (She began to cry.) "Oh, nuts! That's one of the things I can't talk about."

She then explained that Smitty got fired from his factory job. Mrs. Smith had felt ill and had lost weight since going to Maine. After Smitty was fired she had an attack of appendicitis. Smitty did nothing for her; he wouldn't even call a doctor (they had no phone, so Mrs. Smith couldn't call one herself).

Smitty didn't look for work but only stayed around the house. They lived in filth and disorder, but he was content so long as he had plenty of food and sex. Then he got crazy ideas about making pogo sticks out of discarded broom handles and old rubber bands. Eventually, Mrs. Smith went back to her family in S——.

Back in S—— Mrs. Smith had her appendix taken out and, at the same time, had some ovarian cysts removed. When she came out from the anesthetic she was very thirsty. Her father, sitting at the bedside, tried to give her some water on cotton balls that had been provided. In contrast, her mother was unsympathetic, saying to Mrs. Smith after the operation, "You might as well know you may never have any children." Smitty had written to her parents, "Spare no expense"—but he failed to phone her, even though she had a telephone in her hospital room. When a friend suggested to Smitty that he should send her flowers, Smitty reported this suggestion to Mrs. Smith in a letter with the comment, "Isn't that ridiculous?"

It then suddenly dawned on Mrs. Smith, she told the therapist, that she couldn't face returning to Smitty. She wrote him that she wouldn't come back; so he came to S——. She wanted to get a divorce; Smitty insisted that she needed him, and she finally gave in, feeling sorry for him. Smitty still didn't go to work but was content to live with her parents—while she worked. To get out of her parents' home Mrs. Smith finally quit her job and insisted on moving to —— (a very large city).

The therapist announced that their time had run out. He commented, "You seem to have the idea of talking freely quite well."

Mrs. Smith answered him, "I don't see how you can put up with this. I think this is a terrible bore. The more I hear it, the less I think of myself."

NOVEMBER 25: SECOND HOUR OF THERAPY

Mrs. Smith began by saying, "I was wondering about you. Ah . . . you're going to stay here . . . aren't you . . . are you? I'd hate to have you suddenly disappear." The therapist reassured her that he would be around for quite a while.

Mrs. Smith went on to tell of "fleeting encounters" with various boys. "Apparently I pick out a certain type of person," she said, "and get into a situation and then I want to get out of it." She thought that possibly she was afraid of men. She continued, "I always seem to have selected someone who was weaker than myself in some way. And then that weakness would annoy me."

She pointed out that Smitty is very dependent on her. She told him once that she wanted to feel that she could lean on someone, depend on them. "I don't really want to be independent," she told the therapist, "but I don't want to have to depend on someone that I feel is undependable."

She recalled that during her first marriage, as soon as she got a job and had some income of her own, she felt that she wasn't completely at the mercy of the situation and that she could do something about it.

Her first husband, Bertie, was "a blank" to her for a long time after her divorce from him, Mrs. Smith said. "And the funny part about that," she commented, "was that I very frequently would dream about him." In her dreams she became reunited with Bertie —even though he had since remarried. These dreams began when she and Smitty started to break up. After having such a dream she felt depressed.

Mrs. Smith's family, she said, hadn't been able to help her go to college, and she felt a keen disappointment at this. She suspects that her family could have helped her some if they had really wanted to; "I just think my family didn't want me to live away from home." She then gave the therapist examples of how prestigeful people had sometimes tried to help her when she was a child, but she had felt uncomfortable about taking their help.

Her associations led to Wyatt, her steady beau when she was in her teens. Wyatt deferred to her; she had wished that he would be more forceful. She had many beaus at school. "I went from one to the other," she said. "I was looking for something and I don't know what it was."

Mrs. Smith then launched into a recital on her sexual history: "I was rather ignorant about sex . . . I started to menstruate rather late." She went with Wyatt, who was ten years older than she was, for a couple of years. They did some petting but never had intercourse.

She had no friends in high school; she was very shy as a youngster. When she has done a job for someone, she told the therapist, "I'll go out of my way to point out the flaws in it."

Resuming her recital of her sexual history, she recalled going out with another boy with whom she was infatuated. He wanted to have intercourse with her; she refused, believing that people would think less of her; "and," she said, "I didn't want him to think less of me." He dropped her "like a hot potato."

She had an affair with another boy—and confessed it to her father. He didn't condemn her for it but did say that she ought not to be promiscuous.

Mrs. Smith's father and mother didn't get along well at all; they fought constantly. Mrs. Smith recalled, "My mother used to leave home every once in a while for a day or so. She'd get mad. She had a terrible temper."

Mrs. Smith's father confessed to Mrs. Smith, then just an adolescent, that he was having an affair. Her reaction, said Mrs. Smith, was "absolute delight." She was only worried that "I might talk in my sleep and mother'd find out about it."

Memories of dancing with her grandfather then came forward. Grandfather (father's father) didn't get along well with her mother, Mrs. Smith reported. Her mother resented having him and the patient's grandmother in the house.

At this point the therapist announced that the time was up. The patient was asked to sign a permission slip, permitting the clinic to use her records for scientific purposes; she readily agreed and signed it. Going out the door she remarked that the room was warm. "I've heard that people have an impulse to get back to the womb," she said. "I was thinking these rooms are terrific. They're all shut in, absolutely quiet, no windows."

THIRD INTERVIEW: TRANSCRIPT

PATIENT   [1]I missed the bus. [2]And I had to (*Out of breath*) wait about twenty minutes. [3-4](*11-sec. pause*) (*Therapist closes door*) [5]We're locked in.

THERAPIST   [6]Hm?

PATIENT   [7](*Embarrassed laugh*) [8]I'd say all locked in. (*She coughs*)

THERAPIST   [9]Well, that's part of the sound-proofing.

PATIENT   [10](*She sighs*) [11]While I'm catching my breath I'll ask *you* something. [12]Uh . . . you said we'd do this until—to see if it worked. [13]Uh-uh uu-how do you know if it works? [14]I mean . . . (*Still out of breath*) or—or is it working, I should say. [15]I mean, am I doing—

THERAPIST   [16]Well, it's partly—

PATIENT   —the right thing?

THERAPIST   [17]If-if you were not doing the right thing, I would be telling you.

PATIENT   [18]Oh.

THERAPIST   [19]Uh but uh how we tell whether it's working is-is just in terms of what *you* report and what you're thinking about and—

PATIENT   [20]Oh.

THERAPIST   —the insights that you may develop.

PATIENT   [21]Well, let's see, where shall I start? . . . [22]My mind is a blank [23](*Laughing anxiously*) from all this running. Uh—

THERAPIST   [24]Well, you just start when you're ready.

PATIENT   [25]I don't even remember what we were talking about last time.

THERAPIST   [26]Well, you shouldn't necessarily try to link up from one time to the—

PATIENT   [27]Oh.

THERAPIST   —next. [28]You just start whatever happens to be . . . on the top of your mind as you come here.

PATIENT   [29]Well, let's see. [30]I was thinking about something. [31]I think about this a lot in between times. [32]I don't know whether I should or not. [33]Uh . . . I was thinking, there are some snapshops of me when I was a baby.

THERAPIST   [34]Mm-hm.

PATIENT   (*She opens her pocketbook*)   [35]I was a—a very uh . . . bright sort of a baby, I mean, cheerful and happy (*She tears the wrapping off a pack of cigarettes*) and—an aggressive type of baby (*She crumples up the cellophane*), you know?

THERAPIST ³⁶An aggressive-type baby. ³⁷Mm-hmm.

PATIENT ³⁸And uh . . . *all* the pictures of me when I was very small—I was, I mean, a year or two years old—I was laughing or carrying on. And—

THERAPIST ³⁹Mm-hmm.

PATIENT ⁴⁰—and something happened to me. ⁴¹I don't know . . . ⁴²I-I was trying to figure out what it was. ⁴³Maybe it was my brother being born, because I was about two when he was born and then we moved too. ⁴⁴But uh . . . something happened to me when I was very young. ⁴⁵I changed.

THERAPIST (*Softly*) ⁴⁶Mm-hmm.

PATIENT ⁴⁷And . . . uh I never heard my family uh speak of it in this way. ⁴⁸But-but I know that when they talk about me when I was a baby they-they mean when I was . . . around a year or a year and a half. ⁴⁹And . . . uh the uh the pictures uh the—in the—in the albums, now that I think about it, I realize that uh all my early childhood pictures, I was—I was sort of glum and scowling-looking.

THERAPIST ⁵⁰Mm-hmm.

PATIENT ⁵¹Uh and it didn't look like the same baby, about the size of it—

THERAPIST ⁵²And was there anything other than that . . . uh the fact that you noticed that you were different—

PATIENT I just—

THERAPIST —in these pictures that makes you say something must have happened?

PATIENT ⁵³Well, I don't know. ⁵⁴I-I-I was uh I was thinking about it because I have one snapshop that one of my aunts gave me. ⁵⁵And uh uh . . . I had a string of beads on and a pocketbook. ⁵⁶And I think I was about a year or maybe a little older. ⁵⁷And uh . . . I-I was stepping forward towards whoever took the pictures in a—in a very aggressive sort of a way with a big smile on my face.

THERAPIST ⁵⁸Mm-hmm.

PATIENT ⁵⁹And uh . . . I've never been the rest of my life like I was then, I mean right uh—

THERAPIST ⁶⁰How do you mean, could you . . . expand on that a little more?

PATIENT   ⁶¹Uh, well, I don't know. ⁶²Now I act as—⁶³(*She sighs*) as if I was scared to death of everyone. ⁶⁴And uh . . . as a matter of fact I am, I think. ⁶⁵But that's something else I've been thinking about. Uh—

THERAPIST   ⁶⁶Is it that you were aggressive then, as you see it, then, but—

PATIENT   ⁶⁷Why ah—by aggressive, I mean, uh—well, I, uh—I don't know whether that's a good word or not because that has unpleasant uh imp—I-I-I ⁶⁸(*Anxious laughing*) looked like I was going to grow up to be a natural-born salesman. ⁶⁹But—

THERAPIST   ⁷⁰Yeah.

PATIENT   —but someth— but I'm obviously ⁷¹(*Anxious laughing*) not. ⁷²That-that's one of my big troubles now in my work is-is going to see people, and-and talking to them. ⁷³Uh . . . once-once I uh meet someone and I work for them uh it disappears completely. ⁷⁴But-but the initial contact is-is perfectly horrible. ⁷⁵And I know I make a very bad impression. ⁷⁶People have told me that after they've gotten to know me.

THERAPIST   ⁷⁷Mm-hmm.

PATIENT   ⁷⁸But when I meet someone for the first time I look as if I thought they were going to bite my head off. ⁷⁹And-and uh I have no uh—uh I don't know, I-I don't have much confidence in my work. ⁸⁰I uh—now, this is funny. ⁸¹I know-I know uh about what the quality of my work is. ⁸²Uh I would say I'm a good technician. ⁸³That's about the size of it. ⁸⁴But-but that's something because there are plenty of miserable technicians.

THERAPIST   ⁸⁵Yeah.

PATIENT   ⁸⁶But . . . uh uh I-I always feel uh that the job is not as well done as I could have done it if . . . mm—if I'd put a little more effort on it. ⁸⁷And-and that doesn't make any sense, because I just knock myself out anyhow. ⁸⁸And uh I-I do something that I don't suppose many people would believe, because . . . you just don't do it. ⁸⁹I-I trim down my bills quite frequently. ⁹⁰I-I don't tell the customers anything about it. ⁹¹But I just feel that-that I-I'm asking too much. ⁹²And I know that other people get more than I do for the same work. ⁹³And yet I ⁹⁴(*She sighs*) I feel guilty about taking it.

THERAPIST   ⁹⁵Why is th— why is this?

PATIENT   ⁹⁶I don't know. ⁹⁷I think that maybe I'm slow and I'm taking longer than I should. ⁹⁸You see, a lot of it is done on and charged on a time basis.

THERAPIST ⁹⁹Mm-hmm.

PATIENT ¹⁰⁰And uh . . . I don't know uh whether I should be free-lancing at all. ¹⁰¹I—maybe I should have a job. ¹⁰²The reason I want to free-lance is that-that ultimately if it works out, uh . . . I'll make more money than I would on a job. ¹⁰³And as—I-I-I like—I—going around. ¹⁰⁴And-and—this is contradictory—I like to meet people. ¹⁰⁵(*Embarrassed laugh*)

THERAPIST (*Softly*) ¹⁰⁶Mm-hmm.

PATIENT ¹⁰⁷It-it's just that the-the first uh meeting uh that's . . . I don't know how it's going to work out. ¹⁰⁸But . . . the past-past uh two weeks I've been extremely busy. ¹⁰⁹But it's the first time it's happened since I've been doing it really. (*She strikes a match*)

THERAPIST ¹¹⁰Mm-hmm.

PATIENT ¹¹¹Last month I didn't do anything all month long. (*She blows out smoke*) ¹¹²I didn't have one job. Uh . . . ¹¹³(*5-sec. pause*) ¹¹⁴I've gotten to a point—I-it-it's very-very-very hard to explain—and I uh uh . . . I don't have any confidence in my —in anything I do. ¹¹⁵Uh I don't have any-any confidence in my own emotions.

THERAPIST ¹¹⁶Mm-hmm.

PATIENT ¹¹⁷Uh this—this is hard to explain. ¹¹⁸I mean, uh uh for instance, I've been very much upset about my father's illness. ¹¹⁹And uh . . . that's uh really been the—uh well, it's been the first real emotional . . . upset I've had in a long time. ¹²⁰And uh occasionally I-I cry about it when I'm by myself. (*She seems on the verge of tears*) ¹²¹Well, I haven't for a couple of weeks. Uh . . .

THERAPIST ¹²²Mm-hmm.

PATIENT ¹²³ . . . I've-I've sort of—it's-it's hard to explain. ¹²⁴I've sort of stopped thinking about it. ¹²⁵I mean, uh uh . . . I hear a voice. ¹²⁶Uh—I-I ¹²⁷(*Anxious laughing*) don't have auditory hallucinations, I don't think. ¹²⁸But I-I *think* that way. ¹²⁹I hear things. Uh—

THERAPIST ¹³⁰How do you mean? ¹³¹Could you explain that?

PATIENT ¹³²Well, when I think, it seems to me I hear a voice saying something.

THERAPIST ¹³³Mm-hmm. ¹³⁴What sort of things does the voice say?

PATIENT   [135]Uh, well, for instance, I think, "My father is dying."
[136]And uh uh . . . oh . . . then, I-I think uh, "Well, isn't that
curious?" [137]I mean, it's uh . . . when I—when I first found out
about it I just uh—well, I couldn't think about it at all, without-
without going to pieces. [138]And uh . . . and-and then I-I-I
ss-started [139](*She starts to cry; she opens her pocketbook to get
out a handkerchief*) . . . [140](*She sighs*) when-when I cry, for instance, uh . . . I think uh, "What am I crying for?" [141]And uh
. . . [142](*Anxious laughing*) I get in such a state of mind that I
don't know whether I have the right to cry or not. [143]That's about
the size of it.

THERAPIST   [144]Why should it . . .

PATIENT   Uh—

THERAPIST   . . . be wrong for you to cry?

PATIENT   [145]Well, I don't know. [146]Uh . . . I just—I-I think that
possibly it's selfish. I mean—

THERAPIST   [147]How "selfish"? [148]I don't understand why that should
be selfish.

PATIENT   [149]Well, I mean, am I crying for my father? [150]Or am I
crying for myself?

THERAPIST   [151]Well, now, why would you be crying for yourself?
[152]I just don't understand what you mean.

PATIENT   [153](*Almost crying out loud*) [154]Well, because uh because
I'm going to lose the one that I love. I mean—

THERAPIST   [155]Mm-hmm.

PATIENT   [156]It's—you-you see, [157](*Tearfully*) uh that's what I mean,
I have no confidence in my own emotions. [158]If-if I get mad at
someone, I don—I can't *stay* mad, I mean, in-in a state of-of
anger, because uh uh I-I—the first thing I know I'm thinking,
well, am I mad or-or uh am I *not* mad? [159]And-and then I think
well, the other—the other chap has a lot to be said on his side.
And [160](*She sighs*) [161]it's extremely unsatisfactory. [162]I mean, I
wish I could just get into a real rage about something. [163]But uh
. . . this-this business with Smitty, he was around this week. [164]He
stopped in to see me. (*She crushes ash in ash tray*) [165]He has—he
has p-p-periods of depression. [166]And . . . they're very-very severe.
[167]Uh there's-there's always been a-a doubt in my mind how far
the-the word neurosis extends. [168]But uh I don't know whether
he's a neurotic person or not. [169]I think, my-my own feeling is
he goes beyond it.

THERAPIST [170]Mm-hmm.

PATIENT [171]I-I think that uh he's in-in danger of-of uh . . . well, he-he hasn't got much of a grasp on reality *now*. [172]Uh this business that he's trying to-to . . . build up is-is-is just pathetic. [173]It's-it's-it's a heartbreaking thing to see. [174]And uh . . . he's-he's spent almost all his money.

THERAPIST (*Very softly*) [175]Mm-hmm.

PATIENT [176]And . . . I don't know, I've tried to dissuade him. [177]But-but he seems to want to do it to prove something. [178]And-and the whole thing is going to come a cropper. [179]I know it, I mean, it—

THERAPIST [180]Mm-hmm. [181]Which one is this again? [182]This is the one . . .

PATIENT [183]Smitty?

THERAPIST . . . about the pogo sticks, uh—

PATIENT [184]Yes. [185]You know about that?

THERAPIST [186]You mentioned it to me—

PATIENT [187]Did I tell you about that?

THERAPIST [188]Yeah.

PATIENT [189]Yes, the pogo sticks. [190]I mean, he acts really queer about it. [191]He-he-he uh he hides papers and things like that and won't tell people. [192]And . . .

THERAPIST (*Softly*) [193]Mm-hmm.

PATIENT . . . and uh . . . uh as-as far as—as far as our marriage goes i-it's a complete washout. [194]I mean, I-I don't think I could ever get together with him again.

THERAPIST [195]Mm-hmm.

PATIENT [196]But . . . uh-uh when I see him, I feel that-that uh I'm-I'm—I have a responsibility towards him that I'm not fulfilling. [197]And uh—the only way I can [198](*She sighs*) see to do it would be uh be uh uh a-at a cost to myself that I'm not willing to-to-to face.

THERAPIST (*Softly*) [199]Mm-hmm.

PATIENT Uh . . . [200](*5-sec. pause*) [201](*She sighs*) [202]it's uh it-it's such a—you see, I-I'm not—I-I-I don't know enough to-to do anything. [203](*She sighs*) [204]And the only thing that he wa—he wants to do now, he-he's well, he-he seems to—he has moments when he's—when he's optimistic and moments when he's completely down in the dumps. [205]But he wants to-to uh come back. [206]He has for a long time. [207]And uh . . . that's all he wants. [208](*6-sec. pause*)

[209]He need—he—it seems to me he-he needs to succeed at *something*. [210]And-and-and I can't help him to succeed in it. [211]And-and-and I-I ff— [212](*Sighs*) I-I don't know. [213]I-I don't know what I said. (*She blows out smoke, taps cigarette in ash tray*) [214-15](*11-sec. pause*) [216](*Patient weeps*) [217]Why do I do this?

THERAPIST   [218]You are very disturbed about something. [219](*Patient still weeping;* [220]*she sobs*) . . . [221] Maybe if you could just try and tell me what it is you're feeling so disturbed about.

PATIENT   [222-3](*She is crying for 8 secs.; then,* [224]*sobbing*) [225]I'm sorry. [226](*Weeping*) [227]It's aw-it's awfully silly. [228](*Still crying*) [229]It's just this miserable mess.

THERAPIST   [230]People . . . often cry when they feel very miserable and disturbed like this—

PATIENT   [231](*Through tears*) [232]I-I just feel that I-I can't . . . uh I-I don't know what to do. [233](*Still weeping*) [234]And-and I've done so much that's wrong. [235]I-I've made so many mistakes. [236](*She blows her nose in the midst of her crying; then,* [237]*crying*) [238]I can't help Smitty. [239](*Crying*) [240]I don't know what to do for him.

THERAPIST   [241]You feel some kind of responsibility towards him because you're his wife?

PATIENT   [242](*Tearfully*) [243]Yes.

THERAPIST   [244]And yet you feel that [245](*Patient is still weeping*) you are unable to be his wife, and that—

PATIENT   [246](*Still weepy*) [247]Yes.

THERAPIST   —you can't help him. [248]Is that the idea?

PATIENT   [249](*Weepy*) [250]I think so. [251]Yes. [252](*She weeps*) [253]It's-it's . . . I don't know, I tried to—I tried to make things work out. [254]I-I think I did. [255]But I probably didn't or— [256]He-he always s-seemed to me . . . well, after we were married, after the first year we were married, his-his attitude towards life is-is defeat. [257]He-he never starts anything but that he-he thinks, before he starts it he'll fail at it. And—

THERAPIST   [258]Mm-hmm.

PATIENT   [259]—and I thought that it was because he never had much of a break. [260]He-he-he grew up during the worst part of the depression. [261]And he didn't work for a long time. [262]And I thought that it was because he couldn't. [263]But . . . now I don't know whether it was that or something else. [264]And he never had the right kind of education or anything, and . . . and . . . [265](*She sighs*) [266]I-I *tried* to encourage him, and-and show interest, and-

and-and help him along. ²⁶⁷Bu-but I-I did a miserable job. ²⁶⁸I
didn't-didn't do anything. ²⁶⁹And-and now I think that he . . . I
don't know, it seems to me he-he-he's starting some kind of a . . .
of a degeneration of . . . his personality. ²⁷⁰He's—I-I'm afraid
he's going to go off his rocker altogether.

THERAPIST   Tsk—

PATIENT   ²⁷¹And-and I'm afraid of him.

THERAPIST   ²⁷²You're afraid of him? ²⁷³How do you mean?

PATIENT   ²⁷⁴Uh, well, ²⁷⁵(*She sighs*) well, when he comes to see me
—you see, I-I've done a lot of things that I suppose were foolish
feeling the way I do. ²⁷⁶I mean, I-I've-I've uh I've let him come
up and-and talked to him and-and-and uh we've had uh dinner
together a couple of times. ²⁷⁷And-and I've-I've just sort of . . .
oh, I feel when I'm with him that I must cajole him along because if I don't-don't, he'll-he'll lose his temper. ²⁷⁸And-and he,
you see, when we lived together and he lost his temper he didn't
talk to me. ²⁷⁹But-but he had . . . he gets spells a couple of times
a year, two or three times a year when he-he starts to act queer
and then he gets worse, ²⁸⁰and-and-and it's very hard to explain.
²⁸¹Maybe you know about it. ²⁸²I mean, maybe it's in my imagination. ²⁸³But I don't think so. ²⁸⁴When-when he has these spells, it
builds up for a couple of days and then . . . a-and then . . . he
blows up. ²⁸⁵Some—anything will touch it off.

THERAPIST   (*Softly*)   ²⁸⁶Mm-hmm.

PATIENT   ²⁸⁷But he blows up quietly and doesn't say anything.
²⁸⁸And-and this is the part that I-I wanted to tell you. ²⁸⁹H-his
facial expression changes. ²⁹⁰His eyes change. ²⁹¹I don't know how
it happens. ²⁹²But-but sometimes he-he looks positively *insane*.
²⁹³He doesn't look like himself. ²⁹⁴He looks like an entirely different person.

THERAPIST   (*Very softly*)   ²⁹⁵Mm-hmm.

PATIENT   ²⁹⁶And-and when he looks like that I'm-I'm afraid of him.
²⁹⁷(*She sighs*) ²⁹⁸He-he's all alone. ²⁹⁹He has no family. ³⁰⁰And,
well, he-he stopped in to see my family the other night. ³⁰¹He's
going back to New York now. ³⁰²He's going to look for a job in
a pogo-stick factory.

THERAPIST   (*Softly*)   ³⁰³Mm-hmm.

PATIENT   ³⁰⁴(*She sighs*) ³⁰⁵(*Weeping*) ³⁰⁶I don't know what I started
to say. ³⁰⁷(*Tearfully*) ³⁰⁸He says funny things. Well . . . ³⁰⁹(*5-sec.
pause*) ³¹⁰I-I don't know, I just seem to have a complete—I always

—for-for years I've alw—I've always been the-the-the self-reliant one. ³¹¹That's a role that's been imposed on me by my family. ³¹²"Elizabeth can do everything." ³¹³They still do at home if anything is broken. ³¹⁴(*She weeps*) ³¹⁵And I've always taken care of myself. ³¹⁶And I've always worked, supported myself. ³¹⁷And . . . and if there's an emergency I'm-I'm old dependable Elizabeth. ³¹⁸Now I don't know what to do. ³¹⁹(*She laughs through her tears*)

THERAPIST (*Very softly*)   ³²⁰Mm-hmm.

PATIENT   ³²¹(*Weepily*) ³²²It's a joke.

THERAPIST   ³²³Well, you have a *real* problem to face here.

PATIENT   ³²⁴⁻⁶(*She sobs for 10 secs.; then, weeping*) ³²⁷Uh . . . this is ridiculous. ³²⁸(*Weeping*) ³²⁹I never did so much of this in my life in public. (*She blows her nose*)

THERAPIST   ³³⁰Well, you *must* feel that this is quite a different situation from a public situation. ³³¹What you say here—

PATIENT   ³³²Well, I'm afraid of *anyone*. (*Still blowing nose*)

THERAPIST   —and what-what—and the way that you feel—yes, but the way that you *feel* here, too, is quite different from any other kind of situation. ³³³You want to be able to express your emotions as you *are* now, because these are the *real* emotions. ³³⁴And . . . you must feel quite free to let them come out.

PATIENT   ³³⁵(*Weepily*) ³³⁶Well, uh to change the subject abruptly, I've been thinking a lot about my mother.

THERAPIST (*Softly*)   ³³⁷Mm-hmm.

PATIENT   ³³⁸I know enough to realize it, that my relationship with my mother has a great deal to do with this. ³³⁹(*She sighs*) ³⁴⁰And that's something else . . . ³⁴¹(*She sighs*) I don't ³⁴²(*She sighs*) uh uh . . . I don't know if— ³⁴³I don't think I love my mother. ³⁴⁴I-I really don't know.

THERAPIST (*Softly*)   ³⁴⁵Mm-hmm.

PATIENT   ³⁴⁶An-and uh I feel so unfair about it. ³⁴⁷(*Weepily*) ³⁴⁸Everyone tells me what a wonderful person she is. ³⁴⁹And she's had a terrible life. ³⁵⁰(*Weeping*) ³⁵¹I mean, h-her background is-is very bad. ³⁵²(*Weepily*) ³⁵³And the things that she's done . . . she couldn't help herself. ³⁵⁴(*She laughs anxiously*) ³⁵⁵And she had trouble with her mother. ³⁵⁶But she would never admit it. She—

THERAPIST   ³⁵⁷Trouble with—?

PATIENT   ³⁵⁸With her mother, my grandmother—

THERAPIST   ³⁵⁹With her mother, I see. ³⁶⁰Yes—

PATIENT ³⁶¹My-my grandmother was a, I don't know, a very domineering woman. ³⁶²And she had four daughters. ³⁶³Her husband died when Mother was young. ³⁶⁴She was next to the youngest. ³⁶⁵She was two or three, I think, when her father died. ³⁶⁶And her mother brought them up. (*She blows nose*) ³⁶⁷She became a successful businesswoman. (*Still blowing nose; then,* ³⁶⁸*weepily*) ³⁶⁹Very domineering sort of a person. ³⁷⁰I think she was a very selfish old woman. ³⁷¹(*She sighs*) ³⁷²She had four daughters. ³⁷³One-one is a, well, a real hypochondriac. ³⁷⁴And by that I mean that she's made a bedridden invalid of herself. ³⁷⁵She's been in bed for ten or fifteen years. ³⁷⁶The oldest one . . . never got along with her daughters. ³⁷⁷She's sort of mean. ³⁷⁸I don't know, whe——— . . . one of them is an old maid. ³⁷⁹My mother's the most normal one in the family.

THERAPIST ³⁸⁰Mm-hmm. ³⁸¹These are all your aunts?

PATIENT ³⁸²Mm.

THERAPIST ³⁸³Mm-hmm.

PATIENT ³⁸⁴I think that my grandmother did something to all of them. ³⁸⁵I-I think she ruined all of them. ³⁸⁶And-and the things that—the things that-that I feel about Mother I-I don't know, she-she really did have a-a bad time. ³⁸⁷And then—and her marriage wasn't so good, I mean, having her in-laws move in on her. ³⁸⁸And my father, I think, was sort of dominated by his parents. ³⁸⁹And-and it was three against one. ³⁹⁰(*She sighs*) ³⁹¹But . . . I-I have . . . all the—all my-my memories of my mother are unpleasant ones. ³⁹²I don't remember the nice things at all.

THERAPIST ³⁹³Mm-hmm.

PATIENT ³⁹⁴And . . . I-I feel now . . . my brother is—my brother is a lost cause. ³⁹⁵She has no one but me.

THERAPIST ³⁹⁶I didn't quite follow what you said then.

PATIENT ³⁹⁷The-the rest of my—well, my—I say, my brother is a lost cause. ³⁹⁸My brother is a real psycho. ³⁹⁹And he hates my mother quite openly. ⁴⁰⁰He makes no secret of it.

THERAPIST ⁴⁰¹Mm-hmm.

PATIENT ⁴⁰²Between my brother and his wife, between them . . . they have an income of about three hundred dollars a week. ⁴⁰³They never have any money. ⁴⁰⁴My-my sister-in-law is a very nice person. ⁴⁰⁵She's tried to help out at home financially. ⁴⁰⁶My brother was quite annoyed about it. ⁴⁰⁷He didn't think it wa-was her place to help his family. [408]He's never given them a cent since all this trouble has come up. [409]And Father hasn't worked since last year.

THERAPIST   [410]Mm-hmm.

PATIENT   [411]He doesn't give a damn. [412]That's about the size of it. [413]So as far as-as any future plans, he's out of it. [414]He's in the army anyhow. And—

THERAPIST   [415]Mm-hmm.

PATIENT   [416]—and . . . it comes to me. [417]And I'm—I don't know, I guess I don't want the responsibility. [418]But I'll have to take it. [419]That's about the size of it. [420](*Anxious laugh*)

THERAPIST   [421]This responsibility is the responsibility of looking after your . . . mother?

PATIENT   [422]My mother, yes.

THERAPIST   [423]I see.

PATIENT   [424](*Tearfully*) [425]And—poor Mama, she's so innocent. [426]If she—if she . . . she doesn't—I haven't said anything home about-about coming here because . . . I don't think they'd understand it. [427]My father would worry. [428]I mean, he-he would worry there was something the matter. [429]And-and-and one of the troubles is that I've been cut off from him for a long time. [430]I haven't —I haven't been able, well—did you read what I told the social worker? I—

THERAPIST   [431]Yeah, I-I saw the other information that you gave her. [432]But I'd rather you gave me any information personally so that—

PATIENT   [433]—I was just wondering.

THERAPIST   [434]Mm-hmm.

PATIENT (*She coughs*)   [435]I-I started last-last spring, I started to go out with a man. [436]And he—we went for drives. [437]He-he works here. [438]He has his own business. [439]He's a very nice person . . . [440]He's naïve, which is incredible because— [441](*Anxious laugh*) [442]But he's been very nice to me. [443]. . . And-and I really, consciously, I went out with him the first time he asked me to because I was—I was in the middle of all this upset with Smitty. [444]And-and I felt I just had to have-have someone to talk to.

THERAPIST   [445]Mmm.

PATIENT   [446]And-and-and I wanted to talk to my father. [447]But . . . I couldn't. [448]And-and I haven't been able to-to tell him anything for a long time because he's obviously been ill for several years. ⁴⁴⁹He-he's been just d-d-driving himself . . . ⁴⁵⁰And I couldn't-couldn't add to . . . any of his troubles. ⁴⁵¹I didn't know what they were. ⁴⁵²I've known there was something wrong. ⁴⁵³And-and I just had to ha-have someone . . . ⁴⁵⁴⁻⁵(*She breaks down, weeps for 12 secs.*)

THERAPIST ⁴⁵⁶So do you think one of the reasons why you went with this other man was because—

PATIENT ⁴⁵⁷I know it. ⁴⁵⁸I mean now I see it was an extremely foolish thing. ⁴⁵⁹I'm—I've been-been breaking it off gradually. ⁴⁶⁰I don't want to hurt his feelings. ⁴⁶¹I mean, he's been very nice to me. ⁴⁶²And there's no reason to be— ⁴⁶³(*She blows nose while crying; then,* ⁴⁶⁴*laughing through tears*) ⁴⁶⁵And I can't say to any-one, "I went out with you because you reminded me of my father." ⁴⁶⁶(*She weeps*)

THERAPIST ⁴⁶⁷Mm-hmm.

PATIENT So—

THERAPIST ⁴⁶⁸But yet this was true?

PATIENT ⁴⁶⁹Oh, yes, I knew it. ⁴⁷⁰I mean, uh I-I was conscious of it. ⁴⁷¹You see, my father has always been my confidant.

THERAPIST (*Softly*) ⁴⁷²Mm-hmm.

PATIENT ⁴⁷³I-I don't think-think I've ever lied to him. ⁴⁷⁴And-and he knows it. ⁴⁷⁵I've told him practically everything that's ever happened to me, I mean, when I've had troubles.

THERAPIST ⁴⁷⁶Mm-hmm.

PATIENT ⁴⁷⁷My father, I—oh, he-hh—it's-it's not right to say if it sounds as if I were saying that my mother's all bad and my father's all good. ⁴⁷⁸And that isn't so. ⁴⁷⁹My father has a great many faults. ⁴⁸⁰He-he . . . he has had weaknesses. ⁴⁸¹I mean, he was weak with his parents . . . ⁴⁸²But-but he-he's-he's so absolutely good to me. ⁴⁸³(*She begins weeping*)

THERAPIST (*Softly*) ⁴⁸⁴Mm-hmm.

PATIENT ⁴⁸⁵(*Weepily*) ⁴⁸⁶He-he never—I can't ever remember him ever doing anything deliberately to hurt me. ⁴⁸⁷I—sometimes he's done things that I haven't liked . . . in recent years . . . maybe drank too much. ⁴⁸⁸He-he used to drink on weekends. ⁴⁸⁹And I think he drank just to get out of his-his situation. ⁴⁹⁰But I-I got terribly upset about that. ⁴⁹¹I-I hate to see anyone drinking.

THERAPIST ⁴⁹²Mm-hmm.

PATIENT ⁴⁹³And . . . well, but things like that-that he's done that have upset me have not been-been directed against *me*. ⁴⁹⁴I mean,

uh (*She blows nose*) pardon me. [495](*Anxious laugh*) [496]I wonder
what that sounds like on the record. [497](*Laughs anxiously*) [498]Must
be awful. [499](*Still laughing anxiously*)

THERAPIST   [500]Don't worry about that.

PATIENT   [501]Well, I-I . . . I-I don't know, I just—I-I just seem to
have a lop-sided viewpoint about the whole thing. [502]But it seems
to me now when I-I think about it that . . . [503]I don't know.
[504](*She sighs*) [505]And . . . I-I don't want to talk about my mother
any more.

THERAPIST   [506]Why do you want to switch?

PATIENT   [507]. . . Mm, I don't know, it upsets me too much, I
guess.

THERAPIST   [508]Mm-hmm, all right. [509]But if you . . . one of the
things that I would like you to-to realize is that . . . you-you
should try even when things are very *hard* to talk about them.
[510]Uh you—even though it is hard to talk about some things because they are upsetting to you, it *is* important to-to try and fight
off the tendency to-to shy off them if you possibly can. [511]Maybe
you don't feel like talking about it just now.

PATIENT (*Very softly*)   [512]No.

THERAPIST   [513]But at some stage you should try and talk about these
things that are-are so upsetting to you.

PATIENT   [514]Well, I'll start on something else and come right back
to the point because this is . . . connected.

THERAPIST   [515]Mm-hmm.

PATIENT   [516]I told you, I think, last time I had an abortion.

THERAPIST   [517]Mm-hmm.

PATIENT   [518]When I . . . I think when I was young and marrie—
when I had just gotten married, I—you know [519](*Anxious laugh*)
it's funny, I went around a lot. [520]I-I-I went out with boys and
. . . [521]I think some people, I guess, thought I was sophisticated
or something. [522]I-I drank. [523]And I think that when I got married
I was just about as *dumb* as anyone could be. I mean, I was—

THERAPIST   [524]How do you mean "dumb"?

PATIENT   [525]Well, I-I just didn't realize the problems that were
involved in it. [526]I-I thought you got married and . . . and uh
you eventually had a home and children. [527]I mean, it took time.
[528]But it was just something that happened. [529]But uh ww—there
was a crowd of young people I went with [530]and we all drank
quite a bit on weekends.

THERAPIST [531]Mm-hmm.

PATIENT [532]But . . . I did myself. [533]I've had—I mean, that's part of being young. [534]You think it's smart and—[535]and-and yet I don't think I ever really enjoyed it. [536]But-but everyone did it. [537]And-and we'd go out Saturday night and drink [538]and during the week we wouldn't. [539]I mean, it was just something you didn't do [540](*Anxious laugh*) unless you were in a crowd.

THERAPIST [541]Mm-hmm.

PATIENT [542]Well, when I started to go out with my first husband, he-he-he drank very heavily. [543]But . . . he lived a long ways off from me. [544]He lived in-in ————. [545]And we really only saw each other on weekends.

THERAPIST [546]Mm-hmm.

PATIENT [547]And I never realized it until after we were married that he drank all the time. [548]I-I just thought that-that his drinking was like the rest of the crowd did.

THERAPIST [549]Mm-hmm.

PATIENT [550]Well . . . he was a funny person. [551]He-he didn't trust anyone. [552]He was suspicious of everyone. [553]And he didn't want any responsibility. [554]When we got married, he—when we got married he was making thirty dollars a week. [555]And he, well, the first—when we were first married he wanted—he needed new shoes. [556]And he went out and bought a pair of ten-dollar shoes. [557]And they were c-c-cordovan, I think, that heavy—what is it?—cow-uh-horsehide.

THERAPIST [558]Mm-hmm.

PATIENT [559]And they hurt his feet. [560]He wore them one day. [561]And they hurt his feet. [562]And-and he came home. [563]And he said, "These god-damned shoes hurt my feet." [564]And he kicked one of them off, then picked it up and threw it out the window. [565]And we were in a three-story building on the top floor. [566]And he threw it through the window as hard as he could.

THERAPIST [567]Mm-hmm.

PATIENT [568]And I was petrified for fear he'd hit someone on the street. [569]It could've *killed* them.

THERAPIST [570]Mm-hmm.

PATIENT [571]And I looked out. [572]And the shoe—and no one—no one was around. [573]And I went down and got it. [574]And it was all burst open at the seams from hitting the ground.

THERAPIST [575]Mm-hmm.

PATIENT   ⁵⁷⁶I wa—I used to have to go and meet him on pay days because if I didn't he wouldn't come home. ⁵⁷⁷He'd just go on a toot. ⁵⁷⁸And-and I gave him—gave him an allowance every day for his lunch. ⁵⁷⁹He-he couldn't have any money at all. ⁵⁸⁰He wanted me to do it, because if he had more than the car fare he needed, he'd-he'd start drinking.

THERAPIST   ⁵⁸¹Mm-hmm.

PATIENT   ⁵⁸²And-and sometimes things were pretty tough. ⁵⁸³Most of the . . . for a year or so I had . . . practically everything I owned ⁵⁸⁴(*Anxious laugh*) in hock on and off. ⁵⁸⁵I-I used to hock things without saying anything to him about it because if I mentioned it he'd get mad. ⁵⁸⁶I hocked this ring. ⁵⁸⁷This was my father's ring—

THERAPIST   ⁵⁸⁸Mm-hmm.

PATIENT   ⁵⁸⁹(*She weeps*)—baby ring. ⁵⁹⁰Five dollars . . . ⁵⁹¹Well, and he-he didn't want to hear about any of these troubles. ⁵⁹²And he wanted the-the best of everything. ⁵⁹³And if he couldn't have it he didn't want it. ⁵⁹⁴I mean, he had a vacation once. ⁵⁹⁵And I wanted to go on a walking trip. ⁵⁹⁶And he wouldn't go unless he could go to a good hotel and spend a lot of money. ⁵⁹⁷If he didn't have it, he just . . . Well, I-I got pregnant ⁵⁹⁸(*She weeps*) . . . and . . . which was really a miracle because we had practically no sex life. ⁵⁹⁹But it happened anyhow.

THERAPIST   ⁶⁰⁰Mm-hmm.

PATIENT   ⁶⁰¹We did. But—

THERAPIST   ⁶⁰²This was Bertie?

PATIENT   ⁶⁰³Yes, Bertie.

THERAPIST   ⁶⁰⁴You feel you were afraid of him?

PATIENT   ⁶⁰⁵(*Tearfully*) ⁶⁰⁶Afraid of him . . . ⁶⁰⁷(*She sobs*) ⁶⁰⁸I-I think it was from drinking. ⁶⁰⁹But-but-but he couldn't seem to have-have normal intercourse. ⁶¹⁰He didn't have any control over himself.

THERAPIST   ⁶¹¹Mm-hmm.

PATIENT   ⁶¹²Well, anyhow I got pregnant. ⁶¹³(*Weepy*) ⁶¹⁴And . . . I was so happy. ^{615–17}(*She breaks into sobs, which last 13 secs.; then,* ⁶¹⁸*weeping*) . . . ⁶¹⁹I w . . . I went to the doctor. ⁶²⁰(*Weeping*) ⁶²¹And I had a rabbit test. ^{622–3}(*She sobs; then, weeping*) ⁶²⁴An-and then I went home and told him. ⁶²⁵(*Sobbing*) ⁶²⁶And-and he said if I didn't-didn't do something about it I'd never see him again. ⁶²⁷(*Still weeping*) ⁶²⁸He was going to leave. ⁶²⁹(*Still weeping*)

⁶³⁰And he got the name of the doctor from someone he knew who told me about it. ⁶³¹(*Still weeping*) ⁶³²And he didn't-didn't talk to-to me. (*She blows her nose*) ⁶³³(*Weeping*) ⁶³⁴He-he'd come home at night and eat without talking and go to another room and shut the door. ⁶³⁵(*She sighs*) ⁶³⁶So I went and had it done. ⁶³⁷(*She sobs*) ⁶³⁸My mother knew about it. ⁶³⁹She knew I was pregnant . . . ⁶⁴⁰(*She sobs*) ⁶⁴¹(*Weeping*) ⁶⁴²I don't know whether anyone else in the family knew or not. ⁶⁴³I told Mother.

THERAPIST (*Softly*) ⁶⁴⁴Mm-hmm.

PATIENT ⁶⁴⁵⁻⁶(*She cries; then, still weeping, says*) ⁶⁴⁷When, after I had this operation a couple of years ago when I started going to the doctor—you-you see I've always had it on my mind that having the abortion might have done something to me. ⁶⁴⁸And I wanted to find out.

THERAPIST ⁶⁴⁹Mm-hmm.

PATIENT ⁶⁵⁰And . . . and I was upset about it. ⁶⁵¹I mean, I got discouraged. ⁶⁵²And it takes so long and . . . ⁶⁵³I-I was down in the dumps one day. ⁶⁵⁴And Mother asked me what was the matter. ⁶⁵⁵And I-I said, "I don'-I don't know, I wish I had a baby—"

THERAPIST ⁶⁵⁶Mm-hmm.

PATIENT "—and it begins to look as if I never will." ⁶⁵⁷And ⁶⁵⁸⁻⁹(*She sobs, then weeping she says*) and she says, "Well, if you'd come home when I asked you when you were pregnant, you could have had it." ⁶⁶⁰(*Sobbing*) ⁶⁶¹And she says, "You went ahead and did what you did and God's p-punishing you." ⁶⁶²Which is—⁶⁶³(*She sobs*) the whole thing is a complete fabrication. ⁶⁶⁴(*Weeping*) ⁶⁶⁵She never asked me to come home.

THERAPIST ⁶⁶⁶Mm-hmm.

PATIENT ⁶⁶⁷I *couldn't* go home because, well, I don't know, I always —I-I don't know I-I hate to ask for anything. ⁶⁶⁸And . . . now I'm—my family was in . . . bad financial straits. ⁶⁶⁹(*Weepily*) ⁶⁷⁰And I—and I-I just see coming home with a baby. ⁶⁷¹(*Tearfully*) ⁶⁷²And no one ever asked me. ⁶⁷³(*Weeping*) ⁶⁷⁴She never said a word about it. ⁶⁷⁵(*Weeping*) ⁶⁷⁶I remember a long discussion we had in the kitchen about—about various folk remedies for-for . . . getting rid of one . . .

THERAPIST ⁶⁷⁷Yes, well, I-I don't quite understand why *your* feelings didn't count in this, why you gave in to your husband on this matter . . .

PATIENT ⁶⁷⁸(*7-sec. pause*) ⁶⁷⁹I don't know, I guess I was afraid. ⁶⁸⁰I-I

don't know. ⁶⁸¹ . . . I-I wanted to—I wanted to be with him.
⁶⁸² . . . And-and I know that he would . . . go off if—I mean,
I know that, because-because . . . he-he had a habit of going
off anyhow when he'd just . . .

THERAPIST ⁶⁸³Mm-hmm.

PATIENT . . . ⁶⁸⁴(*Tearfully*) at the slightest provocation would disappear. ⁶⁸⁵(*Tearfully*) ⁶⁸⁶We used to go to parties and things together. ⁶⁸⁷(*She sobs*) ⁶⁸⁸And he'd walk off and leave me.

THERAPIST ⁶⁸⁹Mm-hmm.

PATIENT ⁶⁹⁰⁻¹(*She weeps, then continues, weepily*) ⁶⁹²And I had to
go home alone. ⁶⁹³(*She sobs*) ⁶⁹⁴And everyone knew about it . . .
⁶⁹⁵And I—and I-I-I—like I knew this was-was so serious that-that
he would go. ⁶⁹⁶(*Weeping*) ⁶⁹⁷And-and I mean, it wasn't just an
idle threat, I-I think. ⁶⁹⁸But after that, I don't know, nothing was
ever the same. And . . . ⁶⁹⁹(*She sighs*) ⁷⁰⁰(*7-sec. pause*) ⁷⁰¹(*Weeping*) . . . ⁷⁰²Uh I-I don't know. ⁷⁰³I have a-a godson. ⁷⁰⁴(*She
sniffles*) ⁷⁰⁵Have you got a Kleenex? ⁷⁰⁶I haven't got any more.
⁷⁰⁷And I'm in a terrible mess.

THERAPIST ⁷⁰⁸I'm s—I'm sorry, I haven't. Uh-uh—we might go to
the—

PATIENT ⁷⁰⁹Oh, well, ⁷¹⁰(*She laughs*) let it go.

THERAPIST ⁷¹¹Yes. ⁷¹²Well, let—I-I was thinking in any case that
we're coming near the end of the hour and maybe we should begin
to draw things to . . . an end. ⁷¹³There are one or two things I
would like to-to say just before we-we-we do end though. ⁷¹⁴And
uh maybe I'll just try and say them as they come to me. ⁷¹⁵One
of the things that uh that comes out from what you've been saying here today is that you have had quite a number of experiences
which are . . . more than an average person would have—would
have—more than the average person would have to bear or with-
stand. ⁷¹⁶And uh uh this feeling with regard to wanting to have
a child and then not having the child and the doubt in your mind
as to whether or not you *could* have children, this is something
that undoubtedly would cause a great deal of emotional disturbance in you. ⁷¹⁷And uh this is one of the things we'll have to
understand a little more . . . later. ⁷¹⁸I think it's . . . important, too, you've been mentioning at the beginning . . . of the
hour—you were talking about the difficulty that you have in uh
asserting yourself, I think. ⁷¹⁹Uh you used the term "aggressive,"
in the sen—youn—when you were younger. ⁷²⁰You see, you sug-

gested that you were more aggressive even though you don't feel quite happy about that term, but that you're now rather different, you're rather afraid to contact people. ⁷²¹Well, now, we have to understand what it is uh that has le-led you to-to have these fears about asserting yourself. ⁷²²I—it's quite natural when you were young. ⁷²³Quite often your parents are able to-to tell you what you should do and are able to hold you down. ⁷²⁴But now that you are grown up these conditions are past, and you should be in a position to assert yourself more. ⁷²⁵So we have to understand more about these earlier conditions which led you to learn this fear of expression, and expressing yourself. ⁷²⁶Your feelings towards your uh . . . your father and your mother, these are undoubtedly quite uh important, uh because, well . . . you—a-as I see it, you feel that uh you're not very uh—you-you can't have *good* feelings about your mother. ⁷²⁷Uh all of the feelings that you've—that you have about her uh are that, well, you dislike her for this and for that. ⁷²⁸And uh . . . you-you feel that there are some mitigating circumstances to be said in her favor. ⁷²⁹But yet you still dislike her. ⁷³⁰You don't really feel that you-you can have any love *for* her. ⁷³¹Now, undoubtedly this is the kind of thing which you punish yourself for because in our society uh children are supposed to love their parents. ⁷³²And this is something that you must punish yourself for . . . be it to some extent. ⁷³³This is one of the things that-that must be disturbing you, too. ⁷³⁴Then, there is this other big problem that you mentioned. ⁷³⁵There is the problem of-of your uh husband and what you're going to do about that . . . the conflict that you're in there. ⁷³⁶I mean, it's-it's clear that you are in a conflict, that you feel that . . . you want to be able to do something . . . and yet . . . in the way of-of uh shouldering responsibilities towards him, uh to help him along, and yet you feel that uh your—experi—the experiences you've had with him have been so intense uh that you don't want to go back with him. ⁷³⁷Now, this puts you in another conflict situation. ⁷³⁸And these are-are all kinds of situations which uh cannot do anything other than put you in a—in a uh an intense emotional state. This is just a—

PATIENT   ⁷³⁹(*Laughing*) ⁷⁴⁰That about describes it, I would say.

THERAPIST   ⁷⁴¹Yes, well, it's a uh it's a very natural occurrence.

PATIENT   ⁷⁴²I'm so confused I don't know whether I'm coming or going. ⁷⁴³That's about the size of it.

THERAPIST   ⁷⁴⁴Yes, well, as you—what I feel is that you have uh done the right thing in coming to the clinic here, to talk this sort of thing over. ⁷⁴⁵I can understand that uh . . . it could have been one of the—one of the kind of motives that would have led you to go with this other man that you've mentioned earlier, would have been an opportunity to-to talk things over with him. ⁷⁴⁶But in this kind of situation you are able to talk things over with somebody who is a-a disinterested party, and—

PATIENT   ⁷⁴⁷That's-that's the whole point of it exactly. ⁷⁴⁸I know that.

THERAPIST   ⁷⁴⁹Yes . . . where you have the security of the situation and-and know that uh uh well, there's no *involvement* that will get you—

PATIENT   ⁷⁵⁰Yes, I know when you're personally involved with some-body—

THERAPIST   ⁷⁵¹Yes.

PATIENT   —you always distrust their—

THERAPIST   ⁷⁵²Mm-hmm.

PATIENT   —their opinion. ⁷⁵³I mean, it—well, it can't be unbiased—

THERAPIST   ⁷⁵⁴Mm-hmm.

PATIENT   ⁷⁵⁵It's impossible.

THERAPIST   ⁷⁵⁶So I-I think that uh you will find that as you continue coming here uh that . . . more of these feelings of yours will become uh uh dis—well, as you try to explain them to me, that together we will understand what is-is going on here, and that this kind of-of contact will-will be a very rewarding contact to you and your own insights.

PATIENT   ⁷⁵⁷I think, I hope so. ⁷⁵⁸I think it will be . . . that—

THERAPIST   ⁷⁵⁹Yes.

PATIENT   —gets straightened out.

THERAPIST   ⁷⁶⁰Yes, well, I-I think we have to understand more, too, uh about uh well, your-your desire for children and uh just what that means to you, and where the uh where the operations that you've had and where the abortion uh fits into the picture. ⁷⁶¹And maybe there are some things that you may need to do in relation to checking up on just what your . . . status is here. ⁷⁶²I don't know whether this will be necessary or not. ⁷⁶³Maybe you already had all tests you need.

PATIENT   ⁷⁶⁴No, there's one that I didn't have—

THERAPIST   ⁷⁶⁵Mm-hmm.

PATIENT   766—And I still have it on my mind.

THERAPIST   767Yes, well, I-I think these are a whole lot of problems that we have to try and understand a little more. 768But these are the ones that I've—I—that I think I'm beginning to understand a little bit already. (*They both rise*)

PATIENT   769Well, look at me. (*She sees herself in the mirror*) 770(*Embarrassed laugh*) 771I hope there's a washroom around here. 772(*Embarrassed laugh*)

THERAPIST   773Well, now, I don't know whether there is any Kleenex (*He opens the door*) outside or not. I'll just take a—

PATIENT   774Well, that's good. 775Next time I'm going to bring more with me, huh. (*They go out into the waiting room*) 776 . . . I hope I don't need them, but—

THERAPIST   777I don't uh see any just there. 778But we'll find a washroom, and we'll—

PATIENT   779Who's out there, a doctor?

THERAPIST   780No, that's a patient.

PATIENT   781Well, thank you very much.

THERAPIST   782OK.

PATIENT   783(*She laughs anxiously*) 784You have a remarkable grasp on the situation, I would say.

THERAPIST   785Well, it's because you're uh giving me the information that helps me to understand. Uh what I would suggest is that uh you—let's see—(*They go into the corridor and their voices trail off.*)

AUTHORS' SCORING AND COMMENTS ON SMITH CASE, HOUR THREE

1. *A therapist*
2. *A therapist*

Comment: Can one interpret these sentences at all, or must one consider their meaning so ambiguous that they can only be called *Unsc?* We decided, after some conflict, that these first two sentences should be scored *A therapist,* because they were probably motivated by a fear that the therapist would criticize the patient for being late; the patient thus felt called on to explain her lateness.

3. *Res 5*
4. *Res 5*
5. *A therapist*

6. *D*
7. *Lf—*
8. *A therapist*
9. *R*
10. *Sigh*
11. *dep-a*
12. *dep-a*
13. *dep-a*
14. *dep-a*
15. *dep-a*

Comment: When we first scored sentences 10–15, one of us called them *Res,* the other called them *Dep therapist.* The passage does seem resistant, because the patient would presumably move the therapy ahead better by bringing forward all of her thoughts about her internal conflicts rather than by asking questions. Yet her turning to the therapist in this way is in itself an important piece of behavior, deserving notation; and since it is a part of the transference, by our rule of priorities it ought to be scored in preference to scoring "resistance."

The scorer who called these sentences *Dep* was, however, wrong in supposing that the patient was aware of a dependent motive toward the therapist. So far as we can tell, the patient believed that she was just making a reasonable request for information about how the therapy works. She did not understand that her question was prompted by deeper motives. The most important meaning of her utterance is: "Are you going to reject me?" The patient, having a chronic unconscious expectation of rejection, wonders whether the therapist will decide that she is not worthy of therapy and will turn her away.

The mystery here, that calls our attention to the unconscious motive, is the patient's readiness to believe that she is not doing her part in the therapy and that the therapist will reject her, though there has been nothing at all in the therapist's behavior to justify such an expectation. The correct score, therefore, is *dep-a.*

16. *Unsc*
17. *D*
18. *Unsc*
19. *R*
20. *Unsc*
21. *Res*

22. *Res*
23. *Lf—*
24. *R*
25. *Res*
26. *D*
27. *Unsc*
28. *D*
29. *Res*
30. *Res*
31. *Res*
32. *Res*
33. *r*
34. *M*
35. *r*
36. *D*
37. *M*
38. *r*
39. *M*
40. *A*
41. *A*
42. *A*
43. *A*
44. *A*
45. *A*
46. *M*
47. *Unsc*
48. *Unsc*
49. *A*
50. *M*
51. *A*
52. *D*
53. *Res*
54. *r*
55. *r*
56. *r*
57. *r*
58. *M*
59. *A*
60. *D*
61. *Res*

62. *A*
63. *Sigh*
64. *A*
65. *A*
66. *D*
67. *r*
68. *Lf—*
69. *A*
70. *M*
71. *Lf—*
72. *A*
73. *A:r*
74. *A*
75. *A*
76. *A*
77. *M*
78. *A*
79. *h-a/self*
80. *h-a/self*
81. *h-a/self*
82. *h-a/self*
83. *h-a/self*
84. *h-a/self*
85. *M*
86. *h-a/self*
87. *h-a/self*
88. *h-a/self*
89. *h-a/self*
90. *h-a/self*
91. *h-a/self*
92. *h-a/self*
93. *h-a/self*
94. *Sigh*

Comment: There is a mystery in sentences 79–93: Why does the patient have so little confidence in the acceptability of her work, even though she knows that she has done a good job? There must be some inner self-condemnation, uninfluenceable by her reasoning apparatus, that accounts for the patient's feeling that she has not done well. The appropriate score, therefore, is *h-a/self*.

One should not score these sentences as a conscious self-reproach

—*H/self*—because the patient is quite unaware of the source of her negative evaluation of herself and surely does not assess correctly the strength of this force. She knows only the *consequences* of the inner sense of worthlessness and guilt.

95. *D*
96. *Res*
97. *Res*
98. *Res*
99. *M*
100. *Res*
101. *Res*
102. *Res*

Comment: At sentence 95 the therapist tried to open up the subject of the patient's unconscious sense of guilt. Although what he said is not an interpretation, it leads toward the exploration of the behavior influenced by the unconscious motive.

In response to this motivating intervention the patient offered a rationalization. Since acceptance of the rationalization would prevent discovery of the unconscious motive, the patient's response must be considered resistant.

103. *L people*
104. *L people*
105. *Lf—*
106. *M*
107. *A*
108. *Mob:r*
109. *Mob*
110. *M*
111. *Mob*
112. *Mob*
113. *Res 5*
114. *Obs*
115. *Obs*

Comment: These two sentences can only be evaluated in the light of the subsequent sentences, 138 and 141.

116. *M*
117. *Res*
118. *Dep father*
119. *Dep father*
120. *Dep father*

Comment: The scorer must be in conflict here between *A* and *Dep.* Should he recognize the stress of the patient? Should he infer that the loss of her father would be felt as a desertion, a rebuff, an abandonment—and call these sentences *Dep?* In the original scoring of this passage the two scorers made different decisions on this point. Though this is a close one to decide, we have to choose and have chosen *Dep.*

121. *Res*
122. *M*
123. *Res*
124. *Res*

Comment: 121, 123, and 124 show the operation of repressive forces; therefore we use the score *Res.*

125. *Unsc*
126. *A insanity*
127. *Lf—*
128. *Unsc*
129. *Unsc*
130. *D*
131. *D*
132. *Unsc*
133. *M*
134. *D*
135. *Dep father*
136. *Unsc*
137. *Dep father*
138. *Obs*
139. *W*
140. *Sigh*
141. *Obs*
142. *Lf—*
143. *Obs*
144. *D*
145. *Res*
146. *H/self*
147. *D*
148. *D*
149. *H/self*
150. *H/self*
151. *D*

152. *D*
153. *W*
154. *Dep father*
155. *M*
156. *Obs*
157. *W*
158. *Obs*
159. *Obs*
160. *Sigh*
161. *Obs*
162. *Obs*

Comment: Sentences 156, 158, 159, and 162 show ambivalence and vacillation, which is most appropriately scored *Obs*.

163. *A Smitty*
164. *A Smitty*
165. *A Smitty*
166. *A Smitty*
167. *A Smitty*
168. *A Smitty*
169. *A Smitty*
170. *M*
171. *A Smitty*
172. *L Smitty*
173. *L Smitty*
174. *L Smitty*
175. *M*
176. *L Smitty*
177. *L Smitty*
178. *L Smitty*
179. *L Smitty*
180. *M*
181. *D*
182. *D*
183. *Unsc*
184. *Y*
185. *Res*
186. *R*
187. *Res*
188. *R*
189. *Y*

190. *A Smitty*
191. *A Smitty*
192. *H Smitty*
193. *M*
194. *H Smitty*
195. *M*
196. *L Smitty*
197. *H Smitty*
198. *Sigh*
199. *M*
200. *Res 5*
201. *Sigh*
202. *L Smitty*
203. *Sigh*
204. *L Smitty*
205. *L Smitty*
206. *L Smitty*
207. *L Smitty*
208. *Res 5*
209. *L Smitty*
210. *L Smitty*
211. *Res*
212. *Sigh*
213. *Res*
214. *Res 5*
215. *Res 5*
216. *W*
217. *Dep therapist*
218. *R*
219. *W*
220. *W*
221. *D*
222. *W*
223. *W*
224. *W*
225. *Dep therapist*
226. *W*
227. *Dep therapist*
228. *W*
229. *Dep therapist*

230. *R*
231. *W*
232. *L Smitty*
233. *W*
234. *H/self*
235. *H/self*
236. *W*
237. *W*
238. *L Smitty*
239. *W*
240. *L Smitty*
241. *D*
242. *W*
243. *Y*
244. *D*
245. *W*
246. *W*
247. *Y*
248. *D*
249. *W*
250. *Y*
251. *Y*
252. *W*
253. *L Smitty*
254. *L Smitty*
255. *H/self*
256. *L Smitty*
257. *L Smitty*
258. *M*
259. *L Smitty*
260. *L Smitty*
261. *L Smitty*
262. *L Smitty*
263. *L Smitty*
264. *L Smitty*
265. *Sigh*
266. *L Smitty*
267. *H/self*
268. *H/self*
269. *A Smitty*

270. *A Smitty*
271. *A Smitty*
272. *D*
273. *D*
274. *A Smitty*
275. *Sigh*
276. *A Smitty*
277. *A Smitty*
278. *A Smitty*
279. *A Smitty*
280. *Res*
281. *Res*
282. *Res*
283. *Res*
284. *A Smitty*
285. *A Smitty*
286. *M*
287. *A Smitty*
288. *A Smitty*
289. *A Smitty*
290. *A Smitty*
291. *A Smitty*
292. *A Smitty*
293. *A Smitty*
294. *A Smitty*
295. *M*
296. *A Smitty*
297. *Sigh*
298. *L Smitty*
299. *L Smitty*
300. *L Smitty*
301. *L Smitty*
302. *L Smitty*
303. *M*
304. *Sigh*
305. *W*
306. *Res*
307. *W*
308. *A Smitty*
309. *Res 5*

310. *Dep*
311. *Dep*
312. *Dep*
313. *Dep*
314. *W*
315. *Dep*
316. *Dep*
317. *Dep*
318. *Dep*

Comment: Patient is here contrasting her former self-confidence with her current feeling of helplessness. Thus we are obliged to score the intention of her remarks, mainly the expression of her current feeling of helplessness.

319. *Lf—*
320. *M*
321. *W*
322. *H/self*
323. *R*
324. *W*
325. *W*
326. *W*
327. *H/self*
328. *W*
329. *H/self*
330. *R*
331. *R*
332. *A therapist*
333. *D*
334. *D*
335. *W*
336. *H mother*
337. *M*
338. *H mother*
339. *Sigh*
340. *H mother*
341. *Sigh*
342. *Sigh*
343. *H mother*
344. *Res*
345. *M*

346. *H-A mother*
347. *W*
348. *H-A mother*
349. *H-A mother*
350. *W*
351. *H-A mother*
352. *W*
353. *H-A mother*
354. *Lf—*
355. *H-A mother*
356. *H-A mother*
357. *D*
358. *H-A mother*
359. *R*
360. *M*
361. *H grandmother*
362. *H grandmother*
363. *H grandmother*
364. *H grandmother*
365. *H grandmother*
366. *H grandmother*
367. *H grandmother*
368. *W*
369. *H grandmother*
370. *H grandmother*
371. *Sigh*
372. *H grandmother*
373. *H grandmother*
374. *H grandmother*
375. *H grandmother*
376. *H grandmother*
377. *H grandmother*
378. *H grandmother*
379. *H grandmother*
380. *M*
381. *D*
382. *Y*
383. *M*
384. *H grandmother*
385. *H grandmother*

386. *H-A mother*
387. *H-A mother*
388. *H-A mother*
389. *H-A mother*
390. *Sigh*
391. *H mother*
392. *H mother*
393. *M*
394. *H brother*
395. *H brother*
396. *D*
397. *H brother*
398. *H brother*
399. *H brother*
400. *H brother*
401. *M*
402. *H brother*
403. *H brother*
404. *L sister-in-law*
405. *L sister-in-law*
406. *H brother*
407. *H brother*
408. *H brother*
409. *H brother*
410. *M*
411. *H brother*
412. *H brother*
413. *H brother*
414. *H brother*
415. *M*
416. *H mother*
417. *H mother*
418. *H mother*
419. *H mother*
420. *Lf—*
421. *D*
422. *Y*
423. *M*
424. *W*
425. *H mother*

Comment: This statement does not mean, as one might at first suppose, that the patient is sympathetic with her mother; it rather expresses contempt for a stupid and selfish person.

426. *Dep mother*
427. *Dep father*
428. *Dep father*
429. *Dep father*

Comment: Sentences 426–9 express the patient's wish that she could confide in her parents. She is prevented from doing so in the case of her mother by lack of understanding, in the case of her father by her reluctance to burden him with her problems now that he is so sick.

430. *Res*
431. *R*
432. *D*
433. *Res*

Comment: The proposal to leave something out of her account because she had mentioned it previously to the social worker is of course resistant.

434. *M*
435. *Dep older man*
436. *Dep older man*
437. *Dep older man*
438. *Dep older man*
439. *Dep older man*
440. *Dep older man*
441. *Lf—*
442. *Dep older man*
443. *Dep older man*
444. *Dep older man*
445. *M*
446. *Dep father*
447. *Dep father*
448. *Dep father*
449. *Dep father*
450. *Dep father*
451. *Dep father*
452. *Dep father*
453. *Dep older man*
454. *W*

455. *W*
456. *D*
457. *Y*
458. *H/self*
459. *H/self*
460. *L older man*
461. *L older man*
462. *L older man*
463. *W*
464. *Lf—*
465. *L older man*
466. *W*
467. *M*
468. *D*
469. *Dep older man*
470: *Dep older man*
471. *Dep father*
472. *M*
473. *Dep father*
474. *Dep father*
475. *Dep father*
476. *M*
477. *H-A mother*
478. *H-A mother*
479. *L father*
480. *L father*
481. *L father*
482. *L father*

Comment: Sentences 479–81 say critical things of the patient's father, but she is making these qualifications only in order reasonably to assert that he has been good to her. Thus *L father* is an appropriate score for these units as well as for sentence 482. Sentences 477 and 478 seem to indicate an upswelling of guilt at praising her father while she derogates her mother; therefore we thought it appropriate to call these *H-A mother*. An alternative scoring for 477 and 478 would be *L father*.

483. *W*
484. *M*
485. *W*
486. *L father*

487. *L father*
488. *L father*
489. *L father*
490. *L father*
491. *L father*

    Comment: One has some tendency to score these sentences, describing things about her father that the patient doesn't like, as *H father*. But the main point of the utterance is: "I love him despite his faults."

492. *M*
493. *L father*
494. *Res*
495. *Lf—*
496. *Res*
497. *Lf—*
498. *Res*
499. *Lf—*
500. *D*
501. *H/self*
502. *Res*
503. *Res*
504. *Sigh*
505. *Res*
506. *D*
507. *A*
508. *R*
509. *D*
510. *D*
511. *R*
512. *Y*
513. *D*
514. *S-A abortion*
515. *M*
516. *S-A abortion*
517. *M*
518. *S*
519. *Lf—*
520. *S*
521. *S*
522. *S*

523. *H/self*
524. *D*
525. *H/self*
526. *H/self*
527. *H/self*
528. *H/self*
529. *S*
530. *S*
531. *M*
532. *S*
533. *S*
534. *S*
535. *S-a*
536. *S*
537. *S*
538. *S*
539. *S*
540. *Lf—*

Comment: We decided to score the sentences from 518 on that describe her going around with a crowd that drank a good deal, *S*. Her going with this crowd undoubtedly exposed the patient to sexual advances from men in this group. Sentences 523 and 525–8 could be thrown in with the rest as *S;* however, the self-critical reference is so plain that we settled on *H/self*. Alternatively, one could consider all of this material as merely preliminary to the patient's criticism of her first husband which begins with unit 542. She has to establish, one could argue, that she didn't realize that her husband was an alcoholic, because she always saw him in situations where drinking was an accepted thing. But the patient dwells on her relationship to this crowd somewhat more than would be necessary just to make this point.

541. *M*
542. *H Bertie*
543. *H Bertie*
544. *H Bertie*
545. *H Bertie*
546. *M*
547. *H Bertie*
548. *H Bertie*
549. *M*

550. *H Bertie*
551. *H Bertie*
552. *H Bertie*
553. *H Bertie*
554. *H Bertie*
555. *H Bertie*
556. *H Bertie*
557. *H Bertie*
558. *M*
559. *H Bertie*
560. *H Bertie*
561. *H Bertie*
562. *H Bertie*
563. *H Bertie*
564. *H Bertie*
565. *H Bertie*
566. *H Bertie*
567. *M*
568. *H Bertie*
569. *H Bertie*
570. *M*
571. *H Bertie*
572. *H Bertie*
573. *H Bertie*
574. *H Bertie*
575. *M*
576. *H Bertie*
577. *H Bertie*
578. *H Bertie*
579. *H Bertie*
580. *H Bertie*
581. *M*
582. *H Bertie*
583. *H Bertie*
584. *Lf—*
585. *H Bertie*
586. *H Bertie*
587. *H Bertie*
588. *M*
589. *W*

590. *H Bertie*
591. *H Bertie*
592. *H Bertie*
593. *H Bertie*
594. *H Bertie*
595. *H Bertie*
596. *H Bertie*
597. *H Bertie*
598. *W*
599. *H Bertie*
600. *M*
601. *H Bertie*
602. *D*
603. *Y*
604. *D*
605. *W*
606. *Unsc*
607. *W*
608. *H Bertie*
609. *H Bertie*
610. *H Bertie*

Comment: The patient's failure to answer the therapist's question (sentence 604) should not be considered resistant, because the therapist apparently got off the rails a bit here. First he asked which husband Mrs. Smith was talking about, Bertie or Smitty. Then, reacting to her statement a while back that she used to hock things without saying anything about it because she was afraid Bertie would get mad, the therapist asked whether she had been afraid of Bertie. The patient disregarded the question completely, plowing straight on with her recital of her troubles in getting pregnant and her problems after she had gotten pregnant.

611. *M*
612. *S*
613. *W*
614. *r*

Comment: Since we don't know just what drive was reduced when Mrs. S. was happy to be pregnant, we scored it merely *r*. Another possible score for sentence 614 would be *S*. This would be on the ground that pregnancy is closely connected with sex.

615. *W*

616. *W*
617. *W*
618. *W*
619. *S*
620. *W*
621. *S*
622. *W*
623. *W*
624. *S-A*
625. *W*
626. *S-A*
627. *W*
628. *S-A*
629. *W*
630. *S-A*
631. *W*
632. *S-A*
633. *W*
634. *S-A*
635. *Sigh*
636. *S-A*

Comment: One is torn here between recognizing the conflict that her husband's reaction put the patient in and recognizing the strength of the patient's dependence on her husband, which made it impossible for her to resist his wishes and act independently. Wish to have a baby may be considered, in a broad sense, to belong in the realm of sex; therefore getting pregnant earns an *S* score. Conflict about pregnancy therefore becomes *S-A*. If we had considered the patient's dependence on her husband to be overriding here, we would have scored the sentences from 624 on *Dep Bertie*.

637. *W*
638. *Dep mother*
639. *Dep mother*
640. *W*
641. *W*
642. *Dep mother*
643. *Dep mother*

Comment: The patient implies in sentences 638, 639, 642, and 643, "Mother could have saved me; she could have advised me not to have an abortion." Since her mother didn't come through with the needed support for that course of action, the patient felt abandoned. Thus the score is *Dep*.

644. *M*
645. *W*
646. *W*
647. *A abortion*
648. *A abortion*
649. *M*
650. *A abortion*
651. *A abortion*
652. *A abortion*
653. *H mother*
654. *H mother*
655. *H mother*
656. *M*
657. *H mother*
658. *W*
659. *W*
660. *W*
661. *H mother*
662. *H mother*
663. *W*
664. *W*
665. *H mother*

Comment: There is a problem where one should stop scoring *A* and start scoring *H mother*. We resolved the issue by carrying the *A* up to the point where, it seemed to us, the patient launched into her account of the incident in which she told her mother of her wish to have a baby and her mother unjustifiably attacked her.

666. *M*
667. *H mother*
668. *H mother*
669. *W*
670. *H mother*
671. *W*
672. *H mother*
673. *W*
674. *H mother*
675. *W*
676. *H mother*

677. *Interp*
Comment: This is not a classic *Interp,* but it gets by because the therapist does seem to point to an unconscious dependent motive.
678. *Res 5*
679. *Dep Bertie*
680. *Res*
681. *Dep Bertie*
682. *Dep Bertie*
683. *M*
684. *W*
685. *W*
686. *Dep Bertie*
687. *W*
688. *Dep Bertie*
689. *M*
690. *W*
691. *W*
692. *Dep Bertie*
693. *W*
694. *Dep Bertie*
695. *Dep Bertie*
696. *W*
697. *Dep Bertie*
Comment: The scorer's dilemma is: Shall I recognize the patient's dependence on Bertie, which caused her so much to fear abandonment by him, or shall I designate the conflict about her pregnancy that this fear of abandonment put her in? Here the patient's fear of abandonment seems to be emphasized, having been pointed up by the therapist's interpretation at sentence 677.
698. *H Bertie*
699. *Sigh*
700. *Res 5*
701. *W*
702. *Res*
703. *L godson*
Comment: This unit would be *Unsc* except for the fact that the patient previously mentioned how fond she was of the godson.
704. *W*
705. *Dep therapist*

706. *Dep therapist*
707. *Dep therapist*
708. *R*
709. *Unsc*
710. *Lf+*
711. *M*
712. *D*
713. *R*
714. *R*
715. *R*
716. *R*
717. *D*

Comment: Sentences 713–16 seem on the whole to be reassuring; therefore *R* is an appropriate score. Sentence 717 foreshadows more hard work by the patient; thus it is *D*.

718. *Interp*
719. *Interp*
720. *Interp*
721. *Interp*
722. *Interp*
723. *Interp*
724. *Interp*
725. *Interp*
726. *Interp*
727. *Interp*
728. *Interp*
729. *Interp*
730. *Interp*
731. *Interp*
732. *Interp*
733. *Interp*

Comment: This interpretation we believe to be inexact and not wholly correct. However, it is in our opinion not so wide of the mark as to deserve a *Pretni* score. The interpretive elements may be mentioned: first, the contrast of past and present conditions ("It's quite natural when you were young. . . . But now that you are grown up these conditions are past, and you should be in a position to assert yourself more"); second, the labeling of the patient's ambivalence toward her mother ("You feel . . . that you can't have *good* feelings about your mother. . . . You feel that there are some mitigating circumstances to be said in her favor. But yet you still dislike her").

734. *R*
735. *R*
736. *R*
737. *R*
738. *R*

Comment: Sentences 734–8 are a sympathetic paraphrase of what the patient has said. Because of the sympathetic attitude we believe that these sentences should be scored *R*. There is some clarification of the patient's feelings here, but there is no labeling of previously unconscious motives. One may well ask, then, are the preceding sentences dealing with the patient's ambivalence toward her mother any more interpretive than the sentences here? It must be admitted that sentences 726–33 barely qualify as interpretive. One can strengthen the case for calling them interpretive by noting the highlighting of the patient's sense of guilt in sentences 731–3; otherwise they would perhaps be no more than clarifying and would therefore not rate an *Interp* scoring.

739. *Lf+*
740. *L therapist*
741. *R*
742. *Unsc*
743. *Unsc*
744. *R*
745. *Interp*
746. *Interp*
747. *Y*
748. *Y*
749. *Interp*
750. *Reas*
751. *M*
752. *M*
753. *Reas*
754. *M*
755. *Reas*

Comment: The patient's agreement here seems to deserve more than a *Y*. She carries the thought beyond what the therapist has said and shows active reasoning.

756. *D*
757. *Y*
758. *Y*
759. *M*
760. *D*
761. *D*
762. *D*
763. *D*
764. *A abortion*
765. *M*
766. *A abortion*
767. *D*
768. *R*
769. *H/self*
770. *Lf—*
771. *Dep therapist*
772. *Lf—*
773. *R*
774. *L therapist*
775. *H/self*
776. *H/self*
777. *D*
778. *R*
779. *A therapy*
780. *R*
781. *L therapist*
782. *M*
783. *Lf—*
784. *L therapist*
785. *R*

GLOSSARY FOR PATIENT'S SIGNS

A. An internal response-produced stimulus which might be called anxiety, apprehension, distress, tension, or fear.

a. Unconscious anxiety or an unconscious sense of guilt.

A:r. Indicates that anxiety is perceptibly reduced.

a:r. Indicates reduction of unconscious anxiety or guilt.

Conf. A confirmation, a response to an interpretation which shows that the patient understands the interpretation, even if only in a minimal way, and confirms the interpretation by bringing forward either new information or a pertinent emotional reaction.

Dep. Dependence.

dep. Unconscious dependence.

Dep:r. Indicates a reduction of dependent motivation.

Dep-A. Indicates that the patient is aware of and frightened by his dependent motive.

Dep-a. Indicates a conscious dependent motive to which unconscious anxiety is attached.

dep-A. The dependent motive is unconscious but the anxiety is conscious.

dep-a. Both dependent motive and anxiety are unconscious, yet the one elicits the other.

Dep-A:r. Similar to *Dep-A* except that the addition of *r* indicates that the anxiety (but not the *Dep*) component is reduced.

Dep-a:r. Indicates that the unconscious anxiety attached to conscious dependence motives is reduced.

dep-A:r. Indicates that the dependence motive is unconscious and that the conscious anxiety component is reduced.

dep-a:r. Indicates that the unconscious anxiety evoked by unconscious dependence motives is reduced.

Dream. Used for the text of a dream when it is first told, as well as for details which are a part of the dream but are added later.

H. A hostile act or motive.

h. Unconscious hostility.

H-A. Conscious anger and fear.

H-a. Conscious anger, unexpressed because of unconscious anxiety.

h-A. Strong overt anxiety with no apparent reason for it; if one inspects the wider context of the behavior a hostile motive can be inferred.

h-a. Both the hostile motive and the inhibitory force are unconscious.

H:r. Indicates a reduction of conscious angry motivation.

H-A:r. Indicates that the conscious anxiety component of the pair of conflicting motives is reduced.

H-a:r. Indicates that the unconscious anxiety component of conflicting motives is reduced.

h-A:r. Indicates a reduction of conscious anxiety conflicting with unconscious hostility.

h-a:r. The same as above except that both the hostility and anxiety are unconscious.

H/self. Scored when the patient makes critical remarks about himself, expresses negative thoughts concerning himself, or describes punishing himself.

h-a/self. Indicates an unconscious self-critical reaction. (One should never write *h/self,* because if *a* weren't attached to *h* the angry reaction would be conscious and scored as *H/self.*)

H/self:r Indicates that the self-critical reaction is stopped or reduced.

h-a/self:r Indicates that the *a* component is reduced. (When *a* is reduced self-blame would tend to become conscious.)

L. Love, i.e. liking, approaching, taking care of, highly evaluating, sparing, pitying, cherishing, valuing, affiliating with, appreciating persons and activities.

L-A. A conscious loving emotion to which conscious fear is attached.

L-a. A conscious loving emotion to which unconscious fear is attached.

l-A. Indicates that the loving reaction is unconscious and the anxiety conscious.

l-a. Both the loving and anxiety components are unconscious.

L:r. Indicates that loving feelings are stopped or perceptibly reduced.

L-A:r. Indicates that conscious anxiety attached to conscious loving feelings is reduced.

L-a:r. Indicates that unconscious anxiety attached to conscious loving feelings is reduced.

l-A:r. Indicates that the loving component is unconscious and the anxiety factor is conscious and is reduced.

l-a:r. Indicates unconscious loving feeling and reduced unconscious anxiety.

Lf. Laughter.

Lf+. A kind of relaxed laughter which expresses mirth and gaiety.

Lf—. Anxious or embarrassed laughter which expresses tension rather than the tension-release of happy laughter.

Mob. Social mobility, i.e. a change of position in the system of social classes and all activities and habits related to such a change, as well as any reference *to stable status.*

Mob-A. Mobility tendencies elicit conscious fear.

Mob-a. Mobility strivings elicit unconscious fear.

mob-A. The mobility element is unconscious and the anxiety component is conscious.

mob-a. Both the mobility strivings and anxiety are unconscious.

Mob:r. Successful reduction of a mobility motive.

Mob-A:r. Indicates that conscious anxiety about mobility has been reduced.

mob-A:r. Conscious anxiety about unconscious mobility strivings is reduced.

mob-a:r. Unconscious anxiety about unconscious mobility strivings has been reduced.

N. Any negation, not expanded and not considered resistant.

Obs. Obsessional: a thought or act not related to the on-going current of mental events; intrusive; strongly motivated, but the source of motivation unknown; ambivalent behavior showing rapidly alternating feelings of love and hate.

PSS. Psychosomatic symptom.

PSS:r. Indicates the sudden termination of a psychosomatic symptom, accompanied by marked reduction in stress.

r. The sign for reward or reduction in drive, added as a kind of postscript to the sign for the drive that has been reduced. Used alone in one case only: an unanalyzed feeling of well-being.

Reas. Reasoning, insight, covering the unbidden, impulsive emergence of a solution as well as the achievement of it by laborious formal reasoning.

Res and Res 5. Resistance, i.e. any response of the patient that operates against therapeutic process. *Res 5* is any silence of five seconds in length.

S. Sex, erotic feelings or motives.

S-A. Conscious sexual desire opposed by conscious anxiety, which may or may not be strong enough to prevent the occurrence of a sexual act and which may precede, accompany, or follow the act if it occurs.

S-a. A conscious sexual wish which is opposed by unconscious anxiety.

s-A. Unconscious sexual motivation can be safely inferred, but the patient is aware only of the anxiety produced by the unconscious motive.

s-a. Unconscious conflict between thrusting and denying components in the sexual sphere.

S:r. Reduction of sex drive that not only reduces disturbing sexual tension but also reinforces the responses, including thoughts, which have just preceded it. Naturally the sexual orgasm is scored as *S:r.*

S-A:r. A conscious sex conflict in which the anxiety element is reduced.

S-a:r. Unconscious anxiety attached to conscious sexual impulses is reduced.

s-A:r. Conscious anxiety attached to unconscious sexual impulses is reduced.

s-a:r. Unconscious anxiety attached to unconscious sexual wishes is reduced.

S:j. Sexual jealousy, involving sexual and aggressive motives and attendant anxious reactions, and usually precipitating a torturing inner conflict.

S:j:r. A reduction in the motive of sexual jealousy.

Sigh. We do not define *Sigh* in any erudite way but assume that it is easily recognizable.

W. Weeping, i.e. what the transcribing typist can identify and report as weeping.

Y. Any affirmation, not expanded.

Unsc. Unscorable.

GLOSSARY FOR THERAPIST'S SIGNS

D. Drive or demand; any therapist unit which is thought to raise motivation in the patient, such as a question or a comment raising anxiety.

Interp. Interpretation, labeling. Used when the therapist names an unconscious motive, connects such motives to the situation which evokes them, or discriminates unconscious meanings which have been falsely believed to be related.

M. Mild agreement, mild assent, social facilitation on the part of the therapist.

Pretni. The sign for an error by the therapist.

R. Reward or, in our system, tension reduction; therapist's utterance which causes relaxation and reduction of motivation in the patient.

Unsc. Unscorable utterances of the therapist.

BIBLIOGRAPHY

ANDERSON, HAROLD H. (1946) Directive and nondirective psychotherapy: The role of the therapist. *Amer. J. Orthopsychiat., 16,* 608–14.

ARONSON, M. (1953) A study of the relationships between certain counselor and client characteristics in client-centered therapy. In Snyder, 1953, pp. 39–54.

AULD, FRANK, JR., AND MURRAY, EDWARD J. (1955) Content-analysis studies of psychotherapy. *Psychol. Bull., 52,* 377–95.

AULD, FRANK, JR., AND WHITE, ALICE M. (1956) Rules for dividing interviews into sentences. *J. Psychol., 42,* 273–81.

AULD, FRANK, JR., AND WHITE, ALICE MARSDEN (1959) Sequential dependencies in psychotherapy. *J. Abnorm. Soc. Psychol., 58,* 100–4.

BALES, ROBERT F. (1950) *Interaction process analysis.* Cambridge, Mass., Addison-Wesley.

BALINT, MICHAEL (1952) *Primary love and psycho-analytic technique.* London, Hogarth Press and the Institute of Psycho-Analysis.

BELLAK, LEOPOLD, AND SMITH, M. BREWSTER (1956) An experimental exploration of the psychoanalytic process: Exemplification of a method. *Psychoanal. Quart., 25,* 385–414.

BERELSON, BERNARD (1952) *Content analysis in communication research.* Glencoe, Ill., The Free Press.

BIERER, J., AND STRÖM-OLSEN, R. (1948) The recording of psychotherapeutic sessions: Its value in teaching, research, and treatment. *Lancet, 254,* 957–8.

BLAU, B. A. (1953) A comparison of more improved with less improved clients treated by client-centered methods. In Snyder, 1953, pp. 120–6.

BLOOMFIELD, LEONARD (1933) *Language.* New York, Holt.

BOYD, RICHARD W., STANDISH, CHRISTOPHER T., SEMRAD, ELVIN V., AND GREENBLATT, MILTON (1956) The interactive process and changes in psychotherapy. Progress report to National Institute of Mental Health, Public Health Service, on project M-936C2. Boston, Department of Psychiatry, Harvard Medical School.

BREUER, JOSEF, AND FREUD, SIGMUND (1895) *Studies on hysteria.* Translated by James Strachey. New York, Basic Books, Inc., 1957.

COVNER, BERNARD J. (1942) Studies in phonographic recordings of verbal
441

material: I. The use of phonographic recordings in counseling practice and research. *J. Consult. Psychol., 6,* 105–13.

CURRAN, CHARLES A. (1945) *Personality factors in counseling.* New York, Grune & Stratton.

DITTES, JAMES E. (1957) Galvanic skin response as a measure of patient's reaction to therapist's permissiveness. *J. Abnorm. Soc. Psychol., 55,* 295–303.

DOLLARD, JOHN (1943) *Fear in battle.* New Haven, Institute of Human Relations, Yale University.

DOLLARD, JOHN, AULD, FRANK, JR., AND WHITE, ALICE MARSDEN (1953) *Steps in psychotherapy.* New York, Macmillan.

DOLLARD, JOHN, DOOB, LEONARD W., MILLER, NEAL E., MOWRER, O. H., AND SEARS, ROBERT R. (1939) *Frustration and aggression.* New Haven, Yale University Press.

DOLLARD, JOHN, AND MILLER, NEAL E. (1950) *Personality and psychotherapy.* New York, McGraw-Hill.

DOLLARD, JOHN, AND MOWRER, O. HOBART (1947) A method of measuring tension in written documents. *J. Abnorm. Soc. Psychol., 42,* 3–32.

FENICHEL, OTTO (1945) *The psychoanalytic theory of neurosis.* New York, Norton.

FREEDMAN, MERVIN B., LEARY, TIMOTHY F., OSSORIO, ABEL G., AND COFFEY, HUBERT S. (1951) The interpersonal dimension of personality. *J. Pers., 20,* 143–61.

FREUD, SIGMUND (1900) *The interpretation of dreams.* Translated by James Strachey. New York, Basic Books, Inc., 1955.

FREUD, SIGMUND (1905) *Three essays on the theory of sexuality.* Translated by James Strachey. London, Imago Publishing Company, 1949.

FREUD, SIGMUND (1913) The predisposition to obsessional neurosis. Translated by Edward Glover and E. Colburn Mayne. In *Collected papers,* vol. 2. London, Hogarth Press and the Institute of Psycho-Analysis, 1924. Pp. 122–32.

FREUD, SIGMUND (1914) Recollection, repetition and working through (Further recommendations on the technique of psycho-analysis, II). Translated by Joan Riviere. In *Collected papers,* vol. 2. London, Hogarth Press and the Institute of Psycho-Analysis, 1924. Pp. 366–76.

FREUD, SIGMUND (1916–17) *A general introduction to psycho-analysis.* Translated by Joan Riviere. New York, Liveright, 1935.

FREUD, SIGMUND (1926) *The problem of anxiety.* Translated by Henry Alden Bunker. New York, Norton, 1936.

FREUD, SIGMUND (1937) Constructions in analysis. Translated by James Strachey. In *Collected papers,* vol. 5. London, The Hogarth Press and the Institute of Psycho-Analysis, 1950. Pp. 358–71.

FREUD, SIGMUND (1950 [1895]) Project for a scientific psychology. Translated by James Strachey. In *The origins of psycho-analysis,* edited by Marie Bonaparte, Anna Freud, and Ernst Kris. New York, Basic Books, Inc., 1954. Pp. 347–445.

FRIES, CHARLES CARPENTER (1952) *The structure of English.* New York, Harcourt, Brace.

GILL, MERTON, NEWMAN, RICHARD, AND REDLICH, FREDRICK C. (1954) *The initial interview in psychiatric practice.* New York, International Universities Press.

GILLESPIE, J. F. (1953) Verbal signs of resistance in client-centered therapy. In Snyder, 1953, pp. 105–19.

GOODMAN, LEO A., AND KRUSKAL, WILLIAM H. (1954) Measures of association for cross classifications. *J. Amer. Statis. Ass., 49,* 732–64.

HAIGH, GERARD (1949) Defensive behavior in client-centered therapy. *J. Consult. Psychol., 13,* 181–9.

HEINICKE, CHRISTOPH, AND BALES, ROBERT F. (1953) Developmental trends in the structure of small groups. *Sociometry, 16,* 7–38.

HOGAN, RICHARD A. (1952) A measure of client defensiveness. In Wolff, W., and Precker, J. A., eds., *Success in psychotherapy.* New York, Grune & Stratton. Pp. 112–42.

HOLLINGSHEAD, AUGUST B., AND REDLICH, FREDRICK C. (1958) *Social class and mental illness: A community study.* New York, Wiley.

JOHNSON, WENDELL (1944) Studies in language behavior: I. A program of research. *Psychol. Monogr., 56,* No. 2 (Whole No. 255). Pp. 1–15.

KENDALL, MAURICE G. (1948) *Rank correlation methods.* London, Griffin.

KNIGHT, ROBERT P. (1952) An evaluation of psychotherapeutic techniques. *Bull. Menninger Clin., 16,* 113–24.

LAFORGE, ROLFE, LEARY, TIMOTHY F., NABOISEK, HERBERT, COFFEY, HUBERT S., AND FREEDMAN, MERVIN B. (1954) The interpersonal dimension of personality: II. An objective study of repression. *J. Pers., 23,* 129–53.

LASSWELL, HAROLD D. (1935) Verbal references and physiological changes during the psychoanalytic interview: A preliminary communication. *Psychoanal. Rev., 22,* 10–24.

LASSWELL, HAROLD D. (1936) Certain prognostic changes during trial (psychoanalytic) interviews. *Psychoanal. Rev., 23,* 241–7.

LASSWELL, HAROLD D. (1937) Veraenderungen an einer Versuchsperson waehrend einer kuren Folge von psychoanalytischen Interviews. *Imago, 23,* 375–80.

LAZOWICK, L. M., AND YOUNG, N. (1950) A preliminary analysis of a specific patient's personal references to discern movement in psychotherapy. Unpublished manuscript, University of Illinois. (Summarized in Mowrer, 1953.)

LEARY, TIMOTHY (1957) *Interpersonal diagnosis of personality; a func-*

tional theory and methodology for personality evaluation. New York, Ronald.

LEARY, TIMOTHY, AND COFFEY, HUBERT S. (1954) The prediction of interpersonal behavior in group psychotherapy. *Group Psychother., 7,* 7–51.

MAHL, GEORGE F. (1956) Disturbances and silences in the patient's speech in psychotherapy. *J. Abnorm. Soc. Psychol., 53,* 1–15.

MAHL, GEORGE F., DOLLARD, JOHN, AND REDLICH, F. C. (1954) Facilities for the sound recording and observation of interviews. *Science, 120,* 235–9.

MASSERMAN, JULES H. (1943) *Behavior and neurosis.* Chicago, University of Chicago Press.

MATARAZZO, JOSEPH D., SASLOW, GEORGE, AND MATARAZZO, Ruth G. (1956) The Interaction Chronograph as an instrument for objective measurement of interaction patterns during interviews. *J. Psychol., 41,* 347–67.

MOSTELLER, FREDERICK, AND BUSH, ROBERT R. (1954) Selected quantitative techniques. In Lindzey, Gardner, ed., *Handbook of social psychology,* vol. *1.* Cambridge, Mass., Addison-Wesley. Pp. 289–334.

MOWRER, O. HOBART (1953) Changes in verbal behavior during psychotherapy. In *Psychotherapy: Theory and research.* New York, Ronald. Pp. 463–545.

MURRAY, EDWARD J. (1954) A case study in a behavioral analysis of psychotherapy. *J. Abnorm. Soc. Psychol., 49,* 305–10.

MURRAY, EDWARD J. (1955) A method for studying psychotherapy. Unpublished doctor's dissertation, Yale University.

MURRAY, EDWARD J. (1956) A content-analysis method for studying psychotherapy. *Psychol. Monogr., 70,* No. 13 (Whole No. 420).

OKERLUND, GERDA, AND VINSON, ESTHER (1942) *Review exercises in English.* New York, Harper.

PIKE, KENNETH L. (1945) *The intonation of American English.* Ann Arbor, University of Michigan Press.

PORTER, ELIAS HULL, JR. (1943a) The development and evaluation of a measure of counseling interview procedures. I. The development. *Educ. Psychol. Measmt., 3,* 105–26.

PORTER, E. H., JR. (1943b) The development and evaluation of a measure of counseling interview procedures. II. The evaluation. *Educ. Psychol. Measmt., 3,* 215–38.

RAIMY, VICTOR C. (1948) Self reference in counseling interviews. *J. Consult. Psychol., 12,* 153–63.

RAKUSIN, JOHN M. (1953) The role of Rorschach variability in the prediction of client behavior during psychotherapy. In Snyder, 1953, pp. 60–74.

REDLICH, FREDRICK C., DOLLARD, JOHN, AND NEWMAN, RICHARD (1950)

High fidelity recording of psychotherapeutic interviews. *Amer. J. Psychiat., 107,* 42–8.

ROBERTS, BERTRAM H., AND STRODTBECK, FRED L. (1953) Interaction process differences between groups of paranoid schizophrenic and depressed patients. *Int. J. Group Psychother., 3,* 29–41.

ROSHAL, JEAN J. G. (1953) The type-token ratio as a measure of changes in behavior variability during psychotherapy. In Snyder, 1953, pp. 94–104.

RUBINSTEIN, ELI A., AND PARLOFF, MORRIS B., Eds., (1959) *Research in Psychotherapy,* Washington, D.C., American Psychological Association.

SAUL, LEON, AND SHEPPARD, EDITH (1956) An attempt to quantify emotional forces using manifest dreams. *J. Amer. Psychoanal. Ass., 4,* 486–502.

SEEMAN, JULIUS (1949) A study of the process of nondirective therapy. *J. Consult. Psychol., 13,* 157–68.

SNYDER, WILLIAM U. (1945) An investigation of the nature of non-directive psychotherapy. *J. Gen. Psychol., 33,* 193–223.

SNYDER, WILLIAM U. (1953) *Group report of a program of research in psychotherapy.* State College, Pa., Pennsylvania State College.

STEVENS, S. S. (1951) Mathematics, measurement, and psychophysics. In Stevens, S. S., ed., *Handbook of experimental psychology.* New York, Wiley. Pp. 1–49.

STRUPP, HANS H. (1955) An objective comparison of Rogerian and Psychoanalytic techniques. *J. Consult. Psychol. 19,* 1–7.

STRUPP, HANS H. (1957a) A multidimensional system for analyzing psychotherapeutic techniques. *Psychiatry. 20,* 293–306.

STRUPP, HANS H. (1957b) A multidimensional comparison of therapist activity in analytic and client-centered therapy. *J. Consult. Psychol. 21,* 301–308.

STRUPP, HANS H. (1958) The psychotherapist's contribution to the treatment process. *Behavioral Science, 3,* 34–67.

SYMONDS, PERCIVAL M. (1939) Research on the interviewing process. *J. Educ. Psychol., 30,* 346–53.

WARNER, W. LLOYD, AND LUNT, PAUL S. (1941) *The social life of a modern community.* New Haven, Yale University Press.

WILSON, E. BRIGHT, JR. (1952) *An introduction to scientific research.* New York, McGraw-Hill.

ZIMMERMAN, W., AND LANGDON, J. (1949) A preliminary attempt to establish criteria for measuring progress in psychotherapy. Unpublished manuscript, University of Illinois. (Summarized in Mowrer, 1953.)

INDEX

A (anxiety)
 combined with other signs, 49–51
 definition, 44–5
 discriminations from other signs, 52–6
 examples of, 45–8
 theory of, 45
Achievement, scored as *Mob*, 102–4
Actor-action construction, 14
Affection. *See* L
Affirmation. *See* Y
Aggression: produced by frustration, 75;
 see also H
Agreement: measures of, 305–10; by therapist, scored *M*, 199–200; with therapist,
 scored *Y*, 178
Ambivalence, scored as *Obs*, 116
Anacoluthon, 17
Anderson, Harold H., 333
Answers to questions, unitizing of, 16
Anticipatory responses, role in reasoning,
 130–1
Anxiety. *See* A
Aronson, M., 333, 334
Auld, Frank, Jr.: on effect of interpreta-
 tion, 305n.; review of content-analysis
 studies, 327, 330; on rules for unitizing,
 341; on sequential dependencies in psychotherapy, 313, 321–4; on theme or
 episode as a unit, 340

Bales, Robert F.: application of his system by R. W. Boyd, 331, 332; application of his system by Roberts and
 Strodtbeck, 331; application of his system by H. H. Strupp, 332; description
 of his content-analysis system, 331; influence on Hans H. Strupp, 334; little
 influence on Dollard and Auld, 338;
 proposed chi-square as measure of reliability of classification, 343–4; reliability of his content analysis, 298, 344
Balint, Michael, 92
Bellak, Leopold, 334
Berelson, Bernard: on development of
 content analysis, 326; on typical relia-

bility coefficients in content analysis,
 298
Bierer, J., 345n.
Blau, B. A., 334
Bloomfield, Leonard: on definition of
 sentence, 12, 14, 16, 17; on intonational
 contour as cue for sentence, 12; on quo-
 tation device, 18
Bordin, Edwin S., 10
Boyd, Richard W., 332
Breuer, Josef, 9
Bush, Robert R., 303n.

Call, counted as sentence, 17
Categories: for patient, 30–182; for therapist, 183–218
Classification, a primitive kind of measurement, 295
Coffey, Hubert S., 42, 332
Command, counted as sentence, 17
Compound sentence, 15
Conditions-principles framework, 5
Conf (confirmation)
 combined with other signs, 60
 definition, 56–7
 discriminations from other signs, 61
 examples of, 57–60
 theory of, 57
Conflict: aggression-fear, 80–5; depend-
 ence-anxiety, 66–70; love-anxiety, 96;
 mobility-anxiety, 106–10; in Murray's
 content-analysis system, 336; role of
 anxiety in, 45; sex-anxiety, 160–70
Conscious, defined as the named, 32–3
Conscious behavior, description of, 33
Conscious thoughts and feelings, represented by capital letters, 24
Content, latent and manifest, 21–2, 72
Content analysis: history of, 325–38;
 meaning of the term, 27–8; must capture play of feeling and emotion, 2;
 purpose of, 1; sterile if significant variables are omitted, 2
Content-analysis system: aim of, 3; development empirically, 4

447